The Policy-Based Profession

The Policy-Based Profession

*An Introduction
to Social Welfare Policy
for Social Workers*

Philip R. Popple
*School of Social Work
Western Michigan University*

Leslie Leighninger
*School of Social Work
Louisiana State University*

Allyn and Bacon
Boston • London • Toronto • Sydney • Tokyo • Singapore

Editor-in-Chief, Social Sciences: Karen Hansen
Series Editor: Judy Fifer
Marketing Manager: Sue Brown
Editorial Assistant: Jennifer Muroff
Production Administrator: Rob Lawson
Editorial-Production Service: Omegatype Typography, Inc.
Composition and Prepress Buyer: Linda Cox
Manufacturing Buyer: Suzanne Lareau
Cover Administrator: Suzanne Harbison

Library of Congress Cataloging-in-Publication Data

Popple, Philip R.
    The policy-based profession: an introduction to social welfare
policy for social workers / Philip R. Popple, Leslie Leighninger.
      p. cm.
    Includes bibliographical references and index.
    ISBN 0-205-18606-8
    1. Social workers—United States.   2. Public welfare—United
States.   3. Social service—United States.   4. United States—Social
policy.   I. Leighninger, Leslie.   II. Title.
HV91.P677   1998
361.3'2—dc21   97-2260
                                       CIP

Printed in the United States of America
10 9 8 7 6 5 4 3 2   06 05 04 03 02 01 00 99 98

Photo Credits: Chapters 1–3, 5–7, and 12: Robert Harbison; Chapter 4: North Wind Picture Archives; Chapters 8, 11: Mary Ellen Lepionka.

To my kids, Rich and Nancy,
David and Jennifer, and Jeff
—P. R. P.

To Paul Hartrich, Community Activist, and
Toni Hartrich, Policy Analyst
(my father and sister)
—L. L.

Contents

Preface

Social work as a profession has always operated within the context of social policy—whether this policy stems from agency rules and guidelines, the decisions of boards of directors, organizational accreditation or licensing regulations, state and national legislation, court rulings, or administrative and implementation procedures. Social work practice takes place in accordance with policies large and small, such as federal public welfare legislation, state guidelines for Medicaid reimburstments, court orders removing abused children from their homes, or the waiting list practices of a United Way family counseling center. In fact, we argue in this book that social work's intimate connection to social policy makes it unique among the professions, many of which are only now becoming enmeshed in the expectations of external bodies such as the corporation, the state legislature, and the bureaucracy.

Despite the relationship between social welfare policy and social work practice, few students have a good grasp of how to analyze and evaluate the policies that will affect their work, the lives of their clients, and the larger community. The purpose of this book is to help students acquire these policy analysis skills. We are not interested in policy analysis as a mere academic exercise. We are convinced that the understanding of policies—how they have developed, whom they affect, and how—enables social workers to effectively use, implement, and, where necessary, change policies and programs for the good of their clients. One of our students referred to this text as "not overwhelming, as one might expect,...but more of a journey." Our intention is to make this journey as interesting and compelling as possible.

There are particular reasons for social workers to have an informed view of today's social welfare policy world. The policy environment of social work is changing at an extraordinary rate. Economic, demographic, and political developments have opened the way for major welfare reform, re-evaluation of affirmative action, a re-thinking of the purpose and structure of Social Security, and a revolution in health care emanating from the private sector. Social work practitioners need tools to understand and respond to these changes; the profession as a whole needs to revitalize itself as an actor, rather than reactor, in the policy arena.

This book was written in the hopes of making some small steps toward achieving these goals. It is written for students at both the baccalaureate and master's levels of social work education. It begins by outlining a policy-based model of the social work profession which explicitly recognizes the social welfare policy system as a major factor in social work practice. The second section delineates four major facets of the policy context: historical, political, social, and economic. Since both authors were trained as social welfare historians, there is an emphasis on history as an overarching approach to the study of policy. All four facets are then combined in a policy analysis framework which can provide the basis of a practitioner policy analysis.

The final section of the book applies the framework to representative policies in the fields of public welfare, aging, mental health, health, and child welfare. Rather than attempt a comprehensive (and soon outdated) overview of current policies, our intent has been to choose a current example of a major social welfare initiative within each policy area. Most importantly, we have sought to acquaint students with a process for understanding policies that they can continue to apply in their professional practice. We hope that by teaching students to use a policy analysis technique, which we have termed *practitioner policy analysis,* we will equip them with a skill that will be useful throughout their careers.

Acknowledgments

We are grateful to the following people for assistance in researching and writing this text: Laura Dase, Barry Daste, Joseph Delatte, Wendy Franklin, Karen Fraternali, Joe McCarty, Kenneth Millar, Matt Leighninger, Robert D. Leighninger, Jr., Judith Kolb Morris, Shannon Robshaw, Pat Sidmore, the members of the first Ph.D. class of the School of Social Work at Louisiana State University, and the students in the Fall 1994 section of SW 610, Foundations of Social Welfare Policy, School of Social Work at Western Michigan University. Thanks are due to the reviewers who provided feedback at every step of development: David M. Austin, University of Texas at Austin; Richard Blake, Seton Hall University; Ronald B. Dear, University of Washington; George Hoshino, University of Minnesota; Alfred J. Kahn, Columbia University; Ron Manning, University of Montevallo; Nelson Reid, North Carolina State University; Paul H. Stuart, University of Alabama; Susan Vaughn, University of Montevallo; and James L. Wolk, Georgia State University.

We would also like to acknowledge the encouragement and expertise of our several editors, Judy Fifer and Karen Hanson, and the technical assistance of Rob Lawson and Kathy Robinson.

The Policy-Based Profession

Part I

Social Welfare Policy and the Social Work Profession

Chapter 1

The Policy-Based Profession

Our friends in clinical social work tell us that in therapeutic situations when an underlying issue is blocking work on the main issue, it is necessary to deal with the underlying issue before work on the major problem can begin. For example, if a couple is coming to a social agency for marital counseling and the husband believes that the very act of coming for counseling is an admission of weakness and of failure in his role as a husband, this initial resistance to counseling must be dealt with before work on the couple's marital problems can begin. A book on social welfare policy aimed at social workers faces an analogous situation. The major issue to be dealt with, the presenting problem, so to speak, is to develop an understanding of the dynamics of social welfare policy. However, before we can begin to address this subject we must deal with an underlying issue. This issue is that social work students, at least initially, have little interest in the subject of social welfare policy and do not understand why they are required to study this area. In this chapter we address this issue.

Bruce Jansson has identified a phenomena in social work which he refers to as the mythology of autonomous practice. By this he means the tendency of social workers to approach practice in a way which assumes that social workers and their clients are relatively insulated from external policies. This mythology has led the profession to a concern with the development of practice theories which focus heavily on the individual dimension of problems and a general disinterest in the *policy* context of problems. Jansson states that "This notion of autonomous practice has had a curious and persistent strength in the social work profession."[1] In this chapter we argue that the mythology of autonomous practice has been directly related to social work's efforts to achieve professional status. These efforts have been based on a flawed theory of what professionalization means, a theory which equated autonomy with private practice and which assigned primary importance to the development of practice techniques. We will argue that looking at social work within a more up to date and accurate theory of professions leads to the conclusion that not only is policy relevant to the day-to-day activities of social workers, but that it is central to the definition and mission of the profession. Before we can get to this topic, however, we must first look at the function of social work in society and at how policy became relegated to secondary status in the profession, a victim of social work's professional aspirations.

The Target of Social Work—The Individual and Society

When asked to differentiate social work practice from practice in other personal service professions such as psychiatry, psychology, and school counseling, we generally identify social work's distinguishing characteristic as our concern with person-in-environment. By this we mean that we do not limit ourselves to a concern with a person's intrapsychic functioning, but that we also seek to understand and manipulate factors in a person's environment which contribute to his or her problem. Some of these environmental factors are close to the person—for example family, job, and neighborhood. However, people are also affected by factors in the larger environment—affirmative action laws, public welfare programs, United Way fund raising campaigns, church positions on social issues, and the like. The social work profession is distinctive due to its interest in all these factors and issues.

The Social Function of Social Work

Social work's concern with person-in-environment stems from the profession's social function. Social work is the core technology in the social welfare institution, the institution in society which deals with the problem of dependency. By this we mean that every person in society occupies a number of social positions or statuses (mother, teacher, consumer, citizen, etc.) and attached to each of these positions are a number of social roles (nurturing children, communicating information, shopping, voting, etc.). These statuses and roles are located within social institutions which support people in their efforts to successfully meet all role expectations. For example, the role of employee occurs within the economic institution which must be functioning well enough for there to be jobs for most people. When an individual is doing everything necessary to fulfill a role and the appropriate social institutions are functioning well enough to support the person's role performance, we have a situation we refer to as interdependence.[2]

When most people and institutions are functioning interdependently, society operates smoothly. However, when people fail to adequately perform roles, or social institutions fail to adequately support people in their role performance, social stability is threatened. Common examples of individual role failure are:

- A woman is unemployed because she has difficulty controlling her temper.
- A single father leaves his two-year-old son at home alone for an extended period of time while he goes fishing.
- A fifteen-year-old does not attend school because he does not think it is relevant to his life.

Examples of failure of social institutions to support individual role performance are:

- A women is unemployed because, due to plant closings, there are jobs in her town for only seven of every ten people who need to work.
- A single father leaves his two-year-old son at home alone while he is at work because there is no affordable day care available.
- A fifteen-year-old with a learning disability does not attend school because the school does not offer a program that meets his special needs.

The Dual Targets of Social Work

Because of the dual focus of the social welfare institution, the social work profession also has two targets. One target is helping individuals who are having difficulty meeting individual role expectations. This is the type of social work we generally refer to as social work practice with individuals, families, and small groups, or which is sometimes referred to as *micro* practice. The other target of social work is on those aspects of social institutions which fail to support individuals in their efforts to fulfill role expectations.[3] This target of social work, sometimes referred to as *macro* practice, is what we are concerned with in the study of social welfare policy.

The Dominance of Micro Practice

Social workers have long recognized that micro and macro practice are complimentary, but have generally emphasized the micro, individual treatment aspect of the profession. The early social work leader and theoretician Mary Richmond referred to the dual nature of social work as *retail* and *wholesale,* saying "The healthy and well-rounded reform movement usually begins in the retail method and returns to it again, forming in the two curves of its upward push and downward pull a complete circle."[4] Another early leader, Porter R. Lee, referred to these aspects of social work as *cause* (working to effect social change) and *function* (treatment of individual role difficulties). He felt that function was the proper professional concern of social work. Lee argued that a cause, once successful, naturally tended to "transfer its interest and its responsibility to an administrative unit" which justified its existence by the test of efficiency, not zeal; by its "demonstrated possibilities of achievement" rather than by the "faith and purpose of its adherents." The emphasis of the function was on "organization, technique, standards, and efficiency." Fervor inspired the cause, while intelligence directed the function. Lee felt that once the cause had been won it was necessary that it be institutionalized as a function in order that the gains be made permanent. This is what he saw as the primary task of professional social work.[5]

The opinions of Richmond and Lee have continued to represent the position of the vast majority of the social work profession. Practice with individuals, families, and small groups with the goal of treating problems in individual role performance continues to be the focus of most of the social work profession's efforts. Even though most social workers will admit that problems with social institutions are at the root of most client problems, we have tended to persist in dealing primarily with the individual client. There are three main reasons why we as social workers have continued to define our profession in this way. These are (1) the individual is the most immediate target for change, (2) American society is generally conservative, and (3) social work has chosen to follow a particular model of professionalism throughout most of this century.

The Individual Is the Most Immediate Target for Change

An individual with a problem cannot wait for a social policy change to come along and solve the problem. For example, the main reason a welfare mother runs out of money before the end of the month is, no doubt, the extremely small amount of money she receives, an *institutional* problem. If the size of the mother's grant were to increase, her problem might well disappear. However, this is not going to happen in the near future, so the social worker in this case must concentrate on aspects of the mother's behavior that can be changed in order to stretch out the small budget she does have, and on helping her develop skills in manipulating the system in ways which assure that she receives the maximum benefits to which she is entitled.

The Conservative Nature of American Society

Another reason for the social work profession's strong emphasis on individual role performance as the primary practice target is that our society is rather conservative and firmly believes in the notion of individualism. We strongly believe that people deserve all the credit for any success they experience and, conversely, deserve all of the blame for any failures. We resent, and often make fun of, explanations of people's personal situations which attribute anything to factors external to the individual.[6] Explanations which attribute poverty, for example, to factors such as the job market, neighborhood disintegration, racism, and so forth, will often be dismissed as "bleeding heart liberal explanations." In a society characterized by attitudes such as this, a model of social work that concentrates on problems in individual role performance is obviously going to be much more readily accepted and supported than one that seeks environmental change.

Professionalization

The final explanation of social work's emphasis on treating the individual causes of dependency and de-emphasizing the institutional causes is little recognized but of key importance. This is the model of professionalism which social work subscribed to early in the century; social work's efforts to achieve professional status are based on this model. It is to this model that we now turn.

Social Work's Pursuit of Professional Status

Social work as a paid occupation has existed for only a little over one hundred years. From the very beginning, those engaged in the provision of social services have been concerned, some would say preoccupied, with the status of their activities in the world of work, specifically in gaining recognition as a profession rather than simply an occupation. There are several very good reasons for social workers' interest in professionalization.

Social Work Grew Out of Voluntarism

Virtually all of the early social welfare agencies—Charity Organization Societies, state boards of charities, settlement houses—were initially staffed primarily by volunteers. Late in the nineteenth century when it became clear that the complexity and the amount of service required by these organizations was beyond the capacity of volunteer staffs, the boards of these organizations began to hire paid staff. However, the tendency of the boards was to view the staff as volunteers who were receiving a small stipend for their services. The staff, on the other hand, were generally well educated and hard working people, generally women, who believed they were offering a valuable technical service, and should be respected and rewarded for their contribution. Gaining recognition as professionals would accomplish this goal.

The Status of Women in American Society

At the time social work was emerging as a career, the opportunities for smart, ambitious, and well-educated women were very limited. A number of women were graduating from college with a desire to contribute something to society other than in the traditional roles of being a wife and mother. The opportunities for these women were very limited, as most of the established professions such as medicine, law, and business, were closed to women. The professions which were open to women, mainly nursing and teaching, placed women in a position clearly subservient to men and denied them upward mobility (administrators who supervised women in schools and hospitals were in most cases men). The field of social work appeared to offer women the opportunity for success and advancement unimpeded by traditional barriers. However, first social work had to be established as a full-fledged profession.

Professionalization as a Social Movement

The desire of social workers to improve the status of their vocation was occurring at a time when society at large was looking to professionalization as a means of managing problems. The historian Robert Wiebe characterizes the Progressive Era (roughly 1898 to 1918) as a "search for order in a distended society." Social problems associated with massive industrialization, immigration, and urbanization had overwhelmed the traditional means of maintaining social stability, and society was searching for new ways to assure social order. The Progressives were interested in reforms that would increase rationality and order and facilitate business and government planning.

> *A chamber of commerce, mobilized and formidable, desired a cleaner, safer, more beautiful, and more economically operated city. Only the professional administrator, the doctor, the social worker, the architect, the economist, could show the way.*[7]

The Progressives believed that professionalism would bring opportunity, progress, order, and community. The strong desire of social workers to improve their status, combined with the trend in society to view professionalization as the most rational way to manage social problems, resulted in social work becoming a textbook case of a professionalizing occupation.

Professionalization and the Focus of Social Work

When social workers began to actively organize to improve their status, there was a conflict between those who thought the new profession should concentrate on the institutional causes of dependency (social welfare policy) and those who were more interested in developing techniques and knowledge useful in working with individual role failure (social work practice). Social work leaders such as Samuel McCune Lindsey at the New York School of Social Work, Edith Abbott at the Chicago School of Civics and Philanthropy, and George Mangold at the Missouri School of Social Economy argued for a profession based on social and economic theory and with a social reform orientation. Mangold stated:

> *The leaders of social work ... can subordinate technique to an understanding of the social problems that are involved. ... Fundamental principles, both in economics and in sociology are necessary for the development of their plans of community welfare. ... Courses in problems of poverty and in the method and technique of charity organizations are fundamental to our work. But the study of economics of labor is quite as important, and lies at the basis of our living and social condition. ... The gain is but slight if our philanthropy means nothing more than relieving distress here and helping a family there; the permanent gain comes only as we are able to work out policies that mean the permanent improvement of social conditions.*[8]

On the other hand, there were a number of social work leaders who believed that the new profession should concentrate on the development of practical knowledge related to addressing problems in individual role performance. The Charity Organization Society leader Mary Richmond advocated using case records and the experiences of senior social workers to train new workers in practical techniques of work with individuals. Frank Bruno argued that social work should be concerned with "processes ... with all technical methods from the activities of boards of directors to the means used by a probation officer to rectify the conduct of a delinquent child."[9]

The debate regarding the focus of the new social work profession came to a head at the 1915 meeting of the National Conference of Charities and Correction. Abraham Flexner, famed critic of the medical profession, had been asked to prepare a paper for the conference analyzing social work as a profession.

Flexner began his analysis with the first clear statement of traits which differentiate professions from "lesser occupations." He asserted that "Professions involve essentially intellectual operations with large individual responsibility, derive their raw material from science and learning, this material they work up to a practical and definite end, possess an educationally communicable technique, tend to self-organization, and are becoming increasingly altruistic in motivations."[10] Following his definition of profession as a concept, Flexner measured social work against the traits he had developed. He found that social work strongly exhibited some professional traits—it was intellectual, derived its knowledge from science and learning, possessed a "professional self-consciousness," and was altruistic. However, in several important criteria Flexner found social work lacking, mainly those of educationally communicable technique and individual responsibility.

Regarding social work's lack of an educationally communicable technique, Flexner felt the source of the deficiency was the broadness of its boundaries. He believed that professions should have definite and specific ends. However, "the high degree of specialized competency required for action and conditioned on limitation of area cannot possibly go with the width and scope characteristic of social work." Flexner believed that this lack of specificity seriously affected the possibility of professional training. "The occupations of social workers are so numerous and diverse that no compact, purposefully organized educational discipline is possible."[11]

In the area of individual responsibility, Flexner felt that social workers were mediators rather than responsible parties.

> *The social worker takes hold of a case, that of a disintegrating family, a wrecked individual, or an unsocialized industry. Having localized his problem, having decided on its particular nature, is he not usually driven to invoke the specialized agency, professional or other, best equipped to handle it?... To the extent that the social worker mediates the intervention of the particular agent or agency best fitted to deal with the specific emergency which he has encountered, is the social worker himself a professional or is he the intelligence that brings this or that profession or other activity into action?[12]*

Social workers took Flexner's message to heart to the extent that "Is Social Work a Profession?" is probably the most frequently cited paper in the social work literature. David Austin asserts that Flexner's "model of an established profession became the most important organizing concept in the conceptual development of social work and, in particular, social work education."[13] Following the presentation of the paper, social workers consciously set out to remedy the deficiencies identified by Flexner, mainly the development of an educationally communicable technique and the assumption of "large individual responsibility."

In the area of technique the profession choose to emphasize practice with individuals, families, and small groups, or *social casework* as it was then called. The committee that was charged with responding to Flexner's paper stated "...this committee...respectfully suggests that the chief problem facing social work is the development of training methods which will give it [a] technical basis."[14] The committee felt that the social work profession had the beginning of an educationally communicable technique in the area of social casework and the profession should narrow its focus to emphasize this. This view was institutionalized in 1919 when the American Association of Professional Schools of Social Work was founded, dominated by educators who subscribed to the Flexner model for the profession. At an early meeting it was voted that students receive training in casework, statistics, and community service. F. Stuart Chapin, Director of the Smith College Training School for Social Work, proposed that social legislation be included as a fundamental curriculum area. He was voted down based on the argument that social legislation lacked clarity, technique, and was not suitable for field work. Likewise, settlement house work was considered to be unsuitable for professional education. Settlements emphasized "mere neighborliness" and were opposed to the idea that their residents were more expert than their neighbors.[15] Thus, within a relatively few years following Flexner's paper, social work had all but eliminated knowledge and skills related to social policy from the profession's domain, substituting a nearly exclusive focus on techniques which could be demonstrated to be useful in helping individuals solve problems of role functioning.

The second area in which Flexner considered social work deficient in meeting criteria of professionalization is that of "assuming large individual responsibility." By this, Flexner was referring to what is now generally termed professional authority or autonomy. According to Greenwood, "In a professional relationship...the professional dictates what is good or evil for the client, who has no choice but to accede to professional judgement."[16] The criteria of professional autonomy is closely related to professional expertise because it is upon expertise that authority or autonomy is based.

Although neither Flexner or any other theorist said it directly, social workers have historically equated the concept of professional autonomy with a private practice model of service delivery. Two reasons for this interpretation come to mind. The first is that Flexner's model of a profession was based on medicine, which he viewed as the prototypical "true" profession. Because the predominant model of medicine during most of this century has been private practice, social workers naturally assumed that private practice was the key to autonomy. The second reason is that it is obvious on the face of it that a person with no boss—as is the case in private practice—is autonomous. But whatever the reason, the result of this interpretation has been to further push social work away from policy and toward an individual treatment model of practice. As Austin has observed "The emphasis on distinctive method also reinforced a focus on the casework counseling interview as the core professional technique in social work. This was a technique that could most readily be adapted to a private-practice model—a model that has been viewed by many practitioners as a close approximation to the medical model of professionalism that Flexner had in mind."[17]

In summary, for better or for worse, the adoption of a model of professionalization based on the criteria developed by Flexner caused, or perhaps more likely simply accelerated, the trend in social work to define the profession as being focused on role difficulties of individuals (casework) and to de-emphasize concern with the institutional causes of role failure (social welfare policy). Social workers were concerned with identifying and demonstrating an educationally communicable technique, and casework with individuals and families appeared to be a much more promising focus than a concern with social welfare policy, which was, and still is, an amorphous and hard to conceptualize area. Social workers were also concerned with being able to practice autonomously, which they came to interpret as private practice. The types of professional roles associated with social policy almost always occur in large organizations, which traditionally have been viewed as threats to autonomy. The definition of professional autonomy as ideally occurring in a private practice setting has furthered the perception of social welfare policy as an area tangential to the social work profession.

Thus, social workers' concern with professionalization has been an important reason for the relatively low interest in the subject of social welfare policy in the profession. It now appears that the model of professionalism social workers have been following contains some major errors. Flexner's model of what constitutes a profession was based on medicine; it assumed that medicine was a prototype profession, and that as other occupations began to achieve professional status they would more closely resemble medicine. It is now apparent that medicine, rather than being a prototypical profession, was in fact an anomaly.[18] Due to various unique social and political factors, medicine was able to escape both the corporation and the bureaucracy and thus was able to completely control its domain and determine most of its own working conditions.[19] However, rather than social work developing and becoming more like medicine as everyone assumed it would, the movement has been in quite the opposite direction. Medicine is now coming under the control of the corporation and the bureaucracy, and in terms of occupational organization is coming more and more to resemble social work. These developments serve to indicate errors in the Flexner model of professions and call for a re-examination of the concept. This re-examination should develop the concept in such a way that professionalism can be understood without assuming that professionals should be private practitioners and high level technicians. In the following section we will attempt such a re-examination.

The Policy-Based Profession

The model developed by Flexner might well be termed the market-based profession. This model, based on the medical profession in the early part of this century, assumes that the professional is essentially a small business person. The product the professional is selling is his or her expertise. The basic relationship, illustrated in Figure 1.1, is dyadic. The consumer comes to the professional stating a problem, the professional diagnoses the problem and prescribes a solution, the consumer requests the solution which the professional provides, and the consumer pays the bill. The demonstration of specific techniques is key in the market-based model because these represent the "products" the professional is selling. Autonomy is assumed in this model to result from the fact that the professional is his or her own boss.

Two general developments have accelerated over the course of this century which indicate that the market-based model of professions no longer is an accurate reflection of reality, if it ever was. The first is that the trend in all professions has been toward becoming employees in organizations rather than private practitioners. Even medicine, long viewed as the ideal independent profession, shows signs of an eroding independent practice base. Paul Starr observes:

> The AMA [American Medical Association] is no longer as devoted to
> solo practice either. "We are not opposed to the corporate practice of
> medicine," says Dr. Sammons of the AMA. "There is no way that we
> could be," he adds, pointing out that a high proportion of the AMA's
> members are now involved in corporate practice. According to AMA

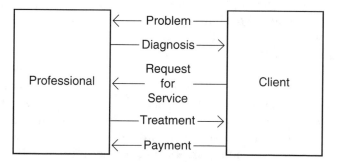

FIGURE 1.1   The Market-Based Profession

data, some 26 percent of physicians have contractual relationships with hospitals; three out of five of these doctors are on salary. . . . Many physicians in private practice receive part of their income through independent practice associations, HMO's, and for-profit hospitals and other health care companies. The growth of corporate medicine has simply gone too far for the AMA to oppose it outright.[20]

Although the number of social workers in private practice has steadily increased in recent years, and to the extent social workers succeed in their efforts to be eligible for third-party reimbursement (insurance) this number may increase even more, it is doubtful that more than a small proportion of social workers will ever earn their living outside of an organizational setting. Thus, the typical work setting for a professional person has become a public or a private bureaucracy rather than a private practice.

The second development which indicates that the market-based model of professions is outdated is that professional practice, even that in private settings, is increasingly subject to the dictates of external bodies. The psychiatry profession developed the *Diagnostic and Statistical Manual* in response to pressure from insurance companies to be able to classify various treatments for insurance reimbursement. This manual is now the bible guiding the practice of mental health professionals regardless of what they may feel is the evil of labeling. The practice of lawyers is subject to the dictates of banks, title companies, state and federal justice departments, as well as the entire court system. Before a physician can hospitalize a patient, an insurance company generally has to approve the proposed treatment for payment; once the patient is in the hospital the length of stay is usually not determined by the patient's physician, but by the insurance company, managed care organization, or governmental agency that will eventually pay most of the bill. The list of examples could go on and on to illustrate our point—even professionals who are in so-called independent practice are now subject to all sorts of influences and controls by external organizations.

The model of professionalism which is reflective of occupational reality in the late twentieth century is what we call the policy-based profession. This model, illustrated in Figure 1.2, is based on a triadic relationship. The triad is comprised of three systems—the professional system, the client system, and the policy system. The policy-based model recognizes the fact that although a professional provides services on behalf of a client, it is often not the client who requests the services, who defines the problem, or who pays the professional.

Recognizing that professions are now predominantly policy-based rather than market-based leads to two major revisions of the traditional way of looking at professions, each contributing to the argument that social welfare policy must be a central concern of the social work profession. The first regards the

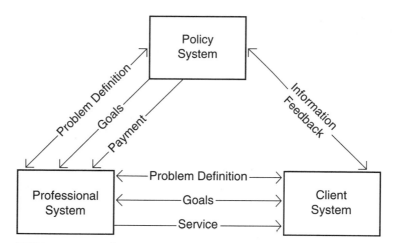

FIGURE 1.2　The Policy-Based Profession

matter of expert technique and the second regards practice within an organizational setting.

Expert Technique

According to Flexner and all the social theorists following him who subscribe to the market-based model, an occupation becomes recognized as a profession by developing techniques in the same way a business develops a product, marketing the technique and, if successful, to use Robert Dingwall's term, "accomplishing profession."[21] This process, however, does not follow what we know of the history of professions. All professions were recognized as professions *before* they had any particularly effective techniques, including medicine which was not particularly effective until the current century. Many professions, the clergy for example, do not now and probably never will have such techniques. As a result of pursuing this trait, social workers have defined a number of areas as outside of the scope of the profession, generally areas related to social welfare policy, because they were not seen as amenable to the development of specific, educationally communicable, technique.

Rather than the possession of expert technique, what appears to be crucial for an occupation to be recognized as a profession is *social assignment.* Professions exist for the purpose of managing problems critical to society; the successful profession is one that is recognized by society as being primarily responsible for a given social problem area. Medicine is charged with dealing with physical health, law with management of deviance and civil relations, engineering with the practical applications of technology, education with the communication of socially critical knowledge and skills, and finally, social work is responsible for the management of dependency. All professions have wide and complex bodies of knowledge and all have a theory base. However, the degree to which this knowledge and theory is translated into educationally communicable techniques varies widely. Medicine and engineering have rather precise, educationally communicable techniques; law and the clergy have techniques which are somewhat less precise. Rather than specific techniques, these professions base their authority on mastery of complex cultural traditions. The important point is that it is not the possession of technique which is crucial for the development of a profession. Rather, what is crucial is the identification of one occupation over others to be given primary responsibility for the management of a social problem.[22]

Professional Practice Within an Organizational Context

Traditional theory, based on Flexner's work, equates professional autonomy with the autonomy of the independent practitioner who is his or her own boss. Over the course of this century, more and more professionals have come to work in traditional bureaucratic organizations and the question has arisen as to whether this development erodes the very basis of professional autonomy. The theoretical position which argues this most forcefully is called *proletarianization*. This thesis emphasizes the loss of control that professionals supposedly experience when they work in large organizations. According to Eliot Freidson, "This thesis stems from Marx's theory of history, in which he asserts that over time the intrinsic characteristics of capitalism will reduce virtually all workers to the status of the proletariat, i.e. dependent on selling their labor in order to survive and stripped of all control over the substance and process of their work."[23] Supposedly, in organizations the authority of the office is substituted for the authority of professional expertise. In other words, a person working in a bureaucracy is required to take direction from any person who occupies a superior position in the organization, regardless of whether the person has equal or greater expertise in the professional task being performed. Thus, when employed in an organization, a professional does not have autonomy.

Sociologists who have studied professionals who work in organizations have found that the fears of loss of professional autonomy in such settings have been greatly exaggerated. What has happened is that the organizations where professionals typically work—hospitals, schools, law firms, social agencies, etc.—have developed as hybrid forms which deviate from the ideal type of bureaucracy in order to accommodate professionals. Freidson states that "... studies [of professionals in organizations], as well as more recent developments in organizational theory, call into question the validity of the assumption that large organizations employing professionals are sufficiently bureaucratic to allow one to assume that professional work within them is ordered and controlled by strictly bureaucratic means."[24]

A number of developments have enabled professionals to work in organizations while maintaining sufficient autonomy to perform their professional
roles. First, professionals have come to be a special group recognized under
U.S. labor law because they are expected to exercise judgment and discretion
on a routine, daily basis in the course of performing their work. In other words,
discretion is a recognized and legitimate part of their work role. Second, professionals are subject to a different type of supervision than are ordinary rank and
file workers. Ordinary workers are generally supervised by someone who has
been trained as a manager, not as a worker in the area being supervised. Professionals, however, generally are entitled to expect that they will only be supervised by a member of their same profession. In social agencies, supervisors,
managers, and often even executive positions are reserved for persons trained
and licensed as social workers.[25]

Summary and Practice Implications

Recognizing that social work is a policy-based rather than a market-based profession clarifies and legitimizes the place of social welfare policy as a central
concern. First, the policy-based model, while recognizing that the development
of technique is important for any profession, also recognizes that functions do
not need to be excluded from a profession's concern simply because they are
not amenable to the development of narrow, specific, procedures. This recognition legitimizes the inclusion of policy content such as policy analysis, administration, negotiation, planning, and so forth. Such inclusion has often been
questioned because it was viewed as not being amenable to the development of
"educationally communicable techniques." Second, the policy-based model
recognizes that the social work profession will probably always exist in an organizational context, and that social work's long experience in providing services
within this context should be viewed as a strength rather than a weakness of the
profession. Finally, the policy-based model explicitly recognizes the policy system as a major factor in social work practice and emphasizes that understanding
this system is every bit as important for social work practitioners as is understanding basic concepts of human behavior.

There are a number of roles within social work which are described as policy practice roles. These are roles such as those mentioned above—planner,
administrator, policy analyst, program evaluator, and so on. In the years following the Flexner report there was a good deal of debate as to whether these were
really social work practice roles or something else, perhaps public administration. Tortured rationales were often developed which defined these roles as
casework techniques applied to different settings and populations. The 1959
Council on Social Work Education curriculum study, for example, concluded

administration project progressed, it became more and more clear that e were discussing in the preparation of social work students for execu- vel positions was social work [practice] in an administrative setting and administration in a social work setting."[26] Over the years, however, these s have come to be defined as legitimate areas of social work practice without resorting to defining them as social casework applied to a different setting. Most graduate schools of social work now offer a concentration in administration, policy, and planning.

This book, however, is not aimed only at social workers preparing for spe- cialized policy practice roles. Rather it is aimed at people interested in more tra- ditional direct practice roles with individuals, families, and small groups. In this chapter we have argued that the study of policy is relevant, in fact a *neces- sity,* for this group because policy is built into the very fabric of social work practice just as much as the study of human behavior. Social work's concern with policy is a logical extension of our person-in-environment perspective. Up to this point this discussion has been rather abstract and theoretical. The reader is justified at this point in looking for specific examples of the ways policy affects direct practice. The following is not intended to be a complete classifi- cation of ways that policy directly relates to practice, but rather to serve as only a few of many possible examples.

Policy Determines the Major Goals of Service

A basic component of social work practice is the setting of case goals. The range of possible goals is not entirely up to the judgement of the individual social work practitioner, but is greatly restricted, and sometimes actually prescribed, by agency policy. A good example of this is in the area of child protective ser- vices. For a number of years, protective service policy was based on goals that have come to be referred to as "child rescue." The idea was that when the level of child care in a home had sunk to the level of neglect or abuse, the family was probably irredeemable and the appropriate strategy was to get the child out of the home and placed in a better setting. Based to a certain degree on case expe- rience and research results, but probably more on the outcomes of a number of lawsuits, policy is now shifting to the goal of family preservation. This means that before a child is removed from the home, the social worker must demon- strate that a reasonable effort has been made to help the family while the child is still in the home. The point is that family preservation now figures promi- nently among the goals of child protection social workers, not because thou- sands of social workers have individually come to the conclusion that this is the most appropriate goal, but because policy now specifies that this be the goal of choice.

Policy Determines Characteristics of Clientele

The policy analyst Alvin Schorr has pointed out how agency policy, often in subtle ways, determines what type of clients social agency staff will deal with. If the agency wishes to serve a middle class clientele, they can attract this type of client and discourage poorer clients by means of several policy decisions. First, by locating in the suburbs the agency services become more accessible to the middle class and less so to poorer segments of the population. Second, what Schorr terms *agency culture* can be designed to appeal to the middle class. By this he means whether the waiting room is plush or bare and functional; whether appointments are insisted on or if drop-in visits are permitted; whether the agency gives priority to clients who can pay for services; whether the agency has evening and weekend hours or is only open during the day, and so forth.[27]

Policy Determines Who Will Get Services

Ira Colby relates the situation where an anonymous caller contacted the Texas Department of Human Services and reported that a fourteen-year-old girl had been at home alone for several days with nothing to eat and the caller wanted the Department to "do something." The supervisor who was working intake that day

> *was torn about what action to take. On the one hand, [she] wanted to send a worker out to verify the referral and provide any and all available services; yet, the department's policy clearly classified this case as a priority three—a letter would be sent to the caretakers outlining parental responsibilities.... In Texas, each child protective services' referral is classified as a priority one, two, or three. A priority one requires that a worker begin work within twenty-four hours after the agency receives a referral; a priority two mandates that contact be made within ten days; a priority three requires no more action than a letter or phone call. Cases are prioritized based on a number of variables, including the alleged victim's age and the type and extent of the alleged abuse.[28]*

Most social workers are employed in agencies with policies which specify who can and who cannot receive services and some method of prioritizing services.

Policy Specifies, or Restricts, Certain Options for Clients

Policy often requires that a social worker either offer, or not offer, certain options. For example, social workers who are employed by Catholic Social Services are generally forbidden to discuss abortion as an option for an unplanned pregnancy. Social workers at a Planned Parenthood Center are required to explore this option. When one of the authors began work for a state welfare department during the first six months of his employment, he was explicitly prohibited by agency policy from discussing birth control with welfare recipients. During the last six months of his employment there, policy was changed to explicitly *require* him to discuss birth control with all welfare recipients.

Policy Determines the Theoretical Focus of Services

Although less common than the other examples, in certain instances agencies will have policies which require that social workers adopt a certain theoretical orientation toward their practice. For a number of years there was a schism in social work between the diagnostic school (followers of Sigmund Freud) and the functional school (followers of Otto Rank). Social agencies sometimes would define themselves as belonging to one school or the other and would not employ social workers who practiced according to the other perspective. Currently there are agencies which define themselves as behavioral, ecosystems, feminist, or whatever, and frown on other approaches being applied by their staff. One of the authors once prepared a training curriculum for child protective services workers on behavioral principles that was rejected by the State Office training division because "this is not the way we wish our staff to practice."

Conclusion

Although few social workers enter the profession because of an interest in social welfare policy, every social work practitioner is, in fact, involved in policy on a daily basis. Social work agencies are created by policies, their goals are specified by policies, social workers are hired to carry out policy-specified tasks, and the whole environment in which social workers and clients exist is policy-determined. We often think of policy in terms of social legislation, but it is much broader than that. As Schorr has noted,

> *Power in terms of policy is not applied on a grand scale only; the term "practitioner" implies consideration of policy in terms of clinical relationships and relatively small groups. These may be as consequential or more consequential for the quality of everyday life than the large-scale government and private hierarchical actions that are more commonly regarded as policy. As practitioners practice policy, they may choose any of a variety of instruments. They may simply decide differ-*

ently about matters that lie within their own control, they may attempt to influence their agencies or they may take on more deep-seated and, chances are, conflict-ridden change. These are also choices that practitioners make.[29]

The problem with which we began this chapter is why social work students who desire to be direct practitioners need to study social welfare policy. The answer should be clear by now. Because social work is a policy-based profession, practitioners need to be sensitive to, and knowledgeable about, the dynamics of three systems—the client system, the practitioner system, and the policy system. The human behavior in the social environment curriculum concentrates on the dynamics of the client system; the social work practice curriculum concentrates on the practitioner system; and the social welfare policy and services curriculum focuses on the policy system. All three are equally important to the preparation of a direct practice social worker.

Notes

1. Bruce Jansson, *Social Welfare Policy: From Theory to Practice* (Belmont, CA: Wadsworth, 1990) p. 2.

2. For a detailed discussion of the social welfare institution and the social work profession's place within it, see Philip R. Popple and Leslie Leighninger, *Social Work, Social Welfare, and American Society,* 3rd ed. (Boston: Allyn & Bacon, 1996) Chapter 2, pp. 23–52.

3. Charles Atherton, "The Social Assignment of Social Work," *Social Service Review* 43 (May 1969) pp. 421–429.

4. Joanna C. Colcord and Ruth Mann, Eds., *Mary E. Richmond, The Long View: Papers and Addresses* (New York: Russel Sage Foundation, 1930) pp. 111–112.

5. Porter R. Lee, *Social Work as Cause and Function, and Other Papers* (New York: New York School of Social Work, 1937) pp. 4–9.

6. For a classic discussion of individualism in American society as it relates to social work and social welfare see Harold Wilensky and Charles Lebeaux, *Industrial Society and Social Welfare,* 2nd ed. (New York: Russell Sage Foundation, 1965).

7. Robert H. Wiebe, *The Search for Order, 1877–1920* (New York: Hill and Wang, 1967) p. 174.

8. George B. Mangold, "The New Profession of Social Service," in J. E. McCullock, Ed., *Battling for Social Betterment,* (Nashville, TN: Southern Sociological Congress, 1914) pp. 86–90.

9. Frank J. Bruno, "The Project of Training for Social Work," *Adult Education Bulletin* 3 (June 1928) p. 4.

10. Abraham Flexner, "Is Social Work A Profession?" *Proceedings of the National Conference of Charities and Correction, 1915* (Chicago: Hildmann Printing Co., 1915) p. 581.

11. Flexner, "Is Social Work a Profession?" pp. 285–288.

12. Flexner, "Is Social Work a Profession?" p. 585.

13. David M. Austin, "The Flexner Myth and the History of Social Work," *Social Service Review* 57 (September 1983) p. 367.

14. Porter R. Lee, "Committee Report: The Professional Basis of Social Work," *Proceedings of the National Conference of Charities and Correction, 1915* (Chicago: Hildmann Printing Co., 1915) p. 600.

15. Roy Lubove, *The Professional Altruist: The Emergence of Social Work as a Career, 1880–1930* (Cambridge: Harvard University Press, 1965) p. 147.

16. Ernest Greenwood, "Attributes of a Profession," *Social Work* 2 (July 1957) p. 46.

17. Austin, "The Flexner Myth," p. 369.

18. George Ritzer, "Professionalization, Bureaucratization, and Rationalization: The Views of Max Weber," *Social Forces* 53 (June 1975) p. 628.

19. See Paul Starr, *The Social Transformation of American Medicine* (New York: Basic Books, 1982).

20. Starr, *The Social Transformation of American Medicine*, p. 446.

21. Robert Dingwall, "Accomplishing Profession," *Sociological Review* 24 (June 1976) pp. 331–49.

22. Philip R. Popple, "The Social Work Profession: A Reconceptualization," *Social Service Review* (December 1985) pp. 560–577.

23. Eliot Freidson, "The Changing Nature of Professional Control," *Annual Review of Sociology* 10 (1984) p. 3.

24. Freidson, "The Changing Nature of Professional Control," pp. 10–11.

25. Freidson, "The Changing Nature of Professional Control," pp. 10–12.

26. Sue Spencer, *The Administration Method in Social Work Education,* Vol. III, Social Work Curriculum Study (New York: Council on Social Work Education, 1959) p. 9.

27. Alvin L. Schorr, "Professional Practice as Policy," *Social Service Review* 59 (June 1985) pp. 185–186.

28. Ira C. Colby, *Social Welfare Policy: Perspectives, Patterns, Insights* (Chicago: The Dorsey Press, 1989) p. v.

29. Schorr, "Professional Policy as Practice," pp. 193–194.

Chapter *2*

Defining Social
Welfare Policy

The last time Bud hit her, something deep inside of Sarah snapped. She yelled, screamed, hit him with a sixteen-ounce can of pork and beans, and finally, after regaining some control, called the police. By the time the officers arrived Bud had agreed to move to his brother's, at least for a while. After four years of physical and emotional abuse Sarah just wanted to take her four-year-old daughter Megan and get out of the situation and begin putting her life back together. However, it seemed that at every step there was some policy or other to contend with.

First, there was the problem of getting untangled from the criminal justice system. Sarah really did not want Bud to go to jail; she just wanted him out of the house. She explained this to the police officers when they arrived and requested that the complaint be dropped. They said that they would like to do that but department policy stated that an arrest had to be made any time there was a domestic violence complaint. After Bud spent the night in jail Sarah explained the same thing to the judge. The judge said that it was his policy in domestic violence cases to send the perpetrator to prison unless the couple agreed to attend marital counseling. Sarah and Bud agreed to do this, even though Sarah was not optimistic about it.

The next problem was in complying with the judge's order. Sarah first called their medical insurance company which explained that their benefits policy paid for marital counseling only if alcohol or drug abuse was the cause of the problem. Simple relationship difficulties were not covered. Sarah then called the mental health unit at the Methodist hospital, which told her that their policy excluded clients who were seeking counseling due to a court order. The hospital board felt that involuntary clients were not motivated and therefore would not benefit from treatment. Finally Sarah was able to get an appointment with a social worker at the local YWCA women's center.

Bud lasted in counseling exactly one session. He said that the social worker, Julie Draughn, was a "feminazi" and he wasn't about to listen to her. Sarah was not surprised at Bud's reaction, but she thought what Julie had to say was kind of nice, and was certainly food for thought. Julie believed that social policy in our country was evolving from a traditionally patriarchal, hierarchical system which forced women into a dependent role, into a more egalitarian system which freed women from subservience, at the same time placing greater demands on them for independent contributions. She tried to explain to Bud that this policy evolution would also eventually free men from burdens that had often crushed them in the past, but he wasn't having any of it. His last words to Sarah were that if she was so damn liberated she had better not count on him for any support at all, financial support included.

After Bud made good on his threat and refused to contribute anything toward Sarah and Megan's expenses, Julie Draughn referred Sarah to the state Department of Human Resources office to apply for assistance. The eligibility worker at DHR told Sarah state policy required that a child support order be obtained before she would be eligible for any help. When she did obtain an order, the amount, $400 per month, when combined with the small income she received from a part time job, exceeded the maximum which eligibility policy allowed for receipt of financial assistance. Eligibility policy for the food stamp program is somewhat less stringent (income less than 125 percent of the poverty level) and so Sarah and Megan at least got some food assistance. In a similar fashion, Sarah found she was eligible for rental assistance under a policy referred to simply as Section VIII, so she was able to get a decent apartment for a very affordable rent.

Two years after her separation and subsequent divorce, Sarah has become somewhat of an expert on social welfare policy. After her living situation became stabilized, Sarah researched educational assistance policy and was able to develop a strategy to obtain assistance with tuition, books, and day care while she studies to become a physician's assistant. She is still working part time but carefully monitors her income to be sure that it does not exceed the maximum allowable for the various benefits she receives. She occasionally feels guilty about not contributing as much as she possibly can to her own support, but she realizes that the purpose of all of these policies is to encourage her to become a self-supporting, tax paying citizen, and that is exactly her own goal.

Sarah's story illustrates the vast impact of policy on social welfare clients, but more important for our purposes in this chapter, it illustrates the multiple meanings of the term *social welfare policy* and hence some of the difficulties in discussing and studying the subject. The term social welfare policy sometimes refers to broad social philosophy, sometimes to the narrowest administrative rule. When people use the term *policy* they are usually referring to the actions of government, but social welfare policy often involves activities of the voluntary sector of the economy, of religious groups, and (more and more) those of profit-making businesses. The purpose of this chapter is to look at the many meanings of the term social welfare policy and to clarify the way the term is used in this book.

Social Welfare Policy—Basic Definition

To define the concept social welfare policy we must break the concept into its two constituent parts—*social welfare* and *policy*. We dealt briefly with the term social welfare in Chapter 1 where it was defined as the institution in society that deals with the problem of dependency. Recall that by *dependency* we mean situations in which individuals are not fulfilling critical social roles (a parent is not adequately caring for a child; a person is unable to financially support him- or herself; a child consistently breaks the law; etc.); or where social institutions are not functioning well enough to support people in their role performance (the unemployment level is so high that a person cannot get a job despite being qualified, etc.).

The social welfare institution deals with these situations in order to help maintain social equilibrium.

Policy is a rather loose and imprecise term for which there is no generally accepted definition in the academic literature.[1] Some frequently cited definitions from political scientists are:

- A purposive course of action followed by an actor or set of actors in dealing with a problem or matter of concern.
- Policy is defined as a "standing decision" characterized by behavioral consistency and repetitiveness on the part of both those who make it and those who abide by it.
- Policy is, in its most general sense, the pattern of action that resolves conflicting claims or provides incentives for cooperation.[2]

As the term is generally used, policy means principles, guidelines, or procedures that serve the purpose of maximizing uniformity in decision making.

Thus, the very simple beginning definition we will use for the term social welfare policy is: principles, guidelines, or procedures that serve the purpose of maximizing uniformity in decision making regarding the problem of dependency in our society. This seems simple enough but, as you will see in the remainder of this chapter, social welfare policy is a most slippery and elusive term.

Factors Complicating the Definition of Social Welfare Policy

Complicating any attempt to reach a clear and simple definition of social welfare policy is the fact that the term is used many different ways by many different people, and to refer to many different things by any one individual. The following are some aspects of the term which often lead to a lack of clarity and precision in its use.

Social Welfare Policy and Social Policy

As you become familiar with the literature of social work and social welfare, you will find that the terms social welfare policy and social policy are often used interchangeably. This practice can be misleading because the terms do not have exactly the same meaning. Social welfare policy is a subcategory of social policy, which has a broader and more general meaning. David Gil, for example, uses the term social welfare policy to refer to societal responses to specific needs or problems such as poverty, child maltreatment, substandard housing, and so forth, and uses social policy to refer to efforts to "shape the overall quality of life in a society, the living conditions of its members, and their relations to one another and to society as a whole." In a similar fashion Kenneth Boulding in his classic essay uses the term social policy to refer to society's "integrative system." By this he means provisions to "build the identity of a person around some community with which he is identified." Martin Rein says that social policy is "not the social services alone, but the social purposes and consequences of agricultural, economic, manpower, fiscal, physical development, and social welfare policies that form the subject matter of social policy."[3]

The term social policy is frequently used in a philosophic sense. As Gil observes, when used in this sense the term refers to the collective struggle to seek enduring social solutions to social problems, and conveys a meaning almost the opposite of the term "rugged individualism." When used in this sense, social policy is equated with the struggle for equality in social and economic life. The term social policy as used by many theorists "goes far beyond conventional social welfare policies and programs. . . . Core functions of social policies [are viewed as] the reduction of social inequalities through redistribution of claims, and access to, resources, rights, and social opportunities."[4]

Thus, social policy is a term that includes some elements which we exclude from our definition of social welfare policy. Items such as libraries, parks and recreation, and various aspects of the tax codes and of family law are included in the domain of social policy because they deal with the integrative system and the overall quality of life. The continuing struggle of humanity for equality is also a central feature of social policy discussions. While these things are clearly related to social welfare policy, they are not central to the way we use the term in this book. We do not include these in our definition of the domain of social welfare policy because they are not related to the problem of dependency or to specific categorical programs.

Social Welfare Policy as an Academic Discipline and a Social Work Curriculum Area

There is an additional complication for the social worker seeking to understand the term social welfare policy: the term has somewhat different meanings when used to refer to an area of academic inquiry as opposed to an area of the social work curriculum. As an area of academic inquiry, social welfare policy is a subfield of political science, history, economics, and—of course—social work. In addition, over the past decade or so a number of academic schools and departments have emerged specifically for the study of policy; social welfare policy is a basic area of study in these schools. As the term social welfare policy is used in these disciplines, it refers nearly exclusively to the activities of government. In addition to the definitions cited above, scholars in these disciplines generally add something to the effect of:

- Public policies are those policies developed by governmental bodies and officials.
- Public policy is whatever governments choose to do or not to do.
- Social welfare policy is anything government chooses to do, or not to do, that effects the quality of life of its people.[5]

Although many social workers in the area of social welfare policy share the traditional academic definition, the term is often used by social workers in a broader fashion. As will be discussed in the next section, many social welfare services are provided by private, non-profit, many times religious, agencies. These have policies which affect social workers and their clients and must be understood if social workers are to fully comprehend their working environments. Also, an increasing number of services are being provided by the profit-making sector. Day care for children, disabled adults, and the elderly; home health services; mental health care; retirement and nursing homes; and low-income housing are only a few examples of rapidly growing social welfare services provided by the profit-making sector. Scholars in the traditional policy areas would be quick to point out that services provided by private non-profit agencies and by private businesses often receive a portion of their funding under government programs and so should probably come under the heading of Actions of Government. This is true, but it is also true that the social workers employed by these organizations are not government employees, and the programs come under a wide range of policies that are entirely nongovernmental in nature.

The term social welfare policy also refers to a specific area of the professional social work curriculum. The accrediting body of social work programs is the Council on Social Work Education (CSWE). The curriculum policy statement of CSWE under the heading of Social Welfare Policy and Services reads:

> *The foundation social welfare policy and services content must include the history, mission, and philosophy of the social work profession. Content must be presented about the history and current patterns of provision of social welfare services, the role of social policy in helping or deterring people in the maintenance or attainment of optimal health and well-being, and the effect of policy on social work practice. Students must be taught to analyze current social policy within the context of historical and contemporary factors that shape policy. Content must be presented about the political and organizational processess used to influence policy, the process of policy formulation, and the frameworks for analyzing social policies in light of principles of social and economic justice.[6]*

This definition encompasses the term social welfare policy as used in traditional academic disciplines, but also contains tangential areas. Thus, in social work programs it is not uncommon to find courses with titles such as The Social Work Profession, or Social Welfare History, included as part of the social welfare policy curriculum.

Also, in the social work curriculum, social welfare policy often refers to a practice method. Policy analysis as taught in the traditional academic disciplines is central to the method, but additional, generally *interpersonal* skills are also included, which are usually not central to these other fields. A well-respected text identifies four general areas of skill needed by the social work policy practitioner:

> Analytic skills *. . . are used to identify policy alternatives, to compare their relative merits, and to develop recommendations.* Political skills *. . . are used to assess the feasibility of enacting specific polices, to identify power resources, and to develop and implement political strategy.* Interactional skills *. . . are used to develop contacts with influential persons, to develop supportive networks, to build personal relationships, to identify old-boy networks, and to use group process to facilitate one's policy objectives.* Value-clarification skills *. . . are used to identify moral considerations that are relevant not only to the shaping of policy proposals but also to political and interactional strategies that are used to obtain support for specific policies.*[7]

Social Workers Are Interested in Social Welfare Policy in All Sectors of the Economy

Although social welfare is generally thought of as the responsibility of government, keep in mind that the social welfare system in the United States grew out of activities of the private sector; the government assumed responsibility very reluctantly. It would not be an overstatement to say that the social work profession itself is a result of policies of private, voluntary, social welfare agencies. In the nineteenth century, private agencies joined to form Charity Organization Societies specifically for the purpose of developing policies and procedures that would rationalize the process of dealing with the growing problem of dependency in large cities. After a short period of time the agencies realized that one of the major barriers to the rationalization of philanthropy was the lack of qualified staff. The agencies then began to formulate policies for training and hiring personnel; this eventually resulted in the emergence of social work as a profession.

During the course of this century the government has assumed a larger and larger role in the provision of social welfare services. However, the private sector still provides a significant proportion of services. In 1992, public social welfare expenditures amounted to over 1,265 billion dollars; private social welfare expenditures were almost 825 billion dollars.[8] Thus, the private sector of the economy still provides approximately 39 percent of all social welfare services and benefits, a very significant proportion.

Private social service agencies have policies that affect their employees and clients in much the same manner as governmental policies. For example, every area United Way agency has policies regarding criteria and procedures for an agency to become affiliated with the United Way; policies regarding the setting of priorities for funding; policies for financial accounting and reporting; personnel policies; and numerous other policies which, to use our earlier definition of policy, set down principles, guidelines, and procedures that maximize uniformity in decision making for member agencies.

It is apparent that the private, for-profit sector is becoming increasingly important in the social welfare enterprise. Nursing homes, adult and child day care, home health services, alcohol and drug treatment centers, managed care mental health systems, phobic and eating disorder clinics—all have appeared on the scene in recent years. Like public and voluntary agencies, these for-profit organizations all have policies that affect clients and staff. As we will discuss in the chapters on physical and mental health, policies of profit-making agencies present a special concern to the social work profession because of the high potential for conflict between providing services that are in the best interest of the client, and services that are most profitable for the organization.

There is a tendency to define policy as only public policy. To fully understand the context in which they practice, social workers need to understand the policies of all three sectors of the social welfare system and the interaction between them.

The Multiple Levels of Social Welfare Policy

An additional point that needs to be dealt with before we can fully define social welfare policy is that policy exists on several levels. These levels are referred to as macro-, mezzo-, and micro-level policy.

Macro-Level Policy

Macro social welfare policy involves the broad laws, regulations, or guidelines that provide the basic framework for the provision of services and benefits. Most macro-level policy is generated by the public and the private non-profit sectors. The macro-level policy arena we most commonly think of is the public sector, in which macro-level policies take the form of laws and regulations. Examples are Title XX of the Social Security Act, the Americans with Disabilities Act, and the Older Americans Act. After passage, all of these acts were translated into detailed Federal Regulations which specify issues of implementation, evaluation, and so forth. The private non-profit sector also generates macro-level policy to guide its efforts to deal with problems of dependency. For example, the 200th General Assembly of the Presbyterian Church (U.S.A.) developed an 83-page policy statement on health care which dealt with health care benefits for church employees and with the church's stand on the general problems of the health care system.[9] The private for-profit sector responds to, and attempts to influence, macro-level policy more than it generates such policy on its own.

Mezzo-Level Policy

Mezzo-level (mid-level) policy refers to the administrative policy that organizations generate to direct and regularize their operations. Every social worker who has ever worked for a state welfare department is familiar with the ritual followed with new employees: a supervisor sets three or four giant manuals before the new employee with instructions to spend the day reviewing them. There will generally be a personnel policy manual, which sets out all the rules and regulations regarding pay, benefits, insurance, office hours, holidays, evaluations, grievances, retirement, and the like. Then there will be a financial policy manual, which outlines budgeting procedures and forms, purchasing, travel, supplies, financial reporting, and so on. Finally, there will be one or more manuals outlining the policies governing the particular program area in which the social worker is employed. For example, the food stamp program will have manuals describing intake, eligibility, record keeping, what is and is not appropriate to discuss with an applicant, referrals, and so forth.

Much of mezzo-level policy is, of course, in direct response to macro-level policy. For example, the food stamp program, as set out in the Federal Regulations, requires that state welfare departments respond to an application within 30 days, except in cases where the family is expected to have an income for the month of less than $150, in which case the department must respond within five days. The macro-level Federal Regulations containing this policy are sent to the state departments which must translate it into mezzo-level policy by setting out specific procedures so the department can comply with the policy of the federal Food and Nutrition Service.

Micro-Level Policy

Micro-level policy refers to what happens when individual line social workers translate macro- and mezzo-level policy into actual service to clients. As we discussed in Chapter 1, social work is a profession with a good deal of autonomy; this means individual social workers have great latitude for interpreting and implementing a given policy. The political scientist Michael Lipsky refers to social workers as "street level bureaucrats" who, he says, "make policy in two related respects. They exercise wide discretion in decisions about citizens with whom they interact. Then, when taken in concert, their individual actions add up to agency behavior."[10] Recognizing the importance of micro-level policy making rests on the question: If Congress passes a law stating that individuals are entitled to a certain benefit (macro-level policy), and state and local agencies develop regulations and procedures for delivering the benefit (mezzo-level policy) but the social workers charged with delivering the benefit do not support the policy and so obstruct the process such that few people actually receive the benefit, what actually is the policy? The policy is that people do not get the benefit.

The following example will illustrate the importance of micro-level policy far better than any theoretical discussion. One of the authors was at one time the training director for a large region of a state welfare department. He would periodically get requests from the state office to conduct training for the food stamp program staff on eligibility policy. The request would be the result of complaints from college students who had applied for food stamps and whose applications had dragged on and on over one technicality after another. The problem, however, had nothing to do with the staff not *understanding* eligibility policy. Rather, the eligibility determination workers tended to be women who, due to one life situation or another (marriage, pregnancy, husband becoming unemployed, etc.) had dropped out of college after two years (the amount of college required for a food stamp eligibility worker position) and taken a job with the welfare department in order to support their families. The attitude of the workers in this particular office was "When I needed money I dropped out of school and got a job; I didn't expect the government to support me." They collectively felt that the policy of permitting college students to be eligible for food stamps was wrong. As a result they had developed techniques to discourage applications from this group, and if a student persisted in applying, the workers would do everything possible to slow the process further. The result? The actual policy in this particular office was that college students were not eligible for food stamps.

Many people would say that the existence of micro-level policy that is significantly different from macro- and mezzo-level policy is an indication of bad management. Effective management should be able to bring individual practice into line with organization policy. Due to the nature of the work of social workers, however, this is not possible. As Lipsky observes, since problems resulting from micro-level policy "would theoretically disappear if workers' discretion were eliminated, one may wonder why discretion remains characteristic of their jobs. The answer is that certain characteristics of the jobs of street-level bureaucrats make it difficult, if not impossible, to severely reduce discretion. They involve complex tasks for which elaboration of rules, guidelines, or instructions cannot circumscribe the alternatives." This situation is the result of two factors: "First, street-level bureaucrats often work in situations too complicated to reduce to programmatic formats...[and] second, street-level bureaucrats work in situations that often require responses to the human dimensions of situations" which are too varied and complex to reduce to routinized procedures.[11]

The recognition of the existence of micro-level policy provides one of the strongest arguments for the promotion of policy-driven professions such as social work. If the performance of workers cannot be controlled by standardized work rules as is the natural practice in bureaucracies, then controls must be internal to the workers. The most effective means of developing these internal controls is through professional training and socialization in certain values and a code of ethics. The food stamp eligibility workers described above, incidentally, were not professional social workers. At one time they would have been, but in the late 1960s in what was known as separation of services, eligibility functions in welfare departments were redesignated from professional social work positions to high level clerical jobs. One of the rationales for this change was that social workers exercised too much individual discretion and that clerical level staff would be more amenable to organizational control. The result appears to have been the implementation of a work force which is effectively under the control of neither organizational rules, nor professional ethics and standards of behavior.

Social Welfare Policy—A Working Definition

By now it should be apparent that there is no one correct (or incorrect for that matter) definition of social welfare policy. The term is broad and general, and its definition is similar to the story of the blind people describing an elephant—how you define it depends on which part you are in contact with. The upshot of this is that it is crucial for people addressing the subject of social welfare policy to be clear on how they are using the term. For our purposes in this book we will use the following definition:

> *Social welfare policy concerns those interrelated, but not necessarily logically consistent, principles, guidelines, and procedures designed to deal with the problem of dependency in our society. Policies may be laws, public or private regulations, formal procedures, or simply normatively sanctioned patterns of behavior. Social welfare policy is a subset of social policy. Social welfare policy as an academic discipline is less concerned with specific policies than it is with the process by which those policies came into being, the societal base and effects of those policies, and the relationship between policies. Those studying social welfare policy as an area of the professional social work curriculum share the concerns of the traditional academic disciplines but have as primary concerns the relationship of policy to social work practice and the ways that social workers both as individuals and as members of an organized profession can influence the policy process.*

This book is aimed mainly at people training to be direct service social work practitioners. Therefore, our major goal is to help develop skills of policy analysis which will enable practitioners to understand and, where possible, affect the policy context of their practice. We will pay a great deal of attention to macro-level policy in the public sector because this is the area having the greatest effect on social work practice. However, recognizing their great impact on social work practice, we will also devote significant attention to mezzo- and micro-level policy and the influence of the voluntary sector and for-profit sector policy.

Notes

1. Leslie Pal, *Public Policy Analysis; An Introduction* (Toronto: Methuen, 1987) p. 2.

2. James E. Anderson, *Public Policy-Making,* 3rd ed. (New York: Holt, Rinehart and Winston, 1984) p. 3; Heinz Eulau and Kenneth Prewitt, *Labyrinths of Democracy* (Indianapolis: Bobbs-Merrill, 1973) p. 465; Fred M. Frohock, *Public Policy: Scope and Logic* (Englewood Cliffs, NJ: Prentice-Hall, 1979) p. 11.

3. David Gil, *Unravelling Social Policy,* 5th ed. (Rochester, Vermont: Schenkman Books, 1992) p. 9; Kenneth Boulding, "The Boundaries of Social Policy," *Social Work* 12 (January 1967) p. 7; Martin Rein, *Social Policy: Issues of Choice and Change* (New York: Random House, 1970) p. 4.

4. Gil, *Unravelling Social Policy,* p. 3.

5. James E. Anderson, *Public Policy-Making,* 3rd ed. (New York: Holt, Rinehart and Winston, 1984) p. 3; Thomas R. Dye, *Understanding Public Policy,* 5th ed. (Englewood Cliffs, NJ: Prentice-Hall, 1984) p. 1; Richard Simeon, "Studying Public Policy," *Canadian Journal of Political Science* 9 (December 1976) p. 548; Ira Sharkansky, "The Political Scientist and Policy Analysis," in Ira Sharkansky, Ed., *Policy Analysis in Political Science,* (Chicago: Markham Publishing Company, 1970) p. 1; Diana M. DiNitto, *Social Welfare: Politics and Public Policy,* 3rd ed. (Englewood Cliffs, NJ: 1991) p. 2.

6. Commission on Accreditation, *Handbook of Accreditation Standards and Procedures,* 4th edition, (Alexandria, VA: Council on Social Work Education, 1994) p. 141.

7. Bruce S. Jansson, *Social Welfare Policy: From Theory to Practice* (Belmont, CA: Wadsworth, 1990) p. 25.

8. Ann Kallman Bixby, "Public Social Welfare Expenditures, Fiscal Year 1992," *Social Security Bulletin* 58 (Summer 1995) p. 65; Wilmer L. Kerns, "Role of the Private Sector in Financing Social Welfare Programs, 1972–92," *Social Security Bulletin* 58 (Spring 1995) pp. 66–73.

9. Office of the General Assembly of the Presbyterian Church (U.S.A.), *Life Abundant: Values, Choices, and Health Care: The Responsibility and Role of the Presbyterian Church (U.S.A.)* (Louisville, KY: Office of the General Assembly of the Presbyterian Church (U.S.A.) 1988).

10. Michael Lipsky, *Street-Level Bureaucracy: Dilemmas of the Individual in Public Services* (New York: Russell Sage Foundation, 1980) p. 13.

11. Lipsky, *Street-Level Bureaucracy,* p. 15.

Social Welfare Policy Analysis

In Part I, we sought to clearly identify policy as central to the social work profession, and to define the term. It logically follows that if policy is as important as we assert it is, then it is important to develop systematic means of studying and understanding policy in all its dimensions. This is the goal of Part II. We begin this section by discussing what policy analysis is (a very slippery subject in its own right), and we then move on to discuss the analysis of various dimensions of social welfare policy. We will basically follow the outline presented below. Before you become overwhelmed with the level of detail presented, note that we are presenting this as a way of discussing the immensely complex subject of policy analysis, not as a model to actually be applied in all of its detail by a social work practitioner. Policy analysts in the real world selectively apply various parts of the outline, guided by the specific policy they are concerned with and the purpose of the analysis. In Part III we will demonstrate how practitioner policy analyses are done.

Policy Analysis Outline

    I. Delineation and Overview of the Policy Under Analysis

       A. What is the policy to be analyzed?
       B. What is the nature of the problem being targeted by the policy?

          1. How is the problem defined?
          2. For whom is it a problem?

C. What is the context of the policy being analyzed (i.e., how does this specific policy fit with other policies seeking to manage a social problem)?

D. Choice Analysis (i.e. what is the design of programs created by a policy and what are alternatives to this design?)

1. What are the bases of social allocation?
2. What are the types of social provisions?
3. What are the strategies for delivery of benefits?
4. What are the methods of financing these provisions?

II. Historical Analysis

A. What policies and programs were developed earlier to deal the problem? In other words, how has this problem been dealt with in the past?

B. How has the specific policy/program under analysis developed over time?

1. What people, or groups of people, initiated and/or promoted the policy?
2. What people, or groups of people, opposed the policy?

C. What does history tell us about effective/ineffective approaches to the problem being addressed?

D. To what extent does the current policy/program incorporate the lessons of history?

E. Are we repeating mistakes from the past and, if so, why?

III. Social Analysis

A. Problem Description

1. Completeness of knowledge related to the problem.
2. Are our efforts to deal with the problem in accord with research findings?
3. Population affected by the problem

    a. Size
    b. Defining characteristics
    c. Distribution

B. What are major social values related to the problem and what value conflicts exist?

C. What are the goals of the policy under analysis?

1. Manifest (stated) goals
2. Latent (unstated) goals
3. Degree of consensus regarding goals.

D. What are the hypotheses implicit or explicit in the statement of the problem and goals?

IV. Economic Analysis

A. What are the effects and/or potential effects of the policy on the functioning of the economy as a whole—output, income, inflation, unemployment, and so forth? (macroeconomic analysis)
B. What are the effects and/or potential effects of the policy on the behavior of individuals, firms, and markets—motivation to work, cost of rent, supply of commodities, etc.? (micro economic analysis)
C. Opportunity Cost; Cost/Benefit Analysis

V. Political Analysis

A. Who are the major stakeholders regarding this particular policy/program?

  1. What is the power base of the policy/program's supporters?
  2. What is the power base of the policy/program's opponents?
  3. How well are the policy/program's intended beneficiaries represented in the ongoing development and implementation of this policy/program?

B. How has the policy/program been legitimized? Is this basis for legitimation still current?
C. To what extent is this policy/program an example of rational decision-making, incremental change, or of change brought about by conflict?
D. What are the political aspects of the implementation of the policy/program?

VI. Policy/Program Evaluation

A. What are the outcomes of the policy/program in relation to the stated goals?
B. What are the unintended consequences of the policy/program?
C. Is the policy/program cost effective?

VII. Current Proposals for Policy Reform

Chapter **3**

Social Welfare Policy Analysis: Basic Concepts

Every once in a while a policy study appears that is so interesting and well-written that people read it for relaxation and enjoyment. Paul Starr's book *The Social Transformation of American Medicine* is one example.[1] This, unfortunately, is a very rare occurrence. Generally, people read policy literature for practical reasons, namely to gain an understanding of the dynamics of our collective response to various social problems. Policy analyses are read to answer questions such as: How do we deal with poverty? What do we do about health care for people who are sick but have no insurance and no money? What is being done to help children who are being mistreated? Is our response to drug abuse the best one and, if not, what other options are available?

When you seek the answers to questions such as those posed above, you will first consult the policy analysis literature. Two aspects about this literature will, at least initially, puzzle you. First, you will notice that the policy analysis literature is spread all over the library. Some is shelved, as you would expect, with the social work literature. You probably won't be too surprised to find some policy material with sociology, political science, history, and economics. A small amount, less predictably, will be with business, and a rather substantial amount will be with religion and philosophy.

Secondly, once you have ferreted out sources on a policy issue (say for example on anti-poverty policy) you will find that, though different sources deal with the same topic, the approaches look very different. Some policy analyses look like literature, being comprised mostly of stories. Some look like mathematics texts, with lengthy and complex formulas, tables, graphs, and so forth. Some look like stories in a newspaper or magazine (in fact, may *be* stories in newspapers and magazines). To help prevent the confusion you may experience in simply identifying and locating sources of policy analysis, we begin with a discussion of the policy analysis field.

The Many Meanings of Policy Analysis

Like most terms and concepts in the study of social welfare policy the term *policy analysis* tends to be used in vague and inconsistent ways. David Bobrow and John Dryzek refer to the policy analysis field as "home to a babel of tongues."[2] The late Aaron Wildavsky, a leading figure in the policy analysis field, argued that it is unwise to even try to define the term, saying "At the Graduate School of Public Policy in Berkeley, I discouraged discussions on the meaning of policy analysis. Hundreds of conversations on this slippery subject had proven futile, even exasperating, possibly dangerous." He referred to policy analysis as that which "could be learned but not explained, that all of us could sometimes do but that none of us could ever define..."[3] While we sympathize with Wildavsky's frustration we believe that, at least for social workers whose primary interest is not policy, it is necessary to deal with the term before any progress can be made in learning policy analysis skills. The definition we like is based on the one offered by the Canadian political scientist Leslie Pal: policy analysis is the disciplined application of intellect to the study of collective responses to public (in our case social welfare) problems. This definition is sufficiently broad to include the wide range of policy analysis approaches we describe, but is still precise enough to exclude many other types of social work knowledge-building activities.[4]

A key to defining and dealing with the term policy analysis is the recognition that it is broad and general. In many ways it is analogous to the term *research,* which we all realize means many different things according to how it is used by different people in different contexts. We all recognize the difference between a husband saying to his wife, "We need to do some research on state parks before we plan our summer vacation," and a social worker saying, "I have received a $250,000 grant to do research on the relationship between drug usage and marital instability." In a similar fashion, the term policy analysis is used to refer to everything from the processes citizens use to familiarize themselves with issues prior to voting, to a multi-year, multi-million dollar project to set up and evaluate programs utilizing different types of financial assistance approaches.

Table 3.1 presents a typology for categorizing different approaches to policy analysis. The table identifies four major dimensions on which policy analysis approaches vary. The first is the sophistication required of the person conducting the analysis. From the top of the table downward, the sophistication required diminishes. For the top two types, academic social science research and applied policy research, the analyst is generally educated at the doctoral level in policy analysis or in a related social science or applied social profession such as public administration or social work. These analysts generally spend a large proportion of their time conducting policy studies which are read and critiqued by other policy researchers and/or by actual policy makers. Because their purpose is to create new knowledge, the results are generally published in fairly accessible sources. These may range from books and articles available in a good library, to proceedings of professional conferences which may be widely circulated, to monographs and reports available in microform, to xeroxed in-house reports which are less widely distributed. Because of the rigorous nature of the methodology and the wide availability of results of these types of analyses, they often form the data base for the other approaches to policy analysis.

The next two approaches, social planning and agency planning/policy management, are generally conducted by professionals educated at the masters or doctoral level in applied social professions, often social work. They generally have specialized in graduate school in policy/planning/administration. Policy

TABLE 3.1   Approaches to Policy Analysis

Policy Analysis Approach	Purpose	Consumer	Method
Academic Social Science Research	Constructing theories for understanding society	Academic community	Rigorous empirical methodology, often quantitative
Applied Policy Research	Predicting or evaluating impacts of changes in variables that can be altered by public and/or private programs	Decision makers in the policy area	Formal research methodology applied to policy-relevant questions
Social Planning	Defining and specifying ways to ameliorate social problems and to achieve a desirable future state	The "public interest" as professionally defined	Survey research, public forums, expert and/or citizen panels
Agency Planning/ Policy Management	Defining and clarifying agency goals; explicating alternatives for achieving those goals; evaluating outcomes of attempts to achieve those goals	Boards of directors, funding agencies, interested citizens	Data bases, management techniques (PERT, flow charting, decision analysis), survey research, public forums, expert and/or citizen panels
Journalistic	Focusing public attention on social welfare problems	General public	Existing documents, expert sources (professionals, scholars, people affected by the problem)
Practitioner Policy Analysis	Understanding the policy context within which an individual social worker functions	The social worker doing the analysis	Existing literature, government and other documents available in microform & documents division of large libraries, expert sources
Citizen Policy Analysis	Clarifying issues for participation as an involved citizen in a democracy	The citizen involved in the analysis of elected officials that citizen wishes to influence	Existing literature, elected and appointed officials

Source: Adapted from David L. Weiner and Aidan R. Vining, *Policy Analysis: Concepts and Practice,* 2nd ed. (Englewood Cliffs, NJ: Prentice-Hall, 1992) p. 4.

analysis usually constitutes only a small proportion of their jobs, with most of their time being devoted to running an agency, coordinating a community social service program, monitoring program compliance, or any of a number of other macro practice roles. The results of these analyses are generally published in-house and are distributed to members of the organization employing the analyst as well as interested community persons.

The next two types are journalistic and practitioner policy analysis. The people who do these analyses generally are not educated specifically in policy analysis, and policy research is only tangential to their primary professional role. However, they need to develop a fairly sophisticated understanding of complex policy issues, the journalist to communicate with the general public, and the social work practitioner to understand and effectively function on a daily basis. Journalistic policy analysis is generally presented in either written or electronic form in the public media and is generally based entirely on the work of academic social science researchers or applied policy researchers. It is important to note that although journalistic policy analysis is not based on original research, this in no way detracts from its importance. The inspiration for the massive social programs of the Kennedy and Johnson administrations in the 1960s is generally credited to an essay review of several policy studies, notably Michael Harrington's *The Other America,* written by journalist Dwight McDonald and published in *New Yorker Magazine.* Randy Shilts' *And the Band Played On: Policy, People, and the AIDS Epidemic* has had a significant impact on AIDS policy.[5] The following section is devoted to a thorough review of the methods used by social work practitioners to do the type of policy analysis relevant to their professional roles, so those won't be described further here.

The lowest level of sophistication is that of the citizen analyst. The purpose of this type of analysis is for a person to obtain the information required to carry out the responsibilities of an informed citizen. Although we classify this as the least sophisticated approach to policy analysis, we should note that many citizens become quite skilled in studying policy.

The next three dimensions of the approaches to policy analysis (purpose, consumer, and method) are sufficiently explained in the table. The main point is that when you read policy analysis literature you need to identify which approach to analysis the author is using. Most of the literature concerns the top two levels of sophistication and is generally read by people who identify themselves as policy analysis professionals. This literature can be very frustrating for the social work practitioner who has neither the time nor the inclination to become skilled in the application of highly sophisticated, often mathematical, techniques such as difference equations, queuing models, simulations, Markov chains, and the like. Fortunately, in recent years a literature has been developing which addresses the needs of practitioners.[6]

Types of Policy Analysis

In addition to there being different approaches to policy analysis, different types may be employed within any of the approaches. A number of different schemes have been developed for differentiating between types of policy analysis. Our discussion categorizes policy analysis as descriptive analysis, process analysis, and evaluation.[7]

Descriptive Analysis

Descriptive policy analysis can be further subdivided into four types. These are content, choice, comparative, and historical analysis.

Content Analysis

Content analysis* is the most straightforward type of policy analysis. It is simply an empirical description of an existing policy in terms of its intentions, problem definition, goals, and means employed for achieving the goals. Content analysis is most often employed by agencies charged with administering a policy and is generally published in manuals, brochures, and annual reports of the agency. Occasionally, special interest groups such as the National Association of Retired Persons will publish content analyses of policies under which members may receive benefits.

Content analysis is generally not widely circulated to the general public and rarely is published in standard academic outlets. A notable exception is a book by Sar Levitan currently in its sixth edition, *Programs in Aid of the Poor.*[8] In this study, originally written in 1973 and updated every three to five years since, Levitan systematically describes cash support programs, programs providing goods and services, programs for children, and programs targeted at the working poor. The book is not, however, purely content analysis because Levitan, like most academics, cannot resist the urge to throw in a little evaluation of the performance of the programs and provide some prescriptive advice as to the direction he thinks antipoverty programs should go.

Choice Analysis

Largely developed by social workers Neil Gilbert and Harry Specht, choice analysis is a systematic process of looking at the options available to planners for dealing with a social welfare problem. Gilbert and Specht describe this type of analysis as dealing with choices which "...may be framed in program proposals, laws and statutes, or standing plans which eventually are transformed into programs. The analytic focus of such studies is upon issues of choice: What is the form and substance of the choices that compose the policy design? What options did these choices foreclose? What values, theories, and assumptions support alternative choices?"[9] The four primary dimensions of choice are described in some detail below.

Bases of Allocations.   The first dimension of choice involves the question *what are the bases of social allocations?* Gilbert and Specht use this phrase to describe decisions about who will benefit from a policy. They draw two major distinctions in allocation: universal and selective provision. In the first case,

*This is not to be confused with the research methodology of content analysis, in which qualitative data, such as words or themes in a text, are subject to quantitative analysis.

"benefits [are] made available to an entire population as a social right." Universalism assumes that all citizens are "at risk," at some point, for common problems.[10] The classic example of universal benefits is Social Security for the elderly and those with disability. Unemployment Insurance is another example of a benefit made available to an entire group of people—those who have worked a specified length of time and are now unemployed. Since the 1930s, provision for these groups of people has been considered a basic right and therefore a responsibility of the government. Eligibility depends solely on characteristics such as age and prior membership in the work force. Factors such as present income or geographic location are irrelevant.

The alternative to universal allocation is selectivity. In the language of social welfare policy, *selectivity* has a specialized meaning: the allocation of benefits based on individual economic need. This is generally determined through an income test; those below a certain income level are eligible to receive benefits. Students often get confused about this concept, since "selectivity" suggests a variety of ways to distinguish who will be provided for (such as all mothers of young children, all nearsighted people, or all intelligent high school students seeking college scholarships). The best way to understand selectivity in social welfare is to remember its tie to income level and the fact that there is no national consensus that the benefits are a fundamental right of the recipient.

Social welfare policymakers also speak of "universal versus categorical" distinctions. In this context, the word *categorical* refers to particular categories of poor people, for example, low-income women and children, elderly individuals, or those with handicaps. Public welfare benefits and Supplemental Security Income (SSI) are examples of categorical public assistance programs. Since these programs are based on need, they are considered a selective approach to allocating benefits.

There are many arguments for and against each type of approach. The universal basis of allocation carries relatively little stigma and fits with democratic notions of equal treatment for all. Recipients can be seen as citizens or consumers. Proponents of selectivity herald its cost effectiveness; instead of resources being spread over a vast population, money or services can be used where they are most needed. This can help fill in the gaps between needy and non-needy groups. Debates over the future shape of Social Security in our society involve these issues, with some observers suggesting that we should stop paying Social Security to those who don't need it, and instead target more money to the less-well-off elderly.

Critics of selectivity argue, however, that it may be more cost effective to provide social welfare benefits across-the-board, rather than to spend time and money sorting out those who are "truly disadvantaged." These critics add that selectivity leads to a two-track system; benefits for low-income groups don't seem as important to society as benefits for the majority and are thus allowed to be of lesser quality. This is a common argument today in discussions of health care; the system people can afford to pay for (on their own or through insurance) is often superior to publically-financed health care for the indigent.

The broad universal–selective distinction is perhaps most helpful in discussing government income maintenance programs. Within the wide variety of public and private social welfare programs, however, there are additional ways of allocating benefits. Benefits can, for example, be provided to groups of people with specific common needs which are not met in the economic market. Such groups might include high school drop–outs or the residents of a deteriorated urban neighborhood. Another principle of allocation is compensation; this is based on membership in a group, such as war veterans, which has made a specific contribution to society. Veterans' benefits are generally made available to individuals without regard to economic need. Finally, people may qualify for assistance through technical diagnosis of a condition such as a physical handicap or mental illness. Table 3.2, developed by Gilbert and Specht, gives a good example of a variety of bases for allocations of benefits.

Types of Benefits.   The second dimension of choice is concerned with the question *what are the types of social benefits to be provided?* A traditional way of categorizing types of provision is to distinguish between "in-cash" or "in-kind" benefits. Monthly unemployment checks are a good example of the former. Indirect forms of cash benefits, although not often viewed as such, include tax credits and exemptions such as the homeowner's deduction for

TABLE 3.2   Alternative Bases for Allocation of Day-Care Services

Conditions of Eligibility	Examples of Alternative Bases for Allocations
Attributed need	All families
	Single-parent families
	Families with working parents
	Families with student parents
Compensation	Minority families
	Families of servicemen and servicewomen
	Families of workers in specified occupational groups
Diagnostic differentiation	Families with physically or emotionally handicapped children
	Families in short-term crises
Means-tested need	Families whose earnings and resources fall beneath a designated standard of economic need

Source: Neil Gilbert, Harry Specht, and Paul Terrell, *Dimensions of Social Welfare Policy,* 3rd ed. (Englewood Cliffs, NJ: Prentice-Hall, 1993) p. 91. Used with permission.

Comparative Analysis

This type of policy analysis involves systematically comparing policies across two or more settings. The most common form is cross national analysis: the policy in one nation (in these examples, the United States) is compared with policies of other nations regarding the same problem. More limited comparisons, between states or communities or between public and private service provision for example, are also possible and useful. This is a very rich approach because it provides policy analysts with "natural experiments" of alternative approaches to social welfare problems.

The recognized masters of this type of analysis in social work are Sheila Kamerman and Alfred Kahn who have produced a number of comparative studies of social welfare policies. An example of a cross national analysis is their study of child care, family benefits, and working parents in which they compared policies in the United States with those of five European countries. They introduce this study as follows:

> *This report...deals with one of the major family policy questions facing industrial urban societies, or perhaps the major question: what is the optimum response, or what are the optimum response alternatives, to a situation in which parents are in the paid labor force, want to have children, and want to rear them successfully? Modern societies have a stake in both childbearing and successful child rearing, but the consequences of different policy responses have not been given detailed, systematic examination. After surveying fourteen country patterns, we selected six countries which have adopted different approaches. The options represent a continuum, with those in the middle involving different mixes. The group also includes a "no policy" option. We have studied social benefits in support of an at-home option, as well as child care services. We have placed all this in societal context, given an overview of where children under three actually are during the day, and assessed the debate and interest group positions in each country. There is a secondary review of research on costs, effects, prices, and who pays. Current trends are depicted."[19]*

An example of comparative analysis of policies within the United States is Kamerman and Kahn's study of child care policy. In this study they compare local child care initiatives, state child care actions, private approaches, public school systems as child care providers, employers and child care, and family day care.[20] Comparative analysis may use any or all of the methods of policy analysis discussed in this chapter.

Historical Analysis

It is difficult, if not impossible, to analyze any current policy without at least a brief review of preceding events. Historical analysis, as a policy analysis type, goes well beyond this and is based on the assumption that current policies can be fully understood only if we have a thorough understanding of their evolution. Content analysis defines *policy* as what currently exists, but the historical orientation views policy as patterns of behavior by the state and private groups extending over a long period of time. If a policy is the continuation of a long trend, as in the case of the recent welfare reform legislation, historical analysis seeks to explicate that trend and to understand why it has continued. On the other hand, if a policy is significantly different from earlier policies in the same area, the Social Security Act of 1935 for example, the purpose of historical analysis is to explain the reasons for the departure from standard practice. Historical policy analysis methods will be discussed in greater detail in Chapter 4.

Process Analysis

Process analysis is less concerned with policy content than with how a policy comes into being. The focus of this analytic approach is on the interactions of the many political actors, which include public officials, bureaucrats, media, professional associations, and special interest groups representing those likely to be affected either positively or negatively by a policy. Although policy content is not the primary focus of this type of analysis, an understanding of the process is necessary to fully understand the content.

One of the better examples of a process analysis is Steiner's study of family policy in the United States. As part of this study Steiner looks at foster care policy, specifically at the process that eventually resulted in the Adoption Assistance and Child Welfare Act of 1980.[21] Steiner found a number of dynamics to be important to the shape of the bill that was eventually passed. These included:

- The Catholic Church, which in the 1930's opposed inclusion in the Social Security Act of federally funded foster care for urban areas. This was to protect already existing agreements between the church and several large urban centers for the funding of Catholic children's homes.
- Academicians, who have failed to develop a useful theory on which to base public policy for children in foster homes.
- Child welfare social workers, who often do not actively seek to involve biological parents in case planning because "...deemphasizing the biological parent is the safest approach for the child welfare worker, who carries in his or her head two injunctions: do the child no harm and do not embarrass the agency."
- Foster parents, who are too diverse a group to be able to get together to support a specific program.

- The Department of Health, Education, and Welfare (now Health and Human Services), which had no new data or new plans to bring to Congress in support of any expansion of services.
- The Child Welfare League of America, whose main concern was opposing any attempt to put a cap on spending for foster care and related services.

The result of all these forces was a piece of legislation that did not break significant new ground in dealing with the problem of children who need substitute care.

Evaluation

If there is a theme that describes social welfare policy over the past two decades, it is increasing skepticism. Voters, elected representatives, bureaucrats, and academics have all ceased to assume that social welfare programs are good simply because they have good intentions. The result is a demand for evaluation of all aspects of social welfare policy. Rather than simply describing or explaining social welfare policy, evaluation is intended to judge it. The evaluation process may judge a policy's logical consistency, empirically evaluate its effectiveness and efficiency, or analyze its ethical character.

Logical Evaluation

Logical evaluation is similar to content analysis in looking at the content of a social welfare policy in detail. It goes beyond content analysis, however, by assessing a policy's internal rigor and consistency. Logical evaluation generally evaluates a policy in terms of three possible dimensions—singly, or in combination. Because social welfare policies generally have more than one goal, the first dimension of logical evaluation entails assessing the internal consistency of a policy's multiple goals. Financial assistance policy, for example, has a goal of getting people to go to work, and also has a goal of enabling mothers to take good care of their children. Because taking good care of children may well involve staying home with them rather than working, these goals are often in conflict.

The second dimension of logical evaluation involves assessing the consistency between a policy's goals and the means for achieving these goals. For example, the recently completed Ford Foundation Project on Social Welfare and the American Future is very critical of the internal logic of our social welfare policies because they do not have the means to achieve the desired ends. The report argues that

> *The current social welfare system appears oriented to picking up pieces rather than preventing the original breakage. Our policies typically do*

not help families with children until there is a crisis and the children are hurt. We spend large amounts to save the life of each low-birth-weight baby, but skimp on the prenatal care that helps avoid future suffering. We stand aside as large numbers of children are damaged intellectually and socially in their first few years of life, and then rush in with remedial school programs and anti-crime measures when the inevitable consequences of such neglect occur. We also ask the poor to go on welfare before health care is made accessible to them. We expect most jobless and very poorly paid workers to exhaust their unemployment benefits and their own resources before they can receive any help with retraining or other means of securing mobility in the labor market.... As taxpayers and as victims of a violent society we end up paying for the social wreckage that results from a lack of earlier investments in other people and their children. We cannot build enough prisons or buy enough home security systems to protect our private worlds from the social decay that spreads when true opportunity is denied to large numbers of people.[22]

The third dimension of logical evaluation involves assessing the difference between intended and unintended consequences. As Pal has observed "Even when goals are consistent and there is a clear logical relationship between ends and means, public policies may have unintended consequences that can be worse than the original problem."[23] Probably the best known current example of this type of evaluation is the 1984 critique of the welfare system conducted by conservative analyst Charles Murray. Murray argues that while the goals of social welfare policy between 1950 and 1980 were to help people become self-sufficient the effect was exactly the opposite. The reason he gives for this is that, in his opinion, the system became so generous in its attempts to help people that it became more attractive to go on welfare, and once on to stay on welfare, than to "tough it out" by getting a job, getting married, and working to rise through the system.[24]

Quantitative Evaluation

Social welfare policies are created to solve pressing social problems, and in so doing they expend large sums of money. Thus it is natural for there to be a demand for a rigorous, data based, evaluation of whether policies achieve their intended goals and at what cost. There are generally two parts to quantitative evaluations: effectiveness (sometimes called outcome) evaluations, and efficiency (sometimes called cost effectiveness) evaluations. These evaluations encompass a wide range of research methodology, and a huge literature has developed related to both the methods and the politics of evaluation.[25]

The most common type of evaluations are ex post facto evaluations of programs which are set up and operating at the time researchers are brought in to assess their effectiveness and efficiency. One of the best known examples of this is the evaluation of the Head Start Program conducted by Westinghouse Learning Corporation and Ohio University in 1968. The Head Start Program was begun in 1964 as one of the main efforts of the Office of Economic Opportunity. The premise of the program (heavily influenced by culture of poverty theory) was that poor children performed at a lower level in school than non-poor children because they came from homes in which adequate cognitive preparation for school was absent. The program originally provided eight weeks of intensive educational preparation, and in many areas this was soon increased to one year. The intent was that poor children would be brought up to the same level of educational readiness as non-poor children and hence would be able to compete successfully in school. The evaluators randomly selected 104 Head Start programs from across the country; about two-thirds were eight-week and one-third were full-year programs. Children who had completed the program and were, at the time of the study, in first, second, or third grade were matched in socioeconomic background with children who had not gone through the program. The children were all given batteries of tests of educational achievement and cognitive development. In addition, parents were interviewed and teachers of both groups were asked to rate the children on achievement and motivation. The results of the evaluation were disappointing because the researchers found little evidence of effectiveness, although the parents of the children in the program voiced great satisfaction with it. In spite of the evidence of low effectiveness Head Start remained, and still remains, a very popular program.* This fact relates to the political nature of policy in general, as discussed in Chapter 6, and of evaluation in particular, which will be discussed later in this chapter.[26]

A less common, but very exciting, type of evaluation is the policy experiment. In this type of evaluation, research questions and hypotheses are developed and a program to test them is designed following generally accepted social science criteria. Perhaps the best example of a policy experiment is a series of studies which will be referred to again in Chapter 7. These studies started in 1967 with the New Jersey Guaranteed Income Experiment, the Rural (1968) and Gary (1969) Guaranteed Income Experiments, and—finally—the largest, the Seattle–Denver Income Maintenance Experiments (SIME/DIME), which began in 1970 and lasted until 1977. In these studies, more than 5,000 families were randomly assigned to experimental and control groups. The experimental groups were placed on what is known as a negative income tax, or guaranteed annual income, and some also were given labor market counseling and training. The control groups were given conventional welfare support. After various periods of time the families were evaluated to see if participants in the more

---

*Note that subsequent studies have indicated the effectiveness of Head Start in improving children's academic performance.

generous guaranteed annual income program were less motivated to work than participants receiving less financial support, if labor market counseling affected labor market participation, and if the program affected marital stability. The results were mixed and, unfortunately, not very encouraging.[27]

Ethical Evaluation

All types of policy analysis discussed thus far are, at least theoretically, value-free. To demonstrate this, Pal uses the following example of an analyst asked to evaluate the Nazi regime's policy of concentration camps:

> *It would be possible to provide a description of the "final solution," an analysis of the processes that caused it, and a logical and empirical evaluation. Auschwitz could be described, its background and establishment detailed, determining political forces as well as its organizational processes outlined, logical consistency of policy probed and even an analysis of efficiency conducted. The analyst's ethical judgement could be withheld while these technical analyses were undertaken. But the concentration camps were and are an effront to civilized ethics, and it is entirely appropriate to judge them in these terms."[28]*

One of the major points we make throughout this book is that social welfare policy is heavily value-laden. The issues that social welfare policy deals with are, at their core, issues of good and bad, right and wrong, should and shouldn't. Therefore ethical evaluation is a common and very important type of social welfare policy analysis. Because there are sharp differences between value systems, ethical policy evaluations are often very controversial. One of the best recent examples is the pastoral letter of the American Catholic bishops, "Economic Justice for All: Catholic Social Teaching and the U.S. Economy."[29] The bishops begin the letter by clearly stating six moral principles that provide an overview for the vision they wish to share:

1. Every economic decision and institution must be judged in light of whether it protects or undermines the dignity of the human person.
2. Human dignity can be realized and protected only in community.
3. All people have a right to participate in the economic life of society.
4. All members of society have a special obligation to the poor and vulnerable.
5. Human rights are the minimum conditions for life in community.
6. Society as a whole, acting through public and private institutions, has the moral responsibility to enhance human dignity and protect human rights.

Based on these moral principles the bishops then analyzed a number of policy issues. They found the U.S. social welfare system deficient in a number of areas and recommended changes such as providing financial assistance recipients with an adequate level of support (they deplored the finding that "only 4 percent of poor families with children receive enough cash welfare benefits to lift them out of poverty"), establishing national eligibility standards and a national minimum welfare benefit level, and making two-parent families eligible for welfare assistance in all states. It is interesting to note that, although the bishops were almost certainly aware of the discouraging final report of the SIME/DIME experiment, one of their concluding recommendations was that the negative income tax "is another major policy proposal that deserves continued discussion." Apparently, based on the moral principles the bishops were using as the framework for their analysis, the fact that a quantitative evaluation had indicated that the negative income tax resulted in lowered labor force participation did not detract from the attractiveness of this approach.

Policy Analysis Approaches as Ideal Types

While reading the preceding discussion of approaches to policy analysis, you may have asked yourself questions such as: How can you do an historical analysis without its also being descriptive? Aren't empirical evaluations based on some ethical principles (for example, SIME/DIME obviously embraces the work ethic)? and Don't ethical evaluations use data as the basis for some of their arguments? These questions point out that none of the approaches we have described actually exist in pure form in the real world. Rather, they are what sociologists refer to as *ideal types.* That is, we have artificially separated them and described what they would look like in pure form, if such a form existed. In reality, there is much overlap between the approaches, and most policy analyses contain elements from several of them. Good policy analysis almost always begins with solid description and historical analysis, always is based on the best empirical data available, and then proceeds to focus on logic, efficiency, effectiveness, or ethics. In addition, good policy analysis is almost always comparative.

Policy Analysis as Science, Art, and Politics

As a rule, policy analysts consider themselves to be social scientists and what they do to be science. Policy analysts generally employ conventional methods of social science beginning with formulating the problem, proceeding to stating the hypotheses, developing data collection procedures, collecting and analyzing data, drawing conclusions, and generalizing from the results. When attempting to read a policy analysis textbook, the lay reader can easily be overwhelmed by the complexity of the technical methods employed.

While there is no doubt that policy analysis seeks to be a science, and there is little doubt as to the appropriateness of this quest, it is important to understand that there are limits to the degree that conclusive knowledge can be obtained regarding policy questions. Charles Lindblom gives four reasons why analysis cannot provide conclusive answers to policy questions:

1. Policy problems are simply beyond the analytic capacities of human beings. Lindblom explains that "The basic difficulty stems from a discrepancy between the limited cognitive capacities of the human animal and the complexities of policy problems. Even when extended by a range of devices from written language to electronic computers, the mind at its best simply cannot grasp the complexity of reality."

2. Policy issues are based on values and interests that are often in conflict. A policy that may be optimal, based on the values and interests of one group, may be in conflict with those of another. For example, what is the correct abortion policy? For one group, the right of a women to choose is the paramount value, and for another, the right of a fetus to live is most important. It is impossible to quantify these values and reach an absolute conclusion.

3. The more a policy analysis approaches complete understanding of an issue, the more time and money will be required to conduct it. Most policy decisions cannot wait until "all the data are in" and therefore are made based on less than complete information. For example, the SIME/DIME studies referred to previously took nine years and many millions of dollars to conduct, yet provided only partial answers to a few rather limited questions regarding the optimal approach to income maintenance.

4. A purely analytic formulation of the question a policy addresses is impossible. What is the problem for antipoverty policy? Is it lack of motivation among the poor? Lack of equal opportunity? Inadequate economic growth? These questions contain moral components and, as such, must be settled by politics rather than analysis.[30]

If policy analysis cannot be purely scientific in the sense that single, definitive answers are rarely found, what does this mean? First it means that we must recognize that policy analysis is as much an art as it is a science. Wildavsky asserts that policy analysis is synonymous with creativity. "Analysis is imagination. Making believe the future has happened in the past, analysts try to imagine events as if those actions already had occurred."[31] One of the means for doing this is what is known as the "thought experiment." This means simply taking a program, either real or imaginary, and—as systematically as possible, based only on logical thought—analyzing the likely effects. The conservative analyst Charles Murray does this to great effect in *Losing Ground*. He describes a young couple, Harold and Phyllis, who are not married but are seriously involved; they have learned that Phyllis is pregnant. Murray proceeds to imagine what their behavior would have been in 1960 when there were few social programs to assist them, and in 1970 when there were generous AFDC benefits (he places them in Pennsylvania, a state with benefits among the highest in the nation), public housing, medicaid, food stamps, as well as other programs. His conclusion from the thought experiment is that in 1960 they would have chosen to get married and to take jobs, even unattractive ones, because there were no other options available. This choice, he argues, would have put them on the first rung of the ladder of success, or at least to participation in mainstream U.S. society. In 1970, Murray imagines, they again would have taken the rational course of action—which now would be to *not* get married so Phyllis could avail herself of all the "generous" social program benefits. This would result in Harold's eventually drifting off because his role had become extraneous to the lives of Phyllis and the baby, and they would be doomed [his view] to a life as a single-parent welfare family. From this, Murray concludes that present social welfare policies result in more harm than good and probably should be discontinued.[32]

Whatever the technique employed, those policy analyses which have had an impact have done so more because of their art than their science. Analyses such as Murray's conservative *Losing Ground,* or Harrington's liberal *The Other America,* or even Edward R. Murrows famous NBC television documentary *Harvest of Shame* have been well-written and well-organized, and because of this have had great impact.

This leads us to introduce an important point that will be noted again in Chapter 6: policy analysis—whether conducted using rigorous, scientific methodology, or more as an art—is, in the final analysis, political. Lindblom argues that analysis, regardless of its form, becomes part of the play of power, a tool of persuasion. He uses the term *partisan policy analysis.* By this he means that effective policy analysts realize that their analysis will be used in the play of power. They therefore target it to people or groups of people they wish to influence. This is done by taking the values of the group or person to be influenced and analyzing the policy in such a way as to show how those values can be furthered. For example, imagine that an advocate for increased economic assistance to the poor was attempting to get support for increased welfare benefits from a member of congress, known for supporting defense spending. The advocate for the poor would attempt to demonstrate that increased welfare benefits would in some way serve the interests of national defense, perhaps by improving the health, education, or social adjustment of the young people who make up the pool of potential soldiers. While this example may be a little far fetched, the point is not. Policy analysis, be it art or science, is used as one of a number of tools of persuasion in the political process.

Conclusion

In this chapter we have knowingly strayed a bit from the major focus of this book; we have addressed policy analysis more from the perspective of professional academic policy analysts and less from the viewpoint of practicing social workers who need to understand the context of their practice. There is a reason for this: when you begin to conduct your own practitioner policy analysis, using the methods described in the following chapters, you will be relying heavily on the work of professional academic analysts. Their work can be very confusing unless you understand a few simple points about it as described in this chapter. Now, with this basic understanding of the policy analysis field, we proceed in the next section to address methods you can use in your own practice.

Notes

1. Paul Starr, *The Social Transformation of American Medicine* (New York: Basic Books, 1982).

2. Davis B. Bobrow and John S. Dryzek, *Policy Analysis by Design* (Pittsburgh: University of Pittsburgh Press, 1987) p. 5.

3. Aaron Wildavsky, *Speaking Truth to Power: The Art and Craft of Policy Analysis* (Boston: Little, Brown and Company, 1979) p. 2.

4. Leslie A. Pal, *Public Policy Analysis: An Introduction* (Toronto: Methuen, 1987) p.19.

5. Michael Harrington, *The Other America: Poverty in the United States* (New York: Penguin Books, 1962); Dwight McDonald, "Our Invisible Poor," *New Yorker Magazine* 38 (19 January 1963) pp. 82–132; Randy Shilts, *And the Band Played On: Politics, People, and the AIDS Epidemic* (New York: St. Martin's Press, 1987).

6. See for example John Flynn, *Social Agency Policy: Analysis and Presentation for Community Practice* (Chicago, IL: Nelson-Hall, 1985); Donald Chambers, *Social Policy and Social Programs: A Method for the Practical Public Policy Analyst* (New York: Macmillan, 1986).

7. See for example Pal, *Public Policy Analysis: An Introduction*, pp. 27–38; Neil Gilbert and Harry Specht, *Dimensions of Social Welfare Policy*, 2nd ed. (Englewood Cliffs, NJ: Prentice-Hall, 1986) pp. 11–15.

8. Sar Levitan, *Programs in Aid of the Poor*, 6th ed. (Baltimore: Johns Hopkins University Press, 1990).

9. Neil Gilbert, Harry Specht, and Paul Terrell, *Dimensions of Social Welfare Policy*, 3rd ed. (Englewood Cliffs, NJ: Prentice Hall, 1993) pp. 42–43.

10. Gilbert, Specht, and Terrell, *Dimensions of Social Welfare Policy*, p. 71.

11. Elizabeth Huttman, *Introduction to Social Policy*, (New York: McGraw-Hill, 1981) p. 123.

12. Chambers, *Social Policy and Social Programs*, pp. 108–115.

13. Chambers, *Social Policy and Social Programs*, pp. 115–116.

14. For a detailed discussion of social service delivery system options see Gilbert, Specht, and Terrell, *Dimensions of Social Welfare Policy*, pp. 125–158.

15. Howard Karger and David Stoesz, *American Social Welfare Policy: A Pluralist Approach,* 2nd ed. (New York: Longman, 1994) pp. 222–231; Mary Ann Jimenez, "Historical Evolution and Future Challenges of the Human Services Professions," *Social Service Review* 67 (March 1993) pp. 3–12.

16. Michael Hill and Glen Bramley, *Analyzing Social Policy* (New York: Basil Blackwell, 1986) pp. 101–106; *Giving and Volunteering in the United States* (Washington, DC: Independent Sector, 1988) p. 5.

17. Michael Sosin, *Private Benefits: Material Assistance in the Private Sector* (Orlando, FL: Academic Press, 1986) p. 166; Hill and Bramley, *Analyzing Social Policy,* pp. 109–110.

18. Susan A. Ostrander and Stuart Langdon, *Shifting the Debate: Public/Private Sector Relations in the Modern Welfare State* (New Brunswick, NJ: Transaction Books, 1987); Lester M. Salamon, "The Marketization of Welfare: Changing Nonprofit and For-Profit Roles in the American Welfare State," *Social Service Review* 67 (March 1993) pp. 16–39.

19. Sheila B. Kamerman and Alfred J. Kahn, *Child Care, Family Benefits, and Working Parents: A Study in Comparative Policy* (New York: Columbia University Press, 1981) p. xi.

20. Alfred J. Kahn and Sheila B. Kamerman, *Child Care: Facing the Hard Choices* (Dover, MA: Auburn House, 1987).

21. Gilbert Y. Steiner, *The Futility of Family Policy* (Washington, DC: The Brookings Institution, 1981) pp. 130–155.

22. Ford Foundation Project on Social Welfare and the American Future, *The Common Good: Social Welfare and the American Future* (New York: Ford Foundation, 1989) pp. 5–6.

23. Pal, *Public Policy Analysis: An Introduction,* p. 33.

24. Charles Murray, *Losing Ground: American Social Policy 1950–1980* (New York: Basic Books, 1984).

25. See for example Jeanne Pietrzak, Malia Ramler, Tayna Renner, Lucy Ford, and Neil Gilbert, *Practical Program Evaluation: Examples from Child Abuse Prevention* (Newbury Park, CA: Sage, 1990); Richard Berk and Peter Rossi, *Thinking about Program Evaluation* (Newbury Park, CA: Sage, 1990); Joseph P. Hornick and Barbara Burrows, "Program Evaluation," in Richard M. Grinnell, Ed., *Social Work Research and Evaluation,* 3rd ed. (Itasca, NY: F. E. Peacock, 1988) pp. 400–420; older but still of value is Carol H. Weiss, *Evaluation Research: Methods for Assessing Program Effectiveness* (Englewood Cliffs, NJ: Prentice-Hall, 1972).

26. Westinghouse Learning Corporation and Ohio University, *The Impact of Head Start: An Evaluation of the Effects of Head Start on Children's Cognitive and Affective Development* (Washington, DC: Office of Economic Opportunity, 1969).

27. Office of Income Security Policy, Office of the Assistant Secretary for Planning and Evaluation, U.S. Department of Health and Human Services, *Overview of the Seattle-Denver Income Maintenance Experiment Final Report* (Washington, DC: U.S. Government Printing Office, 1983).

28. Pal, *Public Policy Analysis: An Introduction,* p. 36.

29. Catholic Church, National Conference of Catholic Bishops, *Economic Justice for All: Pastoral Letter on Catholic Social Teaching and the U.S. Economy* (Washington, DC: Office of Publishing and Promotion Service, United States Catholic Conference, 1986) p. 3.

30. Charles E. Lindblom, *The Policy-Making Process,* 2nd ed. (Englewood Cliffs, NJ: Prentice-Hall, 1980) pp. 19–25.

31. Wildavsky, *Speaking Truth to Power,* pp. 3, 16.

32. Murray, *Losing Ground,* pp. 154–166.

Chapter *4*

Policy Analysis from an Historical Perspective

VIEW OF THE BLIND ASYLUM INSTITUTION, SOUTH BOSTON.

In Chapters 3, 5, and 6 we describe a number of things that are useful to know about particular social welfare policies, including their political implications, their economic contexts, and their social consequences. Historical analysis of policies includes all these elements and more, as they existed in the past. Such analysis helps us understand how and why a particular policy or social welfare program developed. Policy history addresses such questions as: "Why did the federal government (or the state government, or the Greenacres Children's Treatment Center) pick that particular problem to address, and why did they proceed to deal with it the way they did?"

This chapter discusses the historical analysis of policies. We describe the role and usefulness of an historical approach in understanding and dealing with the policies you will encounter on the job. We give examples of policy history, briefly discuss how such histories are developed, and talk about common errors that can lead to misinterpretation of historical evidence. Such errors are particularly troublesome in policy histories, since these studies are often used to support or to criticize existing programs and approaches. When done well, however, historical studies are an indispensable tool for policy analysis.

Historical Context of Social Welfare Policies

The junior staff of a small outpatient mental health center were concerned about a center policy regarding information gathered from clients. When an individual came to the center voluntarily seeking help, or under the direction of a court or other agency, he or she went through a lengthy intake process. As part of this process, the social worker or psychologist interviewing the client prepared an intake form that included personal items such as name, age, marital status, and employment; a short description of the client's perception of his or her current difficulties; a psychiatric diagnosis; and details on any past psychiatric hospitalization. Since the center received the bulk of its funding through the state, a copy of the form was sent to the state Department of Mental Health. The state department used these records in research on such factors as the numbers of persons with a particular diagnosis served in a given year.

The staff members' concern stemmed from the fact that while clients were not identified by name, their social security numbers were to be provided at the top of the form. Fresh out of graduate training which stressed client rights and the importance of maintaining confidentiality, several social workers and psychologists worried that client names and details of their emotional difficulties could be linked through use of their social security numbers. What was to prevent this information from being shared with other departments in the state bureaucracy? The fact that the State Department of Motor Vehicles had a policy of denying drivers' licenses to people who had been hospitalized for psychiatric problems was especially worrisome. What if, the staff members speculated, the Department of Motor Vehicles could gain access to the mental health department records and use them when clients applied for drivers' license renewals? One social worker who had served in the U.S. Army likened this to the past use of military discharge codes to discriminate against job applicants.

These new employees had been taught that evaluating the effects of agency policies on clients was a legitimate part of their job, and that changing policies was sometimes necessary. They reasoned that in order to try to change the intake form policy, they would have to discover its origin. At first they assumed that the State Department of Mental Health mandated the use of social security numbers. This, in fact, is what they were told by several mental health aides and one of the clinic's secretaries. ("Oh, that must be state policy" is a common response when one is looking into an unpopular or cumbersome regulation). Yet when they examined the state mental health handbook, they could not find the policy. They consulted a reference librarian at the local university; he was unable to find any such rule in the published regulations related to state legislation on mental health. The social work supervisor at the mental health center, who had worked there for four years, couldn't supply an answer.

Finally, they approached the psychology supervisor, who had been with the clinic since its founding twelve years earlier. "Oh, that rule," he said, "actually, as far as the state's concerned, the information on social security numbers is optional. But you know how our director is—Dr. Molson is really a very traditional psychiatrist who believes in detailed record keeping and crossing all the t's. I don't think it would occur to him to worry about protecting clients from possible information leaks within the bureaucracy. He's pretty strong-minded, you know—you don't want to suggest changes to him unless it's really serious."

Having discovered the source of the policy, the new staff worked hard to convince the senior psychologist that the practice was unnecessary and potentially harmful to clients. They elicited his help in initiating a discussion of the use of social security numbers at the next staff meeting. With the legitimacy that the psychologist lent to their issue, they were able to convince the clinic director that client identities were not really necessary for mental health research, and that leaks of *information could jeopardize the trust that the clinic attempted to develop with its clients. As a result of this intervention, the space for social security numbers was deleted from the intake form.*

The above incident illustrates the use of historical analysis in understanding and changing a policy. In this case, the staff discovered where the policy came from, who initially promoted it, and why. They used this information in their successful effort to eliminate the policy. Without such information, the staff might have wasted time advocating for change with the wrong people and might have lost credibility by showing ignorance of the policy's origin.

The Role of History in Understanding Policy

All too often, history is treated as a "frill," or as an obligatory but not particularly enlightening preface to the "real analysis" of a social policy, problem, or program. Social work students, for example, may be given a short description of the goals and activities of reformer Dorothea Dix and a review of the Community Mental Health movement of the 1960s before being exposed to a more thorough analysis of current policies and approaches in the field of mental health. This brief introduction often does little to demonstrate the evolution of policies over time, the similarities and differences between policies of different periods, the criticisms levied against particular approaches, the strategies used by policymakers in the past, their underlying assumptions about causes of social problems, and the impact of social, political, and economic factors on the policies they promoted and the programs they designed. Yet knowledge of all these factors is relevant to understanding, evaluating, and even changing current policies.

In the case of today's mental health programs, for example, it is important to understand that the debate over institutionalization versus community treatment of those with mental illness is a long-standing one. Historical analysis increases awareness of the pros and cons of each treatment approach as it has been tried out in the past. In addition, study of Dorothea Dix's techniques in promoting change can inform current attempts to "sell" new approaches. (Dix appealed first to local physicians, who helped her influence state legislators.) More generally, knowledge of the role of underlying assumptions and of the impact of societal factors on past social welfare developments, such as those in mental health, increases our awareness of these factors in current policy making.

What are the consequences of a lack of historical awareness? The absence of an historical perspective can lead to misunderstandings and confusion about contemporary social welfare developments. An example is the incredulity expressed by a student in a social welfare course when she heard that social work's concern about homelessness is a relatively recent phenomenon. She did not realize that the current housing crisis dates back only to the early 1980s and that for most of its history, the social work profession has not been much interested in housing issues. Lacking this knowledge, the student could easily hold unrealistic expectations regarding the degree and effectiveness of social work's current involvement in the problem.

Not understanding the history of an agency policy could lead to serious mistakes on the part of a worker. A new staff member at a family counseling agency might unwittingly walk into an ongoing debate about methods of treatment, a debate which has grown from professional disagreements into personal feuds. If she questions the policy developed to deal with that debate—assignment of clients to particular counselors by the director rather than by group decision—she might be surprised by the strong negative reaction of other staff. Her actions could well be seen as the naive responses of "someone who doesn't know the agency very well."

History, then, helps us understand and deal with current policies. It gives us some sense of how and why particular programs and approaches developed and how well they achieved what they set out to do. Of course, what they "set out to do" is a matter of interpretation. As we will see in Chapter 6, the *manifest* (openly acknowledged) goals of a program are often different from the *latent* (indirect) functions of that same program. For example, the manifest function of a particular drop-in day activities center for those with mental illness was to provide socialization in a therapeutic setting. However, the latent function of such a center was to keep "crazy" people from wandering in the downtown shopping mall. Since historical analysis includes the examination of a policy or program's goals and effects, such analysis is an important tool in recognizing and evaluating both latent and manifest functions.

Despite these arguments regarding the contribution of history to policy analysis, some researchers criticize the historical approach as "too soft," or lacking the "scientific precision" of other methods.[1] These critics are often quantitative methodologists who stress careful construction of hypotheses and the use of statistical data. What they fail to recognize is that much of historical research relies on elements familiar to social scientists: the development of hypotheses or guiding questions, systematic gathering and analysis of evidence to understand the relationships between factors being studied, and the discovery of patterns or the creation of principles to explain these relationships.[2] While historical study can make use of statistical data, it draws also on a rich variety of other sources: interviews, memoirs, government documents, minutes of meetings where policies are debated, and so forth. Overall, as Michael Reisch has persuasively argued, the study of history helps one develop "essential skills of analysis and critical judgement"—elements central to any research endeavor.[3]

Examples of Policy History

What does policy history actually look like? The following examples include both national and regional social welfare policies, and policies developed within social work agencies. Each example includes discussion of the questions asked by the researcher, the sources used, and the conclusions drawn.

Colonial Poor Relief

The problem of dealing with the continued existence of poverty in America dominates much current social policy debate. What is the best way to help individuals off the welfare rolls, what is the most effective way to provide for those who remain on welfare, and how can we structure our economy to provide employment opportunities for all, are questions that policy analysts struggle with almost every day. Geoffrey Guest's study of colonial poor relief documents suggests that these same questions have been asked for several hundred years. As Guest notes, boarding paupers in private homes was the principle method of poor relief in Colonial America. Local governments paid families to house dependent individuals such as widows and the destitute aged. Despite the prevalence of this approach, Guest could find no detailed historical accounts of how the system worked in practice.[4] Most of the surviving county, town, and parish records gave only the names of the householders who kept the poor and the amounts paid to them. Guest argues that lack of detailed evidence to the contrary has allowed historians to assume that people's willingness to take dependent individuals into their own homes was a sign of widespread generosity to the poor during the Colonial period. Historians have posited that a decline in this humanitarian spirit helped lead to a shift in policy during the mid-1800s, in which the boarding system was phased out "in favor of committing the destitute to poorhouses."[5]

The recent discovery of a remarkable collection of court records from Somerset County, Maryland for the period 1725–1759 enabled Guest to examine the boarding-out program more carefully and to come to conclusions that conflict with earlier interpretations of the motives behind colonial poor relief. The new data consisted of the "actual petitions for poor relief by householders who were keeping the poor and by individuals seeking relief for themselves or their dependents."[6] Using these petitions, Guest could ask: How did the boarding-out policy actually work? Why did private householders agree to care for the poor? Did the demise of this system and the development of institutions for the poor signify a decline in the charitable impulse?

Guest found that most householders (usually wealthy planters) who took in paupers did so reluctantly. Many of the boarders were incapacitated and needed constant care. Once individuals had kept a pauper, they almost never volunteered to take in another. Officials rarely considered the wishes of the poor in making placements. To maintain the cooperation of householders, the court paid much more to those who boarded paupers than it did to those recipients of relief who were allowed to remain in their own homes. In other words, care of the dependent poor in Somerset County during the colonial period was not the sympathetic and generous response envisioned by most historians. The large payments made to householders keeping paupers were more indicative of the influence of the householders than of attention to the needs and wants of the poor. Guest concludes that colonial communities used the boarding-out approach primarily because the number of dependent individuals was small and because it was more cost effective to board them than to institutionalize them. The later use of poorhouses did not signify a change in attitude so much as a reaction to the higher costs of boarding an increasing number of poor people.

What Guest has presented is a careful study of the reasons behind the choice of a boarding system that kept poor people in a family setting as opposed to the use of institutions such as poorhouses. Much of social welfare history documents the shift back and forth between community-based and institutional responses to dependency. Case histories such as this one examine the implementation and effects of these responses in the past. They also give us important insights into the motives behind such policy choices. Guest's conclusion that economic considerations played a larger role than humanitarian impulses in the maintenance of a boarding system for the poor is food for thought when we analyze current social welfare programs.

The Use of Orphan Asylums

Guest examined a policy related to a public welfare measure operating in the community. Other researchers have explored the history of various institutional responses to social problems. Eve Smith, for example, analyzed the use of orphan asylums from the latter part of the nineteenth century through the 1930s.[7] She was drawn to this topic in part because problems in the present foster care system have caused some social workers, and even some politicians, to suggest a return to institutions for the care of dependent and neglected children. In what ways, Smith asked, did institutions such as orphanages function in the past? How well did they work? Are they appropriate models for today's needs?

To answer these questions, Smith used annual reports of orphanages from the time, along with magazine articles, government reports, and social welfare conference speeches describing the treatment of children in institutions. In addition, like Guest, she turned to a less-used source of data: the actual case records of children from two different orphan asylums. These records included not only the comments of orphanage workers about children and their families, but letters back and forth between parents, children, and staff. Such sources provide an intriguing insight into daily life in the orphan asylum and the purposes that these asylums served.

You may have noted with surprise the references to parents and families in the preceding paragraph. Smith found, as have earlier researchers, that orphanages dealt more often with children who had parents than with actual orphans. "From the beginning," she explains, "most institutionalized children were 'half-orphaned' children of single or deserted parents and most would eventually return to their families."[8] Smith's contribution to our understanding of the functions of orphanages is her stress on the way single parents were served by such institutions and on the way they themselves used the orphanages to cope with the problems of single parenthood. As the case records show, many parents, usually single mothers, voluntarily placed their children in institutions when they could no longer afford to care for them on their own. Often they contributed a small sum of money toward the children's support. Generally, they maintained contact with their children and orphanage staff, and were involved in decisions about their children's upbringing. If family finances improved, sometimes due to the return of a deserting father, the children left the institution to rejoin the family. (See Box 4.1.) The orphanage thus served as an important resource for poor single parents and as a way for society to deal with children in poverty.

Smith's study suggests several important conclusions. First, she argues there is little evidence that past children's institutions would be appropriate programs for today's foster children. The orphanages served a population of

---

BOX 4.1   Cooperation Between Parents and "Orphanages"

Beginning in the mid-1920s...the [New York] Society for the Relief of Destitute Children of Seamen offered supplementary pensions to a number of parents in order to keep families together. While some parents accepted the assistance and the social work supervision that went with the money, others did not.

An example of a deserted mother who refused the agency's offer, saying she "preferred work to charity" was Mrs. E. When her husband left, she asked for care for her three children, went to work as a domestic (caring for her employer's child), and paid the Society approximately half of her wages. Thereupon

began an eight-year partnership—agency and parent—in raising the children.

Mrs. E. bought the children's clothes, and visited regularly. She took them to the doctor and dentist when she could get time away from her job, and had much to say about the course of their lives. The society supervised the children and their schooling (they were "A" students), eventually placing them in foster homes found by Mrs. E.; arranged for medical and dental services; and supplemented Mrs. E.'s financial contribution. They discontinued assistance in 1933, when Mrs. E.'s salary had increased and the Society was pressed for funds.

Source: Eve Smith, "The Care of Children of Single Parents: The Use of 'Orphan Asylums' Through the 1930's," presented at the Annual Program Meeting of the Council of Social Work Education, March, 1990.

dependent children with parents who generally remained involved in their care, and who, by paying part of the bill and advocating for their children, were able to retain some power over their youngsters' lives. Most children in orphanages were "normal"; their institutionalization was due largely to poverty. Today's foster children, Smith maintains, "are much less likely to have a parent or parents who can or will ever assume their care."[9] In addition, they appear to have higher levels of emotional and physical problems. The two groups of children thus have different needs which will not be served by the same types of programs.

Smith's study also reminds us that the people served by social welfare programs should not be viewed simply as passive recipients of care. Her documentation of parents' use of the orphanage system as a way to provide for their children when their own resources had failed is evidence of the way in which clients can influence the shape of social policies and programs.

Policies for Those with Handicaps

Smith and Guest are both social workers with research competence in social welfare policy history. Historians have also become interested in the examination of social policy, and in fact policy history or "public history" is a newly emerging area of the discipline. Its practitioners seek "to sort out the relationships among policymakers' intentions, the evolution of governmental policy, and the short-range and long-term impact of specific measures."[10] Edward D. Berkowitz presents a good example of public history in his work on the development of state and national policies to deal with disability.[11] Berkowitz, like other public historians, uses his historical analysis to understand current policy problems and to make recommendations for reform.

In his exploration of disability policy in the United States, Berkowitz asks two major questions: 1) How does American public policy respond to the situation of physical disability, and 2) How have these responses developed? The study is based on the hypothesis that the United States has no single disability policy, but rather a set of disparate programs working at cross-purposes.[12] In order to understand the nature of these programs, Berkowitz relied primarily on the records of the U.S. Social Security Administration and of state offices for the handicapped, as well as interviews with past and present policymakers.

Berkowitz studied five major disability programs in the United States, including workers' compensation, national disability insurance, and the state-run vocational rehabilitation system. He found that each program had developed problems, sometimes unanticipated by the policymakers, sometimes emerging despite policymakers' attempts to avoid them. In proposing disability insurance, for example, the Social Security Administration had intended to establish a uniform national program administered by the federal government. Determination of applicants' eligibility was to be carried out by federal examining teams, thus avoiding the inconsistencies created by multiple disability boards and the over-involvement of lawyers in the system. However, private insurance companies, physicians, and state governments lobbied against the plan. The American Medical Association, for example, feared federal disability insurance as an entering wedge for the creation of national health insurance. Political opposition led to a compromise program, Social Security Disability Insurance, in which states play an administrative role. Although the federal government establishes a basic definition of permanent disability, states have the authority to determine who fits the definition and is eligible for benefits. The strictness of the federal definition and the complexity of state eligibility systems have led to increased use of the courts to contest unfavorable rulings. Despite the original intentions of its creators, disability insurance has became a complicated and inconsistent program with frequent reliance on attorneys and the courts.[13]

In reviewing the other disability programs, Berkowitz found similar problems within programs and a lack of coordination between them. The history of disability policy suggests that these problems have arisen because of the lack of a broad political following for disability programs; differences of philosophy between policymakers; conflicting political pressures from state governments, doctors, and other groups; and the difficulties in defining disability.

Berkowitz argues that the system needs reform and that historians can help in that reform. History is important, he argues, because it brings order to a complicated and confusing picture. Historical analysis shows the development of each disability program and the interactions between programs over time. Based on this overview, Berkowitz makes a variety of recommendations to policymakers. He notes, for example, the ongoing failure of disability policy to blend income maintenance and rehabilitation approaches. As a partial remedy, he suggests that the disability insurance program distinguish between individuals, often older, who should be helped to retire on a disability pension, and workers who are capable of returning to the workforce and would like to do so. Disability insurance, he suggests, could provide "independence initiatives" to the latter group, in the form of vouchers for attendant care, modification of transportation and architectural barriers, and so forth. Using his historical training to develop a broad view of disability policy, Berkowitz thus makes an important contribution to the review and potential reform of current approaches.[14]

Historical Analysis of Agency Policy

Unlike the above examples, the history of agency policy is often informal and unwritten. Yet awareness of an agency's development is an important tool for understanding current agency programs and policy. This awareness can help workers and administrators appreciate agency strengths and analyze and deal with agency shortcomings. In addition, social workers often find themselves in situations like the one described in our opening vignette on the mental health center, where a current practice or regulation appears unusual and/or ineffective. Knowing something about the development of the policy and the key actors in that development can be an essential ingredient in getting it changed.

Methods of Policy History

How is policy history carried out? The preceding examples give some sense of the process of historical analysis. In this section, we will provide more specific guidelines for carrying out that process.

One of the most important tasks in historical analysis is the formulation of hypotheses or guiding questions related to the issue or program to be studied. Historians differ somewhat on how structured this formulation should be. Those with a social science orientation tend to stress the development of formal hypotheses, or propositions, regarding what the historical data will reveal. Those with a humanities orientation find it more appropriate to draw up a number of questions, adding perhaps some hunches, to bring to the study of the evidence. In either case, the researcher has developed a guiding framework for approaching a mass of detail. Without this framework, the study might be no more than a descriptive exercise, with little sense of pattern or meaning. The researcher would not know exactly what to look for in the data and how to organize the final document. As Jacques Barzun notes, the historian is like a traveler, who pieces together "the 'scenery' of the past from fragments that lie scattered in many places." To do this, the researcher soon develops "a guiding idea to propel [him or her] along the route, a hypothesis ahead of the facts, which steadily reminds [the traveler] of what to look for."[15]

In a study of the development of sexual harassment policies in social work agencies, for example, the researchers approached the data (interviews with agency administrators and staff, and agency policy documents) with the following questions in mind: 1) How did the policies on sexual harassment in these agencies come about? 2) Why were these policies developed at the time they were? Were they the result of lobbying on the part of female administrators and staff? and 3) what is the past and present nature of these policies? Not only did these questions provide guidance for conducting the study—for example, helping the researchers decide what to ask in their interviews—but they also aided in the structuring and recommendations of the final report.[16] Another way to approach this study would have been to develop a specific hypothesis such as "Sexual harassment policies are most likely to develop in agencies with women administrators at the top level," and to examine the histories of a number of agencies to see if that hypothesis made sense.

The next step in developing the history of a social welfare policy, practice, or organization is to gather evidence related to the major questions or hypotheses. Historians emphasize the use of primary data, that is, records made at the time an event occurs and by participants or direct observers of the events, rather than secondary sources which are reconstructions of an event by a person without first-hand knowledge of the event. A letter from Jane Addams to a colleague regarding strategy for obtaining child labor legislation is a primary source for someone researching child labor history; a chapter in a textbook on labor law describing Addams' involvement would be a secondary source. Primary sources include letters, diaries, board and committee minutes, testimony at congressional hearings, administrative records, newspaper articles about an event written at the time the event was taking place, and similar sources of direct data regarding events.

The best history relies on a variety of kinds of data. Secondary sources summarize and synthesize the historical material, giving you a good place to start. These sources, however, reflect the biases of the writer, both in terms of the selection of material to present and in the interpretation of that material. Such biases are not always made clear to the reader. While primary sources can also include bias (for example, first-hand reporters of political rallies are real people with their own ideological perspective), by examining a number of different primary sources you can strive to develop a balanced picture of what actually occurred. The description of the development of a policy on confidentiality in the agency where you work would be incomplete, for example, if it relied only on the minutes of the committee drawing up the policy. You might also want to consult the written requirements on confidentiality put out by the state organization that funds the agency, and to interview agency staff members and administrators who were present when the policy was constructed and implemented.

Sources of primary and secondary data for historical policy analysis, and means of locating these sources, are described in the appendix on Historical Policy Analysis Research. This material should be useful as you pursue the story of how a policy or program developed over time.

As historical evidence is gathered, it must be evaluated and interpreted. The end product, or conclusions, will relate to the guiding questions or hypotheses with which you began your quest. A number of questions can be asked about the evidence, including:

- Is it authentic? (Was the policy written when it was dated, or inserted later in the agency files when the agency was involved in a legal case? Do the pages of the social worker's diary include material added by the diarist years later?);
- What was the condition of the witness of the event? (Was this person actually present when the committee debated the matter? Did the individual

have strong prejudices regarding the issue? How long after the event did the witness make his or her report?);
- What was the intent of the document in question? (Was it simply to report, or to persuade? Was it for an internal or external audience?)

The use of multiple sources of evidence helps in weeding out inaccuracies and inconsistencies and in recognizing biases. In addition, all historical sources should be read with an understanding of the time and context in which they were written. One should be careful not to evaluate material from the past from a 1990s point of view. For example, flowery, openly affectionate language between women was common at the turn of the century; Jane Addams' correspondence with women friends and colleagues should therefore be read with that thought in mind. Similarly, social workers writing about African Americans in the 1920s rarely questioned the injustices of segregated social agencies. While this appears overtly racist today, these writers reflected the very limited consciousness of racial injustices characteristic of many whites at the time.[17]

The final stage of the analysis is deciding what the evidence has to say in relation to the hypotheses or questions of the study. In history, as in any other research topic, interpretation of the data must be careful and systematic. As Barzun and Graff explain, the historian uses the evidence with "informed common sense" to demonstrate the probability that a certain event occurred for particular reasons and with particular results.[18]

There are a number of common errors that can lead to misinterpretation of historical evidence. One is cross-cultural error, or the lack of understanding of values and customs of another culture. White social welfare historians, for example, have tended until recently to ignore the importance of self-help groups in the African American community as a form of social welfare organization. Similarly, one can make the mistake of assuming that the ideas and lifestyle of a particular group represent all of society. Those who have studied the domestic lives of middle- and upper-class women in the Victorian era, for example, have sometimes falsely concluded that it was typical for women of this period to stay at home providing a nurturing environment for husbands and children. In that same period, however, many poor and working-class women were employed outside the home, took in boarders, or did paid work in the home to help support their families. "Presentism" is yet another error in interpretation. This occurs when we read characteristics of our own time into the past. Historians have sometimes had difficulty, for example, in understanding that the suffragists, while they promoted women's rights, had a different understanding of women's rights and roles in society from that of feminists in the 1990s.

Other types of misinterpretation can be demonstrated by looking at two important books on social welfare, Charles Murray's *Losing Ground* and Frances Fox Piven and Richard Cloward's *Regulating the Poor*. These works are

not strictly histories; they might best be called sociological studies of past policies, situations, and events. They constitute policy analyses that use historical
methods to attempt to make sense of current social issues. It is therefore useful
to analyze them based on some of the same criteria one would use in assessing
the accuracy and usefulness of a historical study.

As we discussed in Chapter 3, Murray's book was published during the
Reagan era and gained immediate popularity among conservatives as a justification for reductions in government social programs. Murray is a former journalist and political scientist now associated with the Manhattan Institute, an
organization that raises corporate money to support the work of conservative
authors. His study focuses on this question: why, after twelve years of greatly
increasing expenditures on government social welfare programs, was the percentage of Americans in poverty in 1980 (13 percent) the same as it had been in
1968? Murray seeks to answer this question through a wealth of statistics, discussion of policy experiments, and reconstructions of the possible motives
behind the actions of the poor. He concludes that government social programs
did worse than fail to alleviate poverty; they were in fact responsible for creating poverty in the United States in the 1960s and 70s.[19]

Murray argues that according to a variety of indicators, including the rate of
poverty, poor people were becoming worse off in the late 1960s, just as the War
on Poverty social programs were beginning to take effect. He describes the
growth in federal spending on social welfare, the development of new programs
such as job training and community action projects, and the loosening of regulations regarding who could receive benefits. He then details increases in crime,
unemployment, divorce, and the number of households headed by single
women, as well as the end to a previous decline in the poverty rate. He
attributes these disturbing phenomena to increased spending, changes in programs, and ultimately to the fact that the "new rules" of welfare made it "profitable for the poor to behave in the short term in ways that were destructive in
the long term." Using the fictitious low-income couple named Harold and Phyllis, who were unmarried and expecting a child, Murray describes a scenario in
which the only reasonable choice for such individuals was to live together on
AFDC rather than seek employment and financial independence.[20]

At first reading, Murray's analysis seems convincing, especially to those
who suspect a connection between welfare and dependency. Yet as numerous
scholars have pointed out, he makes a number of errors in presenting and
interpreting his data. The first of these is what Barzun and Graff call "generalizing beyond the facts." In other words, the writer produces a broad generalization based on limited facts and fails to test the generalization with negative
examples. This occurs, for example, when Murray argues that welfare programs encourage marital breakup and the rise in female single-parent households. To make this generalization, he relies on the results of a social policy

experiment: the implementation of a Negative Income Tax Program in several U.S. localities during the late 1960s and 1970s (the SIME/DIME experiments discussed in Chapters 3 and 7). Using a financial supplement, the program brought the income of selected groups of low-income individuals up to the poverty line for a three-year period; control groups received no supplement. In some of the localities, the rate of divorces among the experimental group was much higher than that of the control group. From this finding, Murray generalizes that "welfare undermines the family." He thus equates the Negative Income Tax with all welfare programs. He does not look for other examples (e.g. the rate of marriage dissolution among AFDC recipients in similar or other time periods) against which to test his findings. In fact, the bulk of research examining the relationship between welfare benefits and marital breakup has been inconclusive, with some studies showing no relation between the two, and others reporting only a small impact of AFDC benefits on divorce. Interestingly, some studies show that women's participation in the labor force *also* increases marital dissolution. [21]

Murray comes to other misinterpretations through inaccuracies in his presentation of the data. Much of his argument regarding the negative results of War on Poverty programs rests on the observation that government welfare spending increased dramatically during the late 1960s and the 1970s. Yet the bulk of these expenditures was in programs for the elderly. Help to the non-elderly poor through means-tested programs showed only modest growth, much of which was in benefits to the disabled. Expenditures for AFDC expanded little in the 1970s; between 1972 and 1980, real benefit levels for AFDC recipients fell by about 30 percent. Thus Murray's linkage between rise in government expenditures for the non-elderly, non-disabled poor and the increase in poverty for this group makes little sense.[22]

Finally, Murray falls into the trap described by Barzun and Graff as reducing all the diversity of history to "one thing," such as characterizing the French Revolution as resulting solely from a conspiracy. "A true researcher," they observe, "shows the parts that make up the complexity." Yet Murray too often fails to examine this complexity or to explore the context within which trends like a rise in poverty or in marital dissolution rates occur. As historian Michael Katz notes, Murray tells us the story of federal social policy in a "contextual vacuum." He ignores factors like changing occupational structures, rising unemployment, and transformations in American cities during the 1960s and 1970s. To illustrate, if we look again at Murray's use of the Negative Income Tax experiment, we note that he is content to present the evidence that divorces increased among some of the experimental groups. He does not question why this happened, or what it was about the particular policy that encouraged or made divorce possible. Did increased financial resources, for example, allow women to escape from stressful marriages? Asking such questions might help us to understand more fully why divorces occur (rather than to pin them to the single cause of welfare policy) and perhaps even guide us in developing policies that would strengthen marriages.[23]

The idea of reducing an historical event to one thing is part of a discussion of the notion of causation and how it might be approached historically. Frances Fox Piven and Richard Cloward's study *Regulating the Poor* is similar to Murray's work in its attempt to trace the causes of a particular phenomenon, in this case increases in welfare benefits, over time. Although Piven and Cloward make comparisons of several historical periods rather than relying on data from only one or two decades, and they provide more of the context of the situation they are studying, they nevertheless can be criticized for presenting an overly simplistic picture of the reasons behind government expansion in welfare programs.

Regulating the Poor was published in 1971; its authors had participated in welfare reform movements during the 1960s. Cloward is a sociologist and social worker, Piven a political scientist and urban planner. As scholar-activists, the two combined social science theory and historical trend analysis in a study of the rise and fall of welfare rolls over time. The central thesis of the book is that public welfare provisions exist primarily to control the poor. Piven and Cloward argue that "relief arrangements are initiated or expanded during the occasional outbreaks of civil disorder produced by mass unemployment, and are then abolished or contracted when political stability is restored.... Expansive relief policies are designed to mute civil disorder, and restrictive ones to reinforce work norms." In other words, public relief programs are based on the need to control dissension among the unemployed (by increasing welfare payments) and to regulate the labor market (by forcing people into low-income work when relief is cut back). This is a social control argument which attributes the development of social policies and programs to the desire of those in power to maintain order for their own advantage.[24]

To arrive at their conclusions, Piven and Cloward trace relief practices in Europe from their beginnings in the sixteenth century through the rise of capitalism. They then look at data on the relief rolls in the U.S. from 1930 through the 1960s. This approach is called historical trend analysis, or the examination of data over time in order to ascertain certain patterns. By comparing the patterns of welfare contraction and expansion to social and political events such as race riots and other unrest, Piven and Cloward conclude that changes in welfare policy were designed primarily by elites to regulate the poor.[25]

Piven and Cloward make a meaningful contribution to our thinking about social welfare policy by alerting us to the fact that the desire to keep low-income people from "causing trouble" can indeed influence the type and amount of welfare that society provides. This understanding prevents us from viewing the development of social policy simply as the story of an ongoing humanitarian march toward progress. Piven and Cloward also help us to appreciate the connections between the purposes of welfare, the political process, the occupational structure, and the market economy. Yet despite providing at least some of the context that Murray lacks, their analysis is problematic because in the end, it sees the social control motive as the primary factor in the shaping of public welfare.[26]

Their conclusion is troublesome on two counts: it stresses a mechanistic, single-factor explanation of a complex phenomenon, and it encourages simple assumptions about cause and effect. A number of writers have criticized *Regulating the Poor* for reducing the growth and decline of public welfare to one element, social control, rather than seeing this factor as one among many. They have questioned whether the model developed can be accurately applied to other historical periods (similar to the argument that Murray neglected to find other examples against which to test his conclusions). If relief rolls do not exhibit the same pattern during the Revolutionary Period in American history, for example, this may cast doubts on Piven and Cloward's findings.[27]

In addition, Piven and Cloward's thesis raises questions about the search for causation in history. Have the two authors shown that the need for social control "causes" change in the welfare rolls? Here Piven and Cloward may have fallen into a dangerous trap, the prediction backwards from results to motives. True, policymakers and public officials may often seek to maintain order and the status quo. But we can't base our conviction that this is so solely on the outcomes of social programs. In addition, much can happen between the creation of a policy and its implementation. Budget committees, rules and regulations, and the actions and personalities of public welfare administration and staff intervene to affect the policy outcome. Given this complexity, the relationship between motives and results becomes unclear in either direction. Finally, we might ask whether it is reasonable to look to history for causes at all? Barzun and Graff have commented that what history shows about the past is not the "cause," but the conditions accompanying an event's emergence. Causation is really the picture of a long chain of events, rather than the notion of a single element, such as the motives of a group of policy makers.[28]

Clarke Chambers, a major social welfare historian, believes "the past is the most practical thing we can study."[29] This is a wise statement, yet not in the way that many think. Too often, we expect history to provide us with neat formulas for avoiding past mistakes and with clear descriptions of what caused certain events. As our critique of Murray and of Piven and Cloward suggests, good history gives us context and a view of complex, interacting forces, rather than single-factor explanations of the past. What can we do with this history? We can analyze the failures and successes of past social programs for suggestions—but only suggestions—of what might work today. We can learn about the relationships between policymakers' intentions, the evolution of policies, and the impact of those policies in the past to try to understand such relationships in the present. We can be alerted to the importance of social, political, and economic factors in policy and program development. Finally, we can try to fathom where we've been, in order to understand where we are.

To give you a real-world sense of all this, we end this chapter with a policy history of a social agency in a middlesized, midwest community. This is the sort of history you might develop yourself as you begin to work at an agency. It is guided by the questions of how an organization developed its policies and programs and how that earlier development affects its operations today. The history is based on interviews with the agency's administration, staff, and board members; local newspaper articles about the organization over the past twenty-five years; and agency records, including a large scrapbook documenting staff training, retreats, and other activities.

The Benton Park Crisis Center

The Benton Park Crisis Center is located in a residential area of a midwest city. It currently functions as a crisis and referral agency with a telephone hotline, outreach mental health services, and educational programs for public school students on substance abuse and suicide prevention. It has a paid professional staff of six and a large body of volunteers. It is in some ways similar, and in other ways quite different, from the center that was established over twenty-five years ago.

The crisis center opened in the summer of 1970. At the time, the main city high school was located a block away. Because of overcrowding in the high school, the lack of after-school recreational facilities, and the general proclivities of teenagers, many young people "hung around" in the neighborhood before and after classroom hours. This was also a time of anxiety about drugs, rebellion, delinquency and a "hippie element" among the young, and while many adult fears were exaggerated, real problems—bad trips, attempted suicides, acting-out—did exist. Responding to the concerns of local residents and of business people in the neighborhood and nearby downtown, a handful of volunteers opened a recreational and drop-in center whose goal was to prevent drug abuse and provide alternative activities for teens. The initial group that backed the center included a Juvenile Court judge, a probation officer, and several local business people and homeowners. The center was located in a building owned by the city and made available at a low rent; it had almost no funding other than some voluntary donations.

The drop-in center offered some rap and counseling groups and various recreational activities, and was open to all on a 24-hour basis. Perhaps not surprisingly, the facility was forced to close down almost immediately. The open-door policy and the small volunteer staff meant a lack of control; overnight "crashing," drinking in closets, and similar events were embarrassing signs that the center was perhaps encouraging rather than preventing problem behavior. However, the agency re-opened shortly, this time with more structure and a federally funded CETA worker to offer services and help coordinate the volunteers. Slowly, the center became a place to go and do particular things, rather than a building in which to hang out.

Within the next two years, the center hired an executive director (paid, but on a minimal level), a substance abuse counselor with a professional degree, and a part-time workshop coordinator. Staff and programs were still funded by donations, and the reliance on community volunteers remained. Being close to the drug abuse problem and other crisis situations promoted a spirit of mutual dependence among volunteers, paid staff, and the young people who frequented the center. A sense of support was established that has lasted throughout the program's history.

Following the hiring of paid staff, the center received some state funding for substance abuse services through the local community mental health board. Staff had not vigorously sought this funding; rather, the mental health board, not too sure about what to do with these state funds, decided to give them to the one agency that had developed a reputation for working on the problem of drug abuse. Increases in funding helped encourage more structure in the organization. There was less reliance on volunteers, and a larger program of counseling by professionals. A drug educator was hired to do preventive work in the schools. Still, an art workshop and other recreational programs remained, as well as a body of volunteers, although these now began to receive formalized training for their activities.

A major focus of volunteer activity was staffing a telephone hot-line to answer crisis calls from the community. Initially, this had simply been a business phone for the center, but as the organization became recognized as "the place that knows about drugs and is willing to help," people facing drug problems themselves, or families and professionals involved at a secondary level, began to call the center for assistance and advice. Gradually, the center again expanded its use of volunteers and developed the extensive system of volunteer screening and training that is one of its hallmarks today. The hotline developed into a 24-hour crisis counseling and referral telephone service, handling not only drug-related problems, but the full range of human difficulties, ranging from suicide calls to mental health problems to requests for information on welfare services and emergency housing. Calls now came from people of all ages.

By the mid-1970s, the recreational and art workshop programs were in decline, spurred by the relocation of the high school to a location on the outskirts of the city. In response to occasional night time use of the center's building by individuals with mental illness looking for shelter, the staff reluctantly decided to lock the facility at night. In the meantime, state funding increased, including some funding specifically for mental health services, and with the increase came more outside control over programming. Drug and mental health programs were emphasized by funding requirements; no special financial aid existed for activities like the art workshop. In addition, state licensing had been developed for substance abuse services. Complying with the licensing brought new restrictions for the center, such as regulations about the sorts of staff needed and detailed rules about the format and content of notes on client contacts. New and innovative programs were harder to launch. Still, volunteers continued to work on the phone line, and an informality and sense of mutual support among staff remained.

Mental health funding led to the hiring of professionally trained "mental health screeners" who could respond to psychiatric emergencies. The fact that their outreach assessment work sometimes led to commitments of individuals to mental hospitals brought a value dilemma to the agency. Was the center, which prided itself on allegiance to the client and to the principle of self-determination, about to become identified with "the system" and with social control? Gradually, however, as emergency calls increased and taxed the skills and energies of volunteers, mental health screeners came to be seen as important backups for the work of the center. The fact that screeners tended to be individuals who were former volunteers with additional training helped in making this transition.

In the past ten years of its history, the Benton Park Crisis Center has added more staff, received additional funding from the local United Way, and shifted program priorities from substance abuse to mental illness, in part due to a change in the types of clientele seeking help. The consolidation of the county substance abuse and mental health planning agencies under a single Human Services umbrella has actually made adaptation of programs to client needs somewhat easier, as funds now come from a common source. For some time, the center had been part of an alcohol and substance abuse council; it recently became incorporated under a separate Board of Directors. This new autonomy helped formalize the move from a drug abuse services mission to a goal of dealing with a broad range of crisis problems in the community. There has been a resurgence of innovative activity in the organization. The phone line remains a strong asset, still staffed primarily by volunteers, including interns from a nearby university's undergraduate social work program. The visitor to the center today is impressed not only by the description of the array of professional services, but also by the cheerful comraderie of the "phone room" and the comfortable informality of staff offices.

The crisis center thus combines innovation and standardization; volunteer and professional help; casualness and regulations concerning paperwork, staff screening, and the like. As a new worker, you might find these combinations confusing. In order to make sense of this milieu, you might seek out the sort of historical information we have presented. The history of the Benton Park Crisis Center would help you see how a variety of elements—the needs of the community and the clientele, the requirements of funding and licensing agencies, the social and economic conditions of the surrounding community, and the traditions embraced by the staff—have all shaped the direction and spirit of the agency.

Notes

1. See the following for descriptions of a traditional "scientific" approach to social work research: Walter W. Hudson, "Scientific Imperatives in Social Work Research and Practice," *Social Service Review* 56 (June 1982) pp. 246–258; William Gordon, "The Professional Base of Social Work Research: Some Essential Elements," *Social Work Journal* 33 (1952) pp. 17–22; William Reid, "Developments in the Use of Organized Data," *Social Work* 19 (September 1974) pp. 585–593. These ideas have lately been challenged. See Martha Brunswick Heineman, "The Obsolete Scientific Imperative in Social Work Research," *Social Service Review* 55 (September 1981) pp. 371–397; Howard Jacob Karger, "Science, Research, and Social Work: Who Controls the Profession?" *Social Work* 28 (May/June 1983) pp. 200–205; and Karen B. Tyson, "A New Approach to Relevant Scientific Research for Practitioners: The Heuristic Paradigm," *Social Work* 37 (November 1992) pp. 541–556.

2. Jacques Barzun and Henry F. Graff, *The Modern Researcher,* 4th ed. (San Diego: Harcourt Brace Jovanovich, 1985) pp. 193–205; Robert Jones Shafer, *A Guide to Historical Method,* 3rd ed. (Homewood, IL: Dorsey Press, 1980) p. 34.

3. Michael Reisch, "The Uses of History in Teaching Social Work," *Journal of Teaching in Social Work* 2 (1988) p. 3.

4. Geoffrey Guest, "The Boarding of the Dependent Poor in Colonial America," *Social Service Review* 63 (March 1989) p. 95.

5. Guest, "The Boarding of the Dependent Poor in Colonial America," p. 93.

6. Guest, "The Boarding of the Dependent Poor in Colonial America," p. 95.

7. Eve P. Smith, "The Care of Children of Single Parents: The Use of 'Orphan Asylums' through the 1930's," presented at the Annual Program Meeting of the Council on Social Work Education, March 1990; see also "Bring Back the Orphanages? What Policymakers of Today Can Learn from the Past," *Child Welfare* 74 (January/February 1995) pp. 115–142.

8. Smith, "The Care of Children of Single Parents," p. 1.

9. Smith, "The Care of Children of Single Parents," p. 1.

10. W. Andrew Achenbaum, "The Making of an Applied Historian: Stage Two," *The Public Historian* 5 (Spring 1983) pp. 21–23.

11. Edward D. Berkowitz, *Disabled Policy: America's Programs for the Handicapped* (Cambridge, England: Cambridge University Press, 1987).

12. Berkowitz, *Disabled Policy: America's Programs for the Handicapped,* p. 1.

13. Berkowitz, *Disabled Policy: America's Programs for the Handicapped,* pp. 43–78.

14. Berkowitz, *Disabled Policy: America's Programs for the Handicapped,* pp. 226, 234–235.

15. Bogart R. Leashore and Jerry R. Cates, "Use of Historical Methods in Social Work Research," *Social Work Research and Abstracts* 21 (Summer 1984) pp. 24–25; Barzun and Graff, *The Modern Researcher,* p. 198.

16. Leslie Leighninger, Norma Jean Barrett, Michelle Ann Debie, Nancy Hallack, Lynn Krol, Clayton Maodush-Pitzer, Janet Richardson, Kathleen Smith, Lisa Vanderwel, Roger Vanderwoude, and Meg Wilson, "Sexual Harassment Policies in Social Service Agencies," Field Studies in Research and Practice, School of Social Work, Western Michigan University, June 1987.

17. Shafer, *A Guide to Historical Method,* pp. 149–170. Unfortunately, of course, that consciousness remains limited for many white Americans today, as we saw in the reactions to the verdict in the O. J. Simpson trial.

18. Barzun and Graff, *The Modern Researcher*, pp. 163–191.

19. Charles Murray, *Losing Ground* (NY: Basic Books, 1984) pp. 3–9; Christopher Jencks, "How Poor Are the Poor?" Book Review of Charles Murray's *Losing Ground*, *New York Review of Books* (9 May 1985) p. 41.

20. Murray, *Losing Ground*, pp. 9, 63, 154–162.

21. Barzun and Graff, *The Modern Researcher*, p. 156; Murray, *Losing Ground*, pp. 148–53; William Julius Wilson and Kathryn M. Neckerman, "Poverty and Family Structure: The Widening Gap between Evidence and Public Policy Issues," in Sheldon H. Danziger and Daniel H. Weinberg, Eds., *Fighting Poverty: What Works and What Doesn't* (Cambridge: Harvard University Press, 1986) pp. 246–252.

22. David T. Ellwood and Lawrence H. Summers, "Poverty in America: Is Welfare the Answer or the Problem?" in Danziger, *Fighting Poverty*, pp. 84–86; Jencks, "How Poor Are the Poor?" pp. 43–44; Michael Katz, *The Undeserving Poor* (NY: Pantheon Books, 1989) pp. 151–156. John E. Schwarz's book *America's Hidden Success* (NY: W. W. Norton and Co., 1983) contains other findings at odds with Murray's presentation. Schwarz contends that Americans have a false perception of the failure of the economy and of social programs in the 1960s and 1970s, and marshals data which indicates that poverty rates had been dramatically reduced by the second half of the 1970s. Government programs, rather than economic growth, were responsible for the bulk of that decline (Schwarz, pp. 1–36).

23. Barzun and Graff, *The Modern Researcher*, pp. 156–157; Katz, *The Undeserving Poor*, p. 155.

24. Frances Fox Piven and Richard A. Cloward, *Regulating the Poor: The Functions of Public Welfare* (New York: Vintage Books, 1971) p. xiii; Achenbaum, "The Making of an Applied Historian: Stage Two," pp. 38–39.

25. Piven and Cloward, *Regulating the Poor*, pp. xv–xvii, 3–41; David A. Rochefort, "Progressive and Social Control Perspectives on Social Welfare," *Social Service Review* 55 (December 1981) pp. 581–582.

26. John K. Alexander, "The Functions of Public Welfare in Late-Eighteenth-Century Philadelphia: Regulating the Poor?" in Walter I. Trattner, Ed., *Social Welfare or Social Control* (Knoxville, TN: The University of Tennessee Press, 1983) p. 69.

27. Raymond A. Mohl, "The Abolition of Public Outdoor Relief, 1870–1900: A Critique of the Piven and Cloward Thesis," in Trattner, *Social Welfare or Social Control*, p. 36; Auchenbaum, "The Making of an Applied Historian," pp. 39–41; Alexander, "The Functions of Public Welfare in Late-Eighteenth-Century Philadelphia," pp. 15, 30.

28. Auchenbaum, "The Making of an Applied Historian," pp. 30–41; Rochefort, "Progressive and Social Control Perspectives on Social Welfare," p. 586; Barzun and Graff, *The Modern Researcher*, pp. 185–191.

29. Clarke A. Chambers, "Doctoral Research and Dissertations on the History of Social Welfare and Social Work," Faculty Development Institute, Council on Social Work Education Annual Program Meeting, March 3, 1990.

Chapter 5

Social/Economic Analysis

Shortly after the Family Support Act of 1988 passed, we had the opportunity to interview a number of people involved in or affected by the bill. Some of the comments were:

A U.S. Representative—This bill places thc cmphasis of our welfare system where it should be, on work. By rewarding people for working and providing supports to make working a realizable goal we will enable a previously disenfranchised segment of our population to rejoin the mainstream and earn a piece of the American dream. The goal of this policy should be the goal of all our social welfare efforts—building individual dignity through individual contribution to society through a job.

A conservative social critic—Unfortunately there is no way to make it easier to get off welfare without also making it more attractive to get on welfare in the first place. If we let welfare mothers keep medicaid and day care benefits after they become employed we will encourage women who have never been on welfare to quit work so as to become eligible for the new benefit. Once again we have adopted a policy on the basis of the people who already exhibit the problem we want to solve, while being blind to the effects of the policy on people who do not yet exhibit the problem. We must stop rewarding people for displaying undesirable behavior.

A left-wing social critic—Once again we are throwing crumbs at the problem. A little day care, a few medical benefits, a lousy job, but no change in the economic system that provides some people with hundreds of times the income they need to live, and lets others starve, go homeless and without health care. This is a policy cleverly designed to give the illusion of progress and concern while changing nothing. The major value expressed in this policy is that the rich deserve all they have and the goal is to maintain the current system.

A business owner/United Way volunteer—I employ two former welfare recipients in my shop and pay them decent wages and benefits. If this new policy results in a tax increase for me I'll probably have to lay one or both of them off. Some way to lower the welfare rolls! If we really want to improve things for the poor let's get government off the backs of employers and free up the power of free enterprise to solve the problem.

These people are all talking about the same policy, they are all knowledgeable about its details and mechanics, yet they have very different interpretations about whether it is good or bad, what values it reflects, what its goals are, and whether its effects are likely to be positive, negative, or nothing at all. Answering these, and similar, questions is the task of the social/economic section of a social welfare policy analysis.

In this chapter we will look at those sections of the outline presented on pages 36–37 under the headings of Social Analysis and Economic Analysis. The basic task of social/economic analysis is fairly straightforward—to gain an in-depth understanding of what our society considers social welfare problems, how we seek to deal with these problems, why we deal with them in the ways we do, and what will be the probable consequences of dealing with them in one way versus another or, perhaps, not dealing with them at all.

Delineation of the Policy Under Analysis

Before the policy analysis process can begin, a critical first step is to carefully specify the boundaries of the policy you intend to analyze. Policies have vague and overlapping boundaries that can easily shift over the course of an analysis unless the analyst has carefully specified them and is constantly aware of the need to maintain focus. For example, imagine that you have been hired as a social worker with a state child protective services agency and you wish to research the policy context of your new job. Before you begin you must decide: Do you wish to analyze the overall topic of child welfare policy? Only policy that concerns child abuse and neglect? Only child abuse and neglect policy in your state? Foster care policy in your agency? If your concern is protective services policy in your agency, are you going to limit your analysis to child protective services, or do you want to include adult protective services? You can, of course, look at several of these, or all of them if you are willing to do the work. However, once you define the topic you must stick with that definition.

Once you have defined your policy topic, the next step is to identify the policy *realm* you are concerned with. Staying with the example of child welfare, you need to decide if you are interested in only government-sector activities, such as state-financed foster care; enterprise-sector activities, such as for-profit therapeutic day care; or voluntary-sector activities such as church-sponsored children's homes. Because of the interaction between the realms of policy, in most cases you will need to look at all three, although you will probably concentrate on only one.

The major problem we find with the work of student policy analysts is that they fail to clearly specify the boundaries of their analysis and therefore tend to change focus, often more than once, during the course of the analysis. In the case of one student's analysis we recently read, for example, when the social analysis was conducted the focus was on public-sector child welfare in general, concentrating on the Adoption Assistance and Child Welfare Act of 1980. When the political analysis was done, the focus changed to adoptions policy of the voluntary sector, looking at changes in private adoption agencies since 1970. The economic analysis concentrated on the development of for-profit day care providers. The focus kept changing until the historical analysis, which dealt with church-sponsored child care institutions. Rather than doing one coherent policy analysis, the student had done one section of each of five separate analyses. The first rule of policy analysis is: specify the policy you wish to analyze as carefully as possible and keep that specification before you all during the analysis. The purpose of this is similar to that of a scientist who states a research question and hypothesis, or a historian who draws up a list of questions, in order to keep the research on one path throughout its course.

Social Problem Analysis

The first step in social/economic analysis is to clearly and completely identify and define the problem the policy addresses. Social welfare policies are hypothetical solutions to perceived social problems. For this reason the definition of the problem is the heart of the policy, the key to understanding its logic. Gerry Brewer and Peter deLeon state that the policy process "begins when a potential problem . . . is first sensed, i.e., problem recognition or identification. Once a problem is recognized, many possible means to alleviate, mitigate, or resolve it may be explored quickly and tentatively."[1] Thus, the first step in practitioner policy analysis is to decipher what problem the formulators of the policy under analysis had in mind when they designed the policy. The definition of the problem addressed by a social welfare policy may be vague and obscure, sometimes even misleading, making problem definition a complex and critical step.

Our initial inclination when faced with the task of defining social problems is to view them as objective conditions that a large number of people think we need to do something about. When problems are defined this way the definitions seem obvious—a policy regarding homelessness deals with the problem of people who have no homes; an antipoverty policy deals with the problem of people without enough money. However, sociologists point out that objective conditions are not, by themselves, sufficient explanations of how we define social problems; that the process of problem definition has other important dimensions. In a work which has come to be considered a classic in the social problem literature, Malcolm Spector and John Kutsuse define social problems as "the activities of individuals or groups making assertions of grievances and claims with respect to some putative conditions."[2] In other words, social problems are labeled, constructed, and defined by individuals and groups, and these labels are accepted or rejected by society based more on the power and skill of the individual or group than on any objective manifestation of the condition being defined. An extreme example of this perspective on social problems is a statement by sociologist Pierre van den Berghe who argues that "There is no such thing as a social problem until someone thinks there is. Social problems have no more objective validity than ghosts. They exist only in the minds of those who believe in them. . . . It seems axiomatic to me that the solution to a "social problem" is for people to stop defining it as such."[3] A number of influential people have proposed exactly this as the solution to the problem of abuse of marijuana—simply stop defining the use of marijuana as a problem and it will cease to be one.

The social construction of social problems is of critical import for understanding social welfare policies. Let's look, for example, at the problem of homelessness. The problem could be defined in terms of the large number of people who are suffering because they have no permanent and decent shelter. From this definition, the obvious policy response would be programs to provide an increased supply of low-cost housing and supportive services to enable people to take advantage of the housing. Using this definition we can understand the policies of an organization such as Habitat for Humanity. But what of the policy of the city of Phoenix where the city council dealt with the homeless by removing their support system including closing shelters, alcohol treatment programs, residential hotels, and ordering the public works department to spray kerosene on trash so as to render any leftover food inedible?[4] Obviously the problem for the city of Phoenix was not that people were suffering due to lack of shelter and needed to be housed, but that homeless people were cluttering up the streets and needed to move elsewhere.

When attempting to define the problem being dealt with by a particular social welfare policy it is helpful to ask ""for whom is this a problem?" and "who will benefit as a result of the policy?" In the case of Phoenix, the problem being dealt with by the policy is clearly not one of those being experienced by the people without any shelter. The intended beneficiaries of the policy appear to be business people and property owners in the areas with large homeless populations, not the homeless people themselves.

It is also helpful to break problems down into primary problems and derivative problems. In the case of mental health policy, the primary problem is that there are a number of people who are suffering because of psychological illness of one sort or another. Derived from this are problems of employers who have employees who are not very productive, children in single-parent homes, people living on the streets of Phoenix, and the list goes on. Most social welfare policies deal with the derivative problems.

Finally, it should be noted that a policy is often a response to more than one problem, and this often creates tensions and inconsistencies in the policy. Financial assistance policy seeks to simultaneously deal with a number of problems, prominent among which are the facts that many people are unable to earn a living, that many poor children are not receiving adequate care, and that the level of family break-up is increasing. Some policy analysts argue that it also deals with the problem of regulating the labor market.[5] Aspects of the policy that address one of these problems may be in direct contradiction with those addressing others. For example, the currently popular policy initiatives that require welfare recipients to take jobs may well result in a deterioration in the quality of care provided to the recipients' children. The reason for this is that the employed parent will not be home with the children but the job provided for the person most likely will not pay enough to purchase adequate child care.

Facts Related to the Problem

In this section of the policy analysis we assess the information we actually "know" about a social welfare problem. Two major areas must be explored in this phase of a policy analysis. The first is an assessment of the completeness of the knowledge regarding the problem—how many facts do we know about it, and what is the state of knowledge regarding cause–effect relationships. The second area is the one in which we generally have quite a lot of knowledge regarding any social welfare problem—what do we know about the population affected by the problem.

Completeness of Knowledge Related to the Problem

One of the most important factors in the understanding of social welfare policy analysis, and in understanding any social welfare policy area, is the realization that there is a tremendous amount we really don't know about most social welfare problems. We have any number of theories and we have a seeming infinite number of discrete facts about any one problem, but when it comes to actually knowing why certain people are poor, why the rate of violent crime is increasing, how we can improve the school performance of inner city kids, our knowledge often is incomplete.

In some areas, the knowledge base is much more complete than in others. We know quite a lot, for example, about health care. We know that by increasing the availability of prenatal care we can reduce the number of birth defects. We can even calculate how much money we need to spend to eliminate a certain number of birth defects, and compare that to the cost of repairing or managing the defects that result from the lack of care. In mental health policy, by comparison, the degree of completeness of knowledge is fairly low. For years we have developed policies that provide psychotherapy to persons suffering from psychological disorders, without much evidence that the provision of these services does any good. However, our knowledge about the causes of mental illness, and particularly its physiological aspects, has been increasing.

Thus it must be recognized that most social welfare policies are actually experiments. Based on the completeness of the knowledge, we can state that some are more experimental than others. The primary questions in health policy revolve around what services we want to provide and how we want to deliver them. We have a pretty good idea regarding the results. In mental health, public assistance, and family policy, the primary questions are, What services should we provide, and Will they work. In many cases we really don't know.

Population Affected by the Problem

The one area about which we know quite a lot regarding most social welfare problems is the characteristics of the population affected by the problem. How large is the population? What are the population trends? We obviously tend to worry more about a problem which affects a large population than we do about a small one, but what probably worries us most is a problem that is rapidly growing. AIDS, for example, does not affect as large a population as cancer, but we are terrified because it is growing and the rate of growth appears to be increasing.

After we have established the population size and the growth trends of the problem under analysis, we then look at the defining characteristics of the population affected—the statistics on age, sex, race, family structure, geographic distribution, and so forth. These characteristics often lead to some very interesting hypotheses about how we deal with the problem. Continuing with the example of AIDS, it is interesting that the level of concern, as indicated by the amount of money spent on AIDS research and treatment, began to increase dramatically when significant numbers of heterosexual, non-drug users began to show up in the statistics.

Social Values Related to the Problem

In the two previous sections we have observed that the definition of social welfare problems is largely socially constructed and that the level of knowledge regarding most problems is incomplete. Based on these observations, it should come as no surprise that values constitute what is probably the most important dimension for understanding social welfare policy. David Easton's definition of politics as "the authoritative allocation of values for society" could just as well apply to social welfare policy.[6] In order to understand our society's response to social welfare problems, you must inquire as to what values support the policy and what values the policy offends.

What major U.S. values lead people to support or oppose various responses to social welfare problems? Probably the best analysis, although now a bit dated, is that developed by sociologist Robin Williams.[7] Williams identifies fifteen major value orientations in U.S. society.* These are discussed below.

Achievement and Success

United States society is marked by a great emphasis on achievement, particularly occupational achievement. This is a very competitive society, and people who don't measure up in the competition are looked down upon. Social welfare policies deal with problems closely related to lack of success. Poor people have not achieved occupationally; people experiencing marital discord have not succeeded in their relationship; people with psychologically disturbed children are viewed as having failed as parents; and so forth. Thus almost any social welfare policy faces an uphill struggle for public support, in that it generally deals with a problem which violates this basic value. A frequent response to this value by social welfare policy makers is to couch policies in terms that indicate that the policy will attempt to instill this value in its clients. A program started by the state of Alabama in response to the welfare reform act of 1988, for example, is entitled Project Success.

Activity and Work

Numerous observers, from Tocqueville up to the most recent, have noted that Americans place a high value on being busy. Even in our leisure activities we emphasize some form of purposeful, action oriented, behavior. However, the primary manifestation of this value is in relation to work. Williams observes "Directed and disciplined activity in a regular occupation is a particular form of this basic orientation."[8] Work has become almost an end in itself, valued even when it is not necessary for economic survival. Observe, for example, that the first thing most winners of large sums of money in lotteries are quoted as

---

*In a later work Williams expanded his list to 19 by separating some of the values into two or three. Tropman has taken Williams' list and condensed the values into seven value dimensions—work, mobility, status, independence, individualism, moralism, and ascription. We do not believe that either of these permutations improves on the 1971 version of the list used as the basis for this discussion. See Robin M. Williams, Jr. "Change and Stability in Values and Value Systems: A Sociological Perspective," in Milton Rokeach, Ed., *Understanding Human Values: Individual and Societal* (New York: The Free Press, 1979) pp. 15–46; and John E. Tropman, *American Values and Social Welfare; Cultural Contradictions in the Welfare State,* (Englewood Cliffs, NJ: Prentice-Hall, 1989).

saying is some variant of the statement "I'm not going to quit my job." Because many social welfare programs provide people with the means of existence without being tied to work, they are immediately suspect in the eyes of many Americans.

Moral Orientation

Americans generally view the world in moral terms—in terms of right and wrong, good and bad, ethical and unethical. The recipients of social welfare benefits are often suspected of having engaged in behavior that is morally bad, or having not engaged in behavior that is morally good. Some welfare mothers, for example, have had children without benefit of marriage, have dropped out of school, and are not working, all behaviors we are likely to condemn as bad, perhaps even sinful. This moral orientation has often led to differentiation between recipients of services and benefits as "worthy" or "unworthy."

Humanitarian Mores

Caring for one another, particularly those who are perceived as less fortunate and suffering through no fault of their own, is a key value in U.S. society. Williams points out that one manifestation of this value is the fact that fully one-third of the adult population participates in some form of voluntary service. This value serves, to a certain extent, to counter punitive social welfare policies that occasionally emerge out of our moral orientation.

Efficiency and Practicality

This society places a high value on good stewardship of time and material resources. We feel a compulsion to continually seek the best means possible for achieving a certain end. This value has several very important consequences for the social work profession. The first is a historic interest in developing better technical means to deal with social welfare problems. For years social workers have sought to develop a "science of social casework." Another way this value manifests itself is in our continual concern with accountability, that is, in demonstrating that social welfare programs are being run efficiently and are having the intended effects. It is ironic that the end result of this value is often antithetical to the value itself. For example, it has been estimated that as much as 40 percent of a social worker's time in public agencies is spent doing paperwork, mostly for the purpose of documenting that the agency is doing its job efficiently and effectively. During training sessions on procedures for completing time documentation forms, a frequent—and legitimate—

question is, "Where on this form do I put down all the time I spend filling out this form?"

Progress

Americans hold charter membership in what Williams has called the "cult of progress," believing that things can, and should, continually be getting better. The historian Henry Steele Commager has observed that "Throughout their history Americans have insisted that the best was yet to be. . . . The American knew that nothing was impossible in his brave new world. . . . Progress was not, to him, a mere philosophical ideal but a commonplace of experience."[9] Because of this belief U.S. society has never accepted the position of many other societies, both past and present, that social problems are simply a part of the natural order of things, and that attempts to change social conditions are as useless as trying to change the ocean's tides. We are continually attempting to do something about conditions such as poverty, ill health, crime, violence, and so forth. An unfortunate side effect of this value is that if a policy or program does not result in immediate results, we tend to quickly grow impatient with it and abandon it in order to try something else. Poverty, for example, has been around for thousands of years; when the War on Poverty didn't eliminate it in three years, Congress became disillusioned and began to dismantle the policy.

Material Comfort

The United States is an acquisitive and materialistic culture. This statement really requires no more justification than to look around yourself at the lifestyles of friends and acquaintances, and to look at what is emphasized in TV commercials and magazine ads. We equate material possessions with happiness and success. The relevance of this value for understanding social welfare policy resides in the fact that people needing social welfare services generally, although not always, are people who are experiencing a low level of material comfort. This raises very difficult questions as to what level of material comfort they have a right to, or that the rest of society has an obligation to provide. We also believe that a lack of material comfort can be a good thing because it will tend to spur people on to solve their own problems to gain the material comforts they desire. (The comedian Red Skelton once said "I've got a solution to poverty—tax the poor; give them an incentive to get rich.") One of the major principles of financial assistance policy ever since the 1601 Elizabethan Poor Laws has been that of less eligibility. This is the notion that the level of material comfort of people receiving the highest level of welfare benefits should always be lower than the level of the least comfortable working person.

Equality

The value of equality constitutes a steady theme throughout American history. Yet, as Williams notes, "few other value complexes are more subject to strain in modern times."[10] We express strong support for the idea of equality as a philosophical principle, but our society is characterized by a high degree of inequality, and most Americans believe this is as it should be. The explanation for this apparent discrepancy is that when most Americans speak of equality they mean equality of opportunity, not of outcome. We believe people should have an equal chance in life, and find elements such as ascribed social status, old boy networks, and the like to be deeply offensive. Social welfare policies that help achieve equality of opportunity, such as Head Start, are warmly supported by most people in the United States. Policies that smack of equality of outcome, whether this is the intent or not, such as guaranteed annual income, racial and sexual hiring quotas, and the like, always face strong opposition.

Freedom

As anyone who has taken a high school civics class is aware, the concept of freedom is complex and multidimensional. Obviously, freedom does not mean freedom from all external control. In the United States, *freedom* generally refers to a preference for control by diffuse social processes rather than by any definite social organization. For example, the practice of neighborhood segregation by race or religion has been made illegal because it violates the value of freedom by forcefully excluding people from certain residences by law. However, few people are totally free to live wherever they wish, simply because they can afford only certain neighborhoods. Thus, in the United States, freedom generally means freedom from excessive and arbitrary external restraint. This way of looking at freedom has resulted in "a tendency to think of rights rather than duties, a suspicion of established (especially personal) authority, a distrust of central government, a deep aversion to acceptance of obviously coercive restraint through visible social organization."[11] The value of freedom has important consequences for understanding almost any social welfare policy. Social welfare policies are often viewed as increasing the rights of one group and decreasing the freedom of another. Child protection laws increase the rights of children to a minimal standard of care, but reduce the freedom of parents to rear children as they see fit without interference by government; financial assistance policies increase the rights of individuals to live with a certain degree of dignity, but decrease the freedom of taxpayers to enjoy the fruits of their own labor; health care policy increases the rights of people to receive medical care, but decreases the freedom of physicians to practice medicine as they wish, and so on.

External Conformity

Even though the American self-image celebrates individualism, it has been frequently noted that we have a rather low tolerance for those who do not conform to accepted standards. Williams observes that "American 'individualism,' taken in broadest terms, has consisted mainly of a rejection of the state and impatience with restraints upon economic activity; it has not tended to set the autonomous individual up in rebellion against his social group."[12] By and large we do not approve of those who vary too far from the norm in dress, behavior, manners, lifestyle, or whatever. Social welfare policies are often directed at people who do not conform to some important standard; they may be unmarried mothers, teenagers who don't go to school, people who use drugs, or people who choose relationships with members of their own sex rather than conforming to the predominant family pattern. Social welfare policies directed at these groups generally are aimed at helping them, but often have an underlying purpose of attempting to control, and sometimes eliminate, the non-conforming behavior.

Science and Secular Rationality

Americans have great faith that the methods of science will eventually solve all, or nearly all, problems of living in our physical and social world. We believe that even the seemingly intractable social problems addressed by social welfare policies will eventually succumb to the onslaught of scientific method. One of the authors had a social work professor who, upon seeing a blackboard covered with formulas from a chemistry class that had met there the previous period, remarked "See that; that's chemistry; it'll really be nice when we can do that." At the present time, however, we are still some way from good, useful knowledge applicable to most social welfare problems, and this causes much frustration among policymakers.

Nationalism-Patriotism

Every society is characterized by some degree of ethnocentrism—that is, the belief that membership in that group is preferable to membership in any other group. In the United States this feeling is quite strong, although probably no stronger than in many other areas of the world. (In some primitive cultures, people outside the culture are not even considered to be human.) In the United States, nationalism-patriotism has one unique dimension: a sense of missionary zeal to spread U.S. economic and governmental institutions throughout the world, generally by nonmilitary means. Many nations have, in the past, sought to conquer other nations in order to dominate them and thereby gain wealth and advantage. The United States wishes for other nations to adopt our way of doing things not for our own advantage but because we feel they, and consequently the rest of the world, will benefit if they do so. Nationalism-patriotism is a value complex that does not have a great relevance for understanding social welfare policy, but it does have some. In Chapter 4 we discussed cross cultural comparison as one approach to policy analysis. Cross cultural comparisons often result in findings that are embarrassing to the United States because they show that we, who like to think of ourselves as world leaders, often rank below some third world nations on social indicators such as infant mortality. Appeals to the value of nationalism-patriotism can often be more effective in engendering sympathy for social welfare proposals than appeals to more obvious values such as humanitarianism.

Democracy

It goes almost without saying that one of the star positions in America's constellation of values is a belief in democratic process, that is, decision making with every person's preferences being weighed. Democracy, however, is sometimes problematic in social welfare policy. The reason for this is related to what Tocqueville referred to as the "tyranny of the majority." This means that if everything is done by majority rule, people, or groups of people, who are not part of the majority can suffer some very harsh consequences as a result of never getting their way. African Americans, Hispanics, gays, and migrant workers have all suffered because the majority has not been sensitive to their problems. Social welfare policies often face strong opposition based on the argument that they are undemocratic because they benefit a minority group against the will of the majority. School integration, while not a social welfare policy as we are defining the term but certainly a social policy, is probably the clearest example of this.

Individual Personality

In the United States we place an extremely high value on the worth and dignity of the individual. We also place a heavy load of responsibility on the individual in the form of credit for success and blame for failure. In many areas of the world—Japan is probably the most frequently cited example—the well-being of the group is the central value, and individuals are expected to defer their own wishes to the collective welfare of the group. This is not the case in the United States. Groups are viewed as collections of individuals formed for the purpose of facilitating the goals and promoting the welfare of individual members. The value of individual personality is critical for understanding social welfare policy in this country. By their very definition, social welfare policies involve collective provisions for the assistance of individuals. Thus they generally involve sacrifice by individuals for the good of the group. For example, public social welfare policies require individuals, sometimes against their will, to sacrifice part of their income, in the form of taxes, to finance provisions for people without enough money to live on. This is deeply offensive to many Americans and guarantees opposition to any proposed expansion of social welfare programs.

Racism, Sexism, and Related Group Superiority Themes

Although the United States is characterized by very strong values of democracy, individualism, humanitarianism, and so forth, we have to recognize that there are what Williams refers to as "deviant themes, contrary to the main thrust of American society," namely racism, sexism, and related prejudices. Because these themes run counter to so many of our other value clusters, we have attempted to resolve them through numerous pieces of legislation. However, we must recognize that they are still present to a much greater degree than we care to admit. Ugly as the value cluster of racism, sexism, and so forth, may be, we must recognize its existence if we are to fully understand social welfare policies. The common perception is that the majority of beneficiaries of most social welfare policies are minorities and women, and thus these policies are often equated with these groups. On the one hand, social welfare policies often receive support from individuals and groups who support attempts to redress the effects of discrimination against minorities and women. In fact, many policies, such as affirmative action and minority scholarships, are often proposed specifically for this purpose. On the other hand, individuals and groups often oppose social welfare policies and, although they generally don't admit this, the reason for the opposition is often directly a result of racism and sexism.

Contradictions in the American Value System

As you may well have figured out from thinking about the values discussed above, they do not result in a uniform pattern, but rather are shot through with conflicts and contradictions. We are motivated to help the poor by our value of humanitarianism, but this is mitigated by other values: *moralism,* which leads us to believe that poverty is somehow related to improper behavior; *individualism,* which places responsibility for problems and for their solution at the feet of the individual affected; and the value of activity and work, which causes us to suspect that welfare programs encourage non-work behavior. Policies to assist groups who are victims of oppression, such as women, African Americans, and gays, are encouraged by our belief in equality, but are retarded by values of *democracy and freedom,* which lead us to suspect that by promoting the rights of one group we will be discriminating against another; and, below the surface, by *racism, sexism,* and *group superiority* themes. Thus our social welfare policies often appear to be schizophrenic because they are attempting to balance numerous conflicting values.

Goals of the Policy Under Analysis

In *Alice in Wonderland,* Alice has the following exchange with the Cheshire Cat—

> *"Would you tell me, please, which way I ought to go from here?"*
> *"That depends a good deal on where you want to get to," said the cat.*
> *"I don't much care where—" said Alice.*
> *"Then it doesn't matter which way you go," said the cat.[13]*

Unlike Alice, the designers of social welfare policies have fairly specific destinations, or goals, in mind. To understand a policy it is necessary to understand just what these goals are. This task constitutes the next stage of the social analysis.

A policy goal is the desired state of affairs that is hoped to be achieved by the policy. As with many areas of policy analysis, the task of determining goals appears simple at the outset, but once you are into it you discover that it can be extremely complex and often misleading. There is a rich sociological literature on the subject of goals that deals with the topic in much greater depth than we need to here.[14]

Policies generally are directed toward more than one goal, and these multiple goals are often in conflict with one another. This is a result of the conflicts in the value structure of United States society discussed above, in combination with the political nature of policy making. Child welfare policy, for example, pursues two often incompatible goals. On the one hand, we seek to assure that all children grow up in a safe home. On the other hand, we seek to assure that a child can grow up in his or her own family. Assuring the safety of children can involve removing them from their families; keeping families intact can involve putting children at risk. In a similar fashion, mental health policy has a goal of preventing mentally ill people from harming themselves and/or others, but also has a goal of putting people in the "least restrictive environment." Obviously, the less restrictive an environment becomes, the greater the risk of disturbed persons harming themselves or others. Financial assistance policy seeks to support people at a adequate level but also has a goal of motivating people to work. If the level of assistance ever becomes such that it truly could be defined as adequate this presumably would lower the recipient's motivation to work.

In almost all cases policies are directed toward different levels of goals, often distinguished as *goals* and *objectives.* The goal of a policy is a general and abstract statement of the state of affairs the policy makers seek to accomplish. A goal is generally difficult to measure and often is not even intended to be accomplished. It is rather a benchmark, a statement that provides general direction to the activities of the programs set up under the policy. For example, the goal of a state policy regarding child welfare staffing was stated as "To assure that all dependent and neglected children in the state receive the highest possible quality services from experienced, professionally trained social workers and allied personnel." Objectives are derived from goals and are specific, concrete, measurable statements. The objectives derived from the state child welfare personnel goals were:

1. Increase the number of competent, practice-ready BSW and MSW candidates applying for employment in child welfare in the Department of Human Resources (DHR).
2. Improve the retention of child welfare staff in DHR.
3. Increase the responsiveness and effectiveness of the State and Departmental Personnel systems in certifying qualified applicants for employment in DHR child welfare positions.[15]

The final, and probably the most important, aspect of goals we must understand in order to do a social analysis is that policies contain unstated, as well as stated, goals. Stated goals are sometimes referred to in the literature as official or manifest goals, and unstated goals are often called operative or latent goals. This is the single most important item in understanding why there are so many policies that seem to make no sense, yet are never effectively reformed. High school teachers, for example, often express their frustration that they have difficulty teaching because so many of their students "have no business in school," in other words are not interested in learning and are not benefiting from being in the classroom. The teachers ask why the school system does not adopt a policy encouraging these young people to leave school, get jobs, and not return to school until they are ready to benefit from it. The reason school systems do not adopt this seemingly rational policy is that, although the stated (official, *manifest*) goal of school systems is to educate young people and prepare them for adult life, an unstated (operative, *latent*) goal of every public school system is to keep young people off the street and out of the full-time job market until they are eighteen years old. Therefore, dropout prevention is always a goal of schools, even though any teacher realizes that the vast majority of prevented dropouts do not benefit in any way from their additional years in school and, in fact, often interfere with the education of other young people.

Another example of the difference, and often conflict, between stated and unstated goals, and one of more relevance to social workers, is public assistance policy. The public welfare system has been reformed again and again, and none of the reforms has ever had much of an impact on our country's dependent population. The Family Support Act of 1988, for example,—

> *sets a new direction for the nation's welfare dependent families by shift-ing the focus from welfare to jobs, education, and training. In addition, the Act also seeks to strengthen parental responsibility and a national system of child support enforcement. The end goal of these changes is to reduce or eliminate welfare dependency in the nation by establishing mechanisms in the states to foster self-support and self-sufficiency.*[16]

As will be further discussed in the chapter on financial assistance policy, the authors are very skeptical regarding the potential of this policy—or of more recent reform measures such as the 1996 Personal Responsibility Act of ever really reducing economic dependency. The reason for our skepticism has to do with our analysis of the unstated goals of the public welfare system. We argue that the primary operative goal of the public welfare system is to manage economic dependency in as efficient a manner as possible while preserving the social and economic status quo in the society. Thus, policies that significantly redistribute power and resources will not be considered. Without significant redistribution of power and resources, there is really no solution to the problem of economic dependency. Our current system, bad though it may be, represents the cheapest possible means of dealing with poor people and thus will not be significantly changed. In other words, the operative goal of the welfare system is not to eliminate dependency, but rather to manage dependency while preserving the wealth and power of the rest of society.

Hypotheses Underlying the Policy

The next step in the analysis of a social welfare policy is to identify the hypotheses or theories on which the policy is based. In most areas of social welfare, the state of knowledge is very incomplete; little is known about cause–effect relationships. Thus, every social policy is, in effect, an experiment and, like all experiments, contains one or more hypotheses. The hypotheses and theories undergirding a policy are rarely explicitly stated and generally must be inferred from other statements.

A hypothesis is an if-then statement; if we do *X*, then *Y* will happen. A careful reading of policy statements will reveal the hypotheses on which the policy is based. The Family Support Act of 1988, for example, hypothesizes that *if* we require welfare recipients to work in return for their grants, *then* they will become self-supporting; *if* we provide basic education and job training, *then* recipients will find jobs and leave the welfare rolls; *if* we require fathers to support their children by setting up mechanisms to enforce child support, *then* a number of women will get off the welfare rolls because their children's fathers will be assuming the responsibility for their support.

Behind every hypothesis is a theory that may be partially or totally incorrect. The theory behind the Family Support Act of 1988 is that welfare dependency is a result of individual shortcomings in the recipients, and that if we address these shortcomings we can reduce the welfare rolls. Social workers, sociologists, and economists have recognized for years that many of the problems behind the "welfare mess" reside in the social and economic structure of society, not in the individual recipient. These are problems involving the number of jobs available, the amount these jobs pay, and the support infrastructure necessary for people to be able to take advantage of the jobs that are available. Social policies will continue to fail unless financial assistance policy begins to address hypotheses such as *if* enough decent paying jobs are made available, and if adequate support services such as day care and transportation networks are put in place, *then* people will become self-supporting.

Economic Analysis

A central concept in the study of economics is that of scarcity. That is, economics is based on the assumption that there is not now, nor will there ever be, enough resources to satisfy all of our needs and wants. Thus, economics is concerned with the matter of choice—how do we choose to distribute scarce resources. Questions of choice in resource allocation revolve around questions of *effectiveness* (Do the measures we support work?), *efficiency* (How much benefit do we get for a given expenditure of resources?), and *equity* (Are resources divided fairly?).

Social welfare policies involve the expenditure of large quantities of money—money that could be spent for alternate social welfare policies or even for other things altogether. Probably the most volatile policy issue is that social welfare benefits are largely financed by tax money, which many people feel would be spent more effectively, efficiently, and equitably if it were left in the taxpayers' pockets to spend as they wish. Thus the economic ramifications of social welfare policies are of critical interest.

As discussed in Chapter 3, economic analysis of social welfare policies can be extremely technical and complex, generally requiring a competence in higher level mathematics. The economic analysis section of a practitioner policy analysis need not be so complex. What this section of an analysis should do is employ the general perspective of an economist to ask questions related to what the effect of a given policy, or policy proposal, might be on the distribution and consumption of scarce resources. In addition, economists have a certain perspective on individual behavior, one that is somewhat different from that of most social workers. In the economic analysis section we look at the macroeconomic ramifications of a policy—the opportunity cost—and assess the implications of the policy for the behavior of individuals, using an economic style of interpretation.

Macroeconomic Analysis

Macroeconomic analysis is concerned with aggregate economic performance. It looks at questions of output, income, inflation, and unemployment. These are the main items of economic interest you view on the evening news—what is happening to the Gross National Product, Gross National Income, the inflation rate, and the unemployment rate. Taken together, these broad measures give us some idea of our collective economic health.

The macroeconomic analysis section of a social welfare policy analysis asks what the effect of an existing or a proposed policy is, or is likely to be, on aggregate economic performance. Will the policy increase or decrease productivity and, consequently, profits? What will the effects be on the rate of employment? Will the policy contribute to an increasing rate of inflation? Minimum wage legislation probably provides the clearest illustration of macroeconomic concerns with a social policy. Every time the minimum wage is increased, critics voice the concern that it will result in higher unemployment due to employers laying off employees they can no longer afford; business failures resulting from marginal enterprises failing under the burden of increased payroll costs; and inflation due to merchants increasing prices to cover the higher cost of doing business which, of course, results in the value of the increased wage eventually being no more than the wage it replaced.

Macroeconomic analysis also asks what the effects of the larger economy are on the social problems the policies seek to redress. Loic Wacquant and William Julius Wilson, for example, assert that welfare reform initiatives have always been failures because they insist on incorrectly identifying the cause of welfare dependency as individual inadequacy. Welfare reform proposals "have paid too little attention to the broader economic and social-structural factors that are responsible for the crystallization of a large underclass and persistent welfare dependency." They argue that an effective welfare policy will need to deal with macroeconomic issues, mainly full employment at an increased minimum wage.[17]

Opportunity Cost

Because social welfare policies involve the expenditure of scarce resources, policy analysis inevitably involves some study of the costs. Cost accounting and auditing are, of course, very important administrative functions, but they are not what we are concerned with here. Rather, we are concerned with how the cost of a certain policy, or proposed policy, compares to policy alternatives. This is referred to by economists as *opportunity cost.*

The opportunity cost of a policy consists of all the outcomes or benefits that must be sacrificed if that particular policy is adopted rather than an alternative policy. In other words, given finite resources, if we spend our money to implement one proposed solution to a social problem we are not able to implement alternate solutions. Although advocates of prevention rarely use the term, opportunity cost is what they are talking about when they criticize social welfare policy in a number of areas. They point out that we spend so much money keeping people in jail, we can't afford community programs that might prevent a number of people from ever getting in trouble with the law; we allocate so many resources to foster care, we are not able to provide adequate family preservation services to prevent foster care being needed in the first place; we spend too much on law enforcement and drug treatment programs, and too little on drug prevention education and counseling.

Opportunity cost is used to assess alternative social welfare policies, but it is also used by critics of the welfare system to argue that the money spent on welfare benefits could be better spent on something altogether different, and that the poor would benefit the most from this alternative allocation. Conservatives such as George Gilder, Martin Anderson, and Charles Murray argue forcefully that spending money on welfare benefits depresses the economy (a macroeconomic analysis) and that if the money was available for investment instead, it would result in economic growth which would make jobs and opportunities for advancement available for the poorest Americans.[18] In other words, the opportunity cost of welfare programs is that businesses cannot expand and provide jobs that would be preferable to welfare.

Effects on Individual Consumer Behavior

The economist looks at behavior in a way that is somewhat different from other social scientists. The economic explanation of behavior is based on an assumption which Gordon Tullock refers to as the "90 percent selfish" hypothesis.[19] This means that while people may occasionally act in generous and selfless ways, in the overwhelming proportion of instances they will seek their own best interest. The economist will add the following disclaimer—economic analysis of behavior makes no claims that it can explain the behavior of any one individual, only behavior in the aggregate. Thus the economist cannot explain the behavior of the individual physician who could make $38 per office visit treating private patients, yet chooses instead to serve Medicaid patients at only $18 per visit. However, economists will predict with a high degree of confidence that, under the conditions described above, most physicians will treat as many private patients as possible and only treat Medicaid patients when they have no private patients available.

Historically, the economic analysis of effects of policy on individual behavior has been one of the driving forces behind financial assistance policy. This policy has been guided by what is known as the doctrine of less eligibility. This refers to the policy principle that a person living on welfare should always be worse off than the lowest paid working person. Guided by the 90 percent selfish hypothesis, this assumes that if people can do as well or better on welfare than they can by working, most people will choose to live on welfare. This was the foundation of critiques of welfare programs during the Reagan administration; that the welfare system had become too generous and the result is that it had sapped people's motivation to work and improve their lives. One author, for example, says "Expanded welfare programs [since the 1960s] made it economically rational for women to have children out of wedlock, for fathers to desert wives and children. By 1970, the package of welfare, food stamps, Medicaid and housing subsidies provided a gross income higher than many working people earned. Small wonder that a sizable number chose the world of welfare."[20]

A rather extreme example of an economic explanation of behavior is regarding the problem of homelessness. Lawrence Schiff (who is a psychiatrist, not an economist) says:

> *In plain English, the welfare state is in essence providing, for a large percentage of the homeless, a lifestyle that would cost roughly $10,000 to $12,000 were it to be purchased in the open market, possibly a little less at some of the worst (read: city-run as opposed to private-contract) shelters. And the greater the monetary value of the benefits in kind— i.e., housing, food, clothing, medical care, etc.—the larger the number of people willing to consider homelessness as a viable option. For the question is not whether the homeless would really prefer to have permanent residences. Of course they would. They are simply subsidized to not obtain the skills and make the sacrifices necessary to obtain such housing, when substandard accommodation is available free.[21]*

Using the economist's perspective on behavior, the policy analyst asks what the effects of a policy are likely to be on individual behavior. The assumption is that people will be utility maximizers. That is, they will behave in the way which will result in the greatest benefit and the lowest cost to them.

Conclusion

In this chapter we have looked in more detail at the social and economic analysis section of our policy analysis model. As should be obvious from the discussion, conducting a social welfare policy analysis is not a simple, straightforward project. Many areas are vague and poorly defined. Because the goals of many policies are not the same as the stated goals, and because policies often reflect values that we as a society do not care to admit we possess, the real goals and values of a policy will often be hidden, and sometimes will not even be recognized by the people actually involved in formulating and implementing the policy. Also, policies seek to solve problems about which there is little agreement as to the definition of the problem or the desirable solution. Uncovering these vague and often highly emotionally charged aspects of a policy is the task of the social/economic analysis. It more often resembles an art than a science.

Notes

1. Gerry D. Brewer and Peter deLeon, *The Foundations of Policy Analysis* (Homewood, IL: The Dorsey Press, 1983) p. 18.

2. Malcolm Spector and John Kutsuse, *Constructing Social Problems* (Menlo Park, CA: The Benjamin/Cummings Co., 1977) p. 75.

3. Pierre L. van den Berghe, "How Problematic Are Social Problems?" *Social Problems Theory Division Newsletter, The Society for the Study of Social Problems* 4 (Summer 1975) p. 17.

4. Michael Higgins, "Tent City: Struggling for Shelter in Phoenix," *Commonweal* (3 September 1983) pp. 494–496.

5. Frances Fox Piven and Richard A. Cloward, *Regulating the Poor: The Functions of Public Welfare* (New York: Vintage Books, 1971).

6. David Easton, "Political Systems," *World Politics* 9 (1956–57) p. 381.

7. Robin Williams, *American Society, A Sociological Interpretation*, 3rd ed., (New York: Alfred A. Knopf, 1970) pp. 454–500.

8. Williams, *American Society*, p. 459.

9. Henry Steele Commager, Ed., *America in Perspective* (New York: Random House, 1947) pp. xi and xiv, quoted in Williams, *American Society*, p. 468.

10. Williams, *American Society*, p. 472.

11. Williams, *American Society*, p. 480.

12. Williams, *American Society*, p. 485.

13. Lewis Carroll, *Alice In Wonderland—Authoritative Texts Of Alice's Adventures In Wonderland, Through The Looking Glass, The Hunting Of The Snark,* Donald J. Gray, Ed. (New York: W. W. Norton & Company, 1971) p. 51.

14. See for example Amitai Etzioni, *Modern Organizations* (Englewood Cliffs, NJ: Prentice-Hall, 1964); Petro Georgiou, "The Goal Paradigm and Notes toward a Counter Paradigm," *Administrative Science Quarterly* 18 (September 1973) pp. 291–310; Charles Perrow, "The Analysis of Goals in Complex Organization," *American Sociological Review* 26 (December 1961) pp. 856–866.

15. Alabama Department of Human Resources, *Task Force on Staffing for Child Welfare Services, Final Report* (Montgomery: photocopy, March, 1991).

16. Ohio United Way Task Force on Welfare Reform, *Task Force Report (Welfare Reform and Welfare Prevention)* (Columbus: Ohio United Way, 1989) p. 1.

17. Loic J. D. Wacquant and William Julius Wilson, "Poverty, Joblessness, and the Social Transformation of the Inner City," in Phoebe H. Cottingham and David T. Ellwood, Eds., *Welfare Policy for the 1990's* (Cambridge: Harvard University Press, 1989) pp. 99–102.

18. Martin Anderson, *Welfare: The Political Economy of Welfare Reform in the United States* (Stanford, CA: Hoover Institution Press, 1978); George Gilder, *Wealth and Poverty* (New York: Basic Books, 1981); Charles Murray, *Losing Ground* (New York: Basic Books, 1984); Lawrence Mead, *Beyond Entitlement: The Social Obligations of Citizenship* (New York: The Free Press, 1986).

19. Gordon Tullock, "Economic Imperialism," in James Buchanan and Robert Tollison, Eds., *Theory of Public Choice: Political Applications of Economics* (Ann Arbor, MI: University of Michigan Press, 1972).

20. Eugene H. Methvin, "How Uncle Sam Robbed America's Poor," An Editorial Review of Charles Murray, *Losing Ground, Readers Digest* (April, 1985).

21. Lawrence Schiff, "Would They Be Better Off in a Home?" *National Review* (5 March 1990) pp. 33–35.

C h a p t e r *6*

Politics and Social Welfare Policy

In Spring, 1993, the Louisiana State Legislature passed six laws grant-ing legal protections and redress to adult survivors of childhood sexual abuse. This package of legislation was enacted largely through the efforts of Carolyn Evans, a graduate student in social work whose field internship experience in a recovery center for survivors of sexual abuse helped convince her that current policies were inadequate for dealing with the problem. The legislation she helped create and pass is a com-prehensive package that broadens the definition of criminal sexual activity with minors and extends the time limit for reporting the crime. Instead of a limit of three years past the age of majority, survivors can now initiate prosecution up until the time they reach age twenty-eight. The legislation also allows survivors to sue for damages (which can compensate for money spent on therapy and for earnings lost due to emotional problems) and requires those convicted of abuse to partici-pate in a sex offender treatment program.

The journey toward enactment of the child sexual abuse legislation began with Evans' exploration of the topic in a social work Independent Readings course. As she studied what remedies were available for indi-viduals like those at the recovery center, she realized that Louisiana law provided inadequate protection for sexually abused children, and little recourse for people who did not fully recognize what had occurred to them until they were adults. She also discovered that some states had developed legislation to fill these gaps. Perhaps Louisiana could adopt similar laws. On the advice of a law student acquaintance, she took her research and her recommendations to a state senator who had a record of concern about family and children's issues. When he expressed an interest in her project, she "gingerly handed him" her eight-inch-thick stack of research findings. At his request, she also summarized the major items she felt ought to be in a protective package. He turned the resulting items over to a legislative aide, who set the recommendations into several bills to submit to the legislature. This package of bills was essentially the same as the final legislation, with one exception: in the bills initially proposed, no time limit was put on when survivors had to report the abuse.

What followed was a complex process of testimony, lobbying, nego-tiation, and collaboration with other state legislators. It began with Sen-ate committee hearings on the bills. In consultation with the senator and his staff, Evans and several other supporters attended the hearings and provided written testimony. As the hearings were being held, she also had the chance to attend a "legislative luncheon" sponsored by the state chapter of the National Association of Social Workers. This is a yearly affair held at the state capital, attended by legislators sympa-

thetic to social work issues. Evans presented her concerns and her leg-islative goals to the group, and was later approached by several women legislators who promised their support if the bills were reported out by the committee to the floor of the legislature.

The first bill to come before a Senate committee, and one that Evans regarded as key, was the bill abolishing the statute of limitations for reporting child sexual abuse; in other words, no matter how late in life people realized they had been abused, they could still initiate pros-ecution of the alleged abusers. This policy, Evans reasoned, would not only help adult survivors but would also deter people from committing abuse in the first place. The senator presented the bill to the committee in a calm and matter-of-fact manner. He had already secured the support of the committee chair. The only objection raised at the hear-ing was voiced by a representative of the insurance industry, who argued that insurance companies might have to bear the costs of suc-cessful suits for damages (since those sued might try to use their home-owners policies to cover their fines.) With no time limit on initiating suits, many more could be filed. However, this argument was not taken seriously enough to prevent the bill from being reported out to the legislature.

The bill was then introduced on the Senate floor. The senator's pre-sentation was again calm and low-key, aimed in part at dispelling the concerns of the insurance industry and predictions of a rash of false accusations. The problem was defined as the need "to protect our women and children from sexual abuse"; this appeal, made by a male legislator to a mostly male Senate (often skittish about what they saw as "feminist issues"), was successful. The bill passed unanimously and proceeded to the House.

"Now," the senator told Evans, "your work really begins." The State House of Representatives presented a formidable challenge, because it contained many powerful and philosophically divided factions. This often led to intense, even rowdy debates in committees and on the floor. Buoyed by the bill's success in the Senate, but nervous about its fate in the House, Evans took advantage of the short period before the House committee hearings to "learn the lay of the land." She spent time observing proceedings on the House floor, determining state represen-tatives' interests from their speeches. With this understanding, she was able to approach legislators individually to explain the importance of the child sexual abuse bills. In each encounter, she tried to tailor her talk to their particular legislative concerns (a tactic known as partisan policy analysis, which we discussed in Chapter 3). She found all but one willing to discuss the issues. She was "surprised and touched at *their treatment of me. I had expected them to treat me like a nuisance. Instead, they were courteous and listened carefully to what I had to say."* Legislators, she learned, appreciated the chance to hear directly from someone at the "grass roots level," who had observed a problem at first-hand.

When the lead bill was introduced in the House committee by its Senate sponsor, it faced more opposition than in the Senate. One particularly adamant woman legislator opposed the bill on the grounds that giving adults the chance to prosecute for sexual abuse they thought they had suffered as children would lead to "a witch hunt" of innocent individuals. Another committee member seemed amused by the issue. This would not be the first time that legislators demonstrated skepticism over the seriousness of the problems faced by survivors of sexual abuse.

In the same hearings, however, one of the women legislators who had earlier promised support spoke favorably about the bill; she was backed by several male legislators. Evans and her supporters sat ready to present testimony, but the senator was able to handle the objections successfully and the bill received enough support to be reported out.

Evans and the senator then had to find a representative who could introduce and defend the bill effectively in the House. The senator originally asked a member of the influential legislative Black Caucus to present the bill. When it turned out that he was unable to do so, Evans was fortunate in locating a legislator from New Orleans who had already proposed legislation similar to hers. Like the senator, this was a man with strong interests in issues involving women and children. A close rapport quickly developed between Evans and the representative and his aides, and he agreed to introduce the bill.

By now, with Evans' help, a coalition was beginning to build around the legislation. The group included the women legislators who had heard her presentation at the NASW luncheon. A human services lobbyist also offered her advice and support. Several social work students and faculty members sat with Evans in the House gallery, waiting for the bill to come up. As they waited, they wrote personal notes to each representative, asking him or her to support this important legislation.

The New Orleans representative presented the bill in a manner similar to that of the senator, stressing its importance as a protection against sexual abuse of children. This time, as in the House committee, debate was spirited. Representatives rose to proclaim the ridiculous nature of a bill that would allow "a sixty-year-old woman to sue her 80-year-old father." The possibility of such lawsuits could "destroy the way, a social worker's involvement in the politics of policy. While this example may be somewhat unusual, social workers are constantly involved in political life in more subtle ways, beginning with their relationships with clients and including their positions in organizations and communities.

The political context of policy is first seen in the politics of problem definition. We have noted the inclination of a legislative body to define the sexual abuse survivor issue as part of a "feminist agenda," an agenda that some see as trivial, radical, or even vindictive. In this situation, both the student and supportive lawmakers were careful to frame the problem primarily in terms of children and the need to protect them from abuse and its potential effects. This is a good example of the way power is involved in language and in the structuring of arguments.

Politics influences the second stage, the development of a proposed policy solution to the problem, in various ways. In this case, the student brought her initial research, including examples of laws in other states, to a legislator; he in turn had it translated into language appropriate for legislation. This was a situation in which existing legislation served as a guide for the policy. In other instances of policy making, the choice and shape of the proposed policy is generally hammered out through debate and compromise.

A third stage in policy development is the enactment or legitimization of a policy; the above example suggests the importance of lobbying, compromise, and other political tools in achieving this goal. The power and interests of the various legislators and lobbies helped dictate what kind of legislation could be passed. Two other stages, which we did not touch on in this particular example, but which are nonetheless of great importance, consist of the implementation and evaluation of policy. Policy evaluation has already been discussed in Chapter 3. We will see later how politics affects the implementation stage.

Finally, our example of child abuse legislation indicates that each step in policy development involves a number of political players. In this case, they included advocates (the student and her supporters), professionals (NASW members), and lawmakers who represented a variety of interests and constituencies (including insurance companies, parents, women concerned about issues of abuse and exploitation, attorneys, people concerned about the strength of families, and the legislative Black Caucus). Political scientists call such people and groups *stakeholders*. Stakeholders are all the actors interested in and potentially affected by a policy, such as interest groups, public officials, individuals and their families, civil servants, businesses and corporations, professional organizations, and labor unions. Each group has particular assumptions and concerns regarding policies and the problems to which they are intended to respond. As we will see, stakeholders play a major role in each of the stages of policy development.

family." While some cried "witch hunt," others re:
of the seriousness of the issue or the need for l
arose about the implications for the insurance in
tative fielded questions knowledgeably; other legi:
port; and Evans and her student/faculty compan
from the gallery, sending notes to lawmakers abc
the issue. In the end, the bill was defeated by one

When the bill was defeated, arrangements we
by the sponsoring representative to have it broug.
close of the legislative session. In the meantime,
women legislators gave Evans a list of all the law1
no, with the directive "now you really need to ge
bied individually with each one, speaking with ¡
the problems of child sexual abuse and its effeci
did so, she discovered that the lack of a limit on r
ticularly troubling to lawmakers; most were ame:
of a ten-year time period for filing a suit. When th
with this change, Evans found she had won ovei
vote. The bill passed 98 to 1.

The other bills in the legislative package prc
ilar process, but this time with much less debat
cern over an unlimited time period for prosecu
resolved, most legislators felt able to support a l
sexual abuse, the right to sue for damages, ana
ment for those convicted of abuse. Within six
ment, this student-inspired package of policies

We tell this story not only as a lesson that polic
from the vision and work of one individual unitin̨
as an example of how policy making takes place wi
haps this seems obvious, since we are using an exa
you would expect to involve politics and politici
policy making in all areas, including social work aḡ
policies of large organizations, court decisions, aı
An important school of thought in political science
itics—the facts of power, the relations of dominati
[very] tissue of reality."[2] The argument is that pc
where and cannot be isolated in the glass case of C
tive proceedings.

We use this particular case, however, because t
ual abuse legislation in Louisiana nicely illustrate
ous stages of policy creation. It also demonstrate

This chapter aims at helping you to understand the politics of policy making. It does this within a larger discussion of *process analysis* of policies. Process analysis looks at the development, enactment, and implementation of policies. All of these areas are influenced by politics in its broadest sense, not just the formal politics of the legislative process.

The chapter begins with an introduction to ideas about the political context of policy making. It then describes and critiques various models of policy development and social change. Finally, it examines political factors as they come into play during the various stages of the policy process: problem definition, the framing of policy solutions, policy enactment, and implementation.

The Politics of Policy Making

Politics is one of those words that is used often and with confidence, yet is rarely defined in a concise manner. The *Random House Dictionary,* for example, gives a circular definition of "politics" as the practice of conducting political affairs and "political" as pertaining to the science of politics. Perhaps the best single statement for our purposes is the general one that "politics has to do with who gets what, when, and how." As Talcott Parsons elaborates, the polity (or government) of a society is the organization of different collectivities for the purpose of attaining their goals. The political process, Parsons notes, "is the process by which the necessary organization is built up and operated, the goals of action are determined and the resources requisite to it are mobilized."[3] So politics is about how groups organize to try to get their needs met and to achieve their goals. Power is a central component of this activity.

The meaning of power has long been a subject of debate among philosophers, political theorists, and others. Many definitions have been offered. Robert Dahl, a political scientist, calls power the control of behavior, in which *A* gets *B* to do something that *B* would not otherwise do. Power has also been described as the ability to influence people through physical power, rewards or punishments, or propaganda and other ways of shaping opinions. Power has been seen as being an attribute of individuals, or groups, or economic classes—or of all three.[4]

A number of theorists have pointed out the interactive nature of power, arguing that the dominated individual or group invests the dominant person with power. As philosopher Hannah Arendt explains, the person "in power" is put there, or empowered, by others. Stated another way, the power of command does not exist unless others accept the commander's authority. College students, for example, generally concede to professors the power to give out grades—even when these might not be the grades they would like. When power is not accepted or is not accorded to the powerful, people may not obey the commands. It has been argued that the common reaction of the powerful—coercion, violence—is no longer power, but a way of responding when power has been lost.[5] The view of power as a relationship should make you think of the various ways in which those exercising power achieve their credibility or legitimacy, including position in an organization or government (CEO, chairperson, elected official), possession of specialized skills or knowledge (engineer, teacher, social worker or physician), or tradition and authority ("kings have always been obeyed").

Most of these conceptions of power have focused on powerful individuals or groups and their effects on those they dominate. Michel Foucault has developed a much broader view of power as something that circulates through society and is never just in one person's hands.[6] Foucault was a French philosopher whose works on power and the nature of knowledge have had a strong influence on political science, history, and other disciplines over the past thirty years. Foucault faulted modern political theorists for their reliance on an idea of power stemming from the development of an absolute monarchy in Europe from the Middle Ages through the sixteenth century. Power, Foucault reasoned, is no longer constituted in the relationship between a king and his subjects, a relationship that stressed laws, limits, and obedience. Although the modern *state* has assumed some of the power of the king, modern relations of power extend beyond the limits of the state. The state lacks total control, and instead operates on the basis of already existing power relations. These power relations go beyond laws, and are embodied in families, institutions, organizations, and bureaucracy.

In his examination of institutions such as the prison and the insane asylum, Foucault focused on the mechanics of power—the small-scale, immediate points at which power is carried out.[7] He came to think of power in terms of a universal surveillance, in which people are kept under constant scrutiny. In the prison and the mental institution, for example, doctors, wardens, chaplains, psychiatrists, and social workers possess the power to discipline, supervise, and socialize people into meeting "normal" expectations of behavior. This new kind of power, Foucault concluded, is everywhere.

The preceding paragraph presents only a few generalizations from a vast and complex body of work. But it points to at least two themes that are useful to think about: the universality of power, and the shape it takes in the bureaucracies and institutions in which social workers are often employed. And while the lesson may seem depressing, Foucault points out that "there is . . . always something which in some way escapes the relations of power; something in the social body [and] in the individuals themselves which is not . . . reactive raw material . . . which responds to every advance of power by a movement to disengage itself."[8] Furthermore, Foucault saw a role to be played by intellectuals or professionals who join in the "everyday struggles" of those with little power at "the precise point where their own conditions of life or work situate them (housing, the hospital, the asylum, the laboratory, the university...)." Foucault's list of intellectuals included social workers.[9]

Other writers have also spoken about the positive aspects of power, and particularly about the possibility that power is not a finite substance but one that can be multiplied. For example, when public officials create democratic institutions, they may fear losing power, but in fact by widening the circle of decision making they are increasing the power that circulates throughout the community. The discussion of social change and empowerment later in this chapter gives insight into the potential of sharing power rather than being bound up in a system with the powerful on one side, and the powerless on the other.[10]

Models of Policy Making

While there is universal agreement that policy making is a political process, there is a lively debate as to how this process works. The debate centers around the interrelated questions of "Who makes policy?" and "How are policies made?".

Who Makes Policy?

In light of the above discussion, this question concerns who has the power to get *their* policy goals adopted rather than the policy goals of competing groups. The most important theories regarding this question are referred to as pluralism, public choice, and elitism.

Pluralism
Traditionally, political scientists have depicted policy as the output of government institutions. The study of policy therefore consisted of the study of governments and what they do. More recently, political scientists have developed other models of policy or decision making which introduce additional actors to the scene. One of the major models, established by Robert Dahl, Nelson Polsby, and others in the 1950s and 1960s, is the pluralist approach. Still a major approach to policy study in the United States, pluralism assumes a sort of "marketplace of ideas," in which numerous groups and interests compete for power and influence in making policy. Individuals are able to participate in decision making through membership in organized groups. These groups have relatively equal power. Some groups may have more power over particular issues than others, but the essential assumption in pluralism is that all voices will be heard.

Power is widely diffused rather than centralized. A pluralist description of the development of health care reform would visualize physicians, allied health professionals, hospitals, insurance companies, businesses, labor unions, health reform advocates, and consumers joining in the debate over health care and each having some say in its resolution.[11]

The pluralist model has been subjected to important critiques. One of the most potent is the argument that not every voice manages to make it to the debate. Certain powerful persons and groups can prevent those with threatening or opposing ideas from reaching an audience and formulating their ideas in public. Those in power may manipulate existing values or use institutional procedures to stifle demands before they get to the relevant decision-making arena. For example, branding a policy proposal as "socialistic" (which happens regularly when people propose a national health care system for the United States like that in England or Scandinavia) is an effective way to discredit the proposal and prevent any serious discussion. Organizational rules can also be manipulated to suppress challenges to the interests of powerful decision makers.[12] In a case study of the difficulties faced by poor coal miners in Appalachia, John Gaventa tells how a group of miners and their families appealed to a state regulatory agency to deny a permit to a strip mine operator who planned to work close to their homes. To thwart their efforts, a state official mailed them information on the appeals procedure after the permit had been granted.[13]

Political scientist Robert Salisbury offers another example of the uneven playing field for political voices. In describing the attempts of various groups to influence public policy in Washington, Salisbury differentiates between interest-based groups with *personal* membership, such as consumer organizations that advocate for health care reform, and *institutions,* such as hospitals and insurance companies, that also seek to influence the reform process. Salisbury observes that institutions have long-time concerns, often with a variety of policies; these concerns tend to be represented by lobbyists. Institutions generally have more resources than interest groups to devote to policy making. They also have less obligation to consult with people other than top management in making decisions about policy issues. Membership groups, on the other hand, "must look far more carefully to the desires of their members, both to assure political legitimacy and to keep their supporters happy." Because of these factors, Salisbury notes, large institutions have come to dominate interest representation in the federal government.[14]

This critique (sometimes referred to as neo-elitism) of pluralism focuses both on "Who gets what—and how, and Who gets left out—and how."[15] Powerful people are said to control the agenda of public discussion and to limit such discussion to relatively unimportant topics. Truly important topics are reserved for private negotiations among only those groups with the required power and influence. One might see this in a private psychiatric hospital for adolescents where staff members try to raise the question "Why do patients get discharged when their private insurance runs out?" and get firmly redirected to what they "ought to be concerned with"—perfecting their therapeutic techniques.

Public Choice Theory

A somewhat different version of the pluralist model is public choice theory, which brings an economic dimension to the discussion. The traditional economist's view of marketplace behavior stresses individuals pursuing their own private interests. Public choice theorists apply this notion to the political arena and assume "that all political actors—voters, taxpayers, candidates, legislators, bureaucrats, interest groups, parties, bureaucracies, and governments—seek to maximize their personal benefits in politics as well." Public choice theorists offer a useful discussion of the separate interests of voters, politicians, and bureaucrats, explaining that the interests of politicians and bureaucrats are to win elections and to expand their power. Voters in turn, are often concerned with how policies will affect them and what benefits they will receive.[16] This understanding of the difference in goals between public officials and voters will be helpful when we talk about policy development and implementation.

Elitist Model

The elitist model of policy development and social change contrasts with the pluralist approach. Rather than conceptualizing policy as the product of a multitude of groups and interests, this model sees it as reflecting the goals of an elite group of individuals—or what C. Wright Mills called the "power elite." The power elite represents the interests of wealthy citizens and the leaders of corporations and military institutions. It may also include the leaders of well-financed interest groups. Sometimes the division between the powerful and the powerless is depicted as a class struggle between capitalists and workers. In the elite model, people on the lower rungs of society are viewed as powerless and therefore apathetic; even if they had strong opinions, they would rarely have the resources to organize as interest groups. As Thomas Dye notes, "policies flow 'downward' from elites to masses; they do not arise from mass demands."[17]

In his study of Appalachian coal miners, Gaventa gives a vivid picture of the control exercised by a large mining company over a several-county area. Company men held offices in local government, miners lived in company houses and had to buy supplies at company stores, and the company hired the people who taught in the schools. Control was so thorough and far-reaching that miners in that area rarely protested low wages or dangerous working conditions. As Gaventa observes, the elite used their power "for the development and maintenance of the quiescence of the non-elite."[18]

Although the pluralist and elitist models seem at opposite ends of the spectrum, it is possible that both can be useful in analysis of policies. Perhaps each side is correct, depending on the situation. In the case of certain foreign policies, for example, some interests and groups—the leaders of the Armed Forces, the defense industry, certain government officials and business interests—have between them enough power to make the crucial decisions. Yet in other cases, such as policy to protect the rights of those with disabilities, many different and opposing groups can enter fairly equally into the debate.[19]

How Are Policies Made?

The models described above focus on *who* makes policy or influences social change. The remaining models seek to address the issue of *how* change comes about. Major theories include rational decision making, incrementalism, and conflict theory.

Rational Decision Making

The rational decision-making approach presents this process in a nice, neat package: concern over an unmet need or social problem leads to development of first informal and then formal groups of concerned persons, who gather information about the problem. These organized groups develop general policy solutions and lobby for change. Decision makers review the range of existing and proposed policies, identify all the relevant social goals and values, and study the consequences of each policy alternative. On the basis of all this information, an operational policy is then formulated, enacted, and, finally, carried out.[20] The rational decision-making model views the policy process as occurring in a manner very similar to the problem-solving approach used in social work practice.

Incrementalism

Many observers of policy development have questioned the seeming logic of the rational decision-making version of how policies come about. In the real world, they argue, policy making is messy. One of the best-known alternative models is presented by political scientist Charles Lindblom. Lindblom describes policy change as "an untidy process" rather than a neat series of steps. It is rarely possible for decision makers to review all policy alternatives and research their costs, benefits, and "fit" with social goals. In addition, the rational model does not take into account people's reluctance to undertake major change. Lindblom proposes an alternate model, the incremental approach, which views change as occurring in small steps, based on a series of compromises. Since rapid change can upset the status quo and shift the balance of power, policy makers tend to do the politically feasible—they propose incremental modifications and variations of existing policies and programs. Lindblom concludes: "Many policy makers . . . see policy making as a never-ending process in which continual nibbling substitutes for the good bite that may never be offered."[21] This model fits with the colloquial definition of politics as the "art of the possible." What is possible is generally a very small change from current policy, even if all rational logic and data indicate that a much larger change is called for. Rather than depicting policy development as rational decision making, Lindblom describes it as "muddling through."

Conflict Theory

While Lindblom's formulation makes a lot of sense, it fails to explain why sudden and major change does occasionally occur. Conflict theorists attempt to deal with the difficult issue of how and why such change takes place. They stress the existence of conflicts and contradictions that are built into society. When these erupt, the result can be major changes in the system. Marxist social theorists describe these conflicts as occurring along class lines, between an oppressed working class and a dominant elite. When conflict builds, and its sources are recognized by those who are exploited, violent revolution can occur, as in Russia in 1917. However, systemic change may also come through nonviolent means, as in Mahatma Ghandi's movement for independence in India.

Some conflict theorists use a political economy perspective. This perspective focuses on political policies and economic processes, on the relations between the two, and on their mutual influence on social institutions such as the family and social welfare. The political economy approach is essentially an offshoot of Marxism, adding a political and social dimension to Marx's stress on class struggle. Feminist writers have used a political economy perspective to describe what they see as the oppression of working women. They assert that under a capitalist system, men have the power to control women's labor both in the home and in the labor market, where women face occupational sex segregation in the form of less prestigious and lower paying jobs. They also argue that welfare policy has been used to reinforce a whole social system of women's subordinance. Similar kinds of observations have been made regarding the situation of African Americans in U.S. society.[22]

Policy analysts don't often talk about revolution (there are relatively few references to oppression, conflict theory, or political class struggle in standard policy texts.)[23] However, U.S. history yields a few examples of policy changes that were influenced, at least to some degree, by antagonism between oppressed and dominant groups. Franklin Roosevelt's New Deal programs after 1935 were justified in part by a rhetoric focusing on political conflict—the people against elite economic groups. The Community Action initiative of Lyndon Johnson's Great Society included a clause mandating the "maximum feasible participation of the poor" in program development, which had the potential of giving people at the bottom rung of the economic ladder some power in making policies. An understanding of conflict theory is helpful in examining these policy developments as well as responses to the student uprisings and the revolts in the Black ghetto in the 1960s.

As in the relationship between pluralism and elite theory, the incremental and conflict models of policy development, although often contradictory, might each be seen as useful in explaining particular instances of social change. Conflict theory helps us to understand periodic occurrences of large-scale structural change, while incrementalism sheds light on a society's ongoing policy shifts.

During the 1960s, social workers talked much more about broad-scale social change than they do today. Awareness of the problems of oppression and powerlessness has taken a different shape in the 1990s, emerging in a stress on "empowerment." This can be defined as "a process of increasing personal, interpersonal, or political power so that individuals can take action to improve their life situation."[24] It can include a union organizer's attempt to bring people together in groups to push for better working conditions, and a school social worker's commitment to helping parents gain more say in school policies. There has been a tendency lately to turn *empowerment* into a "buzz word" and to use it so widely that the original strength of the concept has been lost. Social workers and others have equated empowerment variously with peer counseling, a focus on client strengths, and enhancing people's self concepts—all worthwhile endeavors, but none capturing the significant power gains implied by the concept. The ultimate in misleading and superficial uses of the term is a billboard (seen by one of the authors) in which a large hospital advertises itself as "The Place Where Empowerment Begins." A complex and powerful hospital setting is one of the last places where one would expect people to develop control over their lives.

Nevertheless, empowerment can be an important goal for social workers as they seek to gain more control over their own lives and to assist clients in doing the same. Once people who feel powerless achieve some success in this attempt, they tend to increase their activity in political and other areas. They become involved in an active, self-creative process in which "they are able do things collectively that they could not have done alone."[25]

Phases in the Policy Process

Having discussed broad ways of thinking about policy development, we now move to a more concrete description of how policies come about. At the risk of sounding like the rational decision-making school of policy development (whose sense of precision does not seem to us to accurately reflect the policy process), we have organized the following discussion in terms of separate phases. This is simpler and easier to follow than a portrayal of several steps in policy making going on at the same time. However, in reading this section, you should bear in mind that these different parts of the policy process frequently overlap.

Problem Definition

All policies relate to some sort of perceived problem or issue. How does this issue or problem get defined? For whom does it represent a difficulty? In Chapter 5 we discussed some of the social aspects of problem definition. Here, we need to look at the political dimension by explaining the role of stakeholders in problem definition, and discussing the ways in which definitions get publicized and accepted by a broad audience.

Heffernan describes problem definition as arousing the passion of stakeholders. "From a political perspective," he notes, "a problem is one that touches a significant number of people or a number of significant people and about which a case has been made that a change by the government [or a non-governmental organization] will improve things."[26] Social problems are defined by particular individuals and groups, and acceptance of these definitions by society is based largely on the power of the definers. For example, homelessness began to be defined by various political actors as a pressing social problem in the early 1980s. Homelessness was not a new phenomenon in the United States, but its increased visibility and its ramifications for various groups and interests brought it into the policy limelight.[27] Various economic conditions in the 1980s, including rising unemployment and the decline in supply of low-income housing, led to increases in the numbers of people without permanent homes. With the diminishing use of traditional institutions for handling transient populations (such as flophouses and jails) and the rapid gentrification of urban neighborhoods, more homeless people became visible on the street. This visibility was noted with alarm by a number of disparate groups—police officers, business owners in areas frequented by the homeless, staffs at city missions and other organizations which traditionally offered shelter to "street people," workers at public welfare departments and other social service agencies whose clientele included people without homes, and members of the public whose travels to and from work and shopping brought them in contact with homeless people. In addition, the concerns of the homeless themselves began to be articulated by individual advocates and advocacy groups, which included people with first-hand experience of homelessness.

It is obvious that the above stakeholders worried about the issue for different reasons; business owners often feared that the presence of street people would drive away customers, while social service workers worried about their ability to fund and offer services to an expanding group of people. These differences notwithstanding, the existence of a number of groups concerned about the problem meant that the issue began to achieve general public notice. Note that this would probably not have happened unless at least some of these groups had the resources and power to influence public opinion. A major channel for such influence is the media; business interests, advocates for the homeless, and social service representatives all contributed to widespread publicity about homelessness.

The stage was now set for discussion of ways in which to deal with the issue. Our example so far has dealt with homelessness as a large-scale problem, suggesting the need for interventions on the city, state, or national level. Remember, however, that problems and relevant policies exist on all scales. We could, for instance, discuss homelessness as a problem identified by various stakeholders associated with a mental health facility that needs to discharge clients into the community. In this case, patients, their families, residents and businesses in the surrounding area, and staff members all have an interest in the types of housing options and programs made available to people discharged from the facility.

Policy Formulation

Once public opinion has begun to be mobilized and public officials (or organizational leadership) have taken notice of a particular problem how are potential responses formulated? Here again, stakeholders play an important part, and their different assumptions about the causes of the problem help shape the proposed solutions. The policy formulation stage will often include research into the issue, such as needs assessments, public opinion surveys, and the like. While "research" connotes objective study of a problem, the assumptions of the researchers and their sponsors color their results and thus further influence the development of solutions.

In the case of homelessness, stakeholders such as housing advocates and the staffs of city missions and social service agencies described the problem as the result of institutional flaws (lack of affordable housing and unemployment) or individual difficulties such as physical or mental illness. Their proposals for policy solutions included governmental programs to stimulate creation of low-income housing, employment training, increased social services, and the building and expansion of homeless shelters. Other stakeholders, including members of the police, the business community, and organizations representing community residents, were more likely to picture the problem as the result of "moral defects" within the homeless themselves, such as alcoholism, drug addiction, or the unwillingness to get a regular job. While these stakeholders might back the creation of shelters, they also supported policies leading to substance abuse treatment programs, the removal of street people from public areas such as parks and bus stations, and incarceration.

Each group cited research reinforcing its version of the problem. Some research stressed the rising number of families and marginally employed people needing homes, some reported large percentages of people with mental illness and individuals addicted to drugs or alcohol, and a number of studies conflicted in their assessment of the actual number of homeless in the United States.[28]

The varying degrees of power possessed by stakeholders affects the final choices of policy solutions. Ability to influence the media is an important element. Other factors in stakeholder power include proximity to the official policymakers (legislators, heads of agencies, etc.) and the possession of technical expertise.

A number of these elements can be seen in our homelessness example. In this case, those advocating an increase in supply of affordable housing (which might necessitate a major shift toward government financing of housing development) did not have much influence over policymakers. Generally, these advocates were academics or members of public interest groups. While other housing advocates and a number of social workers supported this approach in principle, in practice they promoted the more feasible and less threatening alternatives of shelter expansion, development of "transitional housing" to bridge the gap between shelter and permanent housing, and use of social service programs. Business and community interests, who had perhaps the most political clout or the greatest access to public policymakers, advocated short-term responses, such as shelters, and regulation of the homeless, including local ordinances to keep them out of public places. While each group reached the media, the gradual decline in stories about the needs of the homeless and the increase in coverage of the "public nuisance" created by street people suggests the power of business and community concerns.[29] The homeless themselves had the least influence in the policy-making process.

The lack of influence of the homeless reminds us of an important factor regarding stakeholders in social welfare policy development. Client (and potential client) stakeholders in this arena generally lack power because they are poor, unorganized, stigmatized, and/or may include a high percentage of women, children, and minorities. Partly for these reasons, lobbies in defense of social welfare programs are often weak. These lobbies include professionals such as social workers. Even when organized professional groups do wield power, they often have their own agendas and do not necessarily support the interests of disadvantaged groups. Many social workers, for example, did feel genuine concern over the problems of the homeless. However, the responses that they as "professional experts" felt were best (for example, placing street people in shelters or in mental health facilities) were not necessarily the ones the homeless themselves would have chosen.

There are exceptions to this picture of the relative weakness of client groups and their organized advocates. In the case of homelessness, as we have noted, advocates for the homeless had a good deal of success in raising initial awareness of the problem. Some client groups, such as the elderly, can have quite a lot of influence over policy proposals. The older U.S. population includes a number of poor people, but the group as a whole is a cross section of American society. It is represented by the American Association of Retired Persons, a large and powerful lobby group. Families of people with developmental disabilities have built a similarly influential organization, the Association for Retarded Citizens. Yet many other social welfare client groups, including mentally ill people and people receiving public assistance (especially women and children receiving AFDC), have little say as stakeholders in the policy process.[30]

Legitimation

In this phase, a generally formalized policy solution or set of solutions is formally enacted or legitimized. In the process, the proposed policy receives further refinement and definition, largely through negotiation and compromise. Individuals and groups seek to influence the decision makers in the final shaping of policy. This often occurs through the formation of coalitions, as in the child sexual abuse legislation. As public choice theory suggests, the personal agendas of policy makers, including reelection or reappointment considerations, come into play along with concern for the public interest. After the final details of the policy are decided—for example, how much will be budgeted for a particular program or initiative and which organizations or departments will carry it out—the policy is enacted through the legislative process or other legitimizing procedure.

Ironically, although one would expect this last phase of policy making to stress the practical aspects of how the policy will be implemented, frequently these details are not given the attention they deserve. The need to respond quickly to demands to "deal with the problem" often takes precedence over figuring out whether the proposed solution can be successfully carried out.[31]

The elements of the legitimization process can be seen in the major national response to the problem of homelessness in the 1980s, the passage of the McKinney Homeless Assistance Act in July, 1987. In this particular case, business and community interests coincided with those of human service professionals and advocates in promoting the need for federal funding for emergency housing and other services for the homeless. Advocacy groups helped set a sense of urgency earlier that year by camping out on the grounds of the U.S. Capitol for seven weeks in December and January to protest inadequate federal attention to the problem. The House Democratic leadership responded by developing a $725 million aid bill; the Senate proposed a less expensive $423 million package. In March, as the bills were being debated, advocates were joined by movie stars and sympathetic legislators in a "Grate America Sleep-Out" demonstration. The main arguments against the aid bills in Congress (echoed in the Reagan White House) were their cost and the fact that they would create "yet another" federal welfare program. However, the feeling of crisis on the homeless issue, promoted by advocates and played upon by the Democratic leadership, particularly in the House, led to large margins for each bill. In conference committee, a compromise was struck to lower the cost to a figure close to the Senate version: $443 million. Reflecting the approach with the broadest consensus, the McKinney bill provided funds for the development of emergency housing but did little to support the creation of permanent affordable housing. An earlier version of the legislation had contained several provisions supporting long-term housing, but most of these were soon eliminated. As predicted, proponents of a structural definition of the causes of homelessness had little impact on the legislation; it did not deal with the need for permanent low-cost housing or with the problems of low wages and unemployment.[32]

As public choice theory suggests, lawmakers debating the McKinney bill were influenced in part by their own agendas—including the need to be reelected. Those constituencies supporting the bill reflected important votes in the next election. More non-traditional approaches to the housing problem (reforming *systems,* rather than providing short-term services and focusing on individual change) would probably be unpopular with large segments of the public.

The policy legitimation process within a social welfare agency is different in scale but essentially the same. Suppose that in a family and children's counseling center, for example, the issue is raised of providing evening hours to accommodate the schedules of working parents. A group of newer staff members has proposed the change, based on feedback from clients. They suggest the agency curtail some of its daytime hours in order to accommodate the new system. Some of the senior staff, long accustomed to daytime work, oppose the idea. Each group has developed its position and presented it in staff meetings. The agency administrator is highly sensitive to public perceptions of her organization, which affect both funding and also her reputation as an agency head. She appears to be leaning toward establishing evening hours in order to show the agency's sensitivity to client needs. The opposing staff members, seeing the writing on the wall, start talking to the other workers about limiting these hours to two nights a week, and rotating them among all agency personnel. Since neither the newer staff nor the administrator relish the idea of a disgruntled group of senior workers, the compromise seems reasonable. After consulting with workers at the agency's weekly staff meeting, the administrator proposes a policy of Monday and Wednesday night hours to the Board of Directors. They concur, and the policy is made official.

Policy Implementation

Many people think that once a policy is enacted, the process of alleviating a problem is well underway and implementation is simply a matter of carrying out a clearly specified program or initiative. This is far from the truth. Policies on both the governmental and private levels are often broadly stated—long on mission and short on detail. The implementation phase is generally a time of filling in the detail through regulations, personnel procedures, program guidelines, and other specifications, all of which further shape the policy. This administrative process is often referred to as "secondary legislation." Heffernan describes it as a phase in which people "strive to translate abstract objectives and complex procedural rules to the street-level reality where the problems are encountered."[33] Flynn observes that in both the government department and private agency, the details of implementation constitute the closest part of the policy world for social work practitioners. Here are the memos, manuals, rules, and verbal directives to which workers must respond. It is also an important area for worker discretion and influence.[34]

There are political as well as organizational aspects to the implementation of the programs or actions called for in a policy. Sometimes the politicians or officials who enacted a policy do not really want it carried out; their activity was intended to convey attention to a problem and they may care less that the proposed solution is actually implemented. Often, the proposed approach is impractical, complicated, or capable of creating hardships that could eventually lead to negative publicity. For example, in the past, state legislators have created the appearance of cracking down on "welfare loafers" by passing legislation imposing stiff regulations that limited eligibility for benefits. Yet these same legislators sometimes looked the other way when state officials interpreted the regulations so as to allow for a number of exceptions. Even the strict federal welfare reform act of 1996 included certain exceptions. For example, although the legislation instituted a five-year lifetime limit on cash assistance, states are allowed to exempt 20 percent of their caseload from this limit. One interesting point about implementation will be just which clients state officials choose to exempt.

Factors such as agency capabilities, like worker skills and computer capacity, and agency resources, such as budget and staff size, also affect policy implementation. In addition, an agency's ideology may color the way in which a program or approach is set up and administered. Martha Derthick, who has written extensively on the administration of government programs, argues that a major problem in implementation is the lack of policymakers' attention to such agency characteristics. She contends that legislators and even presidents tend to attach low priority to administration and are often unable to foresee the administrative consequences of their policy choices. Presidents, particularly early in their terms of office, are often eager to bring about dramatic transformations in domestic policy. As they pursue the "big fix," they do not want to hear that the solution will take time and necessitate changes in organizational mission or structure. Members of Congress must also play to their constituencies, and often have little time to attend to the details of administration. In our federal system of government, both the executive and legislative branches of government are supposed to give guidance to administrative agencies; this guidance is sometimes contradictory. Consequently, government agencies must work in an unpredictable environment, often with little concrete direction and with demands for immediate results. As we will see in Chapter 7, the broad-scale federal welfare reforms of 1996 were expected to be put in place very quickly by the states, even though many states lacked the computer capacity to do the necessary tracking of clients from welfare to jobs.[35]

Derthick illuminates her points through a description of the problems in administering the Supplemental Security Income program (SSI) in 1972. Government bureaucracies are often blamed for poor administration of programs, yet the difficulties may lie in the interaction between policymakers and the agencies whose job it is to implement policy. In the case of SSI, President Nixon and Congress created a program in which the federal government would take over the public assistance payments made by the states to the poor who were blind, elderly, or disabled. The program became the responsibility of the Social Security Administration (SSA). Arguments for this major change included the increased efficiency of centralized administration of benefits and the lessening of stigma of recipients by connecting the program with the broadly accepted Social Security system.

In its administration of the program, however, the SSA was far from efficient. Payments were made, or not made, in error. The new initiative necessitated millions of hours in staff overtime. The agency was overwhelmed by the number of new applicants to the program. These problems occurred, according to Derthick, because the SSA was given little lead time to develop necessary procedures and to train staff (the President was anxious to "make good" on his public promise to abolish poverty, an initiative not restricted to Democrats in that period). The agency lacked adequate numbers of staff and sufficient computer capacity for processing claims. In addition, SSA's traditional mission was to administer institutional welfare, or benefits to which clients were "entitled by right." This was at odds with the needs-tested public welfare approach which characterized SSI, a factor that may have lessened the motivation of field staff to carry out the new program effectively. None of these issues had been considered seriously by the President or Congress, in their emphasis on broad initiatives rather than the details of administration. Implementation suffered because the policymakers paid little attention to the organizational arrangements for carrying out policy.[36]

The details of the implementation process, and its difficulties, can also be seen in an analysis of administration of a "quality assurance program" in a county social services agency in California. Concerns over high welfare costs in the late 1970s led many states to institute "quality control" systems aimed at reducing both client fraud and worker error in determining benefits. In California, the state welfare system imposed a Quality Assurance program which involved a massive audit of the grant computation process. In the agency described here, the program succeeded in lowering error rates from thirty-four to fifteen percent, although the side effects of its implementation included major shifts in the work of middle managers and problems with worker morale.

The state gave county offices leeway in the actual administration of the quality assurance initiative. In the particular office studied, the method selected for identifying errors in benefits was a continuous audit of the case records of all eligibility workers, to be carried out by their supervisors. Choice of this approach over analysis of a smaller sample of worker records and engagement in error prevention planning was due largely to the intense anxiety instilled by federal and state threats to limit the funding of "high error" offices. Long range planning for error prevention took a back seat to the perceived need for masses of data that would impress the state office and let agency management and workers know immediately where they stood in terms of errors. In addition, top agency management decided to report the data separately for each of four eligibility divisions in the agency.

These administrative decisions led to two unanticipated consequences. First, supervisors found themselves devoting an inordinate amount of time to auditing records, often duplicating eligibility worker efforts by recomputing all their figures. Second, the reporting of error rates by division led to intense competition within the agency. The struggle to avoid being seen as the "worst division" undercut worker morale and diminished agency cohesion around common goals. The decision to use a quality assurance system for immediate error reports, in the expectation that this alone would "shock" workers into being more accurate, did, in fact, lower the error rates. But in addition to the reported side effects, this particular form of implementation of error control prevented planning for long-term error prevention approaches, such as improved worker training and lower case loads.[37] A more thoughtful implementation process might have brought about more meaningful and lasting change.

Conclusion

This chapter has indicated the importance of political elements in all stages of the policy making process, including problem definition, the proposal of a policy solution, and legitimatization of the policy. Even in the implementation phase, where it appears that the major task is the technical one of transforming agreed-upon goals into action, political considerations come into play. Stakeholders such as elected officials, staff and administrators of the agencies assigned to implement the policy, and the people to be affected by the policy all help to shape the implementation process and, ultimately, the policy itself. Successful policy creation, implementation, and revision thus demands an understanding of what's at stake, for whom, and why.

Notes

1. Karen Martin, "La. Can Thank Woman for Strides against Child Sexual Abuse," *Baton Rouge Sunday Advocate* (11 July 1993) p. 3 H; Sally T. Kuzenski, "Social Work Student Guides Six Bills through Legislative Session," *LSU Today* (Louisiana State University News Service) (30 July 1993) pp. 1, 7; Interview with Carolyn Evans, December 9, 1993.

2. Charles Chatelet, "Recit," in Meaghan Morris and Paul Patton, Eds., *Michel Foucault: Power, Truth, Strategy* (Sydney, Australia: Feral Publications, 1979) p. 24.

3. A paraphrase of Harold Lasswell in Peter Bachrach and Morton S. Baratz, *Power and Poverty: Theory and Practice* (New York: Oxford University Press, 1970); Talcott Parsons, "Power and the Social System," in Steven Lukes, Ed., *Power* (New York: NY University Press, 1986) p. 96.

4. Robert Dahl, "Power as the Control of Behavior," pp. 37–58; Peter Lukes, "Introduction," pp. 1–18; and Hannah Arendt, "Communicative Power," in Lukes, *Power.*

5. Bertrand Russell, "The Forms of Power," in Lukes, *Power,* pp. 19–22.

6. Michel Foucault, "Disciplinary Power and Subjection," in Lukes, *Power,* pp. 229–242.

7. "Truth and Power," Interview with Michel Foucault by Alessandro Fontano and Pasquale Pasquino, in Morris and Patton, *Michel Foucault,* pp. 38–39; Charles Taylor, "Foucault on Freedom and Truth," in David Couzens Hoy, Ed., *Foucault: A Critical Reader* (Oxford, England: Basil Blackwell, 1986) pp. 74–77.

8. "Powers and Strategies," Interview with Foucault by the Revoltes Logiques Collective, in Morris and Patton, *Michel Foucault,* p. 52.

9. "Truth and Power," in Morris and Patton, *Michael Foucault,* pp. 41–47.

10. We are indebted to Matt Leighninger for his contribution to this discussion.

11. Thomas R. Dye, *Understanding Public Policy* 7th ed.(Englewood Cliffs, New Jersey: Prentice-Hall, 1992) pp. 21–23; B. Guy Peters, *American Public Policy: Promise and Performance* 2nd ed. (Chatham, New Jersey: Chatham House Publishers, 1986) pp. 42–43.

12. Bachrach and Baratz, *Power and Poverty,* pp. 6–51.

13. John Gaventa, *Power and Powerlessness: Quiescence and Rebellion in an Appalachian Valley* (Urbana, Illinois: University of Illinois Press, 1980) pp. 230–235.

14. Robert H. Salisbury, "Interest Representation: The Dominance of Institutions," *American Political Science Review* 78 (March 1984) pp. 64–76.

15. Bachrach and Baratz, *Power and Poverty,* p. 13.

16. Dye, *Understanding Public Policy*, pp. 39–42.

17. Bruce S. Jansson, *Social Welfare Policy: From Theory to Practice* (Belmont, CA: Wadsworth Publishing Company, 1990) pp. 151–153; Dye, *Understanding Public Policy*, p. 28.

18. Gaventa, *Power and Powerlessness*, p. 4.

19. Jansson, *Social Welfare Policy*, p. 153.

20. Beth Huttman, *Introduction to Social Policy* (New York: McGraw-Hill, 1981) pp. 10–12; Dye, *Understanding Public Policy*, pp. 30–33.

21. Charles E. Lindblom, *The Policy-Making Process* 2nd ed. (Englewood Cliffs, New Jersey: Prentice-Hall 1980) pp. 4–5, 38.

22. Patricia Yancey Martin and Rosyln H. Chernesky, "Women's Prospects for Leadership in Social Welfare: A Political Economy Perspective," *Administration in Social Work* 13 (1989) pp. 118–119; Paula Dressel, "Patriarchy and Social Welfare Work," *Social Problems* 34 (1987) p. 295; Mimi Abramovitz, *Regulating the Lives of Women: Social Welfare Policy from Colonial Times to the Present* (Boston, MA: South End Press, 1988); Barbara Nelson, "The Origins of the Two-Channel Welfare State: Workman's Compensation and Mothers' Aid," in Linda Gordon, Ed., *Women, the State, and Welfare* (Madison: The University of Wisconsin Press, 1990) pp. 123–151.

23. Notable exceptions to the neglect of conflict theory in analysis of policy include Frances Fox Piven and Richard A. Cloward (see *Regulating the Poor: The Functions of Public Welfare*, New York: Vintage Books, 1971) and Theda Skocpol (e.g. *The Politics of Social Policy in the United States*, Margaret Weir, Ann Shola Orloff, and Theda Skocpol, Eds. (New Jersey: Princeton University Press, 1988) Introduction, pp. 13–16; W. Joseph Heffernan, *Social Welfare Policy: A Research and Action Strategy* (New York: Longman, 1992); and Howard J. Karger and David Stoesz, *American Social Welfare Policy: A Pluralist Approach* 2nd ed. (New York: Longman, 1994).

24. Lorraine Gutierrez, "Working with Women of Color: An Empowerment Perspective," *Social Work* 35 (1990) pp. 149–153. See also Steven P. Segal, Carol Silverman, and Tanya Temkin, "Empowerment and Self-Help Agency Practice for People with Mental Disabilities," *Social Work* 38 (1993) pp. 707–712.

25. Kathy Ferguson, *The Feminist Case Against Bureaucracy* (Philadelphia: Temple University Press, 1984) p. 103. See also Frances Fox Piven and Richard A. Cloward, *Poor People's Movements: Why They Succeed, How They Fail* (New York: Vintage Books, 1979) and Lawrence Goodwyn, *Democratic Promise: The Populist Movement in America* (New York: Oxford University Press, 1976).

26. Heffernan, *Social Welfare Policy*, pp. 36–39.

27. Dye, *Understanding Public Policy*, pp. 21–23; Peters, *American Public Policy*, pp. 42–43.

28. The official figures produced by the Reagan administration were 350,000, while advocacy groups estimated that three million people were homeless. Note that this discussion is not meant to discourage the use of research, but to remind you to take into account the assumptions of the researchers as you assess its conclusions.

29. It probably also indicates the rise of a "backlash" against the homeless once a certain amount of time and money had been allocated to the problem and it didn't disappear. Note also that discussions of policy solutions for homelessness were taking place during a fairly conservative era in US history, when the poor and disadvantaged were often blamed for their own predicament. See, for example, James J. Kilpatrick, "Just Who

Is Responsible for Nation's Homeless?" *Atlantic Journal* (15 April 1987) p. 15; L. Christopher Awalt, "Brother, Don't Spare a Dime," *Newsweek* (30 September 1991) p. 13; and Stuart D. Bykofsky, "No Heart for the Homeless," *Newsweek* (1 December 1986) pp. 12–13. Kilpatrick argues that some of the homeless "are professional bums."

　　30. Heffernan, *Social Welfare Policy,* pp. 41, 83.

　　31. Martha Derthick, *Agency Under Stress: The Social Security Administration in American Government* (Washington, DC: Brookings Institution, 1990) p. vii.

　　32. "House Approves $725 Million for Homeless," *Congressional Quarterly* 45 (7 March 1987) pp. 422–423; "$443 Million Homeless Aid Bill Cleared for Reagan's Signature," *Congressional Quarterly* 45 (4 July 1987) pp. 1452–1453.

　　33. Heffernan, *Social Welfare Policy,* p. 42.

　　34. John P. Flynn, *Social Agency Policy: Analysis and Presentation for Community Practice* 2nd ed. (Chicago: Nelson Hall, 1992) p. 8; Robert Pruger, "The Good Bureaucrat," *Social Work* 18 (July 1973) pp. 26–40.

　　35. Derthick, *Agency Under Stress,* pp. vii, 51–66, 68–92.

　　36. Derthick, *Agency Under Stress,* pp. 3–92. For additional analysis of the importance of the implementation process, see the many works by Aaron Wildavsky, including the classic *Implementation: How Great Expectations in Washington Are Dashed in Oakland,* Jeffrey L. Pressman and Aaron Wildavsky (Berkeley, CA: University of California Press, 1973).

　　37. Leslie Leighninger and Erica Baum, "Is QA Amiss?" Unpublished study, School of Social Welfare, University of California/Berkeley, April, 1977.

Part **III**

The Framework
Applied

Regardless of how focused on individual practice a social worker is, he or she is often sharply brought back to the realization that practice occurs within a policy context, and that practitioners will experience problems and provide inadequate services if they do not understand this context. Consider the following conversations the authors had with former students at a recent alumni gathering (names have been changed).

Samantha Bowen received her BSW degree four years ago and works as a social worker in the Aid to Families with Dependent Children (AFDC) program in a large northern state. Sam told one of the authors:

> *I've been working since graduation as an AFDC social service worker. I feel very confident of my social work skills in helping my clients problem solve. However, now that I'm considered a senior social worker in the county office I'm being called upon more and more often to do things like address civic groups about the new Temporary Assistance to Needy Families (TANF) program, which will replace AFDC; to serve on community committees and boards related to services to poor people; and I've just been assigned as the practice representative to my department's state office committee charged with the responsibility of developing a welfare reform plan for our state. My knowledge and expertise in social work practice is of little use to me in fulfilling these tasks. These tasks all require knowledge of laws, regulations, economics, program effectiveness, and stuff like that. After four years I'm beginning to realize that there is a lot about my job that I simply don't understand. Also, I'm really tired of people button-holing me at a party, asking my opinion about this-*

or-that welfare program, and then looking at me like I'm some sort of a fool because I don't know much, if anything, about it.

Beth Stapleton reported on her job as a social worker with a large hospital:

I really love my job, particularly dealing with families in crisis. It is so exciting and so satisfying helping them sort out issues, come to grips with the reality of their situations, and make plans for managing in the future. I really feel good when I receive cards or visits from former clients who tell me that they didn't even know what a social worker was before their hospital experience, but that the presence of me and my colleagues was the thing that enabled them to survive the crisis. But it's so depressing that I may not be able to do this much longer. With all the health care reform proposals and the implementation of managed care it looks like social workers are going to be relegated to doing discharge planning with no clinical work at all. I wish I had a better grip on where health care reform is going and how social workers will fit into it.

Janice Kozinski stood out from her colleagues at the reunion largely due to the fact that she arrived driving a Lexus 400 and was wearing a $600 suit. She told a group of classmates from the MSW program:

Being a social worker doesn't mean you can't prosper. After working in community mental health for three years I got together with two of my colleagues and we went into private practice. After we became familiar with government and insurance company policy we opened an outpatient phobic disorders clinic and an inpatient substance abuse clinic. Within four years we had clinics in twelve locations. Last year we were bought out by a national health care corporation. As part of the deal I received a large block of stock in the parent company and the job of chief administrator of treatment services. I find that the efficiency inherent in the profit-making sector results in far more good for clients than the bureaucratic nonsense I had to put up with in community mental health.

Following the reunion, Janice offered one of her classmates, Raphael Ramirez, a job as director of social services at one of her clinics. He called one of the authors and said:

I'm really conflicted about the offer. It's a great job by all of the standard criteria, but I really worry about profit goals interfering with treatment goals. The reputation of Janice's outfit is that every client referred to their clinics is assessed as needing 21 days of inpatient treatment, no more and no less. The reason for this is, of course, that 21 days is the maximum that most insurance plans will pay for this type of thing. It also concerns me that when I told Janice I'm a family therapist and have little expertise in either phobic disorders or substance abuse it didn't really concern her. Her response to my concern was to say, "You're fully licensed aren't you? Then what's the problem?"

Bill Bouchet had been working for a state child protective services program as a child welfare worker for three years since earning his BSW. He told a group of classmates about a discussion he had with a state senator at a political rally:

When I told the senator about my job the senator said "Tell me Bill, do you believe in the philosophy which seems to be dominant now in your department that it is nearly always best to leave a child with the natural parents? This seems unconscionable to me and many of my fellow legislators. Parents who do some of these things to their kids should lose their right to be parents. Surely we can do better by this state's kids then to leave them in unwholesome and often dangerous home environments. All this stuff about family preservation seems to me to be so much liberal pap designed to mask the unpleasant fact that evil does exist, is irreparable, and is present in many of these parents." Fortunately we were interrupted before I could reply because I was stunned. I work in the Families First unit and believe in it. But I feel I should write the senator a letter explaining the approach and correcting his misrepresentations. However, I'm really not sure where to start.

Mustafa Alleem works as a social worker in a large senior citizens center. He told a group of his classmates:

The elderly people who are members of various groups I lead at the center are all feeling really uneasy. It seems like every week one of them comes in with some new rumor about what is going to happen to their entitlements. One week it was the matter of taxing social security benefits, another it was increasing the copay for Medicare services, another time it was lowering the income for eligibility for Medicaid. They were really panicked a while ago when a group of them went to the community center to hear a congressional candidate who advocates the total elimination of entitlement programs and replacing them with means-tested programs, which he estimated would reduce the number of beneficiaries by 40 percent. I spend a lot of time processing these folks' feelings, but I really wish I could give them more concrete information on how real these threats to their security are. I suspect that some of the rumors are just that—rumors. However, some may be real and I feel a responsibility to separate facts from rumors so we could begin to develop strategies to deal with the true threats.

The situations described above are all very different in terms of the people involved, the fields represented, the levels of sophistication, as well as a number of other differences. They have one thing in common however—they all involve social work practitioners who find themselves in the position, whether they would describe it this way or not, of needing to conduct a policy analysis.

The first thing most social workers who find themselves in this situation will do is go to the library and look up policy analyses in the area they are concerned with. What they will find are studies conducted by professional policy analysts of various types. These are fine, but they have two major shortcomings. The first is that—given the time it takes to do a policy study, write, edit, and finally publish a book reporting the findings—much of the material will be dated before it reaches the library shelf. By the time a study reaches the hands of a library patron or a book store customer, the data is at least four years old. Four years may not seem like too long a time until you consider that it represents two sessions of Congress, one Presidential term, four United Way fund raising and planning years, and so forth. As dynamic and fluid as the social welfare policy field is, a four-year-old study may well be completely out of date.

The second shortcoming of analyses by policy professionals from the perspective of the social work practitioner is that they almost always deal only with what we identified in Chapter 2 as macro-level policy. In addition, they almost always deal exclusively with public policy. Mezzo- or agency-level policy, and private sector policy, are rarely dealt with, even though this may be the most important information for the social work practitioner to have.

The solution to the problem of gaining access to current information regarding policies that affect social work practitioners is to become skilled in what we refer to in Chapter 3 as practitioner policy analysis. There is nothing esoteric or complex about conducting a practitioner policy analysis. It is really nothing more than taking a basic framework for analysis, such as the one presented at the beginning of Part II, and filling in the information regarding a specific policy or policy area mainly using library research skills. Sources of information for practitioner policy analysis and skills for accessing these sources are discussed in the appendices.

In the following chapters we demonstrate how our policy analysis framework might be applied by the social workers described in the vignettes above. Each chapter involves either the major program or the hottest current issue in five broad social welfare policy arenas. In the economic assistance arena we look at Aid to Families with Dependent Children and current welfare reform efforts; in the area of aging we discuss entitlement programs, mainly Social Security; in mental health we look at the rapid expansion and increasing influence of managed care and the profit-making sector; in health care we look at Medicare and Medicaid; and in child welfare we direct our attention to family preservation.

As you read the following chapters you will notice that our policy analysis framework provides a guide but not a rigid template for our analyses. Some of the outline sections are important for some of the areas but not for others. For example, economic analysis is central to any discussion of the TANF program which has replaced AFDC, but of only minor importance for understanding family preservation; enterprise sector analysis is important for understanding current trends in mental health policy but is not central to welfare reform. We do, however, believe that historical analysis is central to any policy analysis. There are several reasons for this. The first is our belief that it is virtually impossible to understand any current situation without studying its antecedents. The problem with many current social welfare policy proposals is that the people instigating them have no knowledge or understanding of history. President Reagan's effort to return much of the responsibility for social welfare to private charity, an idea still supported by a number of politicians, is a good example. The assumption seems to be that the public sector assumed responsibility for social welfare out of some misguided liberal desire to extend the scope of government. In reality, the public sector assumed responsibility for social welfare only when the Great Depression bankrupted private charitable agencies and thus demonstrated the inability of a private system to deal with the massive social and economic disruptions characteristic of a modem urban industrial state. Government assumed responsibility not because it wanted to, but because it *had* to. Thus historical policy analysis reveals that proposals to privatize the welfare system are not only wrong-headed, they are just plain foolish.

The second reason we emphasize the historical dimension in practitioner policy analysis is because historical research is manageable for most social work practitioners. Elements of policy analysis such as economic analysis and evaluation are so complex that a complete job generally cannot be done unless one has extensive specialized training and adequate resources. Historical analysis can be successfully done by anyone with a good general education, training in some basic principles as laid out in Chapter 4 and Appendix B, and a willingness to do some careful detective work to uncover the best sources. This is not to say that historical analysis can be done sloppily, or that most historical analysis is well done. It cannot, and it isn't. It constantly amazes us how many people who attempt historical analyses are ignorant of the basic principles discussed in Chapter 4 and Appendix B, or who are too lazy to apply them.

We conclude each chapter with a look at current proposals for policy reform. We include this section even though we realize that by the time this book is off the press this section will have become part of the history section—the proposals we describe will have been acted upon and either have been killed, adopted, modified, or simply abandoned. This brings us back to the reason we are spending so much time discussing how to analyze policy rather than simply providing analyses and leaving it at that. Social welfare policy changes so fast that even the very first person to read this book will have to read our Current Proposals section as the last part of the history section, and will have to go out and do his or her own analysis to find out, as one of our favorite reactionaries, Paul Harvey, says, "The rest of the story."

Chapter 7

Welfare Reform: Temporary Assistance to Needy Families

There is only one type of occasion when I regret my career choice. This is when I go to some type of social gathering where I am among a group of people I don't know and someone says "And what do you do for a living?" It was bad enough when I was a social work practitioner, but now that I'm a professor it's really bad. As soon as I identify my occupation I inevitably get treated to at least one person's thoughts, theories, and philosophy on the social problem *de jour*. Over the years I've more or less patiently listened to lectures, sometimes almost tantrums, on crime, substance abuse, homelessness, AIDS, and numerous other social problems. Often the person seems to hold me personally responsible for the problem, and they certainly hold me responsible for what they see as our society's crack-brained attempts at solving the problem. It used to be that the problem of concern to people I met at these gatherings changed with the individual and, to the extent there was a pattern, with the times. This has now changed. For almost three years the problem identified by every person on every occasion has been the same—public assistance. It seems as though people are almost obsessed with this problem; the sense of frustration and moral outrage is almost palpable.

Welfare reform, always a hot-button issue, has been center stage in the political arena since Bill Clinton, as a candidate, promised to "end welfare as we know it." When the Republican party seized control of the 104th Congress they made the reform of welfare a key plank in their Contract With America. After a protracted fight that included one Presidential veto of a welfare reform bill, President Clinton, on August 22, 1996, signed H.R. 3734, the Personal Responsibility and Work Opportunity Reconciliation Act of 1996. This act replaces the basic architecture of the public assistance system that has been in place since the 1935 signing of the Social Security Act, by replacing the Aid to Families with Dependent Children (AFDC) program with a new program called Temporary Assistance to Needy Families (TANF). This new act leaves us facing an uncharted landscape in public assistance. As President Clinton noted when he signed the act "This is not the end of welfare reform; this is the beginning. We have to fill in the blanks."[1]

As we have noted elsewhere, the term *welfare* conceptually refers to a wide range of programs.[2] Included in the category are programs such as Social Security, Worker's Compensation, Supplemental Security Income, and a number of others. However, it is clear that when speaking of welfare, or welfare reform, only one program is being referred to—public assistance, which used to be the AFDC program and now will be TANF. Public assistance is the public program designed to aid the very poorest members of our society. While it is true that men and married couples could technically qualify for AFDC and will be eligible for TANF, in reality beneficiaries of public assistance have always been, and will continue to be, almost entirely women and their children.

While the trend throughout this century has been to move welfare programs to the federal level, programs for women and their children have remained under tight state control. AFDC was run through a joint federal/state partnership with the federal government providing a set of regulations governing the operation of the program and approximately 75 percent of the funding. The individual states provided the additional 25 percent of funding and set their own eligibility and benefit levels. This situation resulted in wide variations in the program, with average benefits for a woman with one child ranging from a low of $96 per month in Mississippi to a high of $845 per month in Alaska. Under the new TANF program the states will have even more control of the program, with the federal government providing only the most general guidelines. This lack of uniformity between states was considered a weakness of the AFDC program. Under TANF it is defined as a strength because the theory is that each state will experiment with different approaches, increasing the likelihood that some will be found that work.

To qualify for public assistance, a person must be very poor. Under AFDC, total liquid assets for a family could not exceed $1,000; if the family owned a car, its market value was limited to $4,000. If a family had assets exceeding these amounts, they were required to spend these before qualifying for aid. The total average monthly income (including AFDC payment) of all two-person AFDC households in 1993 was $372.[3] Generally, AFDC benefits came in a package that included food stamps and Medicaid. These additional benefits theoretically provided a family sufficient resources to survive. Benefits under TANF may be even stingier because the federal regulations require only that states spend an amount equal to at least 75 percent of their historic spending level, and provide options for the additional 25 percent to be spent for purposes other than direct assistance.

A number of scholars have observed that a major thrust of welfare reform during the later half of this century has been an effort to separate programs believed to be for the "deserving poor" out of the welfare category and to define them as social insurance, a non-stigmatizing category. Donald Norris and Luke Thompson note:

> *First many elderly were covered under Social Security. Later the number of elderly who were covered was expanded. Subsequently, many people with disabilities were given aid through the vocational rehabilitation acts, and later, through Supplementary Security Income. Many of the unemployed were covered under systems of unemployment compensation, either through companies or through state governments. Gradually, these groups of "deserving poor" recipients became isolated from AFDC recipients. . . .[4]*

Feminist scholars such as Linda Gordon and Theresa Funiciello have argued that we have systematically separated programs used by men and whites out from programs largely used by women and minorities and defined the former as social insurance, a category with little stigma, and the latter as welfare, a highly stigmatized category and one always considered in need of reform.[5] The new TANF program reinforces this stigmatization process through its institutionalization of the idea that remaining home to rear children is not a legitimate social role for poor women.

With the passage of the Personal Responsibility and Work Opportunity Reconciliation Act of 1996, we are at the beginning of a new era in public assistance policy. For the past sixty years the receipt of financial assistance by the needy has been considered a right of citizenship; the federal government has cast itself in the role of leading the states toward more progressive and humane social policies; staying home and parenting children has been defined as a legitimate social role for the mothers of small children; and the reality that work was not available for all people was at least implicitly accepted. This has now all changed. Financial assistance is now to be granted only on a temporary basis; the federal government has abdicated its leadership role and now seeks only to get out of the way of the states; women are expected to be in the labor market; and it is assumed that jobs are available for all people if they will just look hard enough and accept whatever comes along. In the following sections we will look at the factors that have lead to the current situation, attempt to make some sense of the situation, and make some projections of where the nation will go from here.

Historical Analysis

The idea of public assistance, defined as the obligation of the government to provide an economic safety net for people, and of people's right to expect such a safety net simply based on citizenship, has a very short history in the United States. As recently as the end of the last century this idea was considered absurd and offensive by most people. The great philanthropic leader of the 19th century, Josephine Shaw Lowell, stated the opinion of many people involved in the early development of social work in this country when, at the 1890 National Conference of Charities and Correction, she said:

> *Every dollar raised by taxation comes out of the pocket of some individual, usually a poor individual, and makes him so much the poorer, and therefore the question is between the man who earned the dollar by hard work, and the man who, however worthy and suffering, did not earn it, but wants it to be given to him to buy himself and his family a day's food. If the man who earned it wishes to divide it with the other man, it is usually a desirable thing that he should do so, and at any rate it is more or less his own business, but that the law, by the hand of a*

public officer, should take it from him and hand it over to the other man, seems to be an act of gross tyranny and injustice.... The less that is given [of public assistance] the better for everyone, the giver and the receiver.[6]

Based on this belief that government had no right to levy taxes in order to provide financial assistance to people, there was really no such thing as a large public assistance system until the current century. Throughout the nineteenth and the early years of the twentieth centuries, poverty and related social problems were dealt with primarily through local voluntary organizations with gifts from wealthy donors (such as Mrs. Lowell) providing most of the financial support. The little public support provided was mostly through a means known as *indoor relief.* This meant that assistance was provided to people only through institutions such as poor houses, orphanages, mental hospitals, schools for the deaf and blind, and so forth. The provision of direct cash benefits to people, a practice known as *outdoor relief,* was frowned upon as it was believed to encourage indolence and dependency. If direct cash relief was provided, it was thought that it should not come from tax revenues, and that only a voluntary organization was capable of the level of scrutiny and supervision of recipients which prudence required.

As the twentieth century dawned, the rapid growth of urbanization, industrialization, and immigration as resulting in a level of poverty and related social problems that threatened to swamp private charities. Many people were becoming concerned with the number of children who were residing in orphanages not due to parental desertion or death, but rather because of parental poverty. These were generally the children of widows who could not earn enough money to support their children and so placed them in orphanages because it was the mother's only option. In response to this problem, developments early in the century began to re-establish financial assistance as a public responsibility. The first development was the establishment in a number of cities, Kansas City being the first in 1908, of boards of public welfare to carry out "duties of the city toward all the poor, the delinquent, the unemployed, and the deserted and unfortunate classes in the community, and to supervise the private agencies which solicited money from the public for these purposes."[7] The second development was the 1909 White House Conference on Children convened by President Theodore Roosevelt. A major recommendation of this conference was that children should not be separated from their parents simply for reasons of poverty. A system of outdoor relief was strongly endorsed as being preferable to institutional placement.

Following the White House Conference on Children, advocates for the poor began to successfully lobby for state welfare laws which became known as "mothers' pensions." This rather strange term was borrowed from the powerful and popular industrial insurance movement which was successfully lobbying for workers compensation, unemployment insurance, and retirement programs as measures to insure workers against the risks of industrial employment. The perspective implied in the name "mothers' pension" was that women with children were productive workers of a sort and had a right to insurance against widowhood, the primary threat to their livelihood, just as men had a right to insurance against industrial accident. The first mothers' pension laws were passed in Missouri and Illinois in 1911. Within two years, similar laws were passed in seventeen additional states, and by 1919 thirty-nine states had mothers' pension programs.

There are two aspects of the mothers' pension movement which are particularly important for understanding the history of public assistance. The first is that these programs were aimed, to quote President Theodore Roosevelt, at "children of parents of worthy character."[8] This meant women who were widowed or who had disabled husbands. A small percentage of recipients were divorced mothers, but these were considered worthy only if it could be demonstrated that the divorce was of no fault of the women, primarily instances in which the husband had deserted the family. The programs were never intended for the children of unwed mothers and very few such children received aid. The second important aspect of these laws is that they were based on a traditional model of the family in which the mother was expected to stay home and care for her children. The very name "mothers' pension" implied that being a wife and mother was analogous to a career and widows were entitled to support when this career was disrupted. There were no work provisions, or even expectations, contained in these laws.

Although mothers' pension programs established an important precedent in the development of public assistance, it was not until the Great Depression of the 1930s that state and federal government actually began to play a major role. Mothers' pensions programs were always quite small; in 1930, for example, fewer than 3 percent of female-headed households received benefits under these programs.[9] Private agencies, with substantial local government support, continued to provide the bulk of financial relief. The central role of private agencies was strongly endorsed by social workers and leaders in philanthropy, who questioned the morality of government providing assistance and doubted the ability of government to provide efficient and effective professional social services. This situation began to change rapidly with the onset of the Depression in 1929 and its increasing severity into the 1930s.

The Depression shocked the nation in general, and social workers in particular, into the realization that local programs supplemented by private relief agencies were not adequate for dealing with the massive economic problems of an urban industrial society. When the Depression hit, private agencies almost immediately ran out of money and began to rely to a much greater extent than previously on state and local governments for assistance. The state and local governments in turn got into financial peril and turned to the federal government for assistance. The realization that private agencies and state and local governments could not cope with the economic crisis, along with the fear that if something dramatic was not done revolution might well occur, resulted in the passage of the Social Security Act in 1935. This act was the first national framework for a social welfare system. The Social Security Act, as it finally emerged after many compromises, was designed to alleviate financial dependency through two lines of defense: contributory social insurance and public assistance. One of the public assistance programs was Aid to Dependent Children (ADC) a program established to serve single mothers with small children, basically the same group targeted by state mothers' pension laws. This is the program which later was called Aid to Families with Dependent Children (AFDC) in recognition of the fact that mothers as well as their children were receiving assistance.

It is not surprising that AFDC has become more and more controversial over the years, because evidence indicates that its designers did not really understand what they were passing and certainly could not predict what the program was going to become. Scholars often romanticize New Deal programs and characterize their designers as humanists and liberals with a far-reaching vision of a just society and a realistic plan for achieving it.[10] Yet evidence indicates that the designers of the AFDC program only supported it because they believed that the program was temporary and would wither away as social insurance came into effect. Further, the designers of AFDC never imagined that the program would support the children of unwed mothers. Franklin Roosevelt characterized welfare as "a narcotic, a subtle destroyer of the human spirit," and argued that federal job creation was far preferable to welfare.[11] Edith Abbott, a social worker and prominent social reformer, advocated for AFDC with the assurance that it would support only "nice" families.[12] Social worker and Secretary of Labor Frances Perkins supported the program under the misunderstanding that the term "dependent mother" referred only to women who were widows, married to disabled workers, or were divorced due to no fault of their own. It never occurred to her that unwed mothers would be included in the definition of dependent.[13] Historian Linda Gordon states "argument suggests that the authors of the New Deal welfare programs, often thought of as spiritual allies of contemporary liberals, would severely disapprove of what the New Deal programs have subsequently become with liberal encouragement: a source of more-or-less permanent support for single mothers who, in many instances, are not white and "not nice.""[14]

By the 1950s, policy makers began to realize that the AFDC program was not going to wither away and was, in fact, providing benefits to a number of people considered undesirable. The fact that the program did not wither but in fact grew, often at an alarming rate, led to calls for welfare reform. Reform strategies can be lumped into two large categories. The first category is attempts to limit the number of people eligible for the program. These policies have taken the form of "suitable home" and "man in the house" rules, and residency requirements. The suitable home and man in the house rules stated that aid would not be given to children who were living in immoral environments, generally defined as home situations where it appeared that the mother was having a sexual relationship with a man to whom she was not married. These rules were struck down by the Supreme Court in 1968 in *King v Smith*. Residency requirements denied assistance to any person who had not resided in a locale for a certain period of time, sometimes as long as five years. These requirements were declared unconstitutional by the Supreme Court in the case of *Shapiro v Thompson* in 1969.

The second group of reform strategies have been efforts to move people off of welfare and onto self-sufficiency through rehabilitating the recipient or else removing environmental barriers. There has been a series of these efforts, beginning in the mid–1950s and continuing to the current reform proposals. The one element that unites all these efforts is their uniform lack of effectiveness. Major strategies have been:[15]

Social Service Strategies

>   *Amendments to the Social Security Act in 1956 and again in 1962 facilitated the provision of social services to welfare recipients. The idea was that social workers would help recipients solve the problems that were preventing them from being self-supporting. This approach lost credibility when welfare rolls not only did not decline, but actually increased at a rapid rate following full implementation of the strategy in the 1960s.*

Institutional Strategies

>   *First attempted in the 1960s as part of Lyndon Johnson's War on Poverty, these attempted to empower individuals and neighborhoods. These programs were based on a "blocked opportunity" thesis which attributed poverty to environmental variables. These programs rapidly ran into political problems, welfare rolls did not decline, and they were discontinued after a very short life. In the 1980s a few institutional strategies were implemented, namely enterprise zones and public housing "ownership" initiatives, but these have also met with little success.*

Human Capital Strategies

>   *In the 1960s, as the social service and institutional strategies were losing popularity, the argument was advanced that a more direct approach*

to poverty was called for. This approach simply said that people were poor because they could not get good jobs, and they could not get good jobs because they did not possess valuable skills. Economists refer to a person's saleable skills and attributes as human capital. *To address this problem, a series of job training programs has been attempted, beginning in the early 1960s with the Manpower Development and Training Act (for the disadvantaged in general) and the Community Work and Training Programs (specifically for welfare recipients). In 1967 the WIN (Work Incentive) program was implemented, which was a joint effort of state welfare departments and employment service offices. This program required all AFDC recipients without preschool age children to participate. As will be discussed in the next section, the human capital approach continues to be popular, its latest manifestation being the 1988 JOBS (Job Opportunity and Basic Skills) program, basically an extension and expansion of WIN.*

Job Creation and Subsidization Strategies

One of the major criticisms of the human capital approach is that there are not jobs available for most of the participants. Various attempts have been made to counter this criticism by creating public service, or publically subsidized private-sector, jobs. The Works Progress Administration and the Civilian Conservation Corps of the Depression era serve as models for this approach. In recent years, the most popular version of this approach has been providing subsidies to employers to offset the costs of creating new jobs for low-skill workers. The Targeted Tax Credit and the WIN Tax Credit are two examples. A popular, if somewhat perverse, twist on this approach in recent years has been to require welfare recipients to perform unpaid community service in return for their grant.

Child Support Strategies

This approach has developed in response to the changing composition of AFDC caseloads, where the majority of cases are children with living fathers who do not provide support. In the mid-1970s the federal Office of Child Support Enforcement was created to assist states in efforts to gain and enforce child support from absent fathers. Federal legislation in 1984 and 1988 strengthened child support provisions. Currently, when a women applies for AFDC she is required to identify the father of her children and file for a child support order if she hasn't already done so; if she has and the father is delinquent, she is required to swear out a warrant for collection.

Recent Welfare Reform Efforts

In the 1980s, with the election of Ronald Reagan to the presidency and the beginning of a long conservative trend in society, pressure for substantial welfare reform began to mount. The first major effort climaxed in 1988 with passage of the Family Support Act, viewed by many to be a major reform of welfare and one that would quiet the calls for reform for many years. This was not to be. Almost before the ink was dry on the Family Support Act, critics began to complain that it had not gone far enough and to demand even more drastic reforms. These efforts resulted in the passage, and subsequent veto by President Clinton, of the Personal Responsibility Act of 1995. Following the veto of this act, the 104th Congress modified the bill slightly and passed the Personal Responsibility and Work Opportunity Reconciliation Act of 1996. In what many viewed as a crass example of political opportunism, President Clinton signed the bill into law on August 22, 1996. These recent welfare reform efforts have been examples of what Thomas Corbett labels the "make work pay" strategy and the "make 'em suffer" strategy.[16] The "make work pay" strategy is based on the idea that people make rational choices and thus, if we want people to choose work over welfare, we need to provide work opportunities that will enable them to be substantially better off than they are while receiving assistance. The "make 'em suffer" strategy is based on the same basic idea but comes at it from the opposite direction. Rather than attempting to provide options more attractive than welfare, these strategies impose penalties on a range of behaviors that are seen as counterproductive to becoming self-sufficient. Welfare recipients are required to attend school, participate in work training, immunize their children, and similar things. If recipients do not accept these responsibilities, they are penalized by reductions in their welfare grants.

The 1988 Family Support Act, primarily a "make work pay" effort, had as its centerpiece an employment and training program called JOBS. The purpose of this program, commonly called "workfare" is to provide the necessary resources (education, training, and child care) to enable welfare recipients who are capable of working to do so, and it includes provisions requiring them to take advantage of these resources. Major provisions of the law are:

- Two-parent families are eligible for welfare assistance in all 50 states and territories. Prior to the act only 23 states had provisions for providing assistance to two-parent families.
- At least one parent in two-parent families receiving assistance must engage in unpaid work for at least 16 hours per week in the Community Work Experience Program.
- States are required to have a minimum of 20 percent of family assistance recipients (minus certain exempt groups such as women with very young children) in jobs or job training.

- States must withhold court-ordered child support from the wages of non-custodial parents.
- Recipients who become self-supporting will be allowed to keep Medicaid and day care benefits for one year after leaving the welfare rolls.[17]

The Community Work Experience provision was supposed to be fully implemented by 1993, and the 20 percent job placement/training provision by 1995. As of 1996, no state had come anywhere close to fully meeting either of these goals.

Due to the apparent failure of the 1988 Family Support Act to meet its initial goals, and to conservative concern that the bill was too soft on recipients, welfare reform was attempted again in the 104th Congress. In 1996, H.R. 3734, the Personal Responsibility and Work Opportunity Reconciliation Act of 1996, was passed and signed into law by President Clinton. Major provisions of H.R. 3734 are:

- The Aid to Families with Dependent Children (AFDC) program will be replaced by the Temporary Assistance to Needy Families (TANF) program.
- Under TANF, states will receive a block grant in an amount calculated to be the highest of: 1) the average payment they received under AFDC in fiscal years 1992 through 1994; 2) the amount they received in fiscal year 1994; or 3) the amount they received in fiscal year 1995. (AFDC was an uncapped entitlement program. The states had a right to reimbursement from the federal government for 75 percent of the cost of AFDC grants up to an unlimited amount, as long as they followed regulations.) States will have much more freedom regarding how to spend TANF money than they had under AFDC, but when it is spent they will have no right to additional funds from the federal government. A contingency fund will be established to help states which exceed their block grant amounts, but this will be available only under specific and limited conditions (i.e., an exceptional increase in unemployment).
- Adults receiving cash benefits are required to work or participate in a state-designed program after two years or their payments will be ended. This work requirement is defined as one individual in a household working at least 30 hours per week.
- States must have at least 50 percent of their total single-parent welfare caseloads in jobs by 2002. States that fail to meet this requirement will have their block grant reduced by 5 percent or more in the following year.
- States are allowed to sanction, through a reduction or termination of cash benefits, people who fail to fulfill the work requirement.
- Payments to recipients using federal funds must end after a maximum of five years for all spells combined, thereby requiring that families become self-supporting at that point.

- Persons immigrating to the United States after the passage of H.R. 3734 will be ineligible for most means-tested programs including TANF, Food Stamps, and Medicaid, for their first five years of residence.
- Illegal aliens will be barred from all means-tested programs.[18]

President Clinton expressed reluctance to sign this bill, saying of it "You can put wings on a pig, but that still does not make it an eagle." He has also expressed the belief that the 105th Congress will repeal or soften significant portions of the bill. However, Senator Danial Patrick Moynihan, probably the leading expert on social welfare policy in the Senate, has strongly asserted his belief that the votes simply will not be there to modify this law.

Social Analysis

From the previous section it is apparent that public assistance in this country has always been very controversial with many strong feelings about what the problem is and about the character of those benefitting from the program. In this section we will attempt to provide an accurate description of the problem, the population affected, the state of our knowledge regarding these, and the social values that shape our public assistance programs. Because the TANF program will not go into effect until July of 1997, all of the data available relates to the AFDC program.

Problem Description

At the heart of our inability to develop a meaningful and effective plan for welfare reform is the fact that public assistance addresses two different problems, and the solutions to these problems are inherently contradictory. On the one hand, public welfare deals with the problem of child poverty. The solution to child poverty is fairly simple and straightforward—the provision of cash and other benefits to poor children in levels sufficient to lift them out of poverty. On the other hand, public assistance is concerned with the problem of adult dependency, people who are perceived as not doing the things necessary to be fully functioning, contributing members of society. The solution to this problem is also fairly straightforward—reduce or completely eliminate benefits in order to force people to support themselves. The difficulty is, of course, that it is not possible to pursue these two goals simultaneously. If we raise benefits in order to reduce child poverty, we risk encouraging adult dependency. If we become harsh and stingy in order to reduce adult dependency, children will inevitably suffer. Because it is not possible to maximize two divergent goals at the same time, we address them serially, first paying attention to one and then to the other.[19] Thus a round of welfare reform that reduces child poverty through increasing benefits will be perceived as increasing adult dependency and will lead to a reform effort to counteract this. The reform effort will attempt to reduce dependency by cutting benefits, which will increase child poverty and lead to calls for reform because of this. The process will go round and round *ad infinitum.*

Population

A large part of the unpopularity of AFDC has to do with the perception by the public of characteristics of the recipients and of the program. The stereotype of the typical recipient is a never-married minority-group woman, living in the inner city of a large urban area, having her first child at a very young age, having a large number of children, and receiving assistance on a more or less permanent basis. In addition, the public perceives the size of the population and cost of the program as being huge and growing at an ever-increasing rate. Like most stereotypes, this one contains a seed of truth but is highly oversimplified. The following is a description of the AFDC population based on the most accurate and recent data available.

Size

In 1993 there were 4,981,250 households with an average size of 2.9 receiving AFDC, for a total of 14,445,625 recipients (Table 7.1). This sounds like a large number, and indeed it is, but it is only 5.3 percent of the households in the country. As shown in Table 7.2, the size of the AFDC caseload rose at a truly alarming rate between 1970 and 1975, but the rate of growth slowed considerably until 1990 when it once again began to grow at a rapid rate.

Cost

Although the AFDC rolls have been steadily growing, the expenditure, adjusted for inflation, has declined since 1976. In 1976, total payments (in 1990 dollars) came to approximately 22 billion dollars. By 1990, this amount had shrunk to about $18.5 billion. The cap for total federal cost of the TANF program is set at $16.5 billion, which was the actual 1994 federal government expenditure on the AFDC program. The reason for this decline in expenditures is that, although the number of AFDC families has expanded, the average size of these families has declined, and the size of the average AFDC grant has also been declining at a rapid rate (Table 7.3). Adjusted for inflation, the average AFDC payment has gone from $676 in 1970, to $434 in 1990, and to $381 by 1993.[20] More detail regarding the cost of the AFDC program will be provided in the section on economic analysis.

TABLE 7.1   Characteristics of the AFDC Population, 1993

Monthly Average Number of AFDC Househods	4,981,250
Average Number of Persons in AFDC Household	2.9
Average Number of Children	1.9
Distribution of Number of Children in AFDC Households:	
One	43%
Two	30%
Three	16%
Four or More	10%
Distribution of Cases by Ethnicity:	
White	38%
African American	37%
Hispanic	19%
Asian	3%
Native American	1%
Marital Status of AFDC Mothers:	
Never Married	48%
Widowed or Divorced	23%
Married, Husbands Absent	17%
Married, Husbands Present	13%
Average Total Monthly Income for a Mother with Two Children	$465
Average Monthly Payment for a Mother with Two Children	$381
Education:	
Not a High School Graduate	43.5%
High School Graduate	37.9%
One or More Years College	18.6%
Enrollment in School:	
Enrolled in School	14.0%
Not Enrolled in School	85.9%
Recent Work History:	
Worked Some Last Month	12.6%
No Job Last Month	87.4%
Residence:	
Central City	56.4%
Suburban	24.6%
Nonmetropolitan	19.0%

Source: Adapted from data in U.S. Department of Health and Human Services, *Characteristics and Financial Circumstances of AFDC Recipients, FY 1993* (Washington, DC: U.S. Government Printing Office, 1995); Bureau of the Census Statistical Brief, *Mothers Who Receive AFDC Payments—Fertility and Socioeconomic Characteristics* (Washington, DC: U.S. Government Printing Office, March 1995).

TABLE 7.2   AFDC Caseload Size 1970–1993

	Average Monthly Number of Families	Percent Change	Average Monthly Number of Recipients	Percent Change
1970	1,909,000		7,429,000	
1975	3,269,000	71.2	11,067,000	48.9
1980	3,574,000	8.5	10,597,000	(4.2)
1985	3,692,000	3.3	10,813,000	2.0
1990	3,974,000	7.6	11,460,000	6.0
1995	4,981,000	25.3	14,144,000	23.4

Source: Committee on Ways and Means, U.S. House of Representatives. *Overview of Entitlement Programs: 1995 Greenbook* (Washington, DC: U.S. Government Printing Office, 1995) p. 325.

TABLE 7.3   Average AFDC Family Size and Monthly Benefit

	Average Family Size	Average Monthly Benefit (In Constant Dollars)
1970	4.0	676
1975	3.2	576
1980	3.0	483
1985	3.0	443
1990	2.9	434
1995	2.9	373

Source: Committee on Ways and Means, U.S. House of Representatives. *Overview of Entitlement Programs: 1995 Greenbook* (Washington, DC: U.S. Government Printing Office, 1995) p. 325.

Race of Recipients

More whites than members of any other ethnic group are on AFDC (Table 7.1). However 61 percent of recipients are members of various minority groups. Also, the proportion of the white population on AFDC is much smaller than that of other ethnic groups. About 81 percent of the total population of the United States is white, while whites constitute only 38 percent of the AFDC population. About 7 percent of white mothers receive aid. African Americans make up about 12 percent of the total population, but account for 37 percent of AFDC caseloads. About 25 percent of African American mothers receive aid. These factors account for the popular stereotype of AFDC being a minority program even though, in absolute numbers, the greatest number of people receiving benefits are white.

Family Size

Another popular stereotype of the AFDC program is that recipients have very large families. Actually, AFDC families are not particularly large. Mothers on

AFDC give birth to an average of 2.6 children compared to mothers not on AFDC who have an average of 2.1 children (Figure 7.1).

Age of Mothers

AFDC mothers are younger than those not receiving AFDC, averaging 30 years of age, compared to 34 years old for mothers not receiving AFDC. Mothers on AFDC are three times as likely as their non-AFDC counterparts to be under 25 years old (28 percent compared to 10 percent). Also, AFDC mothers are significantly younger at the time of the birth of their first child, an average of 20.3 years, compared to 22.9 years for non-AFDC mothers (Figure 7.2).

Monthly Income

The average total monthly income of AFDC mothers in 1993 was $465, with the majority of this amount, $381, coming from the AFDC grant (Table 7.1). Thus it can be seen that AFDC provides a very low level of support, elevating fewer than one out of five mothers over the poverty line.

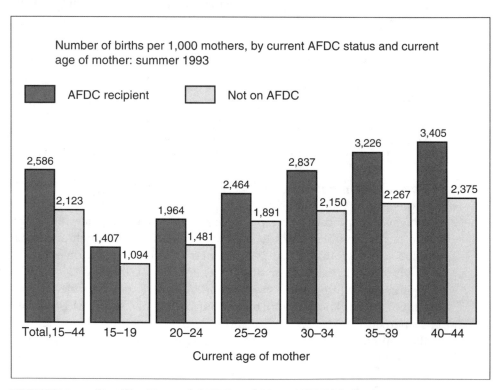

FIGURE 7.1   Fertility Rate of AFDC and Non-AFDC Mothers

Source: Bureau of the Census Statistical Brief, *Mothers Who Receive AFDC Payments—Fertility and Socioeconomic Characteristics* (Washington, DC: U.S. Government Printing Office, March, 1995).

Area of Residence

It is true that AFDC tends to be an urban, largely central city program. Eighty-one percent of cases are in urban areas, with over 56 percent in central city areas (Table 7.1).

Education

The number of years of schooling is significantly less for AFDC mothers than for non-AFDC mothers. Nearly half (43.5 percent) of AFDC mothers never completed high school, compared to only 14.5 percent of non-AFDC mothers. Only 18.6 percent of AFDC mothers attended college for one or more years, compared to 45.3 percent of their non-AFDC counterparts.

Length of Time on AFDC (Spells)

Policy analysts refer to the length of time a person is on assistance as a *spell.* The major concern of policy makers, as well as the general public, about the AFDC program is the belief that AFDC recipients get on the rolls and never

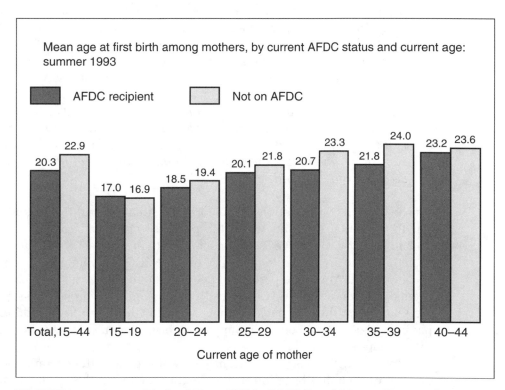

FIGURE 7.2   Age at Birth of First Child of AFDC and Non-AFDC Mothers

Source: Bureau of the Census Statistical Brief, *Mothers Who Receive AFDC Payments—Fertility and Socioeconomic Characteristics* (Washington, DC: U.S. Government Printing Office, March, 1995).

leave. It is precisely this concern that is behind the TANF time limit of two years for any one spell and five years for the total of all spells. This is a somewhat problematic area to discuss, because the terms can be rather confusing and the same data can be presented in ways that create quite different impressions. For example, critics of AFDC will say that 65 percent of recipients of AFDC receive assistance for eight or more years, while defenders of the program will say that nearly 60 percent of people who go on AFDC remain on the rolls for less than two years. Both are, in fact, using the same data, and what both say is equally true. How can this be?

The answer is that statistics regarding AFDC spells look quite different depending upon whether by "time on AFDC" you are referring to everyone who has ever had an AFDC spell, or to the length of the spell of people currently on the rolls. Let us explain by way of the following example:

> *Imagine you are asked to compile statistics on average length of room rental in a small apartment motel in your town. The motel has ten units and you find that eight of the units have been occupied by the same people for the entire previous year. The other two units have been rented by different people each month. Thus the motel has had a total of 32 tenants (the 8 year-long tenants and 24 who each rented one of the other two rooms for a month). If someone were to ask you, based on your analysis, what the typical tenant in the apartment/motel is, you could answer one of two ways. You could say that the typical tenant was a long-term renter because at any one time 80 percent (8 of the 10) was such a person. However, you could just as honestly answer that the typical tenant was a short-term renter because over the past year 75 percent of all guests (24 short-term renters out of a total of 32) rented a room for only a month.*

As can be seen by inspection of Table 7.4, the situation with AFDC spells is similar to the motel example. Of all the persons who ever begin an AFDC spell, 59.25 percent will receive assistance for less than two years. So for the majority of people who are forced to make use of the AFDC program, it works exactly as it is intended. Almost 60 percent of people who receive assistance use it to help them over a temporary life crisis (death in the family, divorce, illness, job layoff, etc.), and then they get back on their feet and continue life as productive, tax paying citizens. Few people in our society begrudge the program as it works for these people.

However, of the people *currently* on the program, the current spell for 49 percent of them has been longer than eight years. If all the spells of the people currently on the program are added together, 65 percent of the current recipients have spell totals of eight or more years. Thus, 65 percent of the people on

TABLE 7.4   Length of Time on AFDC (Spells) (In Percentage)

	Persons Beginning a Spell	Persons on AFDC at a Point in Time (Current Spell)	Persons on AFDC at a Point in Time (Total Spells)
1–2 Years	59.25	15	7
3–7 Years	27.75	36	28
8+ Years	13.00	49	65
Totals	100	100	100

Source: Adapted from Greg J. Duncan and Saul D. Hoffman, "The Use and Effects of Welfare: A Survey of Recent Evidence," *Social Service Review* (June, 1988).

AFDC at any one time are clearly stuck in the program. They have become dependent on it and for some reason, be it personal limitation or lack of opportunity, they are unable to escape. Nearly everyone agrees that something different is needed for this segment of the population.

The Onion Metaphor

As should be apparent from the above information, the welfare population is much more diverse than the popular stereotype. Corbett has developed a useful metaphor relating the various parts of the welfare population to layers of an onion.[21] The outer layer consists of recipients who receive assistance for two or fewer years. These people generally enter welfare due to a discrete and easily observable event in their lives—illness, job loss, divorce, or the like. They generally have comparatively high education, ability, and motivation, and with a few supports will reenter the labor market in a short time. The only thing this group needs is short-term financial help and some assistance in regaining entry into the labor market.

The middle layer of the onion is composed of people who receive assistance for two to eight years, and are often on-and-off-again recipients. These people have limited options. They generally have some basic skills and education, but the employment opportunities do not exist to elevate them out of poverty on a permanent basis. Their fortunes are highly related to the functioning of the economy. When the economy is doing well, members of the middle layer will have opportunities available to them that allow them to escape welfare, if perhaps not poverty. When the economy is doing poorly, because of their relatively low level of education and skills, people in this layer will be the first to be laid off. Appropriate interventions for members of this layer are educational/vocational preparation to help them be more competitive, and measures to strengthen the economy.

The core of the onion is composed of recipients who remain on assistance for eight or more years, a group sometimes referred to as being systems-dependent. This is the group we usually picture when discussing public welfare. In addition to low earning capacity brought on by lack of education, training, and job experience, this group also faces barriers to self-sufficiency such as drug abuse, psychological problems, health problems, abusive personal relationships, etc. This group is also often suspected of lacking basic motivation and of possessing values that are not conducive to work. This group requires far more extensive interventions to achieve self-sufficiency than do members of the two outer layers.

Finally there is the very inner core. These people are permanently functionally limited, due to severe physical or emotional impairment. For these people, self-sufficiency is simply not a realistic objective. The response to this group should be to recognize that they will never be totally self-sufficient and to develop non-stigmatizing ways of providing income support. Corbett believes "An expanded disability program (e.g., a liberalization of Supplemental Security Income) seems an appropriate vehicle through which to assist this group."[22]

Relevant Research

There is a vast amount of research relevant to welfare reform, most of which is systematically ignored by policymakers. In Chapter 3 we briefly mentioned the New Jersey, Seattle, and Denver Income Maintenance Experiments, the largest and most ambitious attempts to test an alternative approach to public assistance. We will only tangentially mention these studies here, even though they are considered landmarks, because the approach they tested, known as a guaranteed annual income or negative income tax, is a liberal welfare reform approach no longer in the public assistance policy arena.* The largest body of research relevant to welfare reform consists of numerous studies being conducted for the purpose of evaluating current reform efforts, generally workfare programs. These will be discussed in some detail in the section on evaluation. There is also a good deal of research on the economics of welfare, some of which will be reviewed in the economic analysis section. In this section we will review research that studies one of the greatest concerns of welfare policy mak-

---

*It is interesting to note that although this approach has been abandoned as a public assistance alternative, it has with almost no fanfare been adopted as the approach of choice for helping the working poor. The Earned Income Tax Credit, first employed in the 1970s, was greatly expanded in 1993. Under this program, workers can deduct job-related expenses, such as child care, from taxes. If the credits exceed taxes due, a refund is paid. In other words, an employed individual can get back from the IRS more than he or she paid in. Refunds from this program now total over $22 billion, making it as expensive a program as AFDC or food stamps.

ers—whether the receipt of welfare promotes undesirable behavior among recipients.

A constant feature of welfare policy is the fear that by giving people assistance, we will somehow damage their moral character. Current concerns are that receipt of public assistance will promote family instability by enabling women to leave their husbands, or to have children without ever being married; that receipt of welfare will damage the recipient's spirit of independence, i.e. will make the person permanently dependent; and, finally, that children who grow up in welfare households will think being on welfare is a normal state of affairs and will hence be more likely to turn to welfare for their own support when they become adults.

David Ellwood and Mary Jo Bane looked at a list of family structure variables and, using several data bases, analyzed the effects of AFDC receipt on these variables. The data indicated no effect of AFDC receipt on births to unmarried mothers, and only a small effect on divorce, separation, or the establishment of female-headed households. Interestingly, the one really significant effect of welfare they found was that in states with low benefit levels, AFDC mothers were more likely to live with their parents than in high-benefit states. Their conclusion was that they found little evidence that receipt of AFDC was a primary cause of variation in family structure.[23]

Mark Plant looked at data from the Seattle and Denver Income Maintenance Experiments (SIME/DIME) to ascertain reasons for prolonged welfare receipt. He specifically looked at the data to see if long-term welfare receipt was: 1) a result of the low earnings available to the families from available jobs, or 2) if people were attracted to leave jobs and enter welfare because of the generosity of the program, or 3) if receipt of welfare led to changes in attitudes and behaviors that favored welfare receipt as a lifestyle as opposed to working for a living (the old "culture of poverty" explanation). His conclusion from this analysis was that the most powerful explanatory variable for long-term welfare receipt was low earnings from available jobs. Plant found the evidence for the "culture of poverty" explanation to be very weak.[24]

A popular stereotype of the AFDC program is that children who grow up in welfare households will be much more likely than non-AFDC children to themselves become welfare dependent adults. This is related to the "culture of poverty" idea referred to above, that children who grow up on welfare will be taught values that are positive toward welfare receipt, and therefore will not have the aversion to welfare that people who did not grow up in welfare households generally have. Consequently, the argument goes, when times get tough these people will be more likely to turn to welfare for support than will people who grew up in non-welfare households. Using fourteen years of data from the University of Michigan's Panel Study of Income Dynamics, Martha Hill and Michael Ponza looked at the intergenerational transmission of welfare dependency. They found that welfare children typically did not become welfare dependent adults. Only 19 percent of the children from African American welfare families and 26 percent of children from white welfare families were heavily welfare dependent in their own homes. In terms of intergenerational transmission of welfare dependency, there were no statistically significant differences for African Americans who grew up in welfare dependent as compared to non–welfare dependent homes. For whites, the only significant difference was for people who grew up in homes with the very highest level of parental welfare dependence, and even these differences were not consistent across all of the models tested.[25]

It should be noted that questions of the relationship between welfare receipt and the behavior/character of recipients are extremely complex and the research results are not clear to the point of being unassailable. However, as Greg Duncan and Saul Hoffman state, "the fact that several million individuals are persistently dependent on welfare raises questions of whether welfare itself promotes divorce or out-of-wedlock births, discourages marriages, or instills counterproductive attitudes and values in recipients. Sparse evidence on the effects of welfare on the attitudes of recipients fails to show any such links."[26]

Has welfare policy making been impacted by relevant research? The evidence does not indicate that it has. Why is this so? The answer is that the research evidence is in direct conflict with some very deeply held American values. We now turn to these.

Values and Welfare Reform

As is the case in most areas of social welfare policy, in public assistance deeply held values supersede empirical knowledge. Public assistance exists at the intersection of two conflicting sets of values, one supportive of welfare and one deeply antagonistic to it. The values that are antagonistic to welfare are:

America as the Land of Opportunity

Most of us sincerely believe that in this country there is opportunity for everyone, if only a person looks for it. Anyone with a good heart and a willing spirit can find work and get ahead. The idea that in our post-industrial, international economy there is no place for many workers offends this belief. Public welfare is seen as an accusation that the economy does not work well and, as such, is seen as almost un-American.

Individualism

Americans believe that individuals are autonomous and have control over their own destinies. We believe that people should get full credit for their successes and take full blame for their problems. We are still fascinated, uplifted, and—more important—believe in, the rags-to-riches American success story. We reject the notion of collective responsibility for individual problems. As public welfare is, by definition, collective responsibility, we think it is a bad thing. Individuals should support themselves and not rely on their neighbors.

Work

Work is considered important because it provides the means for survival. However, beyond this we also think of work as a moral virtue, valuable for its own sake, not just for its contribution to our material well-being. Laziness and idleness are viewed as evidence of weak moral character. Because welfare allows people to survive without working, we tend to suspect that it is a contributor to immorality. As such, public welfare is viewed as more of a moral problem than an economic one.

The Traditional Nuclear Family

The nuclear family—husband, wife, and children—is viewed as the main pillar of a stable, moral, society. This type of family is considered a moral virtue, and the more a family deviates from this ideal the greater the degree of social disapproval. As AFDC is primarily comprised of female-headed families with a very high proportion never having been married, the morality of these families, and by extension the whole program, is suspect.

In support of public welfare are the following values:

Humanitarianism

Although some of our values may be rather harsh, at the core the American people believe that it is wrong, even sinful, to allow other people, especially children, to suffer when we have it in our power to help.

Sense of Community

David Ellwood has stated "The autonomy of the individual and primacy of the family tend to push people in individualistic and often isolating directions. But the desire for community remains strong in everything from religion to neighborhood. Compassion and sympathy for others can be seen as flowing from a sense of connection with and empathy for others."[27]

Thus our values regarding public welfare amount to what Lloyd Free and Hadley Cantril have referred to as a "schizoid combination of operational liberalism with ideological conservatism."[28] On the one hand, strongly held values lead us to conclude that providing financial assistance to people is a very bad thing. Assistance leads, in the public mind, to people giving up individual responsibility for their lives; it allows people to live without working, which encourages the development of sloth and laziness, major character flaws; it allows women to live without husbands, which is seen as contributing to family breakdown. On the other hand, we feel driven to help people who are suffering out of a sense of compassion and of desire for community. This value conflict over AFDC is really not hard to understand. The different values relate to the different objectives of the program discussed earlier. The objective of doing something about the problem of child poverty is addressed by our values of humanitarianism and desire for community. The objective of discouraging adult dependency is addressed by the values of individualism, work, and family. Ellwood asks "Can we design social policies that are consistent with all these values or that at least minimize the conflicts between them?" He concludes that "the conflict is inevitable."[29]

Economic Analysis

Although we generally classify public assistance as social welfare policy, we must recognize that at its core it is *economic* policy. The need for public assistance results from a failure in our economy to provide a place for everyone. Thus, probably the most important questions about public assistance are economic questions. The major macroeconomic questions are, How much does welfare cost?, Is the cost growing?, and What are the employment prospects of welfare recipients in the market economy? The major microeconomic concern is whether welfare receipt serves as a work disincentive, i.e. is the total package of benefits so great that a person is better off on assistance than he or she would be working, thus leading to a rational economic decision to favor welfare over work. A second micro economic concern has to do with the economic effects of welfare receipt on family formation. A final microeconomic concern, one that has not been given much attention but deserves more, is What are the behaviors that welfare recipients actually engage in in order to survive on the minimal grants they receive?

Macreconomic Issues

Listening to politicians and to the popular media leads to the conclusion that public assistance is tremendously expensive and is driving our economy into ruin. It is also frequently alleged that the cost of public assistance has been increasing at a rapid rate and is a major contributor to the federal budget deficit.[30]

How Much Does Public Assistance Actually Cost?

The surprising answer is that, in terms of the total government budget, not very much. The total combined spending of federal and state governments on AFDC in 1995 was a little over 23 billion dollars. In absolute terms, of course, this is a lot of money, and presented with nothing to compare it to it does seem like a reason for major concern. However, when viewed in context the amount seems small. The federal budget alone amounted to over $1.4 trillion dollars. The federal share of AFDC was less than 1 percent of this figure. The average state spent 3.4 percent of its budget on AFDC. By way of comparison, in 1991 the Department of Defense received $300 billion dollars, and $130 billion was spent on the savings and loan bailout.[31] Thus it can be seen that public assistance is not a major contributor to either federal or state deficits, and cutting costs for the program by replacing AFDC with TANF will not result in a great source of savings when viewed in the context of total federal and state budgets.

Is the Cost of Public Assistance Growing?

The other common macro economic concern regarding public assistance is that its cost is growing at a rapid rate and is, in fact, out of control. This is also not true. As we noted earlier, the cost, in constant dollars, has actually declined since 1976, and has increased only moderately since 1980. Probably the reason for this perception of the growth of public assistance has to do with the fact that data on the cost of AFDC has generally been lumped in with general social spending, which has, as can be seen in Figure 7.3, increased significantly since 1980. However, the lion's share of the increase is accounted for by Social Security, Medicare, and Medicaid. AFDC and food stamps have increased at modest levels. Even when looking at total social spending, many economists argue that the rate of growth has been very moderate. Richard Sutch, for example, has analyzed social spending and concludes that "Since the mid-1970s, social spending, has been stable.... The impact of recessions in 1975–76, 1982–83, and 1991–92 can be seen, but overall, social spending has been growing at about the same rate as the economy for twenty years."[32]

Prospects for employment of welfare recipients.

A standard item in nearly all the current proposals for welfare reform is some form of limit on benefits. One of the major provisions of the new TANF program is a limit of two years for any one welfare spell and a lifetime limit of five years for the total of all spells. This has been referred to as a "shock therapy" approach, basically telling recipients that they have only a limited amount of time to get their lives together and then they, and their children, will be on their own. Central to this provision is the assumption that there is work for everyone if they will just do what is necessary to obtain it. Thus a key research question for public assistance policy is whether or not this assumption is true.

Sheldon Danziger, Jeffrey Lehman, and Peter Gottschalk, writing individually and in various combinations, have reviewed the literature and available data bases and developed econometric models to look at the question of the employability of welfare recipients in the current labor market.[33] They conclude that the employer demand for less skilled workers has been rapidly declining and will continue to do so. Of all the new jobs that come available, many require a college degree; of those that don't, the vast majority require that the incumbent be able to read paragraphs, perform basic arithmetic calculations, deal with customers, and use a computer. Only 5 to 10 percent of new non-college jobs do not require these skills on a daily basis. In testimony before congress, Danziger observed that, "In contrast, most welfare recipients, especially long-term recipients who would be subject to time limits, have limited education and labor market experience, score poorly on tests of skills, and are disproportionately

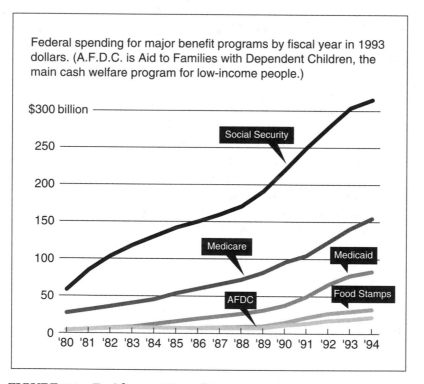

FIGURE 7.3   Entitlement Spending

Source: Congressional Budget Office. Office of Management and Budget.

located in low-income inner city neighborhoods, where there are few job opportunities, and from which they have difficulty commuting."[34]

An interesting opportunity for a natural experiment on this shock therapy approach occurred in Michigan when the state terminated its general assistance (GA) program in 1991. General assistance is a state-financed welfare program intended to benefit people who look very much like the AFDC population but are not eligible for AFDC for one reason or another, generally because they do not have children at home. Sandra Danziger and Sherrie Kossoudji looked at former GA recipients in Michigan two years after their termination from the program to see how they had fared. They found that about one half of former recipients with a high school diploma or GED were working, but fewer than one quarter of those lacking these credentials were employed. Among those who were working, very few were earning enough money to elevate themselves over the poverty line. This study "suggests that welfare recipients who reach the time limit, but are not offered work opportunities, will have difficulty obtaining and holding jobs."[35]

Another relevant and interesting study is by anthropologist Katherine Newman. She looked at job openings at four fast food restaurants in Harlem, New York (a very poor inner city area) and at the work histories of 200 people working in this community. She found that for each job opening, there were fourteen applicants. The people who were hired for the openings were, as might be expected, the applicants with the most education and job-related experience. Of the applicants rejected for the jobs, three quarters were still seeking work when interviewed a year later. It is important to note that the unsuccessful applicants who were interviewed by Newman were less well qualified than the successful applicants, but were on average better educated with more job experience than the typical welfare mother. Newman concluded "that jobs are in extremely short supply in inner city neighborhoods. There are many, many more people pounding the pavement looking for work than there are jobs to be found... [welfare] recipients who must seek employment..., particularly young women who are poorly educated, will have a very difficult time finding work, even in the low-wage sector."[36]

The research on the job prospects of welfare recipients concludes that without some form of intervention in the job market, many, if not most, long-term welfare recipients will not be able to find steady employment. For this approach to be realistic, the government will have to intervene in the job market by becoming the employer of last resort. In other words, if after two years a recipient has not been able to find a job on her own, the government would need to provide one. This approach has many problems, the major one being that it would cost much more to guarantee jobs for all recipients who cannot find work on their own than to simply allow them to stay on the welfare rolls. On the other hand, they could be doing something useful by contributing to upkeep, maintenance, and environmental health and cleanliness in their communities.

The conclusion from an analysis of the macroeconomic aspects of public assistance is that the cost is so small, in relation to other parts of the economy, its effects on the economy are minimal. Neither substantial reductions nor increases in welfare benefits will have any great effect on aggregate measures of the performance of the economy. Also, as the economy is currently structured, there is little room for welfare recipients in the job market.

Microeconomic Analysis

Is Public Assistance a Work Disincentive?

The major microeconomic concern with public assistance is that it serves as a work disincentive. The argument goes that people given a choice between living on welfare or working for a living will only choose to work if they will be significantly better off as a result of doing so. As Sar Levitan and Frank Gallo note, the total package to which a welfare recipient is entitled (cash grant, food stamps, Medicaid, and in some cases subsidized housing) often exceeds the compensation available from low-wage work. They note that in 1991 the average nonworking mother with two children received almost $7,500 in combined AFDC/food stamp benefits, compared with $8,900 earned income from a minimum wage job.[37] If the person received subsidized housing, or if the job did not include free medical coverage, the total welfare package would exceed the minimum wage job by a good margin.

The evidence regarding the degree to which welfare acts as a work disincentive is mixed and generally finds less of an effect than logic would predict. Frank Levy and Richard Michel conducted a longitudinal comparison of AFDC benefits as a proportion of the average wage of workers in the retail trade industry. Their hypothesis was that the higher the ratio of welfare to wages, the more likely it would be that people would choose welfare over work. Thus, if welfare benefits were increasing relative to wages, the size of the welfare rolls should show an increase; if welfare benefits were declining relative to wages, the welfare rolls should shrink. Analyzing 25 years of data, they found that this relationship did not hold. Although the ratio of welfare to wages declined during this period, the welfare rolls expanded.[38] After conducting a thorough review of the literature, economist Robert Moffitt came to a different conclusion. He found that "the available research unequivocally indicates that the AFDC program generates nontrivial work disincentives." The researchers whose work Moffitt reviewed found that the amount of work reduction was small, however, ranging between 1 hour to 9.8 hours per week.[39]

Economic Survival Strategies of Welfare Recipients.

States determine the level of welfare benefits based on a concept called "level of need." Level of need is what the state determines as the minimum amount families of various sizes need to survive. The state then sets a percentage of this amount, usually around 50 percent, as the public assistance grant level. Now, the question the authors have often pondered is this: how in the world do we expect people to survive when, by our own calculations, we provide them with one half of the minimum amount necessary for survival? Sociologist Kathryn Edin and anthropologist Laura Lein have now researched this question and have come up with an answer: people can't and don't survive on welfare benefits alone.

In order to study the question of how welfare mothers survive economically, Edin interviewed a sample of 50 women in Chicago in 1989, and she and Lein interviewed several hundred more in Massachusetts, South Carolina, and Texas between 1990 and 1994.[40] They invested considerable time developing relationships of trust with the women in their sample, and based on these relationships the women were willing to reveal candid details of their economic lives. Edin and Lein collected detailed data on the women's household budgets and on their sources of income. What they found is that the women were not able to come anywhere close to making ends meet on the amount they received from the combination of AFDC and food stamps. In the Chicago sample, for example, the women had average monthly expenses of $864 and average income from AFDC and food stamps of $521. Thus their average monthly shortfall was $343.

With an average monthly shortfall of $343, how did these mothers survive? The answer found by Edin and Lein is that virtually all of the women had additional sources of income they did not report to the welfare department (reported income would result in a reduction of the AFDC grant, although generally not dollar for dollar). The women's sources of income varied. Some income was obtained from family and friends, some from the absent fathers of the children, some was earned in the regular economy and hidden from authorities by means of false Social Security numbers, and some (a very small amount, averaging only $38) was earned in the underground economy through activities such as drug dealing and prostitution. The average family income from the Chicago sample was $897, $521 obtained from AFDC and food stamps, and $376 obtained from unreported sources. Through these means the women were able to cover their basic monthly expenses with an average of $33 of discretionary income left over.

The Effects of Public Assistance on Family Structure.

Between 1979 and 1990 the proportion of the welfare caseload who obtained benefits as a result of out-of-wedlock births increased from 38 to 54 percent. This rate of increase shows no sign of slowing.[41] One explanation for this increase is that it simply reflects changes in American mores which now define unwed parenthood as acceptable, when only a few years ago it clearly was not.

Another explanation, however, is that the increase in the proportion of welfare recipients who are unwed mothers is, at least partially, due to perverse economic incentives to not marry, created by welfare programs. The argument, nicely summarized by economists Levy and Michel, is based on one long-advanced by black writers, first W. E. B. DuBois in 1899, later by E. Franklin Frazier in 1939, and most recently revived by University of Chicago sociologist William Julius Wilson. The idea is that if a man does not have an adequate job and has few prospects for finding one, he will not be viewed as an acceptable prospect for marriage. In inner city areas the number of men who have jobs that pay more than a women can get on public assistance is decreasing. "Thus if welfare benefits are higher than the incomes of a significant portion of men, it may provide an incentive to create more female-headed families."[42]

Levy and Michel analyzed this theory using data from the *Current Population Survey* conducted on an ongoing basis by the Census Bureau. They found that in 1960, 69 percent of black males aged 20–24, and 83 percent aged 25–34, had incomes above the average AFDC grant of $1,269. By 1983, only 38 percent of black males aged 20–24, and 71 percent aged 25–34 had incomes greater than the average AFDC grant, which was $4,741. They conclude that this data confirms Wilson's findings that the increase in female-headed families in black inner city areas is due to the decrease in the number of men who are able to provide an income large enough to support a family at above-welfare levels.

It is important to note that Levy and Michel do not conclude that rising welfare benefits are responsible for the decline in two-parent families. Indeed, as noted previously, in constant dollars the actual amount of welfare benefits has been declining. Rather, the culprit appears to be the lack of employment opportunities available to people with low education, little experience, and few job skills.

Evaluation

For the past thirty years, the primary goal of the AFDC program has been to get recipients into jobs and thereby off of the rolls. Prior to 1967 it was generally accepted that AFDC was intended to allow deserving mothers to remain home with their children. Work was, perhaps unintentionally, discouraged through a policy that reduced the amount of a recipient's grant dollar-for-dollar when that person had earned income. In 1967, the policy of AFDC officially changed to encourage work through the passage of the WIN (Work Incentive) program.* The WIN program employed a carrot-and-stick approach, the carrot being a for-

---

*This was originally to be called the WIP, but this was dropped when policymakers realized that the image conveyed was not what they wanted. Critics of the program, however, felt the original acronym was the more accurate.

mula that decreased a recipient's grant at a rate equal to only a portion of earnings so she would always be better off working than not. The stick was a provision that allowed states to drop people from the rolls who declined to participate in employment or training "without good cause." Various iterations of the WIN program remained in effect until the program was replaced in 1988 with the JOBS (Job Opportunities and Basic Skills) program, the centerpiece of the Family Support Act.[43] The new TANF program emphasizes employment even more heavily, with the new twist of time limits. Recipients will now be eligible to receive assistance for only two years for any single welfare spell and for a lifetime total of five years for all spells combined.

Thus, the most important evaluation questions currently facing public assistance policymakers relate to the effectiveness of employment training and placement programs for welfare recipients. The most critical questions are: Do recipients who are provided with these services actually get jobs? Do those who get jobs earn enough to get them off of the welfare rolls and out of poverty? Do job programs result in cost savings for the programs? Fortunately there has been significant effort expended to evaluate employment programs for welfare recipients. Unfortunately, critics argue that the amount of useful knowledge gained from a substantial monetary investment has been small because of significant methodological flaws with much of the research.[44] Perhaps the major limitation with the evaluation of employment programs is that they have produced what Levitan and Gallo refer to as "bottom line" outcome estimates—that is, they reveal rates of job placements and earnings, but give no information on which aspects of the programs contributed to recipients gaining self-sufficiency, and which did not.[45]

Most evaluations of work-to-welfare programs have found positive results for the programs, but in all cases the results have been slight. The WIN program had very poor results. As summarized by James Patterson, evaluations of WIN found that "of the 2.8 million welfare recipients eligible for WIN in 1967, only about 700,000 were deemed by local authorities to be "appropriate for referral." The rest were ill, needed at home, considered untrainable, or without access to day care. Of the 700,000, only 400,000 were actually enrolled in WIN as of mid-1972, four years after the program got under way. Around a quarter of these completed training, and only 52,000, or less than 2 percent of the total pool, actually were employed—at an average wage of around $2 an hour."[46] Ronald Reagan's work-oriented welfare reform program in California, passed in 1971 when he was that state's governor, has often been cited as a model for national welfare reform efforts. However, an evaluation of that program found that although the stated goal of the program was to place 30,000 welfare recipients in jobs, at its peak it managed only 1,000 placements.[47]

The poster child for welfare-to-work programs is the GAIN program in Riverside, California. This program started under the JOBS program has demonstrated the largest measured impacts to date. Judith Gueron summarizes the evaluation results as "double digit increases in the share of AFDC recipients working, a 50 percent increase in average earnings, a one-sixth reduction in welfare payments, impressive effects on long-term recipients." However, she notes that this is an exceptional program and the difference between it and more typical programs is wide. She concludes, "The more typical program, while achieving positive results, remains severely strapped for funds, does not reach most of the people who could theoretically be subject to its mandates, and has not dramatically changed the message of welfare."[48] Moreover, Theresa Amott reports that although the California program has achieved significant results, the actual earnings of the average participant were only $785 greater over a two-year period than the earnings of members of a control group who did not participate in the program.[49]

Levitan and Gallo reviewed thirteen experimental studies (evaluations that included a treatment/experimental group and a control group) that were conducted on employment programs between 1978 and 1993. They found that the employment rate of the treatment group subjects was statistically higher in five studies, the same or lower in six studies, and unknown in the remaining two. In eleven of the thirteen studies, the experimental group members had statistically higher earnings than the control group. However, once again although earnings increased significantly, the amount was small—ranging for one year from a low of $12 to a high of $1,607.

A review of welfare-to-work evaluations reveals that the basic assumption of these programs is false. This assumption is that welfare recipients do not want to work and that to get them to work requires two things. The first is a stern motivator, such as a time limit on welfare, to scare them into seeking self-sufficiency. The second is the provision of a few resources such as brief education, training, and job counseling programs to help them capitalize on their motivation to become self-sufficient. Virtually every evaluation to date has found no real problem in recipient willingness to work. The problems that have been found all are related to the fact that the programs seriously underestimate the barriers to employment for most long-term welfare recipients. On the one hand, the level of problems which recipients have with health, drug abuse, low ability level, low intelligence, lack of job experience, child care, transportation, and so forth contribute to very low employability of many recipients. On the other hand, the number of jobs available that require few skills and a generally low ability level is small and shrinking. To mount a really successful welfare-to-work program would require two changes. First, many more services and resources would need to be put at the service of clients than is currently the case. Second, the government would need to intervene in the job market and create jobs of last resort. Levitan and Gallo argue: "Society's work is never done. There is no shortage of useful work that could be performed to fulfill needs unmet by the market economy. The limited skills of AFDC recipients would dovetail well with child care, long-term care, and other services that already rely heavily on unskilled low-wage labor."[50]

Why hasn't the shortage of jobs for welfare recipients been addressed in meaningful ways such as government job creation? The reason is that, far from saving money, the implementation of a meaningful welfare-to-work program would cost much more than the present system. Patterson estimates that to fully implement the currently mandated JOBS program would cost over $50 billion, more than three times the federal allocation for the TANF program.[51] As the JOBS program does not include any provision for creating jobs for participants for whom no job is available in the market economy, adding this feature could easily increase the cost to $100 billion. With the country in no mood to increase welfare spending, the likelihood of this happening is virtually nil.

Conclusion

We have presented a large amount of data in a fairly brief space regarding the public welfare system in the United States. Much of this information may seem contradictory and confusing. However, based on the data presented, we think it is possible to come to some pretty firm conclusions. These are outlined below.

The Welfare System Is Not a Giant Failure

Most proposals for reform of the welfare system, and many academic treatises on the subject, begin with the assumption that the system is almost without redeeming features. The data we have reviewed show that this is not true. Most people who use welfare use it exactly as it is intended. That is, they are on assistance for a relatively short period of time, usually responding to some life crisis, and after they weather the crisis they leave welfare as self-supporting people. Evidence shows few clear links between welfare and undesirable behaviors such as divorce, out-of-wedlock births, and loss of motivation to work. To top it all off, the system is cheap. As Christopher Jencks has noted, "Welfare is the cheapest system yet devised for taking care of children whose parents do not live together and whose mothers have few job skills.... A good alternative would cost almost twice as much."[52]

This is not to say that there are not many things wrong with the welfare system. There are. However, the problems with the system are not the ones being addressed by the most recent welfare reform legislation.

Welfare Is Not the Problem, Poverty Is the Problem

It is an obvious, but too often ignored, truism that welfare is a response to poverty. The welfare reform debates in recent years have almost ignored the evidence that poverty in our country is increasing. The distribution of income has become rapidly more unequal in recent decades. Summarizing the data, Danziger and Gottschalk found "In 1989, the real income of a family at the 20th percentile was 5 percent below the 1969 level, while that of a family at the 80th percentile was 19 percent higher."[53] Both the number and the percent of people below the poverty line decreased at a steady rate between 1959 (when we first started counting) and 1978. However, this population has been steadily increasing, rising from 24.5 million people, 11.4 percent of the population in 1978, to 36.9 million people, 14.5 percent of the population in 1992. The reasons for this increase are numerous, complex, and not fully understood. We will not go into them here. Suffice it to say that solving the welfare problem is not the answer to solving the poverty problem, as policymakers often imply. Rather, solving—or at least dealing with—the poverty problem is the answer to solving the welfare problem.

Realistic Welfare Reform Is Possible, but Not Likely

Everyone is in general agreement that people are better off working and supporting themselves rather than living on assistance. Thus, no one opposes the general idea that the best way to reform welfare is to get as many people as possible into the wage economy. It is clear from the data we have reviewed that two requirements would be needed in a plan to accomplish this:

1. It will be necessary for the government to create jobs of last resort. As our economy has become more technical, the number of jobs for people with low skill and education levels has steadily declined. This trend is not going to reverse, so there will continue to be a growing number of people for whom there is no place in the market economy. It will be necessary for the government to create jobs for these people if we seriously want them to work rather than to receive assistance. This will, however, be considerably more costly than simply giving people a subsistence-level welfare grant.

2. It will be necessary to make work pay. If we want welfare recipients to willingly and enthusiastically enter the labor market, it will be necessary to provide them with a package of salary and benefits they can actually live on. The research we reviewed earlier by Edin and Lein, as well as common sense, reveal that a woman with children cannot live on a job that pays minimum wage and no benefits. Lawrence Lynn has summarized what could be done to make work pay:

> *A policy based on making work pay might expand the EITC [Earned Income Tax Credit] and a refundable dependent child-care tax credit. It might seek to increase the value of human capital through cost-effective employment and training programs. It might eliminate possible barriers to labor force participation, such as inadequate child care and racial discrimination. It might ensure universal access to health insurance. It might add a refundable feature, that is, a cash supplement to inade-*

quate support payments, to child support enforcement. It might move welfare recipients toward self-sufficiency by imposing training and job-search mandates without time limits, and it might maintain or enhance food stamp benefits.[54]

A policy to make work pay would also be much more expensive than our current approach.

Public Assistance Is a Social Condition, Not a Social Problem

In the classic book *The Unheavenly City,* Edward Banfield made a useful distinction between urban problems and urban conditions. He defined an urban problem as something that could be fixed, like potholes and broken water mains. Urban conditions are things that are permanent, or very nearly so, and simply must be managed as well as possible. Banfield identified poverty as an urban condition.[55]

We think Banfield's observation is a useful conclusion to the discussion of welfare reform. There are many things about the welfare system that can be improved. However, we need to recognize that in a large, rapidly changing, urban, post-industrial society, we will always need a large welfare system. In other words, welfare is simply a condition with which we should make peace. Leo Perlis, a union organizer, hit the nail on the head when responding to an earlier welfare reform initiative:

> *The current somewhat apologetic emphasis on rehabilitation [of welfare recipients] seems almost obscene—as if rehabilitation would not cost more (at first at least), as if rehabilitation is always possible (in the face of more than 4,000,000 jobless among other things), as if rehabilitation is a substitute for relief for everybody and at all times. I think we all need to make a forthright declaration that direct public assistance in our competitive society is unavoidable, necessary, and even socially useful.*[56]

Notes

1. "Clinton Signs Controversial Welfare Bill," *Dallas Morning News* (23 August 1996) Sec. A, p. 32

2. Philip R. Popple and Leslie Leighninger, *Social Work, Social Welfare, and American Society* 3rd ed. (Boston: Allyn & Bacon, 1996).

3. U.S. Department of Health and Human Services, *Characteristics and Financial Circumstances of AFDC Recipients, FY 1993* (Washington, DC: U.S. Government Printing Office, 1995).

4. Donald F. Norris and Lyke Thompson, Eds., *The Politics of Welfare Reform* (Thousand Oaks, CA: Sage, 1995) p. 4.

5. Linda Gordon, "How We Got 'Welfare': A History of the Mistakes of the Past," *Social Justice* 21 (No. 1) 1995, pp. 13–16; Theresa Funiciello, "The Poverty Industry: Do Government and Charities Create the Poor?" *Ms* (November/December 1990) pp. 33–40.

6. Josephine Shaw Lowell, "The Economic and Moral Effects of Public Outdoor Relief," in *Proceedings of the National Conference of Charities and Correction, 1890* (Boston, 1890) pp. 81–82.

7. L. A. Halbert, "Boards of Public Welfare: A System of Government Social Work," *Proceedings of the National Conference of Social Work, 1918,* pp. 20–21, cited in Roy Lubove, *The Struggle for Social Security, 1900–1935* (Pittsburgh: University of Pittsburgh Press, 1986) p. 94.

8. Roy Lubove, *The Struggle for Social Security, 1900–1935,* p. 98.

9. Joel F. Handler and Yeheskel Hasenfeld, *The Moral Construction of Poverty: Welfare Reform in America* (Newbury Park, CA: Sage Publications, 1991) p. 71.

10. For example see Terry Mizrahi, "The New 'Right' Agenda Decimates Social Programs, Devalues Social Work and Devastates Clients and Communities," *HCSSW Update* (School of Social Work, Hunter College of the City University of New York) (Spring 1996) p. 1.

11. Sar Levitan and Frank Gallo, "Jobs for JOBS: Toward a Work-Based Welfare System," *Occasional Paper 1993–1,* (Washington, DC: Center for Policy Studies, The George Washington University, 1993) (March 1993) p. 1.

12. Linda Gordon, *Pitied but Not Entitled: Single Mothers and the History of Welfare, 1890–1935* (New York: The Free Press, 1994) p. 299.

13. G. D. Reilly, "Madame Secretary," in K. Louchheim, Ed., *The Making of the New Deal: The Insiders Speak* (Cambridge: Harvard University Press, 1983) p. 175.

14. Gordon, *Pitied but Not Entitled,* p. 299.

15. Thomas Corbett, "Child Poverty and Welfare Reform: Progress or Paralysis?" *Focus* 15 (Spring 1993) pp. 4–5.

16. Corbett, "Child Poverty and Welfare Reform: Progress or Paralysis?" p. 5.

17. Carmen D. Solomon, "The Family Support Act of 1988: How it Changes the Aid to Families with Dependent Children (AFDC) and Child Support Enforcement Programs," *CRS Report for Congress* (Washington, DC: Congressional Research Service—The Library of Congress, November 7, 1988).

18. U.S. House of Representatives, "The Conference Report on The Personal Responsibility and Work Opportunity Reconciliation Act of 1996," July 31, 1996.

19. R. M. Cyert and J. G. Marsh, *A Behavioral Theory of the Firm* (Englewood Cliffs, NJ: Prentice-Hall, 1963).

20. U.S. Department of Health and Human Services, *Characteristics and Financial Circumstances of AFDC Recipients, FY 1993* (Washington, D.C.: U.S. Government Printing Office, 1995) p. 1; Kenneth Jost, "Welfare Reform," *CQ Researcher* 2 (10 April 1992) p. 316; Committee on Ways and Means, U.S. House of Representatives, *1995 Green Book* (Washington, D.C.: U.S. Government Printing Office, 1995) p. 325.

21. Corbett, "Child Poverty and Welfare Reform: Progress or Paralysis?" pp. 9–12.

22. Corbett, "Child Poverty and Welfare Reform: Progress or Paralysis?" p. 12.

23. David T. Ellwood and Mary Jo Bane, *The Impact of AFDC on Family Structure and Living Arrangements* (Cambridge: Harvard University, 1984).

24. Mark W. Plant, "An Empirical Analysis of Welfare Dependence," *American Economic Review* 74 (September 1984) pp. 673–684.

25. Martha S. Hill and Michael Ponza, "Does Welfare Dependency Beget Dependency?" Videographed (Ann Arbor, MI: Institute for Social Research, 1984) and "Poverty Across Generations: Is Welfare Dependency a Pathology Passed from One Generation to the Next?" (Paper presented at the Population Association of America Meeting, Pittsburgh, March 1983) cited in Greg V. Duncan and Saul D. Hoffman, "The Use and Effects of Welfare: A Survey of Recent Evidence," *Social Service Review* Vol. 83 (June 1988) pp. 238–257.

26. Duncan and Hoffman, "The Use and Effects of Welfare," p. 254.

27. David Ellwood, *Poor Support: Poverty in the American Family* (New York: Basic Books, 1988) p. 16.

28. Lloyd A. Free and Hadley Cantril, *The Political Beliefs of Americans: A Study of Public Opinion* (New York: Simon and Schuster, 1967) p. 37.

29. Ellwood, *Poor Support,* p. 18.

30. Richard Sutch, "Has Social Spending Grown Out of Control?" *Challenge* (May–June 1996) p. 12.

31. Mimi Abramovitz and Fred Newdom, "Fighting Back! Challenging AFDC Myths with the Facts," xerox prepared for the Bertha Capan Reynolds Society, npnd.

32. Sutch, "Has Social Spending Grown Out of Control?" p. 12.

33. Testimony of Sheldon Danziger, Professor, School of Social Work and School of Public Policy, University of Michigan, before the Senate Finance Committee, February 29, 1996; Sheldon Danziger and Peter Gottschalk, *America Unequal* (Cambridge: Harvard University Press/Russell Sage Foundation, 1995); Sheldon Danziger and Jeffrey Lehman, "How Will Welfare Recipients Fare in the Labor Market?" *Challenge* (March–April 1996) pp. 30–35.

34. Danziger, "Testimony," p. 3.

35. Danziger, "Testimony," p. 6.

36. Katherine S. Newman, "Job Availability," *National Forum: The Phi Kappa Phi Journal* 76 (Summer 1996) pp. 20–23.

37. Levitan and Gallo, "Jobs for JOBS."

38. Frank S. Levy and Richard C. Michel, "Work for Welfare: How Much Good Will it Do?" *The American Economic Review* 76 (May 1986) pp. 399–404.

39. Robert Moffitt, *Incentive Effects of the U.S. Welfare System: A Review* (Madison: Institute for Research on Poverty, University of Wisconsin, March 1990).

40. Kathryn Edin, "Surviving the Welfare System: How AFDC Recipients Make Ends Meet in Chicago," *Social Problems* 38 (November 1991) pp. 462–474; Christopher Jencks, "What's Wrong with Welfare Reform," *Harper's* 288 (April 1974) pp. 19–22.

41. Douglas Besharov, "That Other Clinton Promise—Ending Welfare As We Know It," *The Wall Street Journal* (18 January 1993) p. A10.

42. Levy and Michel, "Work for Welfare," p. 403.

43. James T. Patterson, *America's Struggle Against Poverty, 1900–1994* (Cambridge: Harvard University Press, 1994) pp. 175, 231.

44. David Greenberg and Michael Wiseman, *What Did the Work-Welfare Demonstrations Do?* (Madison: University of Wisconsin Institute for Research on Poverty, April 1992) Discussion Paper 969–92.

45. Levitan and Gallo, "Jobs for JOBS," pp. 45–46.

46. Patterson, *America's Struggle Against Poverty, 1900–1914,* p. 175.

47. David L. Kirp, "The California Work/Welfare Scheme," *The Public Interest* (Spring 1986).

48. Judith M. Gueron, "The Route to Welfare Reform," *The Brookings Review* 12 (Summer 1994) pp. 14–15.

49. Teresa Amott, "Reforming Welfare or Reforming the Labor Market: Lessons from the Massachusetts Employment Training Experience," *Social Justice* 21 (1992) pp. 33–37.

50. Levitan and Gallo, "Jobs for JOBS," p. 51.

51. Patterson, *America's Struggle Against Poverty, 1900–1994,* p. 232.

52. Jencks, "What's Wrong with Welfare Reform," p. 19.

53. Sheldon Danziger and Peter Gottschalk, "Introduction," in Sheldon Danziger and Peter Gottschalk, Eds., *Uneven Tides: Rising Inequality in America* (New York: Russell Sage Foundation, 1993) p. 6.

54. Laurence E. Lynn, Jr. "Welfare Reform: Once More into the Breach: An Essay Review," *Social Service Review* 41 (June 1996) pp. 314–315.

55. Edward C. Banfield, *The Unheavenly City: The Nature and Future of Our Urban Crisis* (Boston: Little, Brown, 1970).

56. Leo Perlis, Statement, January 29, 1962, AFL-CIO Community Services Activities papers, folder 78, Social Welfare History Archives, University of Minnesota—Twin Cities, quoted in Patterson, *America's Struggle Against Poverty, 1900–1994,* p. 133.

Chapter *8*

Aging: Social Security as an Entitlement

Chantelle Wright is a social worker at a senior services center. For several weeks now, she has been doing supportive counseling with Hattie Jordan, a 75-year-old woman who recently lost her husband. Initially, Wright focused on helping Mrs. Jordan deal with the immediate shock and grief following her husband's death. But now Mrs. Jordan is beginning to face the other ramifications of her new situation as a widow. At their most recent meeting, she came in with an envelope stuffed with bills, and apprehensively asked her social worker "I'll still get all of my Social Security, won't I?"

Foster Jones and Heather Breaux are having cappucinos in the coffee house across from the bank where they work. When their conversation turns to earmarking money for personal investments, Foster declares heatedly: "What irks me is that I have to put in so much for Social Security—why don't those liberals and Washington bureaucrats figure out that it makes much more sense to let us all keep that money to invest so we can build our own retirement nest eggs?"

Maggie, a 24-year-old working on her income tax return, comments to her mother: "You know, a lot of money from my paycheck goes for Social Security—but I figure Social Security probably won't be around when I'm older." Her mother, who teaches social work and social policy, is horrified. How could her daughter be so convinced by the scare tactics of people who want to dismantle the Social Security system?

Agnes and Jesse Moorhead have a small apartment and two cats. Mr. Moorhead retired from his custodial job ten years ago. The couple lives modestly, but they go out to dinner and a movie with friends every few weeks and take a short vacation at a nearby lake each summer. Mr. Moorhead has only a small pension, so they rely chiefly on Social Security for their income. "It's not a huge amount," Mrs. Moorhead says, "but it's enough to keep us going. And it certainly gives me peace of mind to know that check will come every month."

Social Security—which some have called the bedrock of the American welfare state—will it still be there when today's 24-year-olds retire?[1] If it does exist in 2038, will it be in the same form? Will people be able to choose between participating in Social Security and investing their own money toward retirement? Will methods of financing benefits be different, and will they be available only to certain groups of people, such as the needy? Will we still think of it as the major entitlement program in our country's social welfare system?

Entitlement is a word much in the news of late. The term has been applied not only to the old-age insurance portion of the Social Security Act, but also to a myriad of other programs that make up the American "safety net." Concerns about the budget deficit, along with ideological conflicts between a Democratic president and Republican majorities in the 104th Congress, have led to close scrutiny of our social welfare system and its costs and benefits, and to a national debate over "who's entitled" and to what?

Some of the participants in this debate have taken the issue to extremes. Robert J. Samuelson, for example, calls our belief in a network of entitlements a fantasy. In his recent book *The Good Life and its Discontents: The American Dream in the Age of Entitlement,* Samuelson pictures post-war America as a time when we expected all social problems to be solved; poverty, racism, and crime to recede; and a "compassionate government" to protect the poor, the old, and the unfortunate. "We not only expected these things," Samuelson notes, "after a while, we thought we were entitled to them."[2] Thus Samuelson recasts the notion of a mutual obligation in our society to achieve security for all into the image of a childish "wish list" in which all of us want gifts and candy that we don't truly "deserve."

Defenders of entitlements view them as the expression of society's obligation to the poor, the elderly, and the unemployed. Some argue that all citizens have a right to economic security, while others stress that certain entitlements, such as Social Security, are in fact earned benefits. Discussions of Social Security thus become inextricably tied up in contemporary debates about the purpose and desirability of entitlements.

This chapter analyzes the Social Security program within the larger context of these debates. It describes the development of Social Security as the first comprehensive effort by the federal government to meet the economic needs of a wide variety of citizens. The chapter concentrates on the social insurance portion of the Social Security Act, the major U.S. policy dealing with the common needs of the elderly. It also touches on the program's provisions for the poor elderly, people with disabilities, and disadvantaged children. It concludes with a discussion of current criticisms of the social insurance program and proposals for policy reform.

The Problem that Social Security Was Developed to Solve

In any society in which the vast majority of people depend on wages for their income, old age will present an economic problem. Once people have stopped working, they must find another source of revenue to pay the rent or mortgage, the grocery bill, and the doctor's bill. Wealthier members of society will have built up savings and acquired other assets for this occasion, and some workers will receive generous pensions from the companies where they worked. But many will enter retirement and old age with only small savings and pension funds, and perhaps a paid-off mortgage—or no assets at all.

Today, almost all people age 65 and over (and in some cases, age 62) have another source of income: their monthly Social Security benefits. Before the Social Security Act was passed in 1935, the only public old-age pensions that existed were limited to certain groups of people—veterans, federal civil service employees, and employees of some state and local governments. Some workers received help through the private pension program of their unions or places of employment. Most elderly people depended for survival on savings, help from their families, assistance from public and private charity (which was generally quite limited), and, as a last resort, the local poorhouse. Not surprisingly, a large proportion of the elderly worked as long as possible to forestall the poverty of old age. In 1930, almost sixty percent of men over 65 were still employed.[3]

The Great Depression decimated most of these sources of income. Bank closures wiped out lifetime savings; unemployed children could not help elderly parents; older people lost their jobs at even higher rates than younger workers; failing companies closed down their pension plans; and the coffers of both private charities and local public assistance programs quickly dried up. Describing the crisis, economist (and later, Senator) Paul Douglas declared that the Depression "... increasingly convinced the majority of the American people that individuals could not themselves provide adequately for their old age and that some sort of greater security should be provided by society."[4]

The Social Security Act of 1935

The economic crisis of the Great Depression brought about a recognition of fundamental economic insecurities in American society. In response, President Franklin D. Roosevelt and his advisors crafted and won passage of the 1935 Social Security Act. This act, perhaps, more than any other major social policy, has been subject to continued change and expansion. We will detail those changes in the historical section of this chapter, presenting here a basic description of the legislation signed by Roosevelt on August 14, 1935.

The 1935 Act is a broad piece of legislation that includes two social insurance programs and three "welfare" or public assistance programs, along with several smaller programs such as vocational rehabilitation and child welfare services. While social insurance benefits were to be made available to people of all income levels, public assistance payments would be made only to those determined by states to be financially needy. The two programs of direct relevance to the elderly are described in Titles I, II, and VIII. Under Title I, "Grants to States of Old-Age Assistance" (OAA), the federal government would reimburse states for fifty percent of the amount they spent on public (cash) assistance to poor people over the age of 65. Each state was required to have a state-wide plan for old-age assistance, and its system of administering the grants would have to be approved by the federal government.[5]

Title II, "Federal Old-Age Benefits," contains what to most Americans is the program synonymous with the term "social security"—a federal system of old age insurance. The program created a federal trust fund, the Old-Age Reserve Account, to which funds would be appropriated each year to provide monthly payments to retired people 65 and over. Excluded from the program were farm laborers, domestic servants, U.S. government employees, state and local government employees, and workers in nonprofit agencies. Old Age Benefit payments would begin in 1942. For workers whose total wages between the start of the program and the time they reached 65 were $3,000 or less, monthly benefits would amount to one-half a percent of these wages. For a person who reached 65 in 1942 and who had worked for the previous five years at $50 a month, for example, this would amount to the munificent sum of $15 a month. As a mild measure of income redistribution, workers making higher salaries would receive a much lower percentage of their salary for all wages in excess of $3,000. No retired worker could receive more than $85 a month.[6]

Title VIII detailed the source of funding for the old age insurance program: federal taxes to be paid by both employers and employees. For the first few years of the program, workers and employers would each pay the federal government one percent of the first $3,000 of the worker's annual wage. The percentage paid would rise every three years thereafter, to a final level of three percent in 1949. Then, as now, workers with lower wages paid proportionately more of their income into Social Security than did people with higher wages.[7]

The other social insurance program of the Social Security Act is a joint federal/state unemployment compensation system detailed in Titles III and IX. Under these titles, the federal government was authorized to appropriate funds to help states administer benefits to unemployed workers. States would collect a payroll tax from employers of eight or more individuals and would give these revenues to the federal government. The federal government would keep the revenues in a central fund for each state; that fund would be used to pay unemployment benefits to workers. Employers would be given federal tax credits to offset most of their payroll taxes. Each state would enact its own unemployment insurance law, which would determine levels and duration of benefits. These laws would have to be approved by the federal government, but the criteria for approval related to administrative matters, rather than to the amount or length of payments.[8]

The Social Security Act also brought into existence joint state/federal programs of public assistance for dependent children and the blind. Title IV,

"Grants to States of Aid to Dependent Children" (ADC), established a system in which the federal government covered one-third of a state's expenditures for the support of needy children in families with one caretaker (usually a widowed or divorced mother). As in unemployment compensation, state plans were to be approved by the federal government, but approval was again limited to administrative procedures and did not include minimum levels of benefits. A similar program for public assistance payments to needy blind persons was included in Title X, with funds provided half by the federal government and half by the state. In both the ADC and Aid to the Blind programs, the percentage paid by the federal government was calculated on benefits up to a certain amount; if states paid more than that amount to beneficiaries, they would have to cover the excess.

Finally, the act established a new federal entity, the Social Security Board, to administer the old age insurance system and the federal portions of the other programs. The board was also responsible for approval of state program plans for unemployment compensation, old age assistance, and aid to children.

Historical Development of Social Security Programs in the United States

While the 1935 Social Security Act may have seemed a bold policy innovation on the part of the Roosevelt administration, each program established by the act drew on precedents dating back at least to the early 1900s. A complex set of social, political, and economic factors influenced the development of the social insurance and public assistance provisions elaborated in 1935. A thorough history of this development, and of the subsequent implementation and amendments of the act, would run to hundreds of pages. We will present a brief analysis here, concentrating primarily on programs related to the elderly.

Precedents of the Social Security Act

The creation of federal old age insurance is often viewed as a watershed in American social welfare history. Historian Mark Leff describes the program as "... both the pearl and the pillar of the American welfare state, a political marvel that has beaten the ideological odds and has allowed Americans to receive government checks without stigma."[9] In developing this "political marvel," the architects of the Social Security Act built on a patchwork of existing programs. The idea of old age pension plans was not new in the 1930s. The public sector had taken the lead in establishing such programs. The federal government established public pensions for United States war veterans after the Civil War. While at first these applied only to financially needy and disabled veterans, by

1912, old age alone could qualify former soldiers to receive benefits. In addition, at the turn of the century, most major U.S. cities provided pensions for firemen and police officers. The majority of states had retirement plans for school teachers by 1916, and in the early 1930s a number of states established mandatory pension laws for their residents. In 1920, a federal Civil Service Retirement System was established.[10]

Businesses and corporations had also developed pension plans, as one part of a private social welfare system that emerged in the U.S. in the 1880s. Based both on moral arguments and the desire for a more efficient and docile work force, employers created a variety of social welfare amenities, including retirement programs. At the same time, some trade unions established pension plans. However, union and corporate programs together covered only about fourteen percent of American workers in 1932.[11]

Nor was the idea of social insurance new in the 1930s. Beginning in the Progressive era, reformers like Isaac Rubinow, Abraham Epstein, and Jane Addams promoted programs based on those developed in Germany and England, in which the government used tax money to protect people against the inevitable hazards of an industrial state: industrial accidents, disability, ill-health, and unemployment. To the reformers, social insurance represented a source of public funds that could spread the cost of dealing with such risks across a large number of people. It also allowed for some redistribution of income from the wealthy to the less well-off. To further these goals, Rubinow helped form the American Association for Labor Legislation. The Association provided research and model bills to states experimenting with various programs to aid unemployed and retired workers.[12]

Despite such activity, the idea of a national public system of old age insurance was slow to catch on. Americans held fast to ingrained beliefs in self-help and private responses to need. Even the developing labor movement did not initially back public old age benefits, preferring to trust the union's ability to improve wages and provide security.

Creation of the Social Security Act

Forces let loose during the Depression changed all this. The 1929 Market Crash led to unprecedented levels of unemployment and was, as we have seen, particularly devastating for the elderly. A relatively small and scattered array of private, state, and local social welfare programs quickly proved inadequate to deal with rising levels of need. Traditional beliefs in independence and self-reliance were badly shaken.

When Roosevelt took office in 1933, he faced the challenge of coping with the country's deepening crisis. While at first pursuing temporary relief measures such as those provided by the Federal Emergency Relief Administration, the President was loath to simply replace the traditional poor law system with federal funds. His belief that more permanent relief should stress jobs over handouts led to the creation of vast public work programs; his commitment to "rebuilding many of the structures of our economic life and reorganizing it in order to prevent a recurrence of collapse" led to a program of social insurance.[13]

Political forces helped shape this move toward social insurance, particularly where it pertained to the problems of old age. The desperation of the elderly was portrayed in numerous letters to the White House. One citizen noted:

> *I am about 75 or 6 years old and Have Labored Hard all My Days until depression Came on and I Had No Job in three years . . . Please Sir do what you Can for me I am to old to be turned out of doors.*[14]

Older people like these formed a major support for increasingly popular flat-rate pension plans, such as that proposed by Dr. Francis Townsend, a retired California physician. Starting in his home state, Townsend built a national movement for a program that promised to end the Depression by giving everyone over 60 a pension of $200 a month. Financed through federal taxation, the plan would bolster the economy by requiring recipients to spend the entire $200 within thirty days. By 1934, Townsend claimed five million supporters. Other Utopian schemes included Louisiana Senator Huey Long's proposal to give $30 a month to every poor person over 60 and to finance this "Share Our Wealth" program through income, inheritance, and other taxes. Long, who had originally supported Roosevelt, was beginning to emerge as a potential political rival. In addition, a bill supported by the Communist party and a number of social workers, other professionals, and unemployed workers was introduced into Congress in 1935 and received wide support. The Lundeen bill would have guaranteed to all persons willing to work but unable to find a job an income equal to the average wages in their district, and would have provided a social insurance scheme for the elderly. Calls for action, especially to deal with unemployment, came also from social work organizations and increasingly powerful unions representing unskilled workers.[15]

Clearly, Roosevelt needed to maintain his political support and to keep control of the reform agenda. In June, 1934, he responded to political pressures and to the country's continued economic distress by announcing to Congress his intent to find a sound means for providing "security against several of the great disturbing factors in life—especially those which relate to unemployment and old age." He proceeded to create the Committee on Economic Security (CES) to make recommendations for a broad program of legislation to ensure that security.[16]

The Committee was chaired by Frances Perkins, Secretary of Labor, and included other cabinet members and Federal Emergency Relief Administrator

Harry Hopkins. Both Perkins and Hopkins were social workers. Two University of Wisconsin labor economists played important roles in the legislative drafting process. One, Edwin E. Witte, served as executive director of the CES, while the other, Arthur J. Altmeyer, chaired an accompanying Technical Board. Experts (government officials and academics) on the Technical Board and on the CES staff did much of the actual work in formulating the legislation and presenting major policy issues to CES members for their review.[17]

Thus a large group of people with different skills and perspectives came together to develop a social insurance program. In their decision-making, CES members brought to bear not only their own points of view, but also their sense of the general thinking of the President. In addition, they were sensitive to issues of constitutionality, since previous Supreme Court decisions had cast doubt on how far the federal government would be allowed to go in enacting social legislation. Administrative feasibility, public and Congressional reactions, and technical problems in financing and implementation were further factors to be considered. The committee's expert advisors, while tuned in to technical issues, were less concerned about constitutionality and congressional acceptance. Perkins referred to working with them as similar to "driving a team of high-strung unbroken horses." In a good example of the messy world of policymaking, academics, politicians, and top officials in the Roosevelt administration all plunged together into uncharted waters to develop a politically, economically, and administratively feasible national economic security program.[18]

To complicate matters, as historian Andrew Achenbaum has noted, there was not a clear consensus about the major thrust of an economic security plan. While some New Deal scholars have portrayed the development and implementation of the Social Security Act as following a set ideology, it seems more accurate to view the process as reflecting a fundamental ambivalence and lack of clarity about goals. Achenbaum describes two potentially conflicting social policy objectives related to Social Security: social adequacy and equity. *Adequacy* referred to assisting people based on their actual need, *equity* to giving assistance based on what people had put into the system. The former was sometimes called welfare, and included a redistribution of income; the latter emphasized principles of self-reliance and fairness: recipients would receive benefits based on what they had contributed.[19]

Roosevelt himself seemed to have had both approaches in mind when delivering his economic security message to Congress. The President spoke of "the security of home, and the security of livelihood" as constituting "a *right* which belongs to every individual and every family *willing to work* [italics added]." This ambivalence between a program which based benefits on citizens' rights, and one which rewarded people for contributions based on work was ingrained in the American Social Security system from the beginning.[20]

The work of the CES and its staff led to a broad program that combined the two approaches. The bill that emerged contained old age insurance and unemployment compensation tied to wage contributions (the equity approach) as well as more traditional public assistance measures (the social adequacy approach). The social adequacy/income redistribution goal even played some part in the old age insurance program, since low-income workers got a larger percentage of their wages back in benefits than did higher income workers.

The bill also drew on existing American values and systems. Wage-based old age insurance and unemployment compensation programs supported the work ethic. A neighborly sense of compassion for deprived children helped justify the ADC proposal, which at the time was considered a rather minor part of the Social Security Act. The same sense of compassion undergirded extra assistance for the poor elderly; in addition, this aid was seen as a justifiable benefit for folks who "deserved help" in their later years. Most parts of the new system fit the American brand of federalism, with its stress on states' rights. While old age insurance broke new ground as a large, nationally administered program, unemployment compensation was shaped by the individual plans of each state, and the federal government was given relatively minimal control over the assistance programs for children and the elderly. For example, states had complete say in determining the level of benefits in the ADC program, leading to a wide range in benefits which still exists today.

Two important issues raised during the bill's development concerned the scope of coverage and financing. For a number of reasons, two groups were excluded from participation in the old age insurance plan: domestic servants and farm workers. CES staff visualized the plan as particularly important for industrial workers who had relatively low salaries. Since these workers tended to have a stable relationship with a single employer, it would be easy to administer a payroll tax on them and their employers. Farm workers and servants might receive in-kind benefits in addition to their wages, such as room and board, and since they were seen as having many employers, collection of a payroll tax might be difficult. An argument could thus be made to exclude these groups, at least for the time being. Yet the fact that many of these workers were African American farm laborers and female domestic servants adds another, more sinister dimension to their exclusion—the influence of Southern legislators anxious to control their work force and the apathy of many of the policymakers regarding the plight of African Americans in the United States. As a result, one-half of the black work force was excluded from benefits.[21]

Financing the old age insurance portion of the Social Security Act through payroll deductions drew fire from progressives and radicals in the 1930s, and the criticism still surfaces today. Detractors asserted that tying benefits to income levels maintained a system of economic inequality and failed to produce the resources needed to give a meaningful amount of aid to all the elderly.

The usual interpretation for this financing decision by the bill's creators is that Roosevelt and his policymakers needed to cast social insurance as an earned benefit, rather than a handout, in order to get it passed. While this was an important factor, other considerations played a part as well. The social insurance systems of European countries were financed out of general tax funds. Roosevelt and the other architects of old age insurance rejected this approach in part because federal tax revenues at the time were quite low—less than five percent of the population paid federal income taxes in the 1930s. In addition, both the President and the expert staffers of the CES were leery of future attempts by Congress to change appropriation levels for social insurance. While we think of old age insurance as the lynchpin of the Social Security Act, the program actually had little support in Congress, and was almost dropped when the bill went through committee. To safeguard the program from politicians in the future, it seemed necessary to create a separate, more easily protected trust fund. Thus for ideological, political, and economic reasons, the opportunity to use general taxes to create substantial income redistribution and a more reasonable level of aid to the elderly was lost.[22]

The bill drew both praise and criticism as it went through Congress. Those supporting the plan included national women's organizations, the American Association of Social Workers, organized labor, liberal politicians, and even the U.S. Chamber of Commerce. However, many businesspeople and Republican politicians opposed it, focusing most of their disapproval on the provisions for old age insurance. Detractors called this "the worst title in the bill . . . a burdensome tax on industry," which would establish "a bureaucracy in the field of insurance in competition with private business." Fears of the oppressive hand of "big government" were added to this strenuous defense of the private market system. From the other end of the political spectrum, radical critics argued that the plan did little to change the negative effects of the market system. Despite these criticisms, Roosevelt and the CES succeeded. Through compromise, careful management in the legislative system, and popular demand for change, the bill passed by wide margins in both House and Senate.[23]

The Social Security Act, for all its flaws, was a milestone in the history of American social welfare programs. It cleverly joined welfare and insurance programs, state and federal levels of financing and implementation, and the often conflicting American values of mutual responsibility and self-reliance. While the old age insurance portion did not attack income inequalities the way some had hoped, it nevertheless included a slightly redistributive measure which paid the poorest workers a higher percentage of their income (note that since this percentage was figured on a lower income, they still got less money than better-off workers). Moreover, as the following section shows, the act created a program capable of slow and steady expansion and reform.

Changes in Social Security

The Social Security system has proved a remarkable example of incremental policy change. Before the first old age insurance benefits were even distributed, a set of amendments had begun to alter the act's balance between equity and social adequacy. Through the years, subsequent changes have broadened the bill's scope and liberalized its benefits.

The first changes, made in 1939, were largely a response to political pressures. Since the first old age benefits were not due to be paid until 1942, there was a long period before the advantages of the new system would be felt. In the meantime, workers' deductions were piling up in a reserve fund, which was, at least in theory, not to be used for anything else. (In reality, the government bought savings bonds with the funds, thus loaning itself money with which to finance current operations.) Workers experiencing their first payroll deductions wondered where their money was going. They also lost some spending power, which hurt the economy. Those who were already elderly had to wait for five years to receive aid; this put pressure on the Social Security Act's state-administered old age assistance program (OAA). The Social Security Board worried that expanding the assistance program would make politicians less likely to support future growth in social insurance. At the same time, older people's groups pressed for programs with broader coverage, and politicians criticized the social insurance financing arrangements.[24]

Roosevelt and the Social Security Board responded with rhetoric that expressed one thing and a set of amendments that did another. In order to keep old age insurance from being overshadowed by OAA, defenders sharpened the distinction between social insurance and welfare and promoted insurance as an effective alternative to welfare. But in order to mollify critics of the program, they proposed a liberalization of social insurance benefits which in fact diminished the work-related aspects of the insurance program and moved it more toward the social adequacy, or "welfare" approach.[25]

A major change was the addition of family benefits. Monthly benefits were established for the survivors of both active and retired workers and for the dependent children of retired workers. By emphasizing care of widows and children who were likely to be needy, the amendments suggested a more paternal role for the government as provider of family support. Encouraging a continued fuzziness regarding the program's actual goals, the new benefits were still couched in the language of work-related insurance. This was not *entirely* misleading, since the new beneficiaries qualified through their relationship to a wage earner who had contributed to the system.

In addition, the 1939 amendments allowed benefit payments to begin in 1940 and lowered the combined worker-employer taxes from 3 to 2 percent. These changes, all voted into law, at the same time liberalized benefits and lowered taxes, not necessarily a winning formula for long-term financing of the program. After 1939, the Social Security program continued to grow incrementally. Extensions in benefits were approved relatively easily in the periods of economic expansion up through the early 1970s. A part of the motivation continued to be the goal of expanding social insurance at the expense of public assistance programs. In 1950, benefits were raised substantially, bringing old age insurance to a parity with OAA. Four years later, regularly employed farm and domestic workers were finally brought into the system, along with people who were self-employed.

Financing was still not satisfactorily addressed, however. While the Social Security Administration recommended that increased benefits be funded by general revenues, Congress chose a plan of gradually rising payroll tax rates, even though it had failed to implement such mandated tax rises in previous years.[26] The continued reliance on payroll deductions to finance the Social Security program reinforced the notion that workers were setting up their own "private savings accounts" for help in old age. Many people did not understand that their deductions were being used to support current retirees.

In 1956, social insurance was extended to workers with permanent disability aged 50 and over; once they reached 65, recipients could receive regular old-age insurance benefits. The initial Social Security Act did not include a basic disability insurance program. It did provide for those who were blind, but only through a federal-state program of means-tested assistance. The changes in 1956 were made acceptable by linking disability with retirement (reflecting the "equity," or work-related approach to social insurance). Benefits were promoted as payments "to unfortunate individuals who had to 'retire early, because of mental or physical impairment'." In 1960, the "social adequacy" goal undergirded an amendment to extend benefits to disabled workers of all ages and their dependents.[27] What was now Old Age, Survivors,' and Disability Insurance (OASDI) also received further boosts in benefits. By 1961, all workers were allowed to retire, with reduced benefits, at age 62. Congress also allowed increases in payroll taxes, to 3 percent, in 1960.

The rediscovery of poverty during the Kennedy and Johnson years brought dramatic changes in Social Security programs for the elderly, changes that an expanding economy seemed well able to support. Three OASDI benefit increases were authorized in five years. In addition, an elusive quest for a federal health care program, which had been proposed intermittently since the 1920s but always rejected as politically insupportable, was finally partially realized through the creation of Medicare and Medicaid in 1965. Medicare provided acute care health benefits to all old age insurance recipients over 65. Medicaid gave health care coverage to those in the Social Security assistance programs, including old age assistance. By now, social insurance had become one of the country's most popular social programs, with a large number of stakeholders.

In 1968, Republicans bent on recapturing the presidency found it politically advantageous to include expansion of the Social Security system in the party platform. Once Nixon was elected, competition between a Republican president and a Democratic Congress to retain the "elderly vote" led to significant reforms and expansion in OASDI. In the presidential election year of 1972, a plan was adopted to tie benefits received after 1975 to rises in the cost of living. This automatic, annual "cost-of-living-adjustment" (COLA) was based on the assumption that wages, and concomitant payroll taxes, would continue to rise. The COLA thus seemed feasible and affordable. Other changes included extending Medicare coverage to the disabled, and transforming the jointly funded state-federal OAA into a federally-funded Supplemental Security Program (SSI). And, most spectacular of all, Congress passed a 20 percent increase in OASDI benefits. But Nixon did not raise the level of the payroll tax. This, along with the stagnation of wages in the mid–1970s, led to a "crisis" mentality regarding the Social Security insurance programs which persists today.[28]

Contemporary Analysis of Social Security

Thanks to the continued expansion of Social Security (as the old age/disability insurance program is now popularly called), the economic position of older citizens has vastly improved. Much of the change occurred in the 1960s. At the beginning of the decade, 35 percent of the elderly were poor despite Social Security benefits; at its end, only 25 percent were below the poverty line. The figure had dropped to 15 percent by 1979. This demonstrates the great success of the Social Security program. Yet the consensus supporting the program is beginning to unravel. Issues regarding Social Security's goals, coverage, and financing are raised by politicians, beneficiaries, and the public. In the following policy analysis, we will pursue these historically-based issues as they are played out in contemporary society.

Social Analysis

Social Security coverage is now close to universal for U.S. workers. Currently, about twenty six million retirees and five million widows and widowers receive benefits. Average monthly payments to retired workers rose to $745 in 1997. Widows and widowers received an average of $707 a month, a disabled worker with a spouse and one or more children, $1,169. This aid constitutes the major source of income for those over 65 (see Figure 8.1). For two-thirds of the elderly, Social Security makes up half or more of their income. The poverty rate for older Americans has continued to decrease, declining to 11.7 percent by 1994. As Figure 8.2 indicates, Social Security has played a notable role in reducing poverty for the elderly.[29]

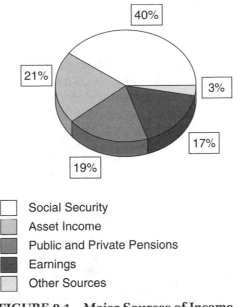

40%

21%

3%

17%

19%

☐ Social Security
▨ Asset Income
▩ Public and Private Pensions
■ Earnings
▨ Other Sources

FIGURE 8.1   **Major Sources of Income for Older Couples and Individuals, 1992**

Source: Adapted from American Association of Retired Persons, *A Profile of Older Americans,* 1995, p. 10.

This is the good news. The bad news is that Social Security remains a supplement to income from other sources for many Americans. Particularly in cases where these other sources don't exist, Social Security benefits are too low to lift all recipients out of poverty or to help the 7 percent of the elderly who are classified as "near-poor." Furthermore, the burden of poverty is unevenly spread among those over 65. Ten percent of older whites were poor in 1994, compared to 27 percent of elderly Blacks and 23 percent of older Hispanics.[30]

Women face particular problems in the Social Security system. Since they were not seen as the primary wage earners in the early years of the program's development, it was expected that their benefits would most likely come through their positions as wives or widows of male beneficiaries. This turned out to be the case, since many women either did not work at all, or worked sporadically. Their lower salaries led to lower contributions to the system, so their own pensions were less than those afforded to them through marriage. However, benefits established for elderly wives and widows were not very generous either—50 percent of a husband's pension for a wife, and 75 percent for a widow. Apparently, women were expected to have lower expenses.

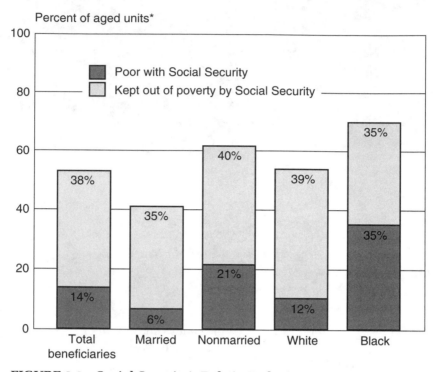

FIGURE 8.2   Social Security's Role in Reducing Poverty, 1992

Source: *Annual Statistical Supplement to the Social Security Bulletin, 1995* (Washington, DC: U.S. Department of Health and Human Services, Social Security Administration, 1995) p. 15.

* An aged unit is either a married couple living together with the husband or wife aged 65 or older, or a person 65 or older who does not live with a spouse.

While some policymakers began to recognize women's problems in the 1950s, to date only small changes have been made, such as the provision of benefits to elderly divorced women in 1965. Due to lower salaries and the more intermittent work histories of wives and homemakers, the average monthly benefit for women was $600 in 1994, compared to $785 for men. African American women averaged $528, African American men $648. Widows as a whole received an average $642; the figure drops to $500 for African Americans. Wives of retired workers averaged $360 a month. In addition, while more than half of all retired men receive pension benefits in addition to Social Security payments, only a third of retired women do.[31]

Social Security's inequities and its inability to provide a firm safety net for lower-wage workers reflect competing social values. As shown in the discussion of the program's history, both the larger social security system and the social insurance plan drew upon ideas of equity and social adequacy. Equity, as you recall, refers to a sense of fairness in the distribution of benefits based on contributions made into the system. The American work ethic undergirds this approach. Social adequacy, in contrast, stresses provision of a "basic floor of protection" or level of income to all who need it, unrelated to contributions. An additional outcome of social adequacy measures is redistribution of income from the better-off to the poor. Principles of mutual responsibility and caring for others foster the adequacy goal.[32]

Sometimes social adequacy is equated with welfare, which may be confusing. Welfare as it exists today provides inadequate benefits, often not lifting recipients above the poverty line. In addition, when it involves people other than the poor elderly, public assistance carries a good deal of stigma. Some critics argue that welfare's main intent is to change behavior, not to protect the poor. Thus our current welfare system is only a partial step toward the goal of social adequacy. To achieve that goal, the system would have to provide higher benefits and promote the legitimacy of recipients' claims to them.

The conflict between equity and social adequacy boils down to the simple question: Do you deserve help because you are poor, or because you worked hard and contributed to the system? Of course, even this question isn't really simple—poor people may work hard and still get low salaries; others, like homemakers, may do unpaid labor and not get the chance to pay anything in. And we also need to remember that Social Security isn't like an individual savings account; the contributions of current workers support the older generation.

In the United States, people generally rank self-reliance over interdependence, thus finding equity a more "legitimate" basis for providing aid. When Social Security began, then, policy makers prudently portrayed the old age insurance plan in the language of work and contributions. However, the notion of helping the less fortunate, particularly those, like the elderly, whose poverty seems no fault of their own, still has a place in the American value system. Thus the Social Security Act combined assistance and insurance programs, and both the act and subsequent changes brought an element of social adequacy into the old age insurance program. Our ambivalence over the relationship between those two goals continues to complicate the debate over how to reform Social Security.

The question of who "deserves" help is closely connected to current discussions of "entitlement." Attacks on the growth of entitlements bring up the same issues of who should be given government assistance and why. While it is becoming popular to portray almost all public assistance and social insurance programs as entitlements, that concept had a more limited meaning when our modern social welfare system began in the 1930s. The architects of the Social Security Act did not even include the term in the act, stressing instead the right of wage earners to benefits. As Roosevelt explained, "We put the payroll contributions there so as to give contributors a legal, moral and political right to collect their pensions." While social insurance was justified as an "earned right," developers of the Social Security Act based the public assistance titles on a different conception of right: a poor person's "statutory right" to assistance, "even though that assistance was conditioned on need." The official rhetoric supporting the act and its later modifications suggests that this was a two-tier model of rights, with earned rights constituting the more legitimate ones.[33]

The use of the term *entitlement* probably originated in legal discussions of welfare in the 1960s. In a 1965 *Yale Law Journal* article, Charles B. Reich used entitlement to describe the idea that "...when individuals have insufficient resources to live under conditions of health and decency, society has obligations to provide support, and the individual is entitled to that support as of right."[34] Legal scholars fleshed this idea out further as they argued that entitlements could be construed as property rights, which could not be denied or cut off without notice and a fair hearing. They contended that ownership could be seen in terms of two different sets of property rights, involving either control over something tangible that one owns, or control rights over income or other resources, such as welfare and social insurance benefits, that one needs to be autonomous. This new interpretation of property as something intangible as well as tangible means, for example, that professionals have a constitutionally protected property right regarding licenses that affect their ability to practice. Such licenses cannot be denied, just as tangible property cannot be taken away or confiscated, without due process. Using similar reasoning, the Supreme Court ruled in 1970 that welfare recipients had certain Constitutional rights to their entitlements, and that the government could not cut these off without due process. The Court argued that it had become realistic "to regard welfare entitlements as more like 'property' than a 'gratuity,'" or charity.[35]

Such sophisticated legal arguments are not in most people's minds when they discuss entitlements today. Neither, probably, are such definitions as "services, goods, or money due to an individual by virtue of a specific status" (*Social Work Dictionary*) or "the state of meeting the applicable requirements for receipt of benefits" (Social Security Administration, 1995). Instead, people tend to think of a two-tiered system that includes "earned entitlements," such as Social Security, and "income-based entitlements" like AFDC, and often to perceive the former as much more legitimate than the latter.[36]

Critics on the left argue that both kinds of entitlement are perfectly legitimate. However, there is a growing movement on the right to lump all types of entitlement together and to characterize the whole notion of entitlement as a false one, which has subtly "subverted personal and institutional responsibility." Under titles like "Escaping the Entitlement Straitjacket," conservatives label entitlements "a problem" and question whether "popularly accepted 'rights'" should be "allowed to destroy the economy." The denigration of entitlements and the claims that they are no longer affordable can be seen as a smoke screen used by those wishing to divert attention from other ways to manage the budget. These ways include increasing taxes, especially for corporations and people with high incomes, and/or decreasing tax breaks, such as the waiver of local property taxes for some businesses and the use of home mortgage interest as a tax deduction. Just as in the equity versus social adequacy debate, confusion and ambivalence over the meaning and role of entitlements cloud public discussion of potential changes and improvements in Social Security.[37]

Political Analysis

As we have seen, the notion of entitlements is politically charged. Now, as in the beginning of Social Security, there are a number of stakeholders concerned about the system and its potential reform. These include beneficiaries, organized lobby groups representing the elderly, current wage earners, employers, the public at large, members of Congress, members of the Executive branch of the federal government, "think tanks" of all ideological persuasions, program administrators, private pension companies, and human service professionals such as social workers.

As Social Security has expanded, both the number and categories of beneficiaries have increased. One of the program's greatest protections is the sheer number and potential voting power of those assisted by it. However, there are various subsets within this group with different agendas and needs. For example, the poor elderly are probably most dependent on Social Security and might not oppose the imposition of means testing for people above certain incomes, whereas this could be anathema to middle-class beneficiaries. While beneficiaries cast individual votes on election day and can write letters to their congresspeople, the more concentrated power of the elderly is exercised through the various citizen and professional organizations that make up the "Gray Lobby." By far the strongest of these is the American Association of Retired Persons (AARP), with a membership of about thirty-four million people. AARP has opposed most attempts to make cuts or other changes in Social Security and the federal health programs, changes which they feel would disadvantage older Americans. By doing so, they have earned the ire of conservative politicians who propose such changes. Speaker of the House Newt Gingrich, for example, launched a campaign in 1995 to deny AARP lobbying privileges based on its status as a non-profit group.[38]

Conservative politicians have wielded a good deal of power in questioning the stability of Social Security funding, discussed in the next section, and in casting doubt on the desirability and legitimacy of entitlements. From the other side of the floor, liberal Democrats have defended the system, although moderate Democrats and Republicans have tempered their support with the conviction that important reforms are needed. "Think tanks," such as the conservative American Enterprise Institute and the liberal Urban Institute, help provide the fodder for politicians' positions. All elected officials, including the President, walk a tight line between awareness of the voting power of older Americans and concerns about balancing the federal budget.[39]

The general public is somewhat ambivalent about support for Social Security and other entitlements, and tends to be leery about what is perceived as the increasing role of "big government" in all of our lives. However, public opinion polls show older voters swinging away from conservative reform plans such as the Republicans' 1995 Contract with America, with its promise to shrink the federal government, and putting more trust in the Democrats' traditional commitment "to protect the Social Security system." Younger workers may fear the demise of Social Security before they can benefit from it and may resent the fact that their payroll deductions support current retirees. There is even an advocacy group, Third Millennium, for people in their twenties who have such concerns. Yet a number of workers, especially middle-aged ones, are cognizant of the important fact that Social Security helps to support their aging parents.[40]

What stakeholders are most concerned about today is the economic viability of the Social Security program as it is currently structured. We turn now to that debate.

Economic Analysis and Proposals for Reform

The major issue regarding Social Security in the late 1990s is the solvency of the reserve fund. Assessments of the financial stability of the fund range from predictions of bankruptcy by about 2030 to confidence that with minor reforms the program will continue to offer a reliable safety net. There was a similar scare in the early 1980s, when it was expected that by mid-1983 there would no longer be enough resources to pay benefits. "This time around," one reporter notes, "the economic and political crisis is coming in slow motion." The forecast is that the system's income from payroll taxes will be greater than outlays until 2013. At about that time, however, the baby boomers will begin to retire, causing a rise in beneficiaries that might engulf the system, leading to complete depletion of the trust fund in 2030.[41]

A foretaste of the current "crisis" in Social Security occurred in the 1980s, when benefit payments were about to exceed incoming tax revenues. This was due to the changing beneficiary/contributor ratio and to serious inflation during the 1970s. Once benefits were tied to the cost of living, whenever people's wages failed to keep up with inflation, their payroll taxes were outstripped by payments to recipients. Congress and the Reagan administration responded to the depletion of the reserve fund with a series of mostly incremental adjustments to the Social Security program. These included advancing the age of eligibility for benefits, to reach 67 in 2017; increasing the payroll deduction; and instituting taxation of benefits received by people with incomes above certain levels. These changes would create large surpluses in the reserve fund, thus preparing the country to handle the retirement of the baby boomers.[42]

Although the 1983 amendments seemed to assure the security of the system for the next 75 years, revised labor force and demographic data now suggest that the current payroll tax will not be enough to forestall depletion in the reserve fund in the next century. What exactly is causing the problem? Is it simply a matter of a big wave of retirees? The answer is, unfortunately, quite complicated—"unfortunately" because this makes it even harder for stakeholders to discuss the situation knowledgeably, accurately assess the severity of the problem, and come up with reasonable responses.

First, the dependency ratio will have changed dramatically over the next 35 years. In 1936, that ratio consisted of 15 workers paying taxes to support each retiree, who generally lived only four to five years after stopping work. Now the ratio is 3.3 to 1, and by 2030 it will have fallen to 2 to 1. Other factors affect the state of the reserve fund, besides the obvious increase in beneficiaries and decline in contributors. In the last several decades, Social Security has been operating on the premise that the best way to deal with the worker/beneficiary imbalance was not large raises in payroll taxes, but the creation of big surpluses in the reserve fund. Planners now forecast that the surplus should rise to a breathtaking $12 trillion in 2030. However, some analysts point out that the surplus exists only on paper. The collected payroll tax revenues, by mandate, are invested in government securities (i.e., U.S. Treasury bonds), which historically produce an average 2.3 percent interest rate. Furthermore, these loans (in the form of bonds) give the Treasury money to use in daily government operations. By doing so, they help disguise the actual size of the federal deficit. This government "I.O.U." to itself during a time of huge deficits makes many observers nervous. As a commentator from the American Enterprise Institute warns, with the federal government in such debt, "it is not immediately obvious whether the Social Security surpluses are being saved and invested for future years or spent on current consumption." A more liberal analyst raises a different issue: by using Social Security surpluses to help pay government expenses, we are putting too much of the burden of financing the government on lower-income workers, who contribute disproportionately to Social Security. It may seem strange to picture those with lower incomes as bearing more of the burden. However, one must remember that the payroll deductions are a regressive tax; that is, income over a certain level is exempt from the deduction. Lower income workers thus have proportionately more of their wages withheld than do higher-paid workers.[43]

Of course, as social policy analyst David Stoesz explains, many factors, such as an expanding economy and a decrease in the deficit, can positively affect the performance of the Social Security system in the next century. It may be that baby boomers will be healthier and in fact work longer, at higher salaries, than their parents. However, the sense of crisis is enhanced by concern about the deficit and the growth in all entitlements, and by Republican attempts to redefine the role of government in solving social and economic problems. This has led to a broad array of suggested reforms. These cover the whole spectrum of political positions, and range from the complete dismantling of Social Security to using income tax increases to help finance the program.[44]

At the conservative end of the continuum, there are various proposals to bring the private market into the system. Those who would dismantle Social Security entirely argue that private pensions and individual savings and investments can in fact replace public mechanisms for old age security. Others suggest conversion to a two-track system, in which only the neediest elderly receive public pensions. More common are plans to combine public and private endeavors. These could involve coupling payroll taxes with various types of individual private investment systems. Another option for privatizing part of the system would be to allow the Social Security Administration to invest some of the program's trust funds in the stock market. This proposition has received support not only from conservatives, but also from such stakeholders as a former Social Security Commissioner and the AARP. Finally, there are suggestions to create a two-track pension system, in which only the neediest elderly receive public pensions.[45]

The idea of introducing some level of privatization into the Social Security System was included in all of the proposals resulting from the recent deliberations of a national blue-ribbon panel of experts. The Social Security Advisory Council was appointed to make recommendations for ensuring the program's future solvency. Reflecting the multiple and often conflicting expectations of Social Security, the Council could not agree on a single, integrated set of recommendations for introducing market-based and other changes into the system. Instead, the Council proposed three alternatives for consideration. The three plans read somewhat like a cafeteria menu, in which one is tempted to choose various options from each.

The first plan recommends slight cuts in Social Security benefits, which would be felt primarily by high-wage workers. It also suggest small increases in the normal retirement age. Each would be a gradual change. All workers would be required to contribute 1.6 percent of their pay to individual investment accounts. These accounts would be managed by the government, and workers would choose among five to ten mutual funds.[46]

The second plan proposes to "turn the workers into investors." Instead of relying on centrally managed funds, workers would have the freedom of Personal Investment Accounts (PSAs) in which they could invest in the financial institutions of their choice. PSAs would replace one-half of the current pay-as-you-go system, with workers getting a rebate of part of their taxes for investment in PSAs. The other half of the Social Security program would consist of a flat benefit for all enrollees, yielding a base level of retirement income *"at or above the poverty level."* (emphasis added) In addition, this plan includes either a small payroll tax increase or a decrease in benefits for high to middle-income wage earners. As the proponents of this proposal explain, in order to get the system up and running there will be long-term transition costs in the form of a supplementary payroll tax of 1.5 percent over a 70-year period coupled with cuts in long-range federal spending. Still, they argue, the potential of the system is worth the high transition costs. [47]

The final plan builds on the premise that fears about the future solvency of the system are exaggerated. It proposes small, "common sense" changes: improve the accuracy of the cost-of-living provision (which some say is set too high), tax those benefits that exceed what the worker has put into the system (a form of taxation of higher income individuals), and make modest cuts in future benefits or increase payroll taxes slightly. Up to this part, the proposal appears modest. However, this plan, too, succumbs to the allure of market investments by suggesting that the Social Security Administration itself invest up to 40 percent of the trust fund in stocks. [48]

These proposals have their advantages and disadvantages. For example, changing from Treasury bonds to stock market investments would yield much higher interest rates, thus increasing the size of the reserve fund. Yet decisions about which stocks the government should invest in could be politically tricky. Individual investment programs can be seen as reinforcing self-reliance, yet investing is a complicated business which not all people have the skills, time, and knowledge to carry out effectively. Historian Edward Berkowitz colorfully depicts the potential horrors of a private investment system:

> *I, for one, hesitate to trade in Social Security for a brave new world of individual freedom in which I get to steer my own course. The economics of scale achieved by the program would vanish in a cacophony of television commercials in which banks, insurance companies, and investment houses all would compete for my retirement dollar. Companies would enter and exit the market, forcing me to decide, again and again, where to put my money. A mistake would be costly, possibly catastrophic, unless I could depend on a bail-out . . . from the federal government.*[49]

Under PSAs or other schemes, Social Security enrollees would exchange political risk for market risk. As one analyst explains, "political risk is that the government will be unable or unwilling to pay you the benefits it promised; market risk is that you will make poor investments or the market generally will not perform well." Low income workers will have much less to invest and so stand to lose the most in a private investment system.[50]

Critics point to still another danger in privatizing part of the system. If the government or individual workers suddenly shifted "an extra $1 trillion into a $6 trillion stock market," stock prices would undoubtedly rise. The price of bonds would fall, with a resulting rise in interest rates. While the investment might put a little more money in the trust fund and in some investors' pockets, the federal government would face higher interest rates and be worse off than before the change.[51]

The suggestion of a minimum flat rate for all enrollees plus a second source of retirement income from investments seems at first glance like a promising combination. Yet what is likely to happen is the creation of a two-track system, with a low-level pension for poorer workers, and a more remunerative arrangement for those with the income and knowledge to take advantage of the market. Similar to plans that restrict Social Security benefits to the neediest retirees, this could create a more stigmatized "second class" group of the elderly and undercut general public support for the program.

The Advisory Council did not stress proposals that would strengthen commitment to a broad, government-regulated program based primarily on tax revenues. One such plan would be to continue to raise Social Security payroll taxes as needed, but to make these taxes more progressive (that is, tax those with larger wages at a higher rate, or raise the amount of income that could be taxed to a much higher level). Or, the United States could use the approach of many European countries, which base old-age insurance on general tax revenues and thus spread the burden of support throughout the entire society. Achenbaum offers a third approach: provide a reasonable flat grant to all individuals meeting broad and universal criteria (such as being 65 or over) and then supplement this with payments directly related to a social security contributor's prior covered earnings. In this way, the values of social adequacy and equity are both recognized. While these proposals would provide much firmer, and in the last two cases, broader sources of revenue, they are obviously dependent on an ideological commitment to our shared responsibility for the welfare of all older Americans.[52]

Conclusion

Thus we have come back to the importance of recognizing which goals and values we want Social Security to stress. The various factors of choice analysis—how and to whom benefits are allocated, what type of provision is made, how benefits are delivered, and the method of financing—all relate to the desired balance between equity and social adequacy, independence and mutual responsibility, and government and private market intervention. Value choices are particularly important in decisions about financing and scope of coverage. As we have seen, proposals for maintaining the financial solvency of the system differ based on ideas about the degree to which people should take the initiative in providing for their retirement and the degree to which this provision should be made through government's use of collective resources. Discussions of the appropriate degree of coverage afforded by the system raise similar value issues.

One example of this relates to both fairness and adequacy of coverage for women in the present Social Security system. A number of working women contribute, but end up receiving a benefit based on their husband's deductions, since this is higher than their own pension would have been. This can seem unfair; women ask "Where has *my* money gone?" In addition, women (or men) who do unpaid work as homemakers are not given the chance to contribute to the program. They are thus unable to build up their own pensions, which because of continuous work might, in fact, be higher than those available to them as a spouse. As a way of expanding the scope and amount of coverage in these situations, proposals have been made to give unpaid homemakers "earnings credits" toward Social Security. These credits would be financed out of general revenues. Another approach, "earnings sharing," would divide the total annual earnings of a married couple equally between them, and calculate contributions accordingly. This would level off inequities between men's and women's salaries in awarding pensions. It would also give a spouse coverage for time spent working in the home.[53]

These provisions promote equity, and they also improve Social Security's ability to diminish poverty among older women. Yet the Social Security system could go much further to achieve social adequacy, as in the creation of a reasonable flat grant for all elderly people, coupled with a secondary pension based on contributions. Or, coverage of the system could be dramatically widened—social insurance in America might be refashioned to include grants for all families to bring them up to a reasonable standard of living, or to include universal children's allowances.

You are now probably asking "How could we afford to do this? How would we do it? Why should we do it?" Beneath all social welfare questions lie our value preferences and our conceptions of the good society. If we chose to put more emphasis on social adequacy as a value, we might reach consensus on enlarging the Social Security system to include children and families and supporting it through general taxation. Taxes, including corporate taxes, would most likely have to be increased to do this. We would, however, have spread the burden of support in a fairer way across a broad social base.

If we chose instead to stress the goal of social equity, and to focus on supporting people who had either worked or were eligible for benefits through relationship to a worker, we could carry out one of the reform proposals aimed at fine tuning the system and keeping it solvent. The best way to do this might be to remove the earnings cap on the payroll deduction and to tax people on 100 percent of their income.

While these suggestions may seem radical or politically unfeasible, it is important to recognize that Social Security is a program that has demonstrated significant progress in reducing poverty among the elderly. It also has a broad base of political support, since the vast majority of Americans are eligible for benefits. The challenges to the program are basically small compared to the good the system accomplishes or could be exanded to accomplish. We think social workers should be out in front of the parade championing Social Security and its potential to reduce poverty among all Americans.

Notes

1. David Stoesz, *Small Change: Domestic Policy under the Clinton Presidency* (White Plains, New York: Longman, 1996) p. 173.

2. Robert Samuelson, "Great Expectations," *Newsweek* (8 January 1996) pp. 24–26.

3. W. Andrew Achenbaum, *Social Security: Visions and Revisions* (NY: Cambridge University Press, 1986) pp. 14–15; Ann Shola Orloff, *The Politics of Pensions: A Comparative Analysis of Britain, Canada, and the United States 1880–1940* (Madison, WI: University of Wisconsin Press, 1993) pp. 269–283.

4. Quoted in Achenbaum, *Social Security: Visions and Revisions,* p. 16.

5. Bruce S. Jansson, *The Reluctant Welfare State: A History of American Social Welfare Policies,* 3rd ed. (Pacific Grove, CA: Brooks/Cole, 1997) pp. 177–179.

6. Eveline Burns, *Toward Social Security* (NY: Whittlesey House, 1936) pp. 244–245.

7. Burns, *Toward Social Security,* pp. 246–247.

8. Jansson, *The Reluctant Welfare State,* pp. 174–175, 178.

9. Mark H. Leff, "Historical Perspectives on Old-Age Insurance: The State of the Art on the Art of the State," in Edward D. Berkowitz, Ed., *Social Security After Fifty: Successes and Failures* (Westport, CT: Greenwood Press, 1987) p. 29.

10. Some states established pension laws in the early 1900s, but these left payment of pensions to county option, and very few people were actually covered. Orloff, *The Politics of Pensions,* pp. 134–135, 269–270; Achenbaum, *Social Security: Visions and Revisions,* p. 15.

11. Edward D. Berkowitz and Kim McQuaid, *Creating the Welfare State: The Political Economy of 20th Century Reform,* rev. ed. (Lawrence, KS: University Press of Kansas, 1992) pp. 1–4, 11–30; Orloff, *The Politics of Pensions,* p. 278.

12. Berkowitz and McQuaid, *Creating the Welfare State,* pp. 38, 112–113; Stoesz, *Small Change,* p. 176.

13. Quoted in Edward D. Berkowitz, *America's Welfare State: From Roosevelt to Reagan* (Baltimore, MD: Johns Hopkins University Press, 1991) p. 15.

14. Quoted in Achenbaum, *Social Security: Visions and Revisions,* p. 17.

15. Jerry R. Cates, *Insuring Inequality: Administrative Leadership in Social Security 1935–54* (Ann Arbor, MI: University of Michigan Press, 1983) pp. 22, 50-51; Achenbaum, *Social Security: Visions and Revisions,* pp. 17–18; Arthur J. Altmeyer, *The Formative Years of Social Security* (Madison: University of Wisconsin Press, 1968) pp. 30–31; Burns, *Toward Social Security,* pp. 136–137.

16. Quoted in Achenbaum, *Social Security: Visions and Revisions,* p. 19.

17. Altmeyer, *The Formative Years of Social Security,* pp. 7–8.

18. Altmeyer, *The Formative Years of Social Security,* pp. 14–15; Berkowitz, *America's Welfare State,* pp. 15–16; Frances Perkins, Foreward to Edwin D. Witte, *The Development of the Social Security Act* (Madison: University of Wisconsin Press, 1963) p. vi.

19. Cates argues that Altmeyer, Witte, and other key figures in the development and implementation of the Social Security Act followed a conservative approach to social insurance that strongly emphasized self-reliance over redistribution of incomes (Cates, *Insuring Inequality*). Achenbaum, Coll, and others describe a broader set of goals. See Achenbaum, *Social Security: Visions and Revisions,* p. 3 and *Shades of Grey: Old Age, American Values and Federal Policies Since 1920* (Boston: Little, Brown, 1983) pp. 42–43; Blanche Coll, "Public Assistance: Reviving the Original Comprehensive Concept of Social Security," in Gerald D. Nash, Noel H. Pugach, and Richard F. Tomasson, Eds., *Social Security: The First Half Century* (Albuquerque: University of New Mexico Press, 1988) pp. 221–241.

20. Achenbaum, *Social Security: Visions and Revisions,* p. 19.

21. Berkowitz, *America's Welfare State,* p. 25; Orloff, *The Politics of Pensions,* p. 294; Linda Gordon, *Pitied but Not Entitled: Single Mothers and the History of Welfare* (NY: The Free Press, 1994) pp. 275–276.

22. Altmeyer, *Formative Years of Social Security,* pp. 11, 34; Anthony Badger, *The New Deal: The Depression Years 1933–40* (NY: Hill and Wang, 1989) pp. 102–104, 231–234; Berkowitz, *America's Welfare State,* pp. 20–21.

23. Altmeyer, *Formative Years of Social Security,* pp. 32–33, 37–42; Witte, *The Development of the Social Security Act,* pp. 87–90; Berkowitz, *America's Welfare State,* p. 14.

24. Berkowitz, *America's Welfare State,* pp. 40–46; Achenbaum, *Social Security: Visions and Revisions,* pp. 26–30.

25. Berkowitz, *America's Welfare State,* pp. 46–48; Achenbaum, *Social Security: Visions and Revisions,* pp. 32–37.

26. Berkowitz, *America's Welfare State,* pp. 25–61.

27. Achenbaum, *Social Security: Visions and Revisions,* pp. 43–44.

28. Achenbaum, *Social Security: Visions and Revisions,* pp. 57–60; Jansson, *The Reluctant Welfare State,* p. 250.

29. Social Security Administration, *Annual Statistical Supplement to the Social Security Bulletin 1995* (Washington, DC: U.S. Department of Health and Human Services, Social Security Administration, 1995) p. 14; "Social Security: Take It While It Lasts," *New York Times* (20 November 1996) p. 2.

30. American Association of Retired Persons, *A Profile of Older Americans* (Washington, DC: AARP, 1995) p. 10.

31. Achenbaum, Social Security: Visions and Revisions, pp. 124–132; *Annual Statistical Supplement to the Social Security Bulletin 1995,* pp. 196–197; Darlene Superville,

"Secretary Cites Need for Pension Parity for Women," *Baton Rouge Advocate,* 10 May 1996) p. 5 C. In 1995, the Social Security benefit gap had widened to an average benefit of $858 for men, $538 for women. Tamar Lewin, "Income Gap Between Sexes Found to Widen in Retirement," *New York Times* (26 April 1995) p. 15 A.

32. Martha Ozawa, quoted in John E. Tropman, *Public Policy Opinion and the Elderly 1952–1978* (NY: Greenwood Press, 1987) p. 39.

33. Witte, *The Development of the Social Security Act,* p. 146; Philip R. Popple and Leslie Leighninger, *Social Work, Social Welfare, and American Society,* 3rd ed. (Boston: Allyn and Bacon, 1996) p. 557; Altmeyer, *The Formative Years of Social Security,* p. 225.

34. Daniel Patrick Moynihan, "The Case Against Entitlement Cuts," *Modern Maturity* 37 (November–December 1994) p. 14.

35. John Brigham, *Property and the Politics of Entitlement* (Philadelphia: Temple University Press, 1990) pp. 4–6, 35–36; John Christman, *The Myth of Property: Toward an Egalitarian Theory of Ownership* (NY: Oxford University Press, 1994) pp. 171–173; Charles Reich, "The New Property," in C. B. Macpherson, Ed., *Property: Mainstream and Critical Positions* (Toronto: University of Toronto Press, 1978) pp. 177–198.

36. Robert L. Barker, *The Social Work Dictionary* (Silver Spring: NASW, 1987) p. 49; *Annual Statistical Supplement to Social Security Bulletin 1995,* p. 374.

37. Samuelson, "Great Expectations," p. 27; Norman Ornstein, "Escaping the Entitlement Straitjacket," *Washington Post Weekly Edition* (7–13 March 1994) p. 25. Note that Orstein is connected with the conservative American Enterprise Institute.

38. Elliot Carlson, "AARP Issues Blunt Warning to Panel," *AARP Bulletin* 35 (November 1994) pp. 4–5; "Senior Power Rides Again, *Newsweek* (20 February 1995) p. 31; Thomas Rosenstiel, "Buying Off the Elderly," *Newsweek* (2 October 1995) pp. 40–41.

39. Spencer Rich, "For the Elderly, A Promise of More Social Security and Less Taxation," *Washington Post Weekly Edition* (12 December 1995–1 January 1996) p. 10.

40. Richard Morin, "The New Deal for '96: Older Voters Give Clinton and the Democrats an Early Lead," *Washington Post Weekly Edition* (15–21 April 1996) p. 38; Richard Morin, "In Washington We Trust," *Washington Post Weekly Edition* (13–19 May 1996) p. 34; Phillip Fiorini, "Poll: OK to Cut Social Security," *USA Today* (16 November 1994) p. 1 B; James Flanigan, "Planning for Social Security's Future in the Market, *The Baton Rouge Advocate* (25 May 1996) p. 2 C.

41. Peter Passell, "Can Retirees' Safety Net Be Saved?" *New York Times* (18 February 1996) sec. 3, p. 1.

42. Wilbur J. Cohen, *Social Security: The Compromise and Beyond* (Washington, DC: SOS Education Fund, June, 1983); Achenbaum, *Social Security: Visions and Revisions,* pp. 61–99.

43. Flanigan, "Planning for Social Security's Future in Market;" Stoesz, *Small Change,* pp. 179–181; Patrick Dattalo, "Social Security's Surpluses: An Update," *Social Work* 37 (July 1992) pp. 377–379.

44. Stoesz, *Small Change,* p. 183; Christopher Farrell, "The Economics of Aging: Why the Growing Number of Elderly Won't Bankrupt America," *Business Week* (12 September 1994) pp. 60–68; Passell, "Can Retirees' Safety Net be Saved?"

45. Passell, "Can Retirees' Safety Net be Saved?"; Miles Benson, "Privatized Social Security May be Proposed," *New Orleans Times Picayune* (15 November 1995) p. 3 A; Eric Pianin, "Lamm Backs Proposal to Partially Privatize Social Security System," *Washington Post* (22 June 1996) p. 11 A; Elliot Carlson, "Panel Floats Ground Breaking Ideas on Investing SS Money," *AARP Bulletin* 37 (April 1996) pp. 4–5.

46. "Promises to Keep: Rethinking the Future of Social Security," *New York Times* (19 January 1997) sec. 3, pp. 12–13; Steven Pearlstein, "Challenging the Myths of Social Security," *Washington Post Weekly Edition* (13 January 1997) pp. 19–20.

47. "Promises to Keep," p. 12.

48. "Promises to Keep," p. 12.

49. Edward D. Berkowitz, "The Insecurity Privatization Would Bring," *Washington Post Weekly Edition* (6 January 1997) p. 23; Albert Crenshaw, "A Stock Answer to Social Security Worries," *Washington Post Weekly Edition* (10–17 June 1996) p. 22.

50. Flanigan, "Planning for Social Security's Future in the Market;" "Americans Speak Out on Retirement Issues," *Viewpoints* (Newsletter, Varible Annuity of Life Insurance Company, Houston, Texas) Fall 1995, p. 1; Berkowitz, "The Insecurity Privatization Would Bring"; Albert Crenshaw, "A Stock Answer to Social Security Worries," *Washington Post Weekly Edition* (10–17 June 1996) p. 22.

51. Pearlstein, "Challenging the Myths of Social Security," p. 20.

52. Achenbaum, *Social Security: Visions and Revisions,* pp. 135–137.

53. Achenbaum, *Social Security: Visions and Revisions,* pp. 133–141.

C h a p t e r 9

Mental Health: Managed Care

Danielle Salley was a troubled youngster from elementary school on. At first, it was dyslexia and motor control problems. By the time she was a teen, these difficulties led to anger and frustration, which Danielle took out on classmates, teachers, and her family. She began to fantasize about suicide. After a psychiatrist diagnosed her as severely depressed, she entered a psychiatric hospital. In and out after several relapses, she checked into the hospital for a third time in 1990, with, according to her father, an immense potential for suicide.

Danielle's father was an executive in a large firm; his health benefit plan covered the bills for the first two hospitalizations. In 1988, however, the firm switched to a managed care company in an effort to curb rising mental health benefits costs. The case managers in this plan pressured Danielle's doctors to keep her hospitalization brief. Once she had been termed "stabilized' by her doctor, the managed care company refused to pay for any additional days, although the doctor warned that she might kill herself if released. Concerned about this possibility, Mr. Salley kept his daughter in the hospital for three more months, and sued his employer to recover the resulting $40,000 in hospital bills. The court sided with Mr. Salley, ruling that "by not thoroughly reviewing Danielle's files before cutting off her benefits," the firm had abused its discretion. The firm still defends its handling of her case, arguing that it is a "needless burden' to review all records in each case and that "the only way companies can keep these costs under control is to manage the cases."[1]

Shirley McNamara is a clinical social worker with a private practice. Although she used to operate on a fee-for-service basis, like many of her colleagues she now has contracts with several managed care companies. When she talks about the way her work has changed, she says she likes the managed care stress on the outcomes of her sessions with clients. "It's extra work and effort to think about what I want to accomplish with each client and to document whether this has occurred," she notes, "but it keeps me on my toes and makes me think very precisely about what I'm trying to do. On the other hand, some of the other aspects of working in managed care drive me absolutely crazy—like the fact that none of the companies I deal with will approve more than six counseling sessions, at most, with a client, unless I convince them that the person is going to go right out and jump off a bridge. And I can spend an hour on the phone, trying to get through to the company's authorization person to get permission to start working with a client in the first place. So it's really a mixed bag, and social workers are going to have to learn to live with it if we want to keep doing therapy."

Jack Prevost is a social worker in the Planning Department of his state's Office of Mental Health. The office has just announced its intention to create a public managed care program in mental health, as part of a larger state effort to convert its Medicaid program into a managed care system. Jack finds himself very ambivalent about this new course. He worries that if the state follows its plan to contract with a private managed care organization to run the new system, the needs of the severely mentally ill won't be met. "What do private, for-profit companies know," he asks, "about working with a chronically ill population that needs frequent hospitalization? And what experience have they had in dealing with people of low incomes and all kinds of practical problems like poor housing and limited job possibilities? How will they cut costs and still do a good job of helping such people?" Yet he also finds himself getting excited about the prospect of change. Managed care companies seem to stress outpatient services and prevention, and to have the flexibility to try new approaches—maybe, with enough direction and controls, he muses, they could be made to work.

Managed care—first in general health services, and now in mental health—is *the* hot topic in health care today. Newspapers, magazines, professional journals, business publications, and the newsletters of associations of social workers and other mental health professionals all cover the tremendous rise of this new model for organizing care. Mental health managed care companies were almost nonexistent ten years ago, yet today they constitute a $2 billion industry. About half of all Americans with health insurance are enrolled in some form of mental health managed care. Some experts predict that by the end of the century, 95 percent of all mental health services will be provided through managed care systems.[2]

What is this "managed care" all about? What are its major goals, its promises and pitfalls? Is it, as a recent *Newsweek* article suggests, the "Walmart of health care?"—the ultimate marriage of business and health care?[3] Is it a cost-cutting mechanism that can also deliver high quality care, or is it a profit-making scheme that will cause health services to deteriorate? What (or whom) does it really manage—care, costs, clients, or the professionals who provide services? As managed care moves into the field of mental health, is it a blessing—or a nightmare?

The following policy analysis explores the many questions surrounding the use of managed care in the mental health arena. It looks both at general trends as well as the great variation among managed care programs. Particular attention is paid to the criticisms and promised benefits of the approach. Finally, since this is a policy that is coming to have major significance for the way social workers practice, the chapter explores managed mental health care's effects on that practice and the variety of ways in which social workers can, in turn, affect the managed care movement.

The Problem that Managed Mental Health Care Was Developed to Solve

The first thing to note is that there is some controversy over *which* problem mental health managed care is meant to deal with. That controversy reflects different ideological perspectives on the appropriate financial support, structure, and goals of health care systems. Is the major problem the rising—some say exorbitant—costs of treatment for mental difficulties? Or is it the need to improve the current state of care for people with emotional problems and mental illness? Perhaps the "problem" is really the perceived need of companies in the health care business to expand into new market areas.

The goal of improving services, expressed most often by consumers of mental health care, their families, advocacy groups, and at least a certain proportion of mental health professionals and policymakers, reflects an expectation that comprehensive, sound, and adequately funded mental health services should be an important priority in our society. Unfortunately, this is not the predominant factor behind the move to managed care. Instead, the problem driving the managed care revolution appears to be widespread concern over costs. These costs are borne not only by individuals, but by businesses and government. While most of us would agree that high costs can be a legitimate problem, the persistent focus on the "financial drain" of mental health services suggests that spending money on good treatment for mental problems is not necessarily a high priority either for the private sector, taxpayers, or the government. The possibility, as some observers suggest, that growth in mental health managed care systems stems from the health industry's search for profits underscores the idea that improvement in mental health care is not the primary issue being addressed. The same questions about priorities, costs, sources of revenue, and issues of quality have been raised for some time in the larger discussion of general health care reform in the United States.[4]

The Costs of Mental Health Care

It would probably be hard to find an American today who doesn't know that U.S. health care costs have risen precipitously over the last several decades. Currently, medical costs increase by about 12 percent a year, well over the costs of food and housing. We now spend 16 percent of the Gross National Product on health care, topping the annual defense budget. Of the nation's estimated $900 billion health care bill, about 10 percent goes to mental health services. The amount spent on mental health care doubled in the 1980s, making it the fastest growing portion of health expenditures. The treatment of substance abuse and mental health problems now accounts for as much as 25 cents of every health care dollar spent by employers. Roughly 70 percent of all mental health expenditures are for inpatient services, which are used by only about 7 percent of all beneficiaries.[5]

Over 40 percent of mental health expenditures are covered by private sources. These include out-of-pocket payments and private charity, but employer-sponsored private insurance plays the major role. The rest of mental health funding comes from government sources, including Medicaid and state expenditures. Obviously, all of these sources have an interest in controlling costs.[6]

Incidence and Treatment of Mental Health Problems

One of the difficulties in planning for and funding mental health services is that, in the eyes of many insurers and employers (among others), mental illness is characterized by the four "uns"—it is "undefinable, untreatable, unpredictable, and unmanageable." In addition to such factors as lack of precision in diagnosis, it is much harder to calculate the number of people with mental illness than those with physical ailments. Nevertheless, broad generalizations can be made about prevalence rates. About 17 percent of all Americans have a mental disorder in any one year, and 12 percent of American children suffer from mental and emotional disturbances. Phobias and major depression account for the largest percentages of major mental difficulties in the United States.[7]

The costs of mental problems to individuals, families, and employers are high. For example, major depression accounts for more days in bed than any other disorder except for cardiovascular disease. In terms of lost productivity, lost earnings, and premature death, mental illnesses cost about $75 billion in 1990. The majority of Americans who commit suicide each year suffer from a mental or addictive disorder. While our discussion so far has focused largely on serious mental illness, it is important to remember that most of us have or will encounter at some point in our lives the kinds of problems—mild depression, anxiety, or stress in our marriages or relationships with parents—that make it difficult to function in our jobs or other areas of daily life.[8]

Despite the aura of unreliability and unchangeability, mental illness *can* be dealt with. On the one hand, the rehospitalization rate among persons with severe mental illness is quite high, and treatments for mental difficulties may take longer than those for other health problems. On the other hand, for example, the National Institute for Mental Health reports that 60 percent of those medicated for schizophrenia improve. Studies have shown that psychiatric rehabilitation services for adults with mental illness can reduce time spent in a psychiatric hospital, raise earning power, and increase the individual's level of independent living. Relatively low-cost outpatient treatment is often effective in helping people with phobias and other anxiety disorders.[9]

Managed Mental Health Care

The managed care movement in health and mental health has brought a whole new vocabulary to health care discussions. In order to understand the new approach and its application to mental health services, one needs to master certain terms. "Managed care" itself is a somewhat slippery term, as there are variations in managed care programs and the concept itself continues to evolve. One definition states "Managed Care is the private regulation and financing of the delivery of health care with the goals of controlling costs while assuring quality." This definition is already outdated in its focus on the private sector; as we will see, managed care is emerging in public forms as well. The focus on cost reduction and quality is, however, a common theme, as in the description of managed care as "A system used by groups to manage costs while maintaining high-quality health and medical services." The National Association of Social Workers adds a further dimension in its statement that managed care plans "cut costs by *monitoring access to* and the quality of medical care" (emphasis added). Here the NASW pinpoints a major approach to cost reduction—limiting the amount and type of services rendered. Sometimes the easiest way to identify managed care is to look for particular mechanisms in the health insurance plan, such as use of a specific set of providers, a contract with a customer based on capitated payments, preauthorization for services, specific guidelines and limits on services, and utilization review.[10]

"That's great," you say; "here's a definition with a whole bunch of additional jargon." We will attempt to demystify the situation by explaining some of the major terms now, and clarifying others later. First, most managed care programs refer to the people delivering health or mental health services, such as physicians, social workers, psychologists, physical therapists, and even entire agencies, as "providers." While you might think of "customers" as the people receiving the services, this term actually refers to the businesses or other bodies, such as state health or Medicaid departments, that contract with a managed care organization (sometimes abbreviated as MCO). These entities pay for the managed care plan through a system of *capitation.* In the traditional fee-for-service approach, the insurance plan pays health care professionals for each specific service they perform, such as a surgical procedure or an eye exam, that is covered in the plan. In capitation, the MCO pays a fixed, per-person amount to its providers for a given time period, regardless of the number of services rendered. The providers assume some or all of the risk in this arrangement. If they've figured correctly, the services they actually give to their clientele in a given month or year will balance the prepayment. The MCO has, in turn, been given a fixed amount by the customer (private employer or public entity) to arrange for care. Less services overall will mean an excess in payment, or profit, for the MCO; more services, a monetary loss.[11]

We've used the words "clientele" or "client" to identify people receiving health or mental health care. Other terms are "consumer," "patient," and in public systems like Medicare, "beneficiary." Under managed care, service to these individuals often requires a "preauthorization review," in which the provider seeks approval from an insurer or other entity before delivering a particular type of care. Care deemed unnecessary will not be authorized. MCO staff people who carry out preauthorization reviews have various titles, including "gatekeeper," "primary physician" (in physical health managed care programs), and "case manager." Many managed care programs also include "utilization reviews." These are evaluations of the "necessity, appropriateness and efficiency of the use of health services, procedures, and facilities." Reviews of the appropriateness of hospitalizations and of length of stay, for example, might be conducted to evaluate the ongoing work of the provider. Finally, even "mental health services" have been given a new name by many MCOs. Mental health treatment has turned into "behavioral health care."[12]

To confuse things further, there are several kinds of MCOs. In Health Maintenance Organizations (HMOs), the consumer must choose a provider from within the system. In Preferred Provider Organizations (PPO), the client has the option of choosing a practitioner from outside the system as well, but at a higher cost. We describe the variety of MCOs further in the history section of this chapter.

You now understand many of the rudiments of managed care policy. We will focus next on the basic context, principles, and structure of managed care plans in general, and then outline the specifics of managed care in the field of mental health.

Managed care in mental health is the latest manifestation of a general revolution in the way health care is financed and structured in the United States. Managed care organizations, particularly HMOs, grew exponentially during the country's recent debate over health care reform. As one analyst wrote in 1994, "Washington may be in gridlock on health care, but Wall Street is in high gear. A private-sector revolution is transforming the nation's medical system." By the end of this revolution, managed care seems firmly entrenched on the national scene. In 1995, 70 percent of Americans with company-provided insurance were enrolled in managed care programs. Most of these were private, for-profit MCOs.[13]

The most important impetus for the managed care revolution is the desire to contain costs. The movement aims to lower costs through managing: (1) access to services, (2) the amount and types of services delivered, and (3) the choice, characteristics, and activities of health care providers. A managed care organization assures its public or corporate customer that for a set fee, based on the number of clients covered over a specific time period, it will provide cost-effective and high-quality health care to enrollees. The assumption is that management of care will make possible reasonable fees for customers and a profit margin for the MCO. (See Figure 9.1 for one company's philosophy of care management.)

How does this work in the mental health arena? Let's say your employer has contracted with an HMO, American Health, that provides both physical and mental health benefits to employees. The HMO's mental health services are arranged through a specialized branch of American Health called HOPE. You have been experiencing a lot of pressure on the job lately, which has led to feelings of anxiety, loss of appetite, and difficulties in concentrating on your work. You call the American Health number listed in your policy, and they refer you to HOPE. Your call to this number is answered by a gatekeeper, who asks you a number of questions about your problems and what's been going on in your life lately. The gatekeeper then gives you the names of two therapists in your area from which to choose; one is a social worker, the other a licensed counselor. She also explains that you will be expected to make a copayment of $25 for each session with the therapist. As in most HMOs, you won't have to pay a deductible.

You choose the social worker and make an appointment with him. This first session allows him to assess your situation and suggest an appropriate treatment approach, or way in which you and he can work together to deal with your difficulty. He explains that the HOPE gatekeeper will probably authorize six sessions over the next three months and that, in his experience, this will be enough to help you learn to understand and manage your anxiety. He outlines the specific goals that the treatment should accomplish, including a substantial decrease in your level of anxiety and the ability to work on job tasks for specified periods without losing concentration.

Several weeks later, the social worker phones to tell you that authorization has been granted for the six appointments, and you proceed with the therapy. At the end of the three-month period, you both feel that the initial treatment goals have been met, although you're a little concerned that the problem will come back. The therapist encourages you to "try it on your own for awhile," but explains that if you later feel the need for more therapy, he can seek authorization for another set of sessions. He also alerts you to the fact that HOPE will be sending you a questionnaire in another month to ask about your satisfaction with the treatment sessions.

This is how managed mental health care can look from the client's perspective. The following interviews with two of our colleagues give you a sense of what it's like from the provider's point of view. The first gives an example of contract work with an HMO as a private practitioner; the second details the experience of practice within a social work agency that contracts with an HMO.

FIGURE 9.1 The Philosophy Behind a Managed Care Company's Treatment Guidelines

MCC Behavioral Care's primary clinical concern is care of our patients. Our goal is that, when emotional issues or behavioral concerns reach the point of needing professional help and intervention, our patients can quickly access quality care, in the most cost-effective manner, from professionals with solid experience and expertise in the field. (The right care at the right time in the right way at the right place by the right people.) To make that happen, certain philosophies guide our care management.

Patients need an opportunity to respond to their difficulties and improve their condition in a setting which affords them the most favorable circumstance. At the same time, their goal and ours is to help them maintain those links with family, friends, community and work which have played a significant role in their previous sense of self-worth and successful coping in the past. As a result, we have developed *Clinical Guidelines for Mental Health and Substance Abuse Treatment* to help patient and practitioner alike reach the best decision about what is "the right place" at "the right time."

Our guidelines are not a mandate for treatment, but, literally, guidelines which aim to encourage and standardize quality care that is available as it is known through scientific literature, professional experience and our own research on what creates successful outcomes for patients. We can also use our experience to continually improve our services by making each encounter an opportunity to learn how to further refine those practices which we consider best at the moment. Our major professional clinical body, the Clinical Senate, incorporates professionals in psychiatry, psychology, social work, nursing and chemical dependency. Through that group, we analyze the latest research and our own best results nationwide to continually update our guidelines so that our patients can feel confident that the care they receive is state of the art and driven by solid dedication to results.

Effective care also requires a collaboration; a collaboration of understanding and purpose between the patient, the clinician and the care manager. Genuine empathy, clinical expertise and commitment to results are the backbone of that care. These guidelines are prepared, in part, to help practitioners explain to patients what they might expect as they go through treatment and the types of decisions they will have to make together on the road to a satisfactory outcome....

MCC wants to return the patient to the highest feasible level of functioning as quickly as possible; that is the cornerstone of the MCC approach. The approach focuses on the present and the future, using the patient's own strengths and resources to develop new patterns of behavior and interaction. Each patient's situation is unique. Therefore, each solution to a presented issue is unique. MCC tailors the therapy to fit the patient, rather than forcing the patient to fit the therapy. MCC clinicians work on goals set by the patient, which helps ensure success.

This philosophy then sets the foundation for what MCC considers the core characteristics of a solution-oriented approach:

1. In addition to a thorough evaluation of any biological contribution to the situation, the first session must be therapeutic. Patients come into therapy because they want something in their life to change....

2. It is important to recognize that the patient has resources and to use those

Continued

FIGURE 9.1   *Continued*

resources to direct change. The focus then becomes the patients' strengths and not their weaknesses. . . .

3. The goals of therapy are focused around the presenting issues. The goals are realistic and reasonable and described in behavioral and interactional terms. Most importantly, these goals are signed off on by the patient. The therapist needs to hear what the patient wants to change. If the therapist does not hear correctly, then change will not occur because the goals of the therapist are not the goals of the patient. That is why it is so important that the therapist and patient both are in complete agreement on the goals so that change can occur easily and rapidly. That patient is a true partner in therapy.

4. The underlying goal of all therapy is to return the patient to their highest previous level of functioning. The therapist does not try to "cure" the patient. The therapist takes the more realistic view that patients can and will return for further treatment as needed.

5. Each patient's situation is unique. So each treatment plan needs to be unique. . . .

6. To ensure an optimal outcome means that the care offered must be quality care; quality is measured through utilization review, quality assurance standards and outcomes measurements. . . .

Expectations of Care Management

All decisions and discussion about level of care are first and foremost clinical. Because each situation is individual the application of rigid algorithms for precise determination will ultimately fail. Nevertheless, certain basic rules and principles guide the decision. Understanding these is essential to effective collaboration in determinations of effective, efficient and appropriate care for our patients.

Adapting the basic assumption of Hoffman et al.,* these assumptions include the belief that (1) treatment should be "individualized, quality clinical care based on patient assessment and treatment planning" (p. 4); that providers must "demonstrate fiscal accountability. . . and a rational clinical decision-making process" (p. 4); that "escalating health care and insurance costs [are] viewed as factors in the treatment of" (p. 4) psychiatric and substance abuse disorders in the same way as other medical problems; and that "the preferred level of care [is] the least intensive level that could accomplish the treatment objectives while providing safety and security for the patients" (p. 6).

*Hoffman, N. G., Halikas, J. A., Mee-Lee, D., et al., *Patient Placement Criteria for the Treatment of Psychoactive Substance Disorders* (Washington, D.C., American Society of Addiction Medicine), 1991.

Source: From *Clinical Guidelines for Mental Health and Substance Abuse Treatment,* MCC Behavioral Care, 1996, pp. vii, x–xi, xiii. Used with permission.

How Does Managed Mental Health Care Work?

Interview With a Social Work Provider

Barry Daste is a professor in a school of social work and also engages in a small private clinical practice. Eight years ago, he was invited to work in a managed care setting. Having heard of his strong skills as a therapist, the regional director of a new mental health component of a large HMO called Daste and asked him to direct a mental health clinic for the organization. In that geographical area, the freestanding clinic was then a common model for the delivery of managed care mental health services. Although Daste declined the directorship, he helped the company set up and staff the clinic, which hired two recent school of social work graduates, a substance abuse counselor, and several other clinicians. Daste became a part-time provider at the clinic.

The clinic's clients were all employed by local companies that had contracted with the HMO to provide health and mental health care. Employees or their family members with mental health problems who called the HMO were referred to the clinic for help. In these early days, clinic workers, including Daste, acted as both gatekeepers and providers. They assessed the problems presented by clients and carried out the appropriate treatment. Much of this consisted of short-term therapy, a model which Daste had long used successfully in his own practice. Group or individual therapy sessions were limited to approximately twenty to thirty a year; clients made a co-payment of $10 to $20 a session, and the employer covered the rest through yearly fixed payments to the HMO.

After five years, in an attempt to lower its costs and to remain competitive with other MCOs, the HMO began downsizing. It closed a number of its mental health clinics, including the one where Daste worked. Daste and other staff became part of the HMO's network of private practitioner providers who practiced in their own offices. Some were full-time; others, like Daste, worked part-time. One clinic remained, functioning as a central office to manage the HMO's mental health services for the entire state. Soon, that too closed, and the coordination function was handed over to a regional office three states away. Now, when clients need services, they call a 1-800 number and are given their choice of a number of providers in their area. While this is clearly less personalized than the original clinic system, the staff person (called a "utilization review technician') in the regional office knows a fair amount about each provider and thus is generally effective in matching client and therapist. The price providers pay for this effectiveness match is the completion of lengthy paper work about their credentials and treatment approaches.

When the client calls Daste or another therapist, he or she generally receives two sessions for assessment and the development of a treatment plan. If the caller appears to be in the midst of a crisis, Daste can get the person into a psychiatric hospital right away. If an immediate consultation with a psychiatrist seems necessary, for example in a case of serious depression necessitating medication, that also can be arranged. Otherwise, Daste sends the treatment plan to the central office for approval. He notes that the social worker has a lot of control over this first phase of the work.

In Daste's company, as in most other mental health managed care systems, the client's condition must fit one of the diagnoses in the American Psychiatric Association's *Diagnostic and Statistical Manual IV* (the *DSM IV*) in order for treatment to be covered. (Authors' note: While the *DSM IV* includes mental problems that are affected by environmental factors, the manual tends to stress a medical model of mental illness. Thus help for situations like "marital difficulties" may not be covered by an MCO, unless the therapist can make a convincing case that the situation represents a crisis).

Daste describes a typical treatment plan as follows: the diagnosis, such as simple phobia, is stated, followed by the treatment goals, such as patient's management of the phobia so it doesn't interfere with normal functioning. The outcomes are operationalized—e.g., "Mr. Jones will be able to return to a manageable level of functioning. Treatment will be designed to enable him to perform his duties at work. This will also involve his being able to drive, both locally and on the highway." Daste feels the specification of how success in treatment will be measured is one of the great benefits of managed care. Finally, the plan includes a description of the treatment to be used, such as systematic desensitization therapy, and a justification of why this particular approach was chosen. The provider may also include "community resource referrals" as part of the treatment; if, for example, Mr. Jones has had difficulties in getting a job, Daste might also refer him to a local job training program. Finally, the treatment plan includes the provider's request for a specific number of sessions; Daste generally asks for six to eight and specifies when therapy will start and finish. Daste shares all the details of the plan with the client before sending it off to the regional office.

In this and most MCOs, the major authorization issue tends to be the number of sessions approved by the utilization review manager. Daste reports that he generally receives the number he asks for, or a few less (e.g., six if he asked for eight). If after the initial series of sessions is completed he feels more are warranted, he submits a new plan to the central office justifying continued treatment. The plan also indicates which therapy goals have already been achieved. If the review manager has questions about the request, he may call Daste for further details. Generally, Daste receives approval for additional sessions. The client is usually allotted a total of twenty sessions a year and would have to pay out of pocket for any additional therapy.

Daste is generally satisfied with the managed care system in which he works. He is comfortable with the emphasis on short-term therapy models and appreciates the fact that the company keeps its providers current with the latest treatment innovations (although he misses the frequent face-to-face inservice training sessions that were carried out in the clinic). He approves of the company's frequent quality control checks with clients, such as client satisfaction surveys and the detailed closing summaries in which therapists document the outcome of treatment. He is impressed with the thoroughness with which the MCO assesses potential providers, even though the review system creates a lot of paperwork. Overall, he feels, these factors "drive good treatment." Therapists must be competent, up-to-date, and accountable in order to remain on provider panels.

The system does have its drawbacks, however. Although there is careful screening of clinicians, the reviewers rarely know the providers; patient-therapist matches can suffer. The vast amount of paperwork and the need for frequent authorization and reauthorization requests can be tiresome. In addition, Daste points out, there are no built-in pay raises, since reimbursements for services are not regularly increased. In the future, in order to get into the provider pool, some therapists may agree to work for less, potentially lowering the rates for all. It is a system, Daste concludes, in which providers need to be assertive in order to deliver the best services to clients and to protect their own practice.

Daste has seen both the pitfalls and strengths of managed care in the private sector. As he watches its recent movement into the public mental health field, he ponders how the approach will work with the chronic mentally ill, including people who need prolonged hospitalization. How will MCOs handle individuals who refuse to take their medications? Will they be able to do outreach work with groups like the homeless mentally ill? These and other questions mark the next stages of the managed care revolution.

Managed Care In an Agency Setting

Interview with a Social Work Staff Member

Judith Kolb Morris has many years of experience working with children and their parents, first as an early childhood educator and now as a social worker. She is currently employed at a private, non-profit child and family services agency in a small city in Massachusetts. Until recently, this 150-year-old agency could be described as a typical example of a traditional social work practice setting: a community agency offering a variety of services to children and families; interacting and consulting with other organizations such as schools and public welfare offices; and supported by the United Way, clients' fees, private insurance, and Medicaid. In the past five years, however, Morris's place of work has become part of the managed care revolution.

The agency has long offered outpatient counseling for people of all ages, adoptions and foster care services, a big brother/big sister program, and various mental health outreach activities. Many of its clients receive welfare and are covered by Medicaid. In the early 1990s, it became clear to the director that the usual sources of funds for these services were changing. The United Way and other charitable organizations had become less able to support social work programs and to compensate for cutbacks in federal and state funding. In addition, private employers were shifting their insurance systems from fee-for-service to managed care. Most significantly, the state of Massachusetts had decided to convert much of its Medicaid system to a public managed care approach. A private

MCO called Mental Health Management of America (MHMA) contracted with the state to cover the health and mental health needs of Medicaid recipients.

The agency board saw two basic choices: to try to resist managed care funding as long as they could, perhaps jeopardizing the existence of the agency, or to join in the new approach, seeking as much agency control over the process as possible. It chose the latter, and the agency signed a contract as a provider for MHMA. Morris recalls that when she was interviewed for her job as a clinical social worker, the director asked her views about managed care. Being a savvy interviewee, she said she saw them as the wave of the future, "like it or not." The director later told her that if she'd complained about MCOs, she wouldn't have been hired.

Although Morris sees a number of current or potential problems with the managed care system as it has developed at her agency, she notes that the director has done much to make it feasible for staff to work within it and to bring out its positive aspects. One of the agency's first steps was to develop an inhouse "Quality Management System" to monitor therapists' clinical decisions, numbers of counseling sessions, and quality and timeliness of paperwork. The agency's clinical director runs the management system. MHMA saw early on that through this mechanism, the agency worked efficiently and was able to offer clients good service in as short a time as possible. Essentially, the agency had taken on many of the monitoring and quality assurance functions usually carried out by MCO staff. In return for its effectiveness in this arena, MHMA gave the agency more leeway in decision making about client treatment.

MHMA has been very generous in what it will authorize for services to clients. New or returning clients may receive sixteen hours of counseling or other help in the first month. This allotment is based on research that indicates that "multiproblem families" (which constitute much of the agency's clientele) benefit from a strong dose of immediate and concentrated assistance. Clients can usually get another thirteen hours of treatment over the next thirteen weeks (sixteen for children). This help is not limited to individual or family counseling; it can include hours spent in vital social work interventions such as consultation with teachers and other people or organizations with whom clients interact. In managed care language, these traditional social work functions of brokerage, advocacy, and case management become "collateral contacts."

If the social worker feels it's warranted, he or she can ask the MCO to authorize another thirteen-hour/thirteen-week stretch. This is generally approved. After seven months, clients are put "on maintenance," a system of one session every two weeks, with no collaterals. While no limit is put on the number of sessions in a given year, MHMA encourages social workers to end their intervention after a year and a half.

Although the MHMA system has offered a good amount of flexibility, Morris still sees several problems. The first (and the one most providers point out) is "all those forms! Everytime you turn around, you have to fill out another one." Forms requesting authorization for treatment must be sent a month in advance, but there is no guarantee they'll be back in time for the sessions to start. In addition, the agency used to wait until services were authorized and payment made by the MCO before it would, in turn, pay the clinicians. The practice was stopped after staff banded together to protest it.

Another problem was the fact that although the agency held the overall contract with the MCO, staff members also had to contract individually with the organization. MHMA could refuse to certify certain clinicians, particularly if they worked with "unreliable" populations such as people who abuse drugs or alcohol. To the MCO, work with clients who often didn't show up for appointments did not fit with managed care's standards of efficiency.

Despite these drawbacks, MHMA has been a reasonably flexible managed care system. It recognizes the importance of environmental or "collateral" work, and its stress on quality control has been positive. While so far quality has been measured largely by assessing the appropriateness of therapists' clinical decisions, the potential exists to use the extensive paperwork on each client to track reduction of symptoms and changes in behavior.

Morris's agency has recently entered a new phase in its involvement with managed care, however. Perhaps because of its flexible benefits, MHMA lost its contract with the state. The company taking its place has contracted with the agency as a provider under more stringent rules. Clients will now be eligible for an initial set of only twelve sessions per calendar year; clinicians must request additional services, and limits and guidelines have not yet been established for further authorization of services. This eliminates the initial intensive treatment approach and leaves less time to do collateral work. Morris fears she will have to cut back on this important function in order to have the time to work with clients directly. She and other staff are also critical of the new MCO's forms, which are lengthier and more complicated. All in all, Morris notes, managed care can present basic ethical conflicts to practitioners. Refusing treatment to people who need it conflicts with both the social work code of ethics and her agency's own policies. "It's a real dilemma," she says, "when you want to help people and do good work, and are told that you have to cut your services."

Managed Mental Health Care in the Public Sector

The agency in which Judith Morris works deals with a managed care plan for Medicaid clients. This is an example of a new venture in managed care: the expansion into services financed by governmental bodies rather than by private employers. The most typical of these are Medicaid managed care plans developed by state governments. Massachusetts was, in fact, the first state to implement a comprehensive privatized public sector health and mental health program for Medicaid beneficiaries.[14]

Medicaid managed care plans, like most of those in the private sector, cover both physical and mental illness. While they have a number of similarities with private employer plans, they also face some specific challenges. These include the need to serve people who are severely and chronically mentally ill and who have traditionally spent long periods of time in mental hospitals. The Medicaid population includes the poor elderly, public welfare clients, and, in many states, people just above the poverty line—groups that lack basic resources and who often have employment, housing, and transportation problems. Some are homeless. These difficulties exacerbate mental illness and make treatment more challenging. Many mental health practitioners and advocates feel such problems call for an emphasis on outreach and community-based services.

It is too early to tell how well public mental health managed care systems are responding to the needs of their particular clientele, but state planners are enthusiastic about the potential for cost cutting and effective treatment. So far, five states have managed care mental health systems up and running; most other states are in the planning stages. States have chosen a variety of formats for their programs. In all of them, participation in managed care is mandatory for most, if not all, of the Medicaid population.[15]

The Massachusetts version of reform offers Medicaid beneficiaries a number of managed care companies from which to choose. Most are commercial MCOs, although the state has also created a Primary Care Clinician plan which is operated by the state Office of Health and Human Services and has the greatest number of enrollees. However, this state-developed MCO contracts with a private company, such as the one used by Morris's agency, to arrange mental health services. In recognition of "the health and access problems that result from such factors as lack of education, poverty, homelessness, fear, drug use, violence, . . . and racism," Massachusetts also contracts with a private company to supply health benefits managers who help Medicaid clients make their managed care choices. The managers speak a variety of languages and are easily accessible. Reflecting a private market approach, their function has been compared to that of "customer service departments." Despite their aid, half of the eligible population did not make a choice of MCO, so the state made the assignment for them. The state also found that many of the private MCOs were poorly prepared to handle clients with severe mental illness who required extended care. Extensive work with these bodies by Health and Human Services staff has not yet solved the problem.[16]

The state of Ohio has chosen a more decentralized approach to public managed care. The fiscal and clinical responsibility for the Medicaid mental health managed care system has been shifted from the state authority to local bodies. The Ohio Department of Mental Health contracts with county mental health boards for a complete array of mental health services. It also provides incentives for reducing the use of hospitalization and for providing less-expensive community-based care. Use of local community mental health centers or mental health boards as MCOs has the potential of enhancing input from people in the community, including professionals, clients, and their families.[17]

As these examples indicate, state managed care systems (or proposed systems) use a combination of public and private elements in their plans. Within the mental health arena, the private MCOs involved are equally split between for-profit and nonprofit ventures. State health authorities can, if they choose, act as their own MCO, contracting directly with providers for services.

Many state plans employ what is termed a mental health "carveout," which allows for delivering services for a particular population, in this case those with mental illness, through distinct and separate organizations or networks of providers. Some plans allow for input into planning from consumers, family members, and advocates; others do not. Finally, most state plans share an interest in increasing outpatient and other community based services and in decreasing the use of mental hospitals. This move appeals both to those interested in cutting costs, since hospitalization is very expensive, and to reformers who see community supports as vital to helping the mentally ill.[18] As the following history shows, these state experiments are the latest chapter in managed care reforms.

The History of Managed Care

The concept of managed health care has been around, in one form or another, for the last sixty years. Health Maintenance Organizations (HMOs) were first developed in the 1930s; these were prepaid medical services, provided initially at a specific clinic or medical center. Fixed monthly fees, usually paid by employers, covered all services provided. HMOs generally gave more comprehensive coverage than existing medical or insurance plans, including preventive services such as annual checkups. One of the best known examples is the Kaiser-Permanente health plan, established by industrialist Henry J. Kaiser in California in 1942. By the 1950s, the Kaiser plan had a growing network of its own physicians, hospitals, and clinics and an enrollment of half a million people. Twenty years later, an alternate type of HMO appeared, in which health organizations contracted with private physicians to deliver services in their own offices rather than in company facilities.[19]

The Nixon administration passed legislation supporting HMO growth in 1971, and the HMO Act of 1973 required all businesses with more than twenty-five employees to offer at least one federally qualified HMO plan as an alternative to conventional insurance programs, if such a plan were available in their locality. President Reagan continued the stress on HMOs as a way to contain costs in the 1980s. Yet while some HMOs were quite successful, particularly on the West Coast, the movement on the whole grew slowly. Prepaid plans lessened physicians' autonomy and were fought by groups like the American

Medical Association. AMA opposition and problems with support in Congress led to various restrictions on HMOs, which initially made it difficult for them to compete with conventional insurance.[20]

As medical costs continued to explode, however, HMOs became more and more attractive to businesses coping with their health care budgets. The growth of for-profit HMOs, generally using the private physician network approach, increased steadily toward the end of the 1980s. By 1991, more than 38 million people were enrolled in 600 HMOs. Generally, these restricted enrollees to the use of specific providers (those of you with such plans are familiar with the list of physicians from which you must choose—either through careful research or by throwing a dart).

As HMOs have evolved and diversified in form, they have become subsumed under the broader rubric of "managed care" or MCOs. MCOs include various types of HMOs, Preferred Provider Organizations (PPO), which offer discounted rates for using providers in a preselected group, and managed mental health firms. The latter, a new development, provide services such as utilization review and management of provider networks to insurance companies or other MCOs. The commonality to look for in deciding whether to describe a program as managed care is whether it is designed to "generate cost savings through the restriction and management of access to health care."[21]

President Clinton included a form of managed care in his massive health care reform plan introduced in 1993. The Clinton proposal called for the administration of health insurance through large purchasing alliances. These alliances would offer several insurance options to consumers, including managed care plans. The alliances would operate under state control, with a national health board setting pricing standards. Yet health reform has never been an easy task in the United States, due to the large number of powerful stakeholders in the current health care system and to the tendency to dichotomize the issue into an either–or debate over the merits of the market system versus the government in dealing with social and economic problems. Bitterly fought by Republican politicians, much of the business community, and the AMA, the President's national health care program was declared "officially dead" in Congress in September, 1994.[22]

While Washington, and the rest of the country, was caught up in the great health care reform debate, insurance companies, corporations, HMOs, and large hospital chains were quietly but steadily creating a private sector, managed care revolution. With the demise of the Clinton health reform initiative, these forces were able to bring about dramatic and rapid change in how health care was financed and delivered in the United States. HMOs and insurance companies merged and grew larger, and hospitals and doctors banded together in alliances and networks of their own. One in six Americans was enrolled in an HMO by September, 1994, and countless others had joined other variations of managed care programs. At the same time several states were turning whole

Medicaid programs over to private MCOs. For now, at least, private sector managed care is becoming the "only show in town" when it comes to delivering health care.[23]

While managed care in the mental health services developed somewhat later than in physical health care, it is now rapidly catching up. Historically, treatment for people with mental illness has been largely the responsibility of the public sector, particularly through state mental hospitals. Only individuals who could afford it saw private therapists or were treated in private mental hospitals. Although commercial health care insurance became available in the 1920s, insurance coverage for mental disorders or substance abuse did not appear until the 1950s. Unlike insurance for physical problems, which covers specific services deemed medically necessary for treatment, mental health benefits are based on duration of treatment. In other words, in the case of cancer, an insurance company generally covers the particular treatment methods necessary to cure or control the cancer, without a time limit; in the case of a condition like manic depressive disorder, benefits are limited to a specific number of sessions with a therapist or days in a mental hospital. As one health policy analyst comments, "This discrimination is 'justified' on the grounds that severely mentally ill people would consume 'unmanageable' (or 'unpredictable') amounts of service," as opposed to the physically ill whose care presumably can be both managed and predicted. Thus a major problem with insurance for mental illness is that it "has remained limited, expensive, and not equivalent to coverage for other medical disorders."[24]

HMOs began to cover mental health and substance abuse services in the 1970s. The 1973 HMO Act required that in order to become a federally qualified HMO, a program had to offer not only basic services for physical disorders, but also short-term outpatient evaluation or crisis intervention mental health services, and referral services for alcohol and drug abuse. Employers became more and more interested in the managed care approach to mental health in the 1980s, because of an unprecedented expansion in mental health services in that decade and a concomitant rise in the insurance costs borne by businesses. By 1986, due to employer interest and federal initiatives, nearly all MCOs offered mental health coverage. At first these benefits were organized by a department within the MCO, but many managed care companies now subcontract with specialized mental health managed care organizations to provide services. Specialized behavioral health care MCOs have now become a huge industry.[25]

The managed care approach has not led to expanded mental health benefits. If anything, as we have seen from the interviews with Barry Daste and Judith Morris, benefits are more tightly controlled under the new structure. The average MCO limits benefits to thirty hospital days and twenty outpatient visits a year.[26]

The most recent chapter in the story of managed care is the move into public managed care systems. As we have noted, a number of states are now experimenting with the use of managed care to serve the health and mental health needs of their Medicaid populations. The impetus for states to move into managed care was the same as that for private businesses—rising costs. Through most of the 1980s, combined state and federal spending on Medicaid grew over 8 percent a year. Since 1988, an expanding number of beneficiaries and spiraling health care costs have driven growth to an annual average of almost 18 percent. The Medicaid share of the average state budget has soared to 13 percent, with some states spending as much as one-third of their resources on the program. Medicaid's average portion of state budgets is second only to that of elementary and secondary education. MCOs have been eager to exploit states' desires to control costs. As the private managed care market has become saturated, companies have come to see the public system as "the next sales frontier."[27]

Managed care has actually been allowed under Medicaid since the 1970s, but was voluntary for Medicaid beneficiaries and few chose to enroll. The major shift to Medicaid managed care systems by the states would not have been possible without the development of a federal waiver system in the 1980s. Under Section 1915(b) and 1115 Medicaid waivers, states can waive various program requirements, such as freedom of choice of providers. The 1115 waiver allows for many different types of changes to Medicaid, including development of statewide managed care plans with mandatory participation of the Medicaid population. States' use of waivers to establish managed care programs has grown rapidly in the 1990s, with twelve states approved in 1995 and ten more applications pending.[28] As in the private sector, experimentation with many varieties of managed care has taken over where the recent proposal for a more centralized and cohesive national health care system has failed.

The Economics of Managed Care

One of the major issues in the economics of managed care is whether it does, in fact, save money, and if so, whether cost reductions are a short-term or ongoing phenomenon. It will be helpful to begin this discussion with a recap of the mechanisms employed by MCOs to curtail health expenditures.

Managed care's major device for cost cutting is a change in the incentive system for providers. Under the traditional fee-for-service practice, doctors and hospitals could pretty much set the going rate for each service that they rendered. Thus there was no economic disincentive for performing many services for each patient, ordering expensive tests, or keeping people in the hospital for lengthy stays. Early attempts at changing incentives included the Diagnostic Related Groups (DRGs) regulations of the Reagan era, in which Medicare began to pay hospitals a set fee for treating each illness, based on the average cost of treating that particular condition. But savings from the DRG approach were short-lived, and applied only to publicly reimbursed care. The capitation system of managed care has proved much more successful in restricting rises in payments to providers. Since doctors, therapists, and health/mental facilities are prepaid a set amount for treating a given number of clients, it is in their interest to limit services as much as possible within whatever quality controls are set by the MCO. Mental health managed care further restricts costs through the use of gatekeepers to regulate the amount and type of therapy provided.

There is a good amount of evidence that managed care cuts health costs, at least in the short run. According to one survey, employers' insurance premiums rose only 2.1 percent in 1995, compared to 11.5 percent in 1991. A study of over 2,500 companies showed that during 1992, employers with traditional insurance coverage averaged a cost of $4,080 per employee, up 14 percent from the year before. Companies using MCOs paid an average $3,313 per employee, only an 8 percent increase (although still above the general inflation rate). In California, where managed care is well developed, hospital spending rose at half the national rate and spending on doctors' bills was 30 percent lower than the national average in the period from 1980 to 1991. When large corporations contracted with mental health MCOs, they saw some dramatic changes. IBM, for example, went from almost $105 million in mental health spending in 1989 to $98 million in 1992 to $59 million in 1993. Perhaps most significantly, the overall cost of medical care rose by just 3 percent in 1996, the smallest rise in thirty years. It is assumed that managed care systems have helped contribute to this leveling off of expenditures.[29]

Other data suggest that costs sometimes rise with the use of managed care. Medicare, for example, pays an average 6 percent more for beneficiaries who choose MCOs than it would if they were in the traditional fee-for-service programs. National surveys on mental health managed care in 1982 and 1986 found substantial increases in hospitalization utilization rates and costs, although this reflected in part the more complete coverage of hospital mental health benefits in MCOs. According to a report by the Bazelon Center for Mental Health Law, the data do not yet exist to show the cost effectiveness of public managed care mental health programs. Some analysts suggest that states will save money in the short run, but after a several year start-up period savings will level off.[30]

Where MCOs do save money, how do they manage it? We've already pointed out a major area, the lowering of payments to physicians, mental health professionals, and other providers. In addition, fewer people may be covered by the plan, more inexpensive services may be used, and less services may be offered overall. The recent uproar over mothers not being covered for more than 24 hours of hospital care after delivery of their babies led to federal legislation to require that insurance plans extend coverage to 48 hours. Coverage for mental health services has always been more limited than that for physical health care, and the situation did not change with the introduction of managed care. A 1986 survey of HMOs found their annual median expenditures for mental health services to be 5 percent of their total medical costs. As we saw in the interview with Judith Morris, MCOs have lately become even more stringent with their alignment of therapy sessions. Many MCOs are now charging more for mental health care premiums and copayments.[31]

The issue of the lack of "parity" or equality between health and mental health coverage has recently attracted attention in Washington. First, a mental health amendment that would have required parity in benefits offered by insurance plans was added to a 1996 Senate health reform bill aimed at making insurance more available to Americans. Under the amendment, insurers would have been prohibited from setting limits on the amount of care or on the levels of guaranteed lifetime benefits that differed from those for physical illnesses. To promote the parity provision, a number of prominent Senators stepped forward to recount their personal experiences with the consequences of mental illness for themselves or family members and the difficulty in getting affordable care. While the exposure of these experiences by respected public figures may have helped lessen the stigma of mental illness, the parity provision was dropped from the final bill. Business groups strongly opposed the proposal because of its presumed cost, while mental health advocacy groups cited data about the affordability and effectiveness of mental health services. Recently, however, a more limited version of parity was passed. Included as an amendment to a 1997 housing bill, it prevents health plans from having different lifetime caps on mental illness benefits than for medical/surgical benefits.[32]

A final consideration in the economics of mental health managed care is the effect of corporate structures and practices on health care costs. Despite their reputation for efficiency and streamlined operations, organizations driven by market forces don't always produce. The *Washington Post* notes that "the typical HMO has been spending a gradually increasing share of its revenue on administrative overhead." Overhead costs now consume an average 12 percent of HMOs' operating revenues. Biodyne, for example, a major mental health MCO, spent $4.7 million on care and $9.3 million on overhead and profits in 1993.[33]

While good business principles often dictate that companies should consolidate to achieve economies of scale, it is unclear whether the increasing merger activity in the field of managed care will lead to greater efficiency and quality of care. Currently, more than 50 percent of the country's HMOs are owned by the top eight insurance companies, and 90 percent of managed mental health care services are carried out by eleven behavioral health firms. Ironically, the most recent mergers have come because medical costs are rising and MCOs are reporting lower profit margins. The tendency now is to attempt to merge with traditional insurance companies in an effort to capture new clients among people with fee-for-service plans. Managed care profits are being reduced somewhat by overhead and rising medical costs. What's left is generally being reinvested or spent on expansion and mergers, rather than on lowering premiums or increasing services.[34]

Social Analysis of Managed Care

In this section we discuss the social values, assumptions, and manifest and latent goals underlying managed care, particularly care for those with mental illness. We will also look at the state of research into this new approach to health care delivery.

Various values and assumptions support efforts to offer treatment to individuals with emotional problems. Humanistic motives compel us to want to help those in difficulty, especially when the problem does not seem to be their fault. While mental illness was once seen as the result of immorality or possession by demons, we have come to view it either as a disease or as a set of reactions to "problems in living." The disease, or medical, model of mental illness is the more prevalent one in our society. It carries with it the assumption that psychological problems are a type of illness that is amenable to treatment by a psychiatrist or other highly trained mental health professional. Treatment can be on an outpatient basis or in a hospital. Medication is often part of the therapist's armament.

The "problems in living" approach is part of what fuels a community mental health model of psychological problems. This model sees psychological difficulties in their broader social and economic context. It stresses interventions in people's environment in order to prevent or at least alleviate mental illness.

Mental health managed care has a stake in both approaches. Private sector MCOs tend to utilize the medical model, perhaps because the image of the highly trained therapist dealing out specialized treatments is a more credible one to "sell" to customers. MCOs working in the public sector with people who have more apparent economic and social stresses are gaining an appreciation of the importance of community-based and preventative services, even though this approach necessitates changes in the ways they have traditionally operated. MCOs in both areas have encouraged greater reliance on outpatient treatment than on hospitalization, in part for therapeutic reasons, in part because outpatient treatment is less expensive.

Managed care also builds on another set of values and assumptions in our society: the belief in the ability of market forces to solve both economic and social problems, and the concomitant suspicion of government's ability to do so. While Clinton's large-scale health reform proposals combined elements of government and private intervention, the plan was seen by many as relying too heavily on "big government." This created a highly favorable environment for entrepreneurial MCOs, which offered to prove the ability of private enterprise to grapple with the enormous problem of health costs in the Unites States. The proliferation of competing MCOs with a variety of structures and services seems to many Americans preferable to a more cohesive national system of health insurance.

The tension between the notion of a collective, societal response to health problems and the idea that market mechanisms should handle health needs is not new. In the United States, health care has always been a mixture of private and public responsibility. In the past few decades, however, there has been a pronounced swing toward private forms of organizing and delivering care. The rise of huge chains of private hospitals, including private psychiatric hospitals, is one manifestation of this swing. The development of MCOs is an even further step in the "commodification" of health care. Much of the language of managed care is the language of business: customers, providers of products, customer service bureaus, market expansion, and so on. A good illustration is an advertisement for a mental health managed care conference for employers, MCO executives, and clinicians, which promises to show participants how to "overcome downward price pressure... by enhancing behavioral healthcare value and implementing value-based pricing strategies." Participants will also learn how to "take advantage of 'focused factory' service production methods."[35]

The manifest goal of mental health managed care programs is to cut health costs while maintaining quality care. Latent goals include expanding into new markets, particularly at a time when the general health market is becoming saturated, and gaining control over providers. While this is particularly true of the for-profit MCOs that dominate the field, even non-profits need to pay attention to maintaining a market share of enrollees. While MCOs, as we have noted, do cut costs in many situations, critics describe latent effects of denying needed care, lessening client control, and avoiding accountability to the public at large.[36]

This discussion of assumptions and goals leads us to important research questions. Where managed care has cut costs, what is the source of these savings? Do they come from greater efficiency or from reduced access and/or quality? What kinds of interventions do MCOs promote for the treatment of mental illness? How effective are these interventions? How does usage of services compare between managed and fee-for-service care plans? How effective and efficient are MCOs' organizational structures? There are two sources of research on these issues: studies and surveys produced by outsiders like academics and members of think tanks, and the in-house outcome assessments conducted by the MCOs. So far, the research has been sketchy and a broad, comprehensive data base has not yet been established. However, based in part on three national surveys of managed care, some trends are becoming evident.[37]

In the late 1970s, HMOs were reporting lower mental hospitalization rates and higher outpatient rates than were fee-for-service insurance plans. Managed care hospitalization rates have continued to fall; annual admissions per 1,000 members dropped from 6 to a little over 3 between 1978 and 1986. However, the length of average stay in a mental hospital increased from 32 days to 37 between 1982 and 1986. Interestingly, non-profit HMOs reported the lowest managed care hospitalization rates.[38]

Comparative studies in the mid-1980s suggested that HMO enrollees generally used fewer mental health services than did their fee-for-service counterparts. However, they were about as likely to make initial contact with a mental health provider, and twice as likely to be referred for mental health services as were individuals with traditional insurance. This suggests an interesting slip between referral or initial contact and actual engagement in therapy for HMO enrollees. As yet there is no explanation as to why this occurs, due in part to the fact that there has been little research on the effectiveness of the referral process in HMOs and other MCOs.[39]

Not much is known about the cost of treatment for severely mentally ill people under a managed care system. These are the clients most likely to be served by Medicaid managed care programs. There is some indication that such programs can reduce the use of state mental hospitals and that they can lower the average per-patient cost of care. However, a Medicaid mental health managed care project in Minnesota was closed down after one year, largely because the MCOs involved concluded that their costs for serving Medicaid clients were greater than the rates paid to them by the state.[40]

There are relatively few published studies comparing the efficacy of mental health treatment for clients of managed care and fee-for-service systems. Several projects look at the outcomes for individuals with depression. Of people treated by regular physicians for their depression, 61 percent were deemed appropriately treated in fee-for-service programs, as opposed to 42 percent in managed care. Those seeing a psychiatrist were left with more functional limitations from their depression in managed care systems than in traditional insurance arrangements. There was also a higher rate of use of minor tranquilizers and a lower rate of counseling sessions in the managed care population.[41]

You will notice that the studies cited above do not fully answer any of the research questions. Two questions, those about the source of savings and the efficiency of particular MCO structures, have not been answered at all. One policy analyst asserts that "ultimately, outcome oriented studies will be conducted to assist in determining which (if any) of the managed care options help contain service utilization and costs of mental health...care" without compromising quality. Yet he also notes that such research will be difficult until a better national data base on managed care operations is developed.[42]

What of the internal research conducted by MCOs, which tend to stress accountability and outcome-driven treatment guidelines? It is difficult to judge the extent of this research, since it is not easily accessible. An extensive study of MCOs providing mental health care to children and adolescents in the Medicaid population does indicate that companies put much greater emphasis on measuring costs, access, and utilization patterns than on ascertaining treatment effectiveness. For example, 83 percent of the companies surveyed studied costs, while only 51 percent studied treatment outcomes. It is encouraging to note, however, that over 80 percent of the specialized mental health MCOs researched treatment effectiveness, compared to only one-third of MCOs offering both health and mental health care. An important question is how this research measures treatment success. It appears that a number of MCOs rely primarily on client satisfaction surveys for such data. In public sector managed care particularly, these surveys tap only the people who "stay in the system," and not those who don't come to their appointments. Although providers produce a variety of information on measurable outcomes such as symptom reduction and the achievement of behavioral goals, it is not clear that many MCOs actually analyze such data in any comprehensive way.[43]

Lack of a definitive body of research on the effectiveness of their mental health interventions by MCOs lends credence to the suggestion that issues of quality are not paramount in the move to the new approach. Speaking of the rise of public managed care, health analysts Essock and Goldman note that this new chapter in mental health policymaking, "proceeds in the absence of data" and in the context of political and fiscal pressures to cut costs.[44]

The Political Context of Managed Care

By now you are no doubt well aware that the managed care revolution is a "high stakes" phenomenon involving many different organizations and constituencies. It is a two billion dollar industry, tackling a national problem, built on a specific ideology, and affecting Americans of all walks of life. The list of stakeholders is lengthy, including clients, employers, state health officials, providers, MCOs, federal and state legislators and other government leaders, advocacy groups, and the broader public. This section provides a brief overview of the major players and their points of view.

Clients and their families are at the receiving end of mental health managed care. They want effective and accessible help, and most would like some control over the type of assistance they get and the way it is delivered. Some are the people who provide the horror stories to newspapers and magazines—"After my allotted sessions were over, I could only see a psychiatrist 15 minutes every three months to have my depression medication checked." Some may be concerned about confidentiality issues that arise when details of their problems are discussed between their therapist and an unknown gatekeeper. Others are largely satisfied with their care. Most are not organized with other clients or families to advocate for good treatment, although many have access as individuals to at least a rudimentary grievance procedure in their MCO. Some, however, join the ranks of client groups or organizations for family members, such as the National Association for the Mentally Ill, in order to influence MCO practices.

Employers and state health officials might be called the cogs that drive the mental health managed care revolution, in that their direct concern about dealing with mental health costs underlies the move to MCOs. Private employers generally prefer market-oriented solutions to problems rather than government programs and mandates. Yet they would also like to maintain some control over the premiums and practices of the MCOs with which they contract. In Minnesota, for example, an employer coalition called the Business Health Care Action Group recently criticized several large HMOs for "spending millions of dollars on business matters instead of medicine... engaging in destructive price wars and... stifling rather than stimulating new approaches to care." Many of the groups' members have begun to contract with smaller HMOs instead. While saving money is the bottom line, most businesses recognize the importance of adequate health care for their employees. (Interestingly, however, executives in many large companies receive much fuller health coverage than their employees, with no restriction on choice of provider). State Medicaid and mental health officials, who are more publicly accountable and whose health care planning decisions are more visible, are even more likely to address concerns about the quality of care.[45]

Mental health providers sound like a unified group, but actually represent a number of professions, with somewhat different perspectives on managed care. Psychiatrists are particularly incensed at a phenomenon that reduces their autonomy in treatment decisions and in setting their own fees. An article entitled "Organized Psychiatry and Managed Care: Quality Improvement or Holy War?" pictures psychiatrists as at war with the "Great Satan" of managed care. A managed-care opponent recently elected to the presidency of the American Psychiatric Association called MCOs "greed-driven sharks" that "manage health care for a profit." Many psychiatrists see managed care as interposing a third party into the previously sacred and confidential relationship between doctor and mental health patient. They, like other mental health providers, are also concerned about the ability of MCOs to drop providers from their lists, to set limits on the amount of treatment that can be delivered, to make decisions about what constitutes appropriate and effective therapy for clients, and to lower therapists' customary fees. In New York City, for example, MCOs pay about 60 percent of psychiatrists' usual charges. Psychiatrists' complaints are similar to the complaints of physicians working in general health managed care systems. Some physicians are even turning to unions to help them fight managed care plans.[46]

Social workers are another major provider group with concerns about managed care. They are perhaps less flamboyant than psychiatrists in their criticisms of MCOs. While many psychiatrists see their autonomy at stake in the move to managed care, most social workers in private practice, and increasingly their colleagues in agencies, depend on insurance coverage for their very livelihood. Increasingly, for these practitioners, managed care is the major source of insurance payments. Partly because they charge less than psychiatrists and psychologists, social workers have been able to carve out a large space in managed care systems. MCO plans rely heavily on social workers, giving them over 50 percent of mental health referrals. We will go into detail about social worker reactions to managed care and their activities as providers in the next section of this chapter.[47]

One of the protective mechanisms used by the various providers in behavioral health managed care, including psychiatrists, social workers, psychologists, and counselors, is the formation of independent group practices or networks which then contract with MCOs. Psychologists participate most frequently in such groups, followed by social workers, psychiatrists, and counselors. Many of these groups are "independent practice associations" (IPAs), in which providers share the risk in managed care contracts but also compete with each other for non-IPA business. Group membership can give practitioners more power in negotiating with MCOs.[48]

At the center of the managed care revolution, of course, are the MCOs themselves and, if they are for-profit, their investors. We have already described the cost-cutting goal of MCOs and their need to establish remunerative markets. While most don't intend to diminish the quality of mental health care, they base much of their cost reduction on restricting people's access to care and limiting the amounts that providers can charge. MCOs maintain that shorter, more purposeful, and more efficient therapy may in fact be of higher quality than traditional treatment, and that some clients don't need the assistance they ask for. However, there is as of yet little conclusive research supporting the contention that managed care brings better therapeutic results.

Legislators, governors, presidents, and presidential candidates have a large investment in the development of health care policies such as managed care. They must respond to the conflicting demands of powerful, well-organized stakeholders like employers, MCOs, and physicians. They are sensitive to the voters' call to keep down taxes and to make health care affordable. They are also aware of public concerns related to the effects of health care changes on accessibility and quality.

Legislators and public officials must also respond to the pressures of health care advocacy groups. Many such groups have taken an interest in managed care. They include the National Association of Mental Health, a large and well-established organization that lobbies for increased funding for mental health programs and effective treatment for those with mental illness; the National Alliance for the Mentally Ill, a group composed of the families and friends of the mentally ill; the Bazelon Center for Mental Health Law, the leading national legal advocate for people with emotional problems; children's advocacy organizations like the Federation of Families for Children's Mental Health; and client support and advocacy groups, such as the National Mental Health Consumers' Self Help Clearinghouse. Many national advocacy organizations have state branches that lobby for effective public managed mental health programs. In addition, professional associations, such as nurses' groups and the National Association of Social Workers, advocate regarding both client and provider issues.[49]

All of these groups have at least some skepticism about the effectiveness of managed care arrangements for delivering mental health services. Yet all see the potential of bringing about long-sought reforms in mental health care through influencing the current managed care movement. Many groups note a particular opportunity to help shape the developing Medicaid programs.

Mental health advocacy reflects the strong commitment that clients should receive adequate services from an accountable managed care entity. They urge the following types of improvements, changes, and protections in managed care:

1. effective grievance and appeal procedures in all MCOs
2. client and family input into planning, implementation, and oversight of state-sponsored managed care mental health programs
3. client and family participation in treatment planning
4. coverage of the full array of treatments and interventions, including greater attention to community-based services such as supported housing, daily living skills, and vocational training, especially in public mental health managed care programs
5. development of prevention measures
6. greater development and use of outcome measures (which focus on changes such as symptom reduction, the ability to get and keep a job, and improved quality of life)
7. parity between benefits to the physically and mentally ill, and adequate attention to the needs of those with severe and chronic mental illness
8. attention to the mental health needs of children and provision of appropriate services, including coordination with child welfare, schools, and juvenile justice programs

As we will see in the conclusion of this chapter, advocates, providers, consumers, and clients have already had some success in bringing about changes in managed care practices.

Social Workers and Managed Care

Social workers play a variety of roles in managed care systems, including those of provider, gatekeeper, planner, and advocate. Although the movement first affected social workers in private practice, its impact has spread rapidly. Any social work setting that relies on third-party insurance reimbursement is likely to become involved in the managed care revolution, as we saw earlier in the interview with Judith Morris. There is even talk of introducing managed care principles into public child welfare programs. It is therefore vital for social workers to strive to make the system work well for their clients and themselves, and to call for reforms where necessary.

Private practitioners, called social work vendors in insurance parlance, bore the brunt of the initial move to managed mental health care. Providers like Barry Daste had to adjust to new expectations regarding treatment plans and their approval, types of therapy used, and reporting procedures, as well as to new systems of payment. They also encountered different, often lower, reimbursement rates for their services. Like doctors, they were not uniformly pleased. Some referred to managed care as "the plague," and many complained that it drained their autonomy, complicated their work, and interfered with their ability to help clients. They were disturbed by clients' loss of confidentiality when providers had to discuss intimate details of their problems with gatekeepers, and they questioned whether all the reviewers had the professional credentials to make decisions about therapy. Finally, not all private practitioners were able to make it onto MCO provider lists; some of those who did were afraid "to make waves" for fear they would be terminated without cause, a cost saving device used by some MCOs.[50]

While most private practitioners still have these concerns, many have decided to make the best of it, adapting to and/or trying to change the system. One response has been to increase their own marketing skills in order to compete for and keep contracts; the *National Association of Social Work News* now regularly carries articles like "Market Savvy Opens Managed-Care Doors," which describe the ins and outs of targeting the MCO audience, marketing their skills and specialties, designing business letterheads, and using elaborate billing and management software. Social workers who chose private practice in part for the autonomy it offered now find themselves joining provider networks, including large, multidisciplinary practices called "Supergroups" in order to wield greater power in a system dominated by MCOs.[51] In addition, as the next interview shows, some social workers have taken the next step up in the managed care chain, joining MCO staffs as the gatekeepers who conduct authorization reviews.

Conducting PreAuthorization Reviews

Interview with a Gatekeeper

Michael Breaux (not his real name) is a social worker in private practice whose speciality is working with children and families. His involvement with managed care companies began as a provider when MCOs were proliferating in the mid-1980s. He recalls that "in those days, the companies were sending out applications about once a week to practitioners. You could end up on several dozen provider lists." He worked with several different MCOs for a number of years. Then one of the companies asked him to fill in, on a part-time basis, for a staff member who received clients' initial calls and made assignments to therapists.

Breaux agreed, and received "quick and dirty" on-the-job training. Another worker was there to give him advice and support as he received his first calls. Breaux's many years of clinical practice made the job easier. Under the title of Triage Specialist, his job functions were to do quick face-to-face assessments of the nature and severity of clients' problems and to choose an appropriate therapist for treatment. The work entailed both diagnosis as well as making judgments about the kind of therapy clients should receive, so providers with the appropriate therapeutic skills could be chosen. In picking a provider, Breaux generally took geography into account, selecting someone in a location convenient to the client. Clients also had input into the process; they could request that the provider come from a particular discipline, such as social work or psychology, or they could ask for a specific type of professional, such as a Christian therapist.

In addition to his work as triage specialist, Breaux also spent some time authorizing providers' treatment plans. I asked how it felt to be working "on the other side of the fence," expecting that it might be difficult to be put in the position of restricting the amount of treatment a client could receive. Actually, he replied, it wasn't much of a problem. In dealing with outpatients, at least, "no managed care personnel turned down extra visits," as long as the client didn't exceed the contracted number of annual visits, such as twenty-five per year. Within the limits of the ceiling, authorizations for any amount below that number became a kind of rubber stamp, a process which Breaux saw as not particularly efficient. Once the yearly limit was reached, however, the MCO adhered strictly to the cut-off policy.

From his perspective both as provider and as part of the managed care gatekeeping system, Breaux had a number of observations to make about the strengths and weaknesses of the managed care approach. He noted that MCOs have probably reined in costs, particularly by requiring physicians and hospital administrators to clearly document a patient's need for hospitalization. This has helped lead to lower hospitalization rates. Perhaps cost reductions will translate into lower insurance premiums for clients. In addition, managed care may control the tendency of some clients to shop around for a therapist who "says what they want to hear." As a triage specialist, Breaux always encouraged clients to try to work out difficulties with their therapists before they sought a transfer to another provider. This may have kept clients focused, and cut down on the tendency to therapist-shop.

On the other hand, the lack of consistency among MCOS regarding rules and paperwork requirements makes it difficult for the many providers who work with more than one company. In addition, because companies sometimes contract out various parts of the managed care process, a therapist might have to deal with three different entities regarding a single client: one to precertify assistance, another to authorize additional therapy, and a third to pay the therapist's bill. Finally, practices within the managed care organization are not always straightforward. For example, providers can sometimes be kept on the company's list, but never used. This can happen when a MCO decides that a therapist is too outspoken, or isn't "playing by the rules." Rather than going through the messy process of removing someone from the list, the company may simply decide to maintain the provider in name only.

Breaux would probably echo Barry Daste's observation that social workers working within MCOs or serving as providers need to be assertive, in order to maintain as much autonomy in decision making as possible. He also points out the importance of the social work code of ethics as a safeguard against abuses both by therapists, such as exploiting clients, and by the MCO, such as withholding needed treatment. MCOs need to recognize that their providers must operate within such professional codes and that organizational regulations should not put them at risk for unethical behavior.

While many of the private practitioners' responses are focused on providers' issues regarding autonomy, levels of payment, and job security, private practitioners and their organizations attend also to client issues (and it should be noted that provider concerns, such as the need for some independence in clinical decision making, can affect clients as well). Groups like the National Federation of Societies for Clinical Social Work have lobbied companies about such issues as client confidentiality and the denial of needed services by intrusive utilization reviews. Local clinical organizations have also been active. For example, the New Jersey Society for Clinical Social Work organized a panel of legislators, social workers, and other mental health professionals to discuss problems in managed care. The discussion led to a plan to further legislation protecting consumers.[52]

As the managed care movement has grown and broadened into the social service agency and public mental health arena, what was initially seen as a private practice concern has become a major interest of the profession as a whole. As the broadest and probably the most powerful voice of social work, the NASW has undertaken a variety of educational and advocacy activities. Echoing Breaux's emphasis on the importance of the NASW Code of Ethics, the NASW grounds much of its work on managed care in an emphasis on accountable and ethical professional practice. The association has produced numerous publications outlining practice guidelines and responsibilities for social workers in managed care. These responsibilities include the obligation to ensure that necessary services are made available to clients who still need help after their benefits have been used up. The organization's membership, through the Delegate Assembly, approved a comprehensive policy statement on managed care in 1993. The statement's section on advocacy calls on social workers to "promote state and federal legislation that supports basic standards of care that include universality, accessibility, affordability, comprehensive and adequate services, and portability." In coalition with other professional groups, NASW lobbies for such legislation at the national level.[53]

What can you, as an individual social worker, do to affect managed care policy and practices? If you work in an agency, you can join in advocacy and change efforts at that level, such as the development of an inhouse quality assurance system which gave more autonomy to Judith Morris's organization. You can band with other staff members to influence the agency's policy and practices as a provider and to protect your ability to carry out ethical practice in as secure an employment situation as possible. When you encounter situations like the following, you can work to empower clients to grieve harmful decisions by MCOs.

A practitioner recently told us this story: "I have been working with a seven-year-old boy who was severely sexually abused by his father. His mother, who works for a large manufacturer, has insurance that covers twelve therapy sessions in a calendar year. The child has so far told no one but his mother about the abuse. I have finally begun to gain his trust, and I think that soon he'll be able to talk with me about what happened. This will help him cope with the situation, and it will also help his mother in her attempts to press charges against his father. Unfortunately, she has used up almost all of her yearly allotment of therapy sessions, and won't qualify for new ones until four months from now. Last week, she came to talk to me about leaving her job and going on welfare, so she might qualify for better mental health benefits." The therapist in this situation was planning to present this to the MCO as an emergency case and to ask for additional treatment sessions. She was also urging the mother to pursue a grievance with the MCO.

Beyond such agency or individual practice-based activities, you can play a role in one of the many organized professional or advocacy groups. Local NASW chapters often have social action committees that would welcome new members. States developing Medicaid managed care programs have aroused the interest of numerous advocacy associations and lobbying coalitions that are eager for involvement by citizens, clients and family members, and professionals. These groups have a real chance to affect change at the local and state level, both by exerting outside pressure on legislators and state health officials and by gaining representation on internal public managed care program planning groups. This last interview with a social worker gives an excellent picture of the sort of work that is there to be done.

Influencing the System

Interview with an Advocate

Shannon Robshaw is a recent graduate of an MSW program. Before she pursued her master's degree, she volunteered in a local chapter of the Mental Health Association of Louisiana, in order to pursue her interest in improving mental health treatment for children with serious emotional disturbance. Her strong commitment to making the mental health system more responsive to children's needs helped propel her to the Presidency of the association chapter. Along the way, she also discovered that she had a talent for lobbying. At her first visit to the Louisiana State Legislature, representing her chapter, she sat in on a legislative committee session to observe the hearings on a piece of mental health legislation. She had no plans to testify, but did submit a written note stating her opposition to one provision of the bill. To her surprise, legislative aides sought her out at a recess to explain her objections. Because of their discussion, the bill was changed in line with Robshaw's suggestions.

At the School of Social Work, Robshaw did one of her internships with a children's services planning unit within the state Office of Mental Health. After graduation, she continued her involvement with the Mental Health Association, this time with the state chapter in Baton Rouge. She is now employed part-time as the chapter's Executive Director. In this capacity, she engages in lobbying and educational efforts to enhance public understanding of mental illness and to improve services for those with psychological problems. As Louisiana begins to plan a managed care program for its Medicaid clients, Robshaw has played a pivotal role in organizing the Mental Health Reform Coalition. This is a coalition of advocacy groups, including the state chapter of NASW, with the goal of influencing the goals and provisions of the proposed program.

Robshaw feels that states are currently seeing managed care as a panacea, or a magic wand that will "take care of" all problems of mental illness. The promise of cost savings reassures planners and legislators that there will be enough money to provide all needed services. But if there isn't enough money allocated now for mental health, she muses, there won't be enough under managed care either, particularly if private MCOs skim off the profits. Robshaw and others have already lobbied successfully at the legislature to restore some money that was being cut from a psychological rehabilitation services option within the Medicaid program.

When she visualizes a new public mental health managed care system in Louisiana, Robshaw argues persuasively that MCOs should provide a full range of services, including a hospitalization safety net, but maintain a strong emphasis on community based care. Outpatient clinics will provide some of this care, but mentally ill adults will also need help in areas like housing and employment. Children could be assisted through school-based counseling, crisis residential centers, and other interventions. For children particularly, services will need to be coordinated across multiple providers and agencies, including child welfare and the juvenile justice system. Presently, more state money is allocated to the state hospital system than to community care; Robshaw feels this ratio needs to be reversed. A sound system should also include responsive grievance procedures and an independent obmudsman program for people to appeal denials of service.

What does Robshaw feel is the best tactic for achieving these goals? First, consumers and their advocates need to be included at the planning table. This is the first goal the new Mental Health Reform Coalition will pursue. The next step is to work to outline good contracts in which the state specifies what particular services it expects an MCO to deliver. Consumer, family, and advocate involvement can make sure these contracts stress community services and don't rely strictly on a medical model. As representatives on a planning board, they can also help develop appropriate outcome measures and quality assurance mechanisms.

As Robshaw notes, "managed care is riddled with problems, but it's not as if we've had a really good system up to now." The dream of people like Robshaw is that through strong advocacy efforts, the managed care movement can be used to create an effective, coordinated, and innovative public mental health program.

Conclusion

Is managed mental health care here to stay? Or will the promise of significant and sustained cost savings go unfulfilled, leading to a search for other solutions to the problems associated with effective and affordable treatment for those with psychological problems? While we can't answer these questions, we *can* predict that managed care will continue to change, and that many of these changes will be imposed on the system by outside forces.

Already the publicized complaints of clients, the concerns of providers, and the efforts of advocate groups have led to proposed federal and state regulation of health and mental health MCOs. Major proposals being introduced around the country include bills prohibiting the practice of restricting the choice of provider and requiring MCOs to set up speedy and simple appeals processes. In some cases, legislation has already been enacted. Sixteen states, for example, have outlawed the use of "gag clauses," in which HMOs ban doctors from disclosing the bonuses they receive for restricting care or discussing treatments the MCO doesn't cover. The federal government recently followed suit, stating that MCOs may not limit what doctors tell Medicare patients about treatment options. The federal Substance Abuse and Mental Health Services Administration (SAMHSA) has launched a Managed Care Initiative to collect data from state programs in order to evaluate managed care's impact on service delivery. The U.S. General Accounting Office has called for more oversight and quality assurance monitoring of MCO activities in the public sector. Within the managed care industry, a National Committee for Quality Assurance (NCQA) has been formed to accredit HMOs based on various standards of quality (although only half of all HMOs have even applied). Finally, clients and providers are becoming more knowledgeable about managed care and how to influence its practices.[54]

None of this activity will necessarily halt the revolution. As social workers, no doubt you too will be affected in one way or another by managed care. We hope that you will use your policy skills to enhance the positives and to work to change the negatives of this latest approach to mental health care.

Notes

1. Joan O' C. Hamilton and Michele Galen, "A Furor over Mental Health," *Business Week* (8 August 1994) p. 66.

2. Hamilton and Galen, "A Furor Over Mental Health," p. 67; Jane Hiebert-White, "From the Editor: Managed Care and the New Economics of Mental Health," *Health Affairs* 14 (Fall 1995) pp. 5–6; *Third-Party Reimbursement for Clinical Social Work Services* (Washington, DC: National Association of Social Workers, 1995) p. 6.

3. Ellyn Spragins, "Does Your HMO Stack Up?" *Newsweek* (24 June 1996) p. 56.

4. Bruce Lubotsky Levin, "Managed Mental Health Care: A National Perspective," in *Health United States 1992,* National Center for Health Statistics (Hyattsville, MD: Public Health Service, 1993) p. 208; Daniel Goleman, "Battle of Insurers vs. Therapists," *New York Times* (24 October 1991) sec. D, p. 1; Susan M. Essock and Howard H. Goldman, "States' Embrace of Managed Mental Health Care," *Health Affairs* 14 (Fall 1995) p. 37; Philip J. Boyle and Daniel Callahan, "Managed Care in Mental Health: The Ethical Issues," *Health Affairs* 14 (Fall 1996) pp. 9–10.

5. Philip R. Popple and Leslie Leighninger, *Social Work, Social Welfare and American Society* (Boston: Allyn and Bacon, 1996) pp. 406–408; Levin, "Managed Mental Health Care: A National Perspective," p. 208; Hamilton and Galen, "A Furor Over Mental Health," p. 66; Michael Malloy, *Mental Illness and Managed Care: A Primer for Families and Consumers* (Arlington, VA: National Alliance for the Mentally Ill, April, 1995) p. 24.

6. Richard G. Frank and Thomas G. McGuire, "Health Care Reform and Financing of Mental Health Services: Distributional Consequences," in R. W. Manderscheid and M. A. Sonnenschein, Eds., *Mental Health United States 1994,* Center for Mental Health Services (Washington, DC: U.S. Govt. Print. Off., 1994) p. 8.

7. Bentson H. McFarland, "Health Maintenance Organizations and Persons with Severe Mental Illness," *Community Mental Health Journal* 30 (1994) p. 224; Mental Health Association in Louisiana, "Mental Health Fact Sheet," May 1993; Jolie Solomon, "Breaking the Silence," *Newsweek* (20 May 1996) p. 20.

8. Mental Health Association in Louisiana, "Fact Sheet."

9. Frank and McGuire, "Health Care Reform and Financing of Mental Health Services," p. 13; Solomon, "Breaking the Silence," p. 22; Mental Health Association in Louisiana, "Fact Sheet."

10. Malloy, *Mental Illness and Managed Care; Social Work Speaks: NASW Policy Statements,* 3rd ed. (Washington, DC: NASW Press, 1994) p. 169.

11. Malloy, *Mental Illness and Managed Care; Managing Managed Care for Publicly Financed Mental Health Services* (Washington, DC: Bazelon Center for Mental Health Law, November 1995) pp. 44–48.

12. *Managing Managed Care,* p. 48.

13. David S. Hilzenrath, "Putting Their Money Where Their Health Is: Wall Street Is Betting on Firms That Are Revolutionizing the Medical Marketplace," *Washington Post Weekly Edition* (31 October–6 November 1994) p. 19; Robert J. Samuelson, "The Revolution's Started," *Washington Post Weekly Edition* (30 October 5–November 1995) p. 5.

14. Kenneth Minkoff, "Community Mental Health in the Nineties: Public Sector Managed Care," *Community Mental Health Journal* 30 (August 1994) pp. 317–318.

15. Susan Landers, "Managed Medicaid: Care in the Balance," *NASW News* 40 (April 1995) p. 3.

16. Bruce M. Bullen, "Managed Care in Massachusetts," *Public Welfare* 53 (Spring 1995) pp. 6–9.

17. Essock and Goldman, "States' Embracing of Managed Mental Health Care," p. 38.

18. Sheila A. Pires, et al., *Health Care Reform Tracking Project: The 1995 State Survey* (University of South Florida: Florida Mental Health Institute, November 1995) pp. 32–33, 57.

19. Paul Starr, *The Social Transformation of American Medicine* (NY: Basic Books, 1982) pp. 320–327.

20. Popple and Leighninger, *Social Work Social Welfare and American Society,* p. 427; Starr, *The Social Transformation of American Medicine,* pp. 400–401.

21. Levin, "Managed Mental Health Care: A National Perspective," pp. 208–209; *Third-Party Reimbursement for Clinical Social Work Services,* p. 5.

22. Popple and Leighninger, *Social Work, Social Welfare, and American Society,* pp. 437–439.

23. Dan Morgan, "While Washington Talked: Health Care Reform is Taking Shape in the Private Sector without Help from Congress," *Washington Post Weekly Edition* (12–18 September 1994) p. 31.

24. McFarland, "Health Maintenance Organizations and Persons with Severe Mental Illness," p. 225; Levin, "Managed Mental Health Care: A National Perspective," p. 209.

25. Levin, "Managed Mental Health Care: A National Perspective," p. 210; Philip J. Boyle and Daniel Callahan, "Managed Care in Mental Health: The Ethical Issues," *Health Affairs* 14 (Fall 1996) pp. 7–8; Essock and Goldman, "States' Embrace of Managed Mental Health Care," p. 37; Malloy, *Mental Illness and Managed Care,* pp. 17–18.

26. Levin, "Managed Mental Health Care: A National Perspective," p. 211.

27. Richard Wolf, "States Grabbing the Rope in Medicaid 'Tug of War'," *USA Today* (3 November 1995) sec. A, p. 19; Colette Fraley, "The Blossoming of Medicaid," *Congressional Quarterly* (10 June 1995) p. 1638; Rita Vandivort Warren, "Merging Managed Care and Medicaid: Private Regulation of Public Health Care," *NASW Social Work Practice Update* (Washington, DC: NASW, June 1995) p. 1; Essock and Goldman, "States' Embrace of Managed Health Care," p. 37.

28. Warren, "Merging Managed Care and Medicaid," pp. 3–4.

29. Essock and Goldman, "States' Embrace of Managed Mental Health Care," pp. 36–37; Samuelson, "The Revolution's Started," p. 5; "Health Insurance," *Standard and Poor's Industry Surveys* 163 (2 March 1995) pp. 1–44; Robert Pear, "Medicine Panel Advises a Freeze on Hospital Pay," *New York Times* (19 January 1997) pp. 1, 11.

30. Leah K. Glasheen and Susan L. Crowly, "Taking a Slower Path: Many States Turn Away from Bold Reform Measures," *AARP Bulletin* 36 (July/August 1995) pp. 6–7; Levin, "Managed Mental Health Care: A National Perspective," 212.

30. Levin, "Managed Mental Health Care: A National Perspective," p. 212; *Managing Managed Care,* p. 10.

31. Levin, "Managed Mental Health Care," p. 211.

32. "The Mental Health Amendment," *Washington Post Weekly Edition* (April 6–12, 1996) p. 25; Melinda Back, "Follow the Money," *Newsweek* (20 May 1996) pp. 23–24; "Congress Approves Key First Step Toward Parity of Mental Health Benefits," *Legislative Alert* (Washington, DC: Bazelon Center for Mental Health Law, 26 September 1996).

33. David S. Hilzenrath, "HMOs are Gaining Steadily by Squeezing Others," *Washington Post Weekly Edition* (19–25 September 1994) p. 20; "Healthcare Services Rapidly Adapt to Change," *Standard and Poor's Industry Surveys* 164 (11 January 1996) p. H 5; Carol Hymowitz and Ellen Joan Pollock, "The New Economy of Mental Health," *The Wall Street Journal* (13 July 1995) sec A. pp. 1, 4.

34. "Healthcare Services Rapidly Adapt to Change;" Hilzenrath, "HMOs are Gaining Steadily by Squeezing Others;" Hilzenrath, "Putting Their Money Where Their Health Is."

35. Popple and Leighninger, *Social Work, Social Welfare, and American Society,* pp. 429–431; Lloyd M. Krieger, "How Managed Health Care Will Allow Market Forces to Solve the Problem," *New York Times* (13 August 1995) p. 12; The Institute for Behavioral Health Care, Final Program, Eighth Annual National Dialogue Conference on Mental Health Benefits and Practice in the Era of Managed Care: Behavioral Healthcare Tomorrow (September 1996).

36. Robert M. Johnson, "Ethics and Managed Care," *Health Decisions,* Publication of the Vermont Ethics Network (September 1995); Sharon R. King, "Mental Health Ventures May Gain from New Law," *New York Times* (20 October 1996) sec. 3, p. 3.

37. Samuelson, "The Revolution's Started," p. 5; Levin, "Managed Mental Health Care," pp. 213–214.

38. Levin, "Managed Mental Health Care," pp. 212–217.

39. McFarland, "Health Maintenance Organizations and Persons with Severe Mental Illness," p. 230; Levin, "Managed Mental Health Care," p. 212.

40. McFarland, "Health Maintenance Organizations and Persons with Severe Mental Illness," pp. 231–235.

41. "Medical Outcomes Study," *Journal of the American Medical Association* 262 (1989) p. 3298; *Archives of General Psychiatry* 50 (1993) p. 517; Kenneth B. Wells and Roland Sturm, "Care for Depression in a Changing Environment," *Health Affairs* 14 (Fall 1995) pp. 83–88.

42. Levin, "Managed Mental Health Care," p. 214.

43. Pires, *Health Reform Tracking Project,* pp. 66, 69.

44. Essock and Goldman, "States' Embrace of Managed Mental Health Care," pp. 38–39.

45. Ron Winslow, "Employer Group Rethinks Commitment to Big HMOs," *Wall Street Journal* (21 July 1995) sec. B, p. 1; Allen R. Myerson, "A Double Standard in

Health Coverage: Executives are Cradled While Medical Benefits are Cut for Rank and File," *New York Times* (17 March 1996) sec. 3, pp. 1, 13.

46. James Sabin, "Organized Psychiatry and Managed Care: Quality Improvement or Holy War?" *Health Affairs* 14 (Fall 1995) pp. 5–6; Goleman, "Battle of Insurers vs. Therapists;" Melinda Hennenberger, "Managed Care Changing Practice of Psychotherapy," *New York Times* (9 October 1994) pp. 1, 19; Peter T. Kilborn, "Devalued by Growth of H.M.O.'s, Some Doctors Seek Union Banner," *New York Times* (3 May 1996) p. 1.

47. Beck, "Follow the Money," p. 24.

48. Behavioral-Health Involvement High," *NASW News* 41 (July 1996) p. 14.

49. Nat Hentoff, "Harry and Louise Go to California," *The Washington Post* (22 June 1996) sec. A, p. 17.

50. *Managed Care Information Booklet* (Managed Care Committee of the Association of Clinical Social Work Vendorship, no date), p. 1.

51. Roger Rose, "Market Savvy Opens Managed-Care Doors," *NASW News* 39 (January 1994) p. 5; Roger Rose, "Matter of Marketing: Do-It-Yourself Design," *NASW News* 41 (July 1996) p. 5; Susan Landers, "Supergroups: A 'Big Pond' Survival Tactic," *NASW News* 39 (November 1994) p. 3.

52. Chad Breckenridge, "President's Report," *Progress Report* 13, Newsletter of the National Federation of Societies for Clinical Social Work (December 1995) p. 3; Luba Shagawat, "New Jersey Speaks Out on Regulation," *Managed Care News,* Newsletter of the National Federation of Societies for Clinical Social Work's Health Care Systems Committee (November 1995) p. 4.

53. *Third-Party Reimbursement for Clinical Social Work Services* (Washington, D.C.: NASW, 1995); *A Brief Look at Managed Health Care* (Washington, DC: NASW, 1994); *Third Party Reimbursement for Clinical Social Work Services,* p. 12; *Social Work Speaks: NASW Policy Statements,* 3rd ed. (Washington, DC: NASW Press, 1994) pp. 169–175.

54. Milt Freudenheim, "HMO's Cope with a Backlash on Cost Cutting," *New York Times* (19 May 1996) p. 1; Robert Pear, "Laws Won't Let H.M.O.'s Tell Doctors What to Say," *New York Times* (17 September 1996) sec. A, p. 9; Susan Landers, "'Spinning Dry' with Managed Care," *NASW News* 40 (November, 1995) p. 3; U.S. General Accounting Office, "Medicaid Managed Care: More Competition and Oversight Would Improve California's Expansion Plan" (April 1995); Robert Pear, "HMOs Ordered to Remove Doctors' Gags," *New Orleans Times-Picayune* (7 December 1996) sec. A, p. 4; Jane Bryant Quinn "What's a Good HMO? Right Now There's No Good Way to Tell," *Baton Rouge Advocate* (21 March 1997) sec. C, p. 5.

Chapter 10

Health: Medicaid and Medicare Changes in the Context of Health Care Reform

All the talk these days about cuts in Medicare has older Americans worried. Seventy-one-year old Inez Byrd is afraid her medical bills will rise if Congress carries out its proposed overhaul of the Medicare program. "Worried? Of course I'm worried," she exclaims. "I'm barely existing now. If they cut very much, I don't know how I'm going to make it." Alberta Green, 79, concurs. "I really can't pay any more because I don't have anything left over each month. Social Security only goes so far."[1]

Legislators and taxpayers who worry about the growing portion of federal and state budgets dedicated to Medicaid payments sometimes suggest that it would help if more people took care of their elderly family members. Grace Solomon, who is 69, disagrees. Solomon lives on the 14th floor of a run-down New York City housing project. Quiet and self-possessed, she is blind and has many health problems. She's very thankful for the assistance she gets from her son and from members of her church. Yet, she explains, "they all have their families" to look after. So far, it's been possible for Solomon to remain independent, due to the twelve hours of Medicaid-sponsored personal help she receives each week. During those twelve hours, Solomon's Medicaid aide helps her get to the doctor, pay the bills, and do other essential chores. Without this help, she asks, "What will I do?"[2]

Maria Ruiz is a social work student doing her internship at a private counseling center. Many of the clients at the center are from poor families and are eligible for Medicaid. Ruiz is becoming more and more concerned about something going on at the center that at first she couldn't figure out. Several times now, she's noticed billing forms on the secretary's desk that show her name attached to home visits to various clients. But these are clients that she has only spoken to on the telephone, and several are people that she's never met at all. Much as she tries to convince herself otherwise, she has come to realize that her agency is engaging in Medicaid fraud. "But what am I going to do?" she agonizes. "If I tell my supervisor, I might get in big trouble. Maybe I'd better go to my faculty field liaison—maybe he can help me out."

This chapter is somewhat different from the others. They focused on specific, fairly discrete policies, such as Social Security and Family Preservation. Here we will concentrate less on the details of any one policy or policy proposal and more on the broader policy framework of which they are a part. We will examine two policies in the health care arena, Medicare and Medicaid, but we will do so in the context of the interconnectedness of all health care provisions in the U.S. As you saw in the opening vignettes, both Medicare and Medicaid face problems in the 1990s; this chapter will analyze proposed solutions to those problems. The underlying theme, however, will be the shortcomings of piecemeal attempts to achieve a needed restructuring of the U.S. health care system.

The Problem that Medicare and Medicaid Were Developed to Solve

The problem that Medicare and Medicaid were expected to address is actually a multilevel one. On the first level, it consists of the inability of poor people and many older individuals to pay for adequate health care. But on the second level, it can be described as the lack of affordable and accessible health care for Americans from many walks of life. Medicare and Medicaid were developed with an eye to tackling both problems. While both are programs aimed at specific populations, a number of the architects of the two policies also saw them as important first steps toward a national health care system.

The Health Needs of Poor and Older Americans

As we described in the chapter on Social Security, once members of our society have retired from work, they tend to have fewer financial resources. Although Social Security was well established by the time Medicare was developed in the 1960s, many older Americans still lived on limited means. Their health care needs had generally increased with age, so medical expenses often took larger proportions of their resources than when they were young. Many could not afford the higher premiums that private insurance companies charged for older people. Medicare was established to meet their needs. Poor families, especially those receiving public welfare, faced even greater difficulties in getting good health care. Because they could not afford private care, they were often dependent on the services of overcrowded, understaffed and ill-equipped public hospitals and clinics. Elderly people living below the poverty line were in a similar situation. Medicaid was the solution proposed for the health care needs of poor families and older people who were still poor after receiving Social Security and who could not afford to pay for the health services which Medicare did not cover.

The second problem that at least some policymakers expected Medicare and Medicaid to help solve was the lack of any broad-scale program to provide basic health care services for the average American. European countries such as England and Sweden had developed comprehensive national health care systems early in the 1900s, but the United States, with its stress on private approaches to health care provision, had failed to do so. Under Medicaid and Medicare, some policymakers saw the chance to establish the idea of health care as an entitlement, at least for the elderly, and to broaden government-financed health care for the poor.

The Medicare and Medicaid Legislation of 1965

Medicare and Medicaid reflect the dual approaches to social welfare policy in the United States. Medicare is a universal program available to anyone eligible for Social Security, including people of all ages with disabilities. Medicaid is a means-tested approach, designed initially with recipients of Aid to Families with Dependent Children in mind, but available also to the poor elderly. Each program has a different governmental home, with Medicare operating on a federal level and Medicaid based on a joint federal–state system of funding and administration. Medicare is a social insurance program, a broad entitlement like Social Security. Medicaid, while often referred to as an entitlement in current discussions of the welfare system, is not generally seen as an "earned right" in our society.

The Provisions of Medicare

Medicare is divided into two parts. Part A funds hospital services, is mandatory, and is financed by a payroll tax on employers and employees (the "Medicare Tax" you see on your pay stubs). Part A covers the first 60 days of hospitalization after a deductible of about $700. Beneficiaries make a copayment for each day beyond 60. Part A also covers short stays in nursing homes after release from the hospital. Part B is a voluntary program, funded in part by premiums paid by beneficiaries and in part by funds from general federal revenues. Premiums are currently $46 a month, and almost all those eligible for Medicare choose to enroll. Part B covers physicians' fees and other outpatient services. These fees are also subject to deductibles and copayments.[3]

It is important to note the gaps in Medicare, since these fuel part of the current interest in reforms. Medicare does not pay for prescription drugs, dental or eye examinations, or immunizations. It thus excludes treatments for many of the medical problems of older people. It also makes no provision for long-term care, such as extended stays in nursing homes. To cover gaps in Medicare coverage, better-off senior citizens buy supplementary "medigap" health insurance from private companies.[4]

The Provisions of Medicaid

Medicaid is the country's largest publicly financed program providing health care to low-income individuals. In 1996, the program covered thirty-six million people. It is paid for by the state and federal governments and administered by the states. Federal reimbursement for state payments ranges from 50 to 80 percent of the bill, depending on a state's per capita income. Federal guidelines require states to cover specific groups of people and benefits. Being poor is not an automatic qualification for Medicaid. Instead, the program covers categories such as AFDC recipients; people in other public assistance programs, including those who receive Supplemental Security Income (SSI); and the "medically indigent." The Medicaid category of "medically indigent" was intended to include those who do not qualify for public assistance but who lack sufficient income to cover necessary medical expenses. States differ in their definition of "medically indigent," with some states covering more non-welfare recipients than others. Medicaid currently covers only 62 percent of poor Americans.[5]

Now that AFDC has been phased out, all people eligible for aid under the new Temporary Assistance for Needy Families Block Grant (TANF) will be eligible for Medicaid. Their eligibility will not be contingent upon their actually receiving benefits through TANF, but they *will* have to complete a separate application for Medicaid. Since AFDC recipients were automatically enrolled in Medicaid, the new welfare legislation has thus made it a little more difficult to receive health care insurance.

The Medicaid population is diverse, including older Americans, people with disabilities, and children. The program mandates states to cover a broad range of services for its various beneficiaries. These services include: inpatient hospitalization; outpatient hospital visits; care from physicians and allied health professionals; laboratory work; nursing homes and home health care; early and periodic screening, diagnosis, and treatment (DPSDT) for children under 21; and family planning. States that meet the federal eligibility and benefit guidelines receive matching payments from the federal government based on the state's per capita income. States can also cover additional services and receive the federal match. These optional services include prescription drugs, hearing aids, intermediate care facilities for those with developmental disability, and the Psychiatric Rehabilitation Option, which provides for community services for the mentally ill.[6]

Currently, while adults and children in low-income families make up about three-fourths of Medicaid recipients, they account for less than a third of the program's spending. The elderly and those with disabilities account for about 60 percent of expenditures, due to their intensive use of acute and long-term care services. Nationally, Medicaid covers one-half of all nursing home bills. In 1994, the average payment for recipient served was $8,200 for persons aged 65 or older, $7,700 for people with disabilities, and $1,000 for children.[7]

Like the Medicare program, Medicaid has gaps. As we have noted, it does not cover all poor Americans. In addition, states vary widely in the types of services included in the Medicaid "package."

The History of Medicare and Medicaid

Both the Medicare and Medicaid programs were enacted during the War on Poverty in the 1960s. Their creation followed about five decades of efforts to develop some type of national health insurance in the United States. Health insurance first became a political issue in America in about 1913, after most of the major European countries had adopted some sort of governmental program. Reformers of the Progressive era hoped that the United States would also see fit to enact legislation that would provide compulsory insurance against illness. But, as we have seen in the chapter on Social Security, the American ideologies of self-help, limited government, and the superiority of market solutions to social and economic problems mitigated against passage of social insurance programs such as health insurance. In addition, physicians, particularly through the organized power of the American Medical Association, constituted a strong lobby against any reform that might weaken their professional autonomy or change the fee-for-service system through which they were paid.[8]

Reformers made other attempts to create national programs, coming closest under President Truman in the mid–1940s. Largely neglected for political reasons during the New Deal, the health insurance issue "finally moved into the center arena of national politics and received the unreserved support of an American president." Legislation was proposed in 1943 making national health insurance a part of Social Security; it was to be universal and comprehensive in its coverage. Yet as health historian Paul Starr notes, the idea of compulsory health insurance became embroiled in the ideological battles of the cold war. Opponents were able "to make 'socialized medicine' a symbolic issue in the growing crusade against communist influence in America." During committee hearings on the bill in the Senate, Senator Robert Taft of Ohio suggested that compulsory health insurance came right out of the Soviet constitution. And once again, the AMA, along with organizations like the American Hospital Association, opposed incursions into its territory. The Truman administration's health initiative was defeated.[9]

National health insurance was intended to deal with the problems of a predominantly private health system, in which the poor and working classes were often at a disadvantage. Lack of access to medical care, particularly for low-income and elderly Americans, had become an increasing problem as medical costs rose after World War II. The attempt to fashion a solution to the problem was unsuccessful during Truman's presidency, but the "discovery" of poverty and racism in the 1960s brought a new appreciation of the connections between poverty and poor health, and of the ways in which discrimination against minorities undercuts their access to adequate medical care. It was within this context that President Lyndon Johnson was able to bring about government health insurance for Social Security beneficiaries and certain categories of poor Americans as part of the War on Poverty.[10]

Even though concentration on poverty in the 1960s created a more conducive atmosphere for health care changes, we should note the limited parameters of health reform thinking in the United States. American policymakers have never really entertained the idea of a national system such as that of England and some other European countries, in which health care is delivered by doctors and other health care professionals paid by the government. American values and ideologies have instead dictated that any U.S. health care program would have to be limited to government-supported health insurance, and that even that insurance would need some limitations in order to receive widespread support.[11]

This is the type of policy compromise that was begun during the Kennedy administration and which culminated in the passage of Medicare under President Johnson. As historian Edward D. Berkowitz notes, the history of national health insurance in the United States shows a close alliance between the public and private sectors. While Social Security was the keystone of the U.S. version of the welfare state, health care was the product of modern welfare capitalism. Health care, in other words, "was a matter of vital concern to [private sector] professional providers, such as doctors and hospitals, and to organized consumers, such as private employers." These important stakeholders had to be mollified for health insurance to be passed.[12]

Lyndon Johnson benefited from the momentum for health insurance built up during the Eisenhower and Kennedy administrations. When Eisenhower was president, labor leaders and Social Security officials had begun to promote a Social Security–linked insurance initiative. This more limited social insurance approach, designed to benefit the aged, was much more acceptable to politicians than Truman's plan of the previous decade. Legislation for such an approach was initially blocked, however, by Congressman Wilbur Mills. Mills, a conservative Southern Democrat, was an important member of the House Ways and Means Committee, soon to become its chairman. He was a strong supporter of Social Security and feared that a social insurance–linked health care plan would weaken that program. Funding needs for health insurance might well lead to the use of general tax revenues, to constant raises in Social Security taxes, and to smaller increases in Social Security benefits. In a prophetic insight, Mills pictured Congress as constantly needing to feed the Medicare program with more funds.[13]

Health care insurance figured as an important issue in the 1960 Presidential campaign, with Kennedy giving it strong support. A limited bill for the elderly poor, which provided grants-in-aid to the states for a new category of public assistance called Medical Aid for the Elderly, was enacted in 1960 during the heat of the Presidential race. However, because of continuing opposition from the AMA and conservative members of Congress, no broad social insurance–linked legislation emerged during Kennedy's term of office or in Johnson's completion of that term.

During this time, however, federal policymakers, particularly officials in HEW and Social Security such as Wilbur Cohen and Robert Ball, continued to create the internal compromises that would make legislation possible. To woo Wilbur Mills, they reduced the proposal to its bare essentials, limiting its benefits to the elderly and assigning only a small administrative role to the federal government. Hospitals would be allowed to transact Medicare business through private intermediaries such as the Blue Cross rather than through a federal bureaucracy. Another concession, particularly appealing to the AMA, was the decision that Medicare would cover hospital bills but not physicians' bills. Doctor's services were excluded from the proposal in large part because the fear of a government-imposed medical fee schedule was one of the driving forces behind physicians' continued opposition to a national program. Cohen, Ball, and other creators of Medicare and Medicaid felt that this more limited legislation would lead to much more comprehensive national health insurance in the future.[14]

With the Democratic sweep of Congress in 1964, a full Medicare bill received the highest priority among Johnson's Great Society programs. By this time, Mills had conceded its inevitability. Out of the numerous proposals, including a voluntary program proposed by the Republicans, a composite bill finally emerged. In 1965, Congress passed Medicare and Medicaid, as Titles XVIII and XIX of the Social Security Act. In order to include both private and public approaches to health care, to meet the objections of doctors and hospitals, and to maintain the support of Social Security officials, the legislation offered three main provisions. These represented an "ingenious compromise fashioned by the administration and Wilbur Mills, powerful chairman of the House Ways and Means Committee." In the proposal, Medicaid, or subsidized medicine for welfare recipients, followed the traditional and generally accepted approach of government assistance for the "bona fide" poor. Medicare, or hospital insurance, was built on the social insurance principle of Social Security, with the American twist of being legitimate because it was "earned" by recipients. Part B of Medicare reflected the Republicans voluntary plan. This part of the program, which was optional and paid doctors' bills, fit with notions of self-reliance because beneficiaries paid extra to receive it.[15]

While it was the first major step toward national health insurance in the United States, the Medicare program actually made little change in existing systems of providing and paying for medical care, except "to pump more money into the systems and bid up costs." In a move that would have serious consequences for the rate of national health care expenditures, Medicare set no limits on fees charged by hospitals or physicians. Payments were made according to the provider's costs; the more a hospital spent, for example, the more money the government would pay out. Berkowitz and McQuaid call this "the American version of national health insurance: federal money and private control."[16]

Several important changes have been made in the Medicare and Medicaid programs since 1965. One was a response to the fact that the lack of any government limits on hospital and doctor bills helped fuel large rises in costs. Between 1970 and 1980, for example, federal Medicare expenditures increased from $15 to $38 billion. By the time of the Reagan administration, these outlays were increasing faster than the revenues from the Medicare payroll taxes. To remedy the situation, Reagan's advisors developed a system of national payment levels based on "diagnostic-related groups," or DRGs. The program was adopted in 1983. Under it, hospitals are paid an established fee for all patients with a particular diagnosis, no matter how long they stay in the hospital. A similar system for doctors was established in 1989. In addition, under the budget-cutting efforts of Reagan and Bush, the government increased the money that beneficiaries had to pay toward their medical care. For example, the amount of the Medicare deductible was more than doubled.

The Medicaid program was broadened in the 1970s, when coverage was expanded to include screening and treatment of low-income children and to help pregnant women. However, the same rising medical costs that plagued the Medicare program had also caught up with Medicaid by the 1980s. The federal government responded by cutting the federal share of Medicaid funding and offering incentives to states to reduce their rates of Medicaid growth. Ironically, a few years before, lawmakers had responded to reports of hospitals in inner city areas that were on the brink of financial collapse by adding a new line in the 1981 budget that dealt with Medicaid. This described a mechanism called "disproportionate share." The new mechanism allowed states, in setting their Medicaid rates, to "take into account the situation of hospitals which serve a disproportionate number of low-income patients with special needs." Such hospitals could then collect a higher rate of Medicaid reimbursement. Since the state payments were matched by federal monies, this meant the potential for higher costs. While the move extended health services to more needy people, and helped keep hospitals with a low-income clientele afloat, the accompanying rise in expenditures led the federal government to shut the practice down in 1994.[17]

As we will see, continued and rapid rises in expenditures in both Medicare and Medicaid have recently spearheaded a number of proposals for major changes. Before discussing these proposals, we will look briefly at various social, economic, and political aspects of the two programs, as well as at problems that the proposals attempt to address.

Social Analysis of Medicare and Medicaid

You can probably already recite the assumptions and values underlying Medicare and Medicaid, which combine a belief in a limited role for government in the social welfare arena with an emphasis on the importance of preserving the role of the private sector—in this case, hospitals and physicians—in dealing with illness and other social problems. While Americans are still not united in a belief that affordable health care is a right for all, to be guaranteed by government, they have generally accepted an approach that grants this right to people who are perceived as having earned it (retirees in the Social Security program) and to people whose difficulties do not seem to arise from any fault of their own, such as individuals with physical disabilities. Americans tend to be ambivalent about the legitimacy of government aid to poor people, single mothers, and to those whose disabilities relate to dependency on alcohol or drugs. There is probably a consensus that at least a minimum safety net should be preserved for these groups, but we differ among ourselves about the size and purpose of that safety net. In addition, all of these values and our attitudes toward social programs like health insurance are affected by the strength of the economy.

To turn to matters of effectiveness of these programs, how much is known about the effects of Medicare and Medicaid on national health indicators? Jansson points out that although medical researchers have attempted to evaluate the impact of Medicare on the health and health practices of elderly persons, conflicting findings and methodological issues have made evaluation difficult. It is difficult to structure a control group, since most older Americans participate in the program. Therefore, we can't really ascertain whether they would have been more or less healthy without it. The program does seem to have increased the utilization of physicians and hospitals by poor people, and without Medicare, it is likely that many more of the elderly would have been forced onto the welfare rolls.[18]

Assessing the effects of Medicaid is also a challenge. Through the program, the use of outpatient services by low-income people has increased dramatically, although poor people continue to use the emergency room for their care much more frequently than those who are better off. Medicaid appears to have had little impact on the existence of a two-track medical system. Middle class Americans generally use nonprofit or for-profit hospitals. Low-income Americans use public hospitals, inner city clinics, and "Medicaid mills," staffed by physicians who turn high-volume services into large profits. As in research on Medicare, not a lot is known about the extent to which Medicaid improves the health status of its clientele.[19]

Economic Analysis of Medicare and Medicaid

Currently, Medicare spending represents 11 percent of the federal budget. In addition, costs keep rising. In 1991, they increased a dramatic 14 percent, although now they have slowed to a still-uncomfortable 10 percent a year. The worst news is yet to come: in June, 1996, an official government report confirmed that because of slower rises in payroll deductions, the Medicare Trust Fund is projected to run out of money by 2001.[20]

What are the reasons for this potential crisis in Medicare funding? Is it caused primarily by the growth of the proportion of elderly in our country? True, spending on Social Security and Medicare, the large majority of whose recipients are older Americans, has now reached about 36 percent of the federal budget. Yet health care analysts like Vicente Navarro argue that the growth in Medicare expenditures is not primarily the result of an increase in the number of elderly. Navarro and others assert that the growth is caused largely by price inflation in hospital and medical services. As we have seen in the history of Medicare, the program was designed to allow physicians and hospitals to charge whatever they determined to be a reasonable fee and to add associated indirect costs. The decision to reimburse private providers in this way became a powerful force in driving costs upward. One analyst characterizes Medicare as "a windfall for health providers."[21]

This would suggest that the main economic difficulty with Medicare is that, unlike national health insurance schemes in other countries, it maintained the traditional fee-for-service system of reimbursement. Although the program carried out a slight adjustment to that system through the DRG mechanism in the mid 1980s, the rate of rise in expenditures dropped only temporarily. Internally, however, Medicare is an efficient operation, at least judged in terms of administrative overhead. Medicare's administrative expenses run about 3 percent or less a year, well under those of private health insurance plans, including MCOs.[22]

Major cuts are now being proposed to bail out Medicare. Yet the implications of these cuts illustrate the interconnectedness of all health care provision in the United States, and the ultimate futility of trying to make changes one program or one governmental level at a time. Cuts in Medicare will no doubt send more people to the Medicaid program, which is itself in economic difficulty. This will further swell the ranks of that program, which has also long been used by states to get help for their residents who don't qualify for SSI. The existence of Medicaid has also allowed states to cut back on some of their own state-funded health programs.

In addition, Congress's attempts to slow Medicare growth by reducing payments to providers have inadvertently exacerbated the problem of the explosion of the country's overall health costs. This is because doctors and hospitals squeezed by Medicare often respond to cuts by raising prices for private patients. This, in turn, raises costs for insurance companies. Any change in one part of the U.S. health care system thus reverberates in other parts of the system.[23]

Medicaid's expenditure picture looks similar to that of Medicare, except that costs are rising even faster. Although Medicaid constitutes a smaller portion of the federal budget, only 6 percent, its overall rise in expenditures has recently been averaging almost 18 percent annually. In fact, from its inception, Medicaid has witnessed double-digit growth in all years but one. Part of this cost, of course, is shared by state governments. As we noted in the chapter on managed care, the proportion of state budgets dedicated to Medicaid is booming, now constituting an average 20 percent of state spending.[24]

Again, a major question is why the rate of expenditures keeps accelerating. Part of the answer lies in the expansion of covered services and the moves of some states to create more liberal eligibility standards. The addition of programs like coverage of child health and services to pregnant women has increased costs. So have the attempts of some states to bring more of the "medically indigent" (people who are not receiving public assistance) into the program. Undoubtedly, however, a major and growing part of the cost can be attributed to payments to nursing homes for long term care for the elderly. In 1990, the cost of institutional care for the elderly and some younger people was an impressive 68 percent of total Medicaid spending, even though these two groups made up only a fifth of the Medicaid population.[25]

Lurking beneath all of these costs, of course, are the fees charged by doctors, hospitals, nursing homes, and other institutional treatment facilities, such as psychiatric hospitals. Inflation in these fees plays an important role in the continued growth of Medicaid spending. Furthermore, as we noted in the discussion of Medicare, any attempt to limit the payments made to Medicaid providers results in cost-shifting to other, generally private, payers. It is such cost shifting, a writer in the *Congressional Quarterly* points out, that "has led policymakers to conclude that the only way to get a handle on Medicare and Medicaid is to get control of the entire health system." Interestingly, this assessment was made in 1993, at the height of the national debate over "real" health care reform. The failure of that attempt at comprehensive reform has left us floundering in efforts to do the job piecemeal.[26]

Political Analysis of Medicare and Medicaid

Attempts at current reform of Medicare and Medicaid involve and affect a plethora of stakeholders. First of course, there are the hospitals, clinics, and long-term care institutions, such as nursing homes, that deliver services. Each of these groups maintains an organized lobby effort regarding Medicare and Medicaid. The nursing home industry, for example, can wield strong influence over decisions regarding Medicaid funding. At recent legislative hearings about Medicaid cuts in Louisiana, nursing home lobbyists and other representatives crowded the corridors and hearing rooms of the State Capitol. This occurs because Medicaid is the largest financier of nursing homes. Even though the program's reimbursement rates are relatively low, most nursing homes would not be able to operate without Medicaid money.[27]

We've also talked a lot in this chapter about the health professionals who are reimbursed for care. They include, of course, physicians, who within their ranks contain a number of specific categories of stakeholders: psychiatrists, general practitioners, specialists, and others. Specialists have noted strong concern about their situation in any Medicare or Medicaid changes, since many of the proposals for reform rely on some type of managed care. They are well aware that MCOs tend to favor general practitioners over the more expensive medical specialists.

The role of physicians in the cost structure of Medicare and Medicaid has been well publicized. To be fair, we should note here that a number of physicians testify that they are unable to give adequate care to Medicaid or Medicare clients, due to low levels of reimbursement.

In addition to physicians, professionals who receive program reimbursement themselves, or who work within entities that do, include nurses, psychologists, physical therapists, pharmacists, and social workers. Social workers are found in all sorts of medical and health settings that receive Medicare and Medicaid funding. These include hospitals, mental health clinics, child and family counseling agencies, private practice groups, and nursing homes. Social workers are also quite likely to be employed in settings that work with clients who are on Medicaid, whether or not the agency itself delivers reimbursable services.

In their roles as frontline workers and supervisors, social workers see the effects of the present system on clients and the impact of any changes. They have an ethical obligation to advocate for clients and client groups who are not receiving appropriate and effective services. Such advocacy can take place both within agencies and in the political arena (the chapter on mental health has detailed some of the ways in which this can be done). Social workers can also make a valuable contribution to the policymaking process, since they can testify at first hand about client needs and are skilled in looking at the whole picture when evaluating policies that relate to people's health. Social workers, in their roles as case managers and referral persons, need to know about how Medicare and Medicaid operate. Those who work with the elderly, for example, need to understand what Medicare will and won't cover as they make referrals for their clients.

The National Association of Social Workers is the major professional organization for the field. The association is located in Washington, DC, and maintains a variety of lobbying efforts in Congress and the Executive Branch. The NASW often joins with other social work groups, such as the Council on Social

Work Education and the associations of social work deans and of undergraduate program directors, in its lobbying efforts. The letter in Figure 10.1 is an example of the response to lobbying work done by the dean of a school of social work as part of a collective effort to affect legislation regarding appropriations to health and social welfare programs.

Beneficiaries constitute another large group of stakeholders. Some types of beneficiaries carry more weight than others. The elderly, for example, are much less likely than people receiving public welfare to be stigmatized by politicians and the public for receiving aid. They have one of the largest and most powerful lobby organizations, the American Association of Retired People (AARP). Despite attempts by Speaker of the House Newt Gingrich first to muzzle, and then to coopt the AARP with various compromises, the association has maintained a fairly consistent effort to oppose Medicare and Medicaid cuts and some of the other proposals that they see as disadvantaging the elderly.

People receiving public welfare are more frequently stigmatized by the public. Particularly during this era of concern over budget deficits, they present a tempting scapegoat to politicians, radio talk show hosts, and conservative columnists. (Ironically, welfare recipients receive a relatively small proportion of Medicaid money.) Unfortunately, those receiving public assistance are not a cohesive and well-organized group. They have no equivalent of the AARP to speak for them, though a variety of smaller advocacy groups do seek to represent their concerns. These include the Children's Defense Fund, the many mental health advocacy groups, the Association for Retarded Citizens, and organizations of welfare clients. There are also groups, often working on the local level, that attempt to speak for all people who are affected by Medicaid and Medicare. The Louisiana Health Campaign is a good example of such a group. It has held frequent press conferences to publicize the impact of the state's proposed Medicaid cutbacks on the many client groups involved. (See Figure 10.2.)

Administrators in state Medicaid offices and departments of health are vitally involved in any change to the system, as are federal officials in the Social Security Administration. State legislators and governors are the people who must make the hard decisions about how to deal with what seem like uncontrollable Medicaid increases. These decisions involve balancing the interests of many groups, and finding a way to fund health care while maintaining adequate resources for education and other state needs. The National Governors' Conference has played an important role in recent debates about Medicaid, making its own proposals for change. Finally, state elected officials must answer to the largest stakeholder group of all—taxpayers.[28]

There is one set of stakeholders whose members are drawn from the ranks of other groups. It includes people who are hospital and clinic administrators and staff, health care professionals, business investors, and state-appointed and elected officials. The interest that binds these particular individuals

THE WHITE HOUSE

WASHINGTON

June 20, 1996

Kenneth I. Millar, Ph.D.
Dean
School of Social Work
Louisiana State University and
   Agriculture and Mechanical College
311 Huey P. Long Field House
Baton Rouge, Louisiana 70803

Dear Ken:

Thank you so much for your letter regarding the interests and concerns of social work practitioners and educators. I am glad to know that you have met with members of my staff, and I am sorry that I was unable to respond sooner.

I was pleased to sign the Omnibus Consolidated Rescissions and Appropriations Act of 1996, which preserved many of the important investments that you wrote about. This legislation will not only keep the deficit on the downward path we started in 1993, but it will also uphold America's most basic values by honoring our national commitment to the elderly, children, and to the future. We are protecting Medicare and Medicaid, strengthening our fight against crime, investing in education, and continuing our protection of the environment.

I share your belief that the federal government must continue to play a central role in responding to problems such as AIDS, child abuse, and teenage pregnancy. Be assured that in each of these crucial areas, I have continued to press for further investment and to seek innovative solutions.

I appreciate your continued involvement in this important effort.

Sincerely,

Bill Clinton

FIGURE 10.1   Letter from the President

FIGURE 10.2   State Newsletter

Medicaid Update   June 21, 1996

Louisiana Health Care Campaign

sicu100uflcio

LOUISIANA GOES OVERBOARD WITH MEDICAID CUTS

As you probably already know, the bite of some of the state's most severe Medicaid cuts will soon be felt by thousands of Louisiana residents. According to DHH, more than 15,000 recipients are (were) eligible for Medicaid under "optional" eligibility categories. People who qualified for Medicaid under optional categories are scheduled to be terminated as of July 1, 1996. The exception appears to be people who currently qualify as medically needy, including some 400–500 elderly nursing home residents. In effect, the State is saying that there isn't enough room in the Medicaid lifeboat, so they're throwing you overboard.

As the state throws these people over the side, the ranks of the state's already high number of uninsured will swell by another 15,000 people. Unfortunately, doing so does not reduce illness or disability, or the expense of providing care when people show up in the hospital emergency rooms. The action simply shifts those costs outside of the responsibility of the Medicaid program.

WHAT CAN WE DO?

If we hope to reverse these cuts in the short run or in the long run, we must make certain that they do not go into effect without a lot of noise, and without legislators, DHH officials, and the public understanding very clearly how much these budget cuts hurt Louisiana families. There has already been news coverage about people in the Medically Needy program being terminated. It is no accident that DHH's response has been to try to find money to keep the program going for another year.

The Louisiana Health Care Campaign, the DD Council, and many other groups are working to fight these and further cuts as effectively as possible, but we need your help.

1) If you are getting calls from people whose Medicaid coverage is being taken away, we need to know about it.
- The LHCC office will be checking with many of you to find out more about the people who are being hurt by these cuts. We will be looking for more information about these people: how many have you heard from, what problems will be caused, are they willing to tell their story to our friends with the news media, are they people who the average newspaper reader or TV viewer might identify or empathize with?

2) Work with us to make certain people's stories are told: These are some of our ideas and suggestions:
- Work with us to get news coverage and stories told in the news media on July 1st, the first day the cuts go into effect. We will be working on both TV and on print news.

Continued

FIGURE 10.2 *Continued*

- Work with the LHCC to put together some kind of news event on July 1, to compliment the personal stories. In Baton Rouge, we are thinking about a news event focusing on how the state is pushing people overboard, out of the lifeboat and something to throw overboard to dramatize the harm being done.

3) Keep in mind that everything we do to help the public better understand the harm being done now will help us down the road as we approach the next two pivotal discussions about the fate of people who depend on Medicaid:

- Fall elections, in which the Medicaid budget will be a major topic of discussion. Block grants, budget cuts, and other changes that further shred the safety net will be a big part of the debate. Do we want the discussion to be about how to save money, or how to protect Louisiana families and citizens?
- Next year's Medicaid budget, where there is already talk about having to make another $300–400 million in cuts. The better people understand the problems caused by this year's cutbacks, the better protection we have against even more damage being done next year.

P.O. Box 2228 ✦ Baton Rouge, LA ✦ 70821-2228 ✦ (504)383-8518

---

together is fraud. Unfortunately, Medicare and especially Medicaid—like all large and complex systems that involve money—have relatively few controls, are hard to police, and invite abuse. While fraudulent operators no doubt represent a small portion of providers and government officials, the amount of money they drain from the system makes the level of "cheating" by Medicaid clients pale by comparison. These are stakeholders with a negative mission: keep the flaws and loopholes in the system that allow the perpetration of fraud.

The *New Orleans Times Picayune* recently published an exposé of the misuse of Medicaid money in Louisiana. In its opening paragraph, a special report on "Medicaid Madness" warns the reader:

> *It's a nightmare scenario: with the connivance of state bureaucrats, public spending on private psychiatric hospitalization for the poor explodes 9,000 percent in five years. A new breed of politically connected, for-profit hospitals steps in and earns millions of dollars, as much as 10 times the national average. Many deliver skimpy care that sometimes makes the patients worse. And most of the beds the new hospitals provide weren't needed in the first place.*[29]

Among the many examples that the report describes is the story of a small rural hospital facility that was going unused until a former official in a high elective office leased it. He rented the building on a monthly basis, and with a group of other investors set up a psychiatric hospital. Interestingly, the hospital quickly began making money, to the tune of a profit of almost $1 million in the first year. The vehicle for this impressive accumulation of wealth was Medicaid.

The hospital and similar institutions in Louisiana were able to take advantage of loopholes, special rules, and lax oversight created by the governor of the state. Many of the hospitals were also able to bill Medicaid at a legally higher rate by gaining disproportionate share status. All of these measures "cleared the way for millions of dollars of taxpayer money to flow to a new cadre of psychiatric hospital owners." In this particular case, much of the profit came through large Medicaid reimbursements for what appears to have been low-cost care. A 1994 inspection showed that the hospital had far too few professional personnel; for example, one psychiatrist was responsible for 98 patients, more than twice what mental health experts recommend.[30]

All in all, psychiatric facilities like these received millions of dollars from taxpayers for treating the poor. The growth in these hospitals is one reason why the state's Medicaid program "skyrocketed from $1.1 billion in 1989 to more than $4 billion in 1994, most of it in federal dollars."[31]

While we have presented only the economic disaster caused by Medicaid fraud, it is important to note the human side of its existence. As social workers and others have observed, fraud often involves the denial of good mental health and health services to clients. As we described in one of the opening vignettes, such malpractice in the places where they work constitutes an ethical challenge for social workers and other professionals. To help deal with the problem, some states have now established "Medicaid fraud hotlines" where abuses can be reported.

As the country debates solutions to the Medicare and Medicaid "problem," the most dramatic and visible stakeholders are members of Congress and the President. The Republican-controlled House of Representatives in the 196th Congress, following the precepts of the party's Contract with America, made deficit reduction and tax raises the foundation of its work. Ardent new conservative Representatives joined in, and sometimes surpassed, Speaker Gingrich's efforts to "get America going again." These efforts were aimed at slashing the deficit and balancing the budget by 2002, promoting business growth, creating a much leaner federal government, and legislating tax cuts. In order to fund tax cuts and to reduce the deficit, Congress had to find large areas of spending that they could cut. This invariably meant concentrating on the huge entitlement programs—Social Security, Medicare, and Medicaid. Early on in this campaign, political pressures led Congress to back away from changes in Social Security, just as President Reagan had been forced to do a decade earlier. This left the Medicare and Medicaid programs as the main source for budget cuts and reforms.

The Senate, also with a Republican majority, followed the House's general program, but in a more temperate way. A more deliberative and slow-moving body, the Senate generally softened some of the cuts and changes proposed by the House. There was a certain dissonance between the goals and approaches of Speaker Gingrich and then-Leader of the Senate Bob Dole. When Presidential vetoes of Republican budget measures caused a government shutdown in Fall of 1995, Dole was ready to work out a compromise to get the government back to work. Gingrich and hardliners in the House were at first prepared to sit the crisis out. But President Clinton's refusal to give way, and public backlash against the government shutdowns (which were blamed largely on the Republican-led Congress) eventually led to compromises and to a slowing of efforts to slash social spending and curtail "big government."

These efforts have also been diluted by Presidential vetoes. While Democrats have opposed the size of budget cuts sought by Republicans, they rarely have had the votes to defeat the majority party's measures. The spotlight has been largely on the President, who has played the role of "protector" of entitlements and other social spending. While he has proposed his own budget reductions, these have been more modest and cast within a longer timeframe. Although he signed a welfare reform bill that was much closer to Republican ideas about welfare than to those of most Democrats, the President held firm against major limits on Medicare and Medicaid's scope and funding.

These are the most visible players, then, in the national drama of deficit reduction, tax cuts, and health program reforms. The 1996 Presidential campaign temporarily diverted attempts to deal with critical health care issues, and dealt instead with charges and countercharges about which party would destroy Medicare. But the problems of keeping Medicare and Medicaid solvent have not gone away, and will have to be dealt with in the next several years.

Proposals for Reform

Proposals for changes in Medicare and Medicaid are complex, and the debates surrounding them have taken place in a volatile political environment. It would take a much lengthier policy analysis to detail the many moves and counter moves on the part of Democratic and Republican members of Congress, the Clinton administration, and state governors. What follows, then, is a brief description of the details and the pros and cons of the various suggestions for reform.

The one proposal that has been adopted by both parties, although at different levels, has been the reduction of funding for Medicare and Medicaid. The details of both the Republican and the Democratic versions of Medicare cuts have changed in the political process. Due to strong opposition to reductions from older Americans and others, and the veto of their first $279 billion reduction plan by President Clinton during his first administration, the Republicans have scaled back to a proposed $158 billion cut over a six-year period. This would be accomplished mainly through paying less to doctors and hospitals and by facilitating seniors' use of managed care plans. Originally, the Republicans had planned to increase premiums in Part B of Medicare and to raise deductibles. This met with a fire storm of protest from the elderly, which was strongly expressed by the AARP.[32]

Clinton has proposed a savings of $124 billion in Medicare spending. He, too, is relying largely on reductions in payments to providers. "Philosophically," writes Colette Fraley in the *Congressional Quarterly,* "the divide is wide." Republicans want older Americans to choose the coverage they can afford and to make greater use of private MCOs. This will "let market competition help control costs. Clinton's...concept of health care is to guarantee coverage for everyone and use the government to ensure quality and availability."[33]

Following a market approach, the Republicans have proposed another reform, the introduction of special medical savings accounts. While not a direct part of Medicare reform, these accounts would theoretically enable people to save money to cover more of their own medical costs, thus reducing the amount needed for federal funding of health care insurance. The special accounts would allow individuals enrolling in high-deductible health insurance plans to accrue tax deductible savings that would be used solely for medical expenses.[34]

As can be expected, there has been strong debate over the pros and cons of these approaches to changing Medicare. Seizing on the Republicans' intention to cut taxes and to reduce the deficit in just six years, Democrats argue that they are balancing the budget and granting tax breaks to the rich "on the backs of the elderly." Republicans point to the impending bankruptcy in Medicare and the need to take strong and immediate action. Beneficiaries and their advocates fear that slowing Medicare growth will of necessity bring reductions in medical coverage. Providers contend that they will have even more difficulty meeting people's health care needs with lower Medicare fees.

The idea of greater use of managed care by seniors and the notion of special savings accounts have also been defended and attacked. Republicans see these measures as in keeping with a market approach to solving problems. Both provide consumer choice. MCOs work on sound business principles, and savings accounts would encourage individuals to be more frugal in making decisions about medical care. Democrats and other opponents argue that medical savings accounts would favor the "healthy and wealthy" while adversely affecting the poor and the sick. Healthy people would choose to join the savings program, while the ill and those with more limited means would remain in traditional health care. Older Americans may be particularly wary of pressure to join MCOs, due to their desire to maintain the choice of a doctor who knows them and understands their needs. In addition, experts are concerned that aggressive sales tactics and strong profit motives may turn the elderly into targets of abuse.[35]

The Republicans have also made reductions in Medicaid spending a priority. They have proposed to cut some $170 billion from the Medicaid budget by capping the program's growth over the next seven years. These have been presented not as out-and-out program cuts, but as savings through letting the program grow more slowly. Again due to political pressure, the initial amount has been pared down to $85 billion. The President has similarly proposed cuts in spending, setting a target of $59 billion. Clinton would get these savings by capping the amount spent for each beneficiary, reducing hospital payments, and giving states more flexibility in designing their Medicaid programs. Republicans propose instead to cap a state's total Medicaid spending and give states much greater leeway in determining whom to cover.[36]

The Republican notion of a block grant to states would bring about a major change in the Medicaid system. Instead of the federal oversight and required categories of beneficiaries and coverage, states would have the freedom to spend this money as they wished. Many of the governors argue that this would allow them to approach health care provision in much more innovative ways, free from restrictive federal regulations. A number of governors, however, would be willing to accept federal requirements for basic coverage of the health needs of low-income people.[37]

On the other hand, say opponents, the health block grant approach would not allow for increases in the need for health coverage for low-income people, caused, for example, by a state's population growth or a sudden rise in unemployment. Critics also note that the block grant's flexibility would mean that the needs of certain vulnerable groups might not be met; children with disabilities, for example, would no longer be guaranteed treatment. Clinton's counterproposal has been to ease the requirements for Medicaid waivers. As discussed in Chapter 9, this allows states to experiment with their Medicaid programs, converting them into managed care systems, for example. The President and Congressional Democrats have also sponsored a capped entitlement, which would guarantee certain categories of beneficiaries coverage of a basic set of health services, but with a ceiling on the federal government's total spending for Medicaid.[38]

Conclusion

Although Republicans and Democrats differ on a variety of proposals to reform Medicare and Medicaid, their positions on reductions in spending are not that far apart. Both the Republican Congress and the President have embraced the notion that a major way to cut rising health costs is to rein in the growth of these two programs. Yet piecemeal changes in specific programs will not be enough to solve America's health care problems. As we have noted, reductions in one program may send recipients scrambling to another; savings in one area can mean higher costs in a different part of the health care arena. Since the problems in the system are comprehensive ones, the solutions must also be broad.

During the great debate on health care reform several years ago, an argument was made that the market is not the best mechanism for organizing the nation's health system. A decentralized and competitive approach may not be an effective framework for constructing a coherent system that will deal with the health care needs of a variety of people, and which will offer a basic level of health care services to all Americans.

At the moment, suggestions of a broader role for government in planning and monitoring the nation's health care system are politically unfeasible. Yet the challenge of creating an effective and efficient approach to national health insurance remains a critical item on the national agenda.

Notes

1. Bruce Alpert, "Medicare Worries Seniors," *New Orleans Times Picayune* (22 September 1995) sec. A, p. 1.

2. Leah K. Glasheen, "N.Y.'s Poor Brace for the Budget Axe," *AARP Bulletin* 36 (April 1995) p. 17.

3. Bruce S. Jansson, *The Reluctant Welfare State: A History of American Social Welfare Policies,* 3rd ed. (Pacific Grove, CA: Brooks\Cole, 1997) p. 216; *Annual Statistical Supplement to the Social Security Bulletin 1995* (Washington, DC: U.S. Department of Health and Human Services, Social Security Administration, 1995) p. 320.

4. B. Guy Peters, *American Public Policy: Promise and Performance,* 2nd ed. (Chatham, NJ: Chatham House Publishers, 1986) pp. 191–192.

5. "Medicaid Facts," The Kaiser Commission on the Future of Medicaid (December 1995).

6. "Medicaid Facts"

7. "Medicaid Facts" p. 338.

8. Paul Starr, *The Social Transformation of American Medicine* (NY: Basic Books, 1982) pp. 236–249; Martha Derthick, *Policymaking for Social Security* (Washington, DC: The Brookings Institute, 1979) p. 316.

9. Starr, *Social Transformation of American Medicine,* pp. 280–286.

10. Philip R. Popple and Leslie Leighninger, *Social Work, Social Welfare, and American Society,* 3rd ed. (Boston: Allyn and Bacon, 1996) pp. 422–423.

11. Edward D. Berkowitz and Kim McQuaid, *Creating the Welfare State: The Political Economy of 20th-Century Reform,* rev. ed. (Lawrence, KS: University of Kansas Press, 1992) p. 211.

12. Berkowitz and McQuaid, *Creating the Welfare State,* 211.

13. Derthick, *Policymaking for Social Security,* pp. 321–328; Edward D. Berkowitz, *America's Welfare State: From Roosevelt to Reagan* (Baltimore: Johns Hopkins University Press, 1991) p. 171.

14. Starr, *The Social Transformation of American Medicine,* p. 369; Berkowitz, *America's Welfare State: From Roosevelt to Reagan,* pp. 168, 171–172.

15. Jansson, *The Reluctant Welfare State,* p. 216; Berkowitz and McQuaid, *Creating the Welfare State,* p. 213.

16. Berkowitz and McQuaid, *Creating the Welfare State,* pp. 213–214.

17. Chris Adams, "Medicaid Madness," *Times-Picayune* (13 August 1995) sec. A, p. 13.

18. Jansson, *The Reluctant Welfare State,* p. 216.

19. Jansson, *The Reluctant Welfare State,* pp. 217–218.

20. U.S. Bureau of the Census, *Statistical Abstract of the United States: 1996,* 116th ed. (Washington, DC: 1996) p. 332; David E. Rosenbaum, "Gloomy Forecast Touches off Feud on Medicare Fund," *New York Times* (6 June 1996) sec. A, p. 1.

21. Vincente Navarro, *The Politics of Health Policy: The U.S. Reforms, 1980-1994* (Cambridge, MA: Blackwell, 1994) p. 40; David Stoesz, *Small Change: Domestic Policy Under the Clinton Presidency* (White Plains, NY: Longman, 1996) pp. 31–32.

22. Robert Pear, "Medicare Prognosis: Unwieldy Growth Fueled by More Fees and Beneficiaries," *New York Times* (10 March 1991) sec. E, p. 4.

23. Julie Rovner, "A Job for the Deficit Bomb Squad...Defusing Exploding Health-Care Costs," *Congressional Quarterly* (2 January 1993) pp. 28–29.

24. Colette Fraley, "The Blossoming of Medicaid," *Congressional Quarterly* (10 June 1995) p. 1638.

25. Rovner, "A Job for the Deficit Bomb Squad," p. 28.

26. Rovner, "A Job for the Deficit Bomb Squad," p. 29.

27. "Who Pays for Nursing Homes?" *Consumer Reports* (September 1995) pp. 591–593.

28. "States Grabbing the Rope in Medicaid 'Tug of War,'" *USA Today* (3 November 1995) sec. A, p. 4.

29. Adams, "Medicaid Madness," p. 1.

30. Adams, "Medicaid Madness," pp. 1, 12–13.

31. Adams, "Medicaid Madness," p. 13.

32. Steve Langdon, "Gloomy Medicare Report Causes Partisan Finger-Pointing," *Congressional Quarterly* (8 June 1996) p. 1603; "States Grabbing the Rope in Medicaid 'Tug of War'"; Colette Fraley, "GOP Scores on Medicare, But Foes Aren't Done," *Congressional Quarterly* (18 November 1995) p. 3536; Robert P. Hey, "Cuts Loom for Medicare Enrollees," *AARP Bulletin* 36 (June 1995) pp. 1, 15; Richard W. Stevenson, "Sharp Differences and Compromise are Likely on Budget," *New York Times* (12 January 1997) p. 11.

33. Colette Fraley, "Clinton, GOP are Far Apart as Medicare Talks Begin," *Congressional Quarterly* (2 December 1995) p. 3664; Stevenson, "Sharp Differences and Compromise are Likely on Budget."

34. Robert P. Hey, "Who Gets a Ride on the MSA?" *AARP Bulletin* 37 (June 1996) pp. 4–5.

35. Fraley, "Clinton, GOP Are Far Apart," p. 3664; Hey, "Who Gets a Ride on the MSA?"; Robert Kuttner, "The Great HMO Hope," *Washington Post National Weekly Edition* (10–16 April 1995) p. 5; Ellyn E. Spragins, "Simon Says, Join Us!" *Newsweek* (19 July 1995) pp. 55–58.

36. Fraley, "Medicaid Differences Portend Tough Budget Talks Ahead," p. 3663.

37. Colette Fraley, "Governors Looking for the Key to Open Way for Medicaid," *Congressional Quarterly* (16 December 1995) p. 3813.

38. "Medicaid Reform Stalls," *Action Alert,* Bazelon Center for Mental Health Law (15 February 1996).

Chapter 11

Child Welfare: Family Preservation Policy

Life for many children in America is far more difficult than it should be. The Children's Defense Fund has gathered data indicating that on an average day in this country, 1,849 children are abused or neglected, 3,288 children run away, 6 teenagers commit suicide, 30 teenagers are wounded by guns, 10 children die from gunshot wounds, 13,500 children take a gun to school, 211 children are arrested for drug abuse, 437 children are arrested for drinking and driving, and 1,629 children are in adult jails.[1] To these figures could be added the millions of children who each day suffer under conditions of extreme poverty or are afflicted by severe mental or behavioral disorders. Our society's concern for these problems is expressed in a formal service delivery system known as child welfare. This system is comprised of government and private agencies that are given the responsibility to:

- protect and promote the well-being of all children
- support families and seek to prevent problems that may result in neglect, abuse, and exploitation
- promote family stability by assessing and building on family strengths while addressing needs
- support the full array of out-of-home care services for children who require them
- take responsibility for addressing social conditions that negatively affect children and families, such as inadequate housing, poverty, chemical dependence, and lack of access to health care
- support the strengths of families whenever possible
- intervene when necessary to ensure the safety and well-being of children[2]

Although child welfare has a very broad mandate, as a field of social work and of social welfare policy it has in recent decades focused more and more on the problems of child neglect and, even more so, abuse, providing what are known as child protective services. This narrowing of focus has been driven by two developments. The first is a rapidly increasing awareness among the general populace of the problem of child abuse, resulting in an ever-more efficient system for reporting abuse, and laws in every state mandating that professionals who deal with children report suspicions of abuse. The result of this is that abuse reports have increased from 9,563 in 1967 to nearly 3,000,000 in 1992.[3] The other development contributing to the narrowing of focus is that funding for child welfare has not increased fast enough to allow agencies to deal with the massive increase in reports while still attending to broader child welfare concerns. Thus, broader concerns such as day care and child health have been pushed aside while agencies spend an ever-increasing proportion of their resources on child protection.

It is an old truism that every solution contains within it the seeds of a new problem. This has proven to be true in child protective services. One of the obvious ways to deal with a child in a home situation perceived to be dangerous is to move the child from the home into substitute care. After the child is placed the home can be assessed and, if there is hope for remediation, services can be delivered to strengthen the family with the child eventually being returned home. Predictably, as the number of reports of child abuse and neglect skyrocketed, the number of children in foster care kept pace. Ironically, as the number of children needing foster care has increased, the number of licensed foster homes has decreased. Between 1985 and 1990, the number of children in foster care increased by 47 percent while the number of foster homes decreased by 27 percent.[4]

At the same time the child welfare system is being subjected to increasing pressure to protect abused and neglected children, it is also being severely criticized for breaking up families and then not providing services to rebuild them. The child welfare system has been criticized for being overzealous, not following due process, and trampling on the rights of parents accused of abuse and neglect of their children. A political action group has been formed, VOCAL (Victims of Child Abuse Laws) to champion the cause of parents involved in the child welfare system.[5] While many of these critics greatly overstate their case, it is true that the system deserves criticism for not putting enough effort into helping families resolve problems once a child has been removed. Child welfare researchers have found that once a child is removed from the biological parents, the amount of clinical services provided to the child and parents actually declines.[6]

The combination of these factors, as well as others that will be discussed later in this chapter, has lead to great pressure on the child welfare system to reduce the number of children placed in foster care. One possible remedy, enthusiastically embraced by almost all stakeholders in the system, is an approach known as family preservation. This approach is based on the belief that in many cases where placement appears to be imminent, it is possible to prevent placement by the provision of intense services delivered in the child's home over a brief, time-limited period. Elizabeth Tracy lists five primary goals of family preservation services:

- to allow children to remain safely in their own homes
- to maintain and strengthen family bonds
- to stabilize the crisis situation that precipitated the need for placement
- to increase the family's coping skills and competencies
- to facilitate the family's use of appropriate formal and informal helping resources[7]

Family preservation services begin, as do most child welfare interventions, with a child being referred to an agency as being in danger of serious harm. A social worker investigates the complaint and, if the complaint is confirmed, decides if the family is a good candidate for family preservation services. For the family to be considered an appropriate case for family preservation services the child must be at risk of placement, but the social worker must be convinced that the child can remain safely in his or her own home if intensive services are provided. Depending on the model of family preservation being applied, the family is given services for periods ranging from four to six weeks in the most intensive, to three months or longer in the less intensive models. The social workers providing services have small caseloads and work with each family for many hours each week, sometimes twenty or more. After the provision of the brief, intensive, services, the agency withdraws to a supervisory role and leaves the family to function—presumably with a greatly increased problem solving capacity.

The several models of family preservation differ in length and intensity of service and also in psychosocial theory base. The original model, called Homebuilders, provides the shortest and most intense services. In this model, social workers carry only two cases at a time, spend as many as twenty hours per week with each case, are available twenty-four hours a day, and generally complete services within four to six weeks. This approach is based on cognitive–behavioral

FIGURE 11.1   Service Delivery Contrasts

Traditional Social Services	Family Preservation Services
Services in office	Services in client's home
Waiting list	Immediate response
50-minute hour	As long as session is needed
Weekly or less	Frequent—often daily
Business-only hours	7 days a week, 24 hours a day
Selective intake	Accept almost all cases
Worker defines solutions	Family selects solutions
Indefinite duration	Predetermined length
Long-term, often years	Short-term, four to six seeks
Large caseloads, 12 to 50	Small caseloads, 2 to 3
Focus on individual	Focus on family system
Concentrate on immediate symptom	Concentrate on underlying skills and interactions
Soft services only	Blend of hard and soft services
No special use of crisis	Use crisis as teachable moment
Solve problem for client	Help client solve own problem

Source: *For Children's Sake: The Promise of Family Preservation,* by Joan Barthel. Published by the Edna McConnell Clark Foundation.

theory and relies heavily on devices such as behavioral checklists. The Home-builders approach also focuses on concrete services. Another approach is based on structural family therapy, utilizes family systems theory, and emphasizes the relationship between the family and other systems. Special attention is given to improving the relations of the family with the community. In this model, social workers have somewhat larger caseloads and work with each family over a longer period of time, generally three to twelve months. Other variations of family preservation utilize psychodynamic and behavioral approaches and involve longer periods of contact with families.[8]

Since its inception in 1974 with the original Homebuilders program, family preservation has grown in popularity until it can now be said to be the policy of choice for dealing with child abuse and neglect. Some form of family preservation service is now in place in every state of the Union. The services are provided by both public and private agencies, generally in some form of partnership. The approach is specified in laws at both the federal and state level and in the policies of public and private agencies. The approach is probably undergoing the most thorough evaluation of any social welfare innovation in history; it has become so popular that a backlash is developing against it. We will now turn to a detailed discussion of the development of child protective services and the growth and current dominance of family preservation as the service of choice.

Historical Analysis

If a time machine were to transport someone from the early nineteenth century into the present age, they would find child protective services almost as baffling as all of our technological marvels. Although few people during this earlier age would have approved of unnecessary cruelty or neglect towards children, the notion of children as a group with the right to protection, and of the government as having the right to provide such protection, was entirely foreign to the thinking of the era. By the end of the nineteenth century, thinking on this matter had undergone a remarkable transformation. Many people, particularly those in the middle and upper classes, had begun to firmly believe in the right of children to a certain level of care and the right of government to step in and enforce the provision of adequate care in cases where parents were judged to be unable, or unwilling, to provide such care.

Two general developments during the nineteenth century account for the changing attitude toward the rights of children to protection and of government to provide it. The first is that during this century the position of children in the economy changed radically, and along with this the method of valuing children. During the early years of the century children had direct economic worth and their rights and value were judged accordingly. Viviana Zelizer in her book *Pricing the Priceless Child* documents how during the nineteenth century the concept of the "useful" child who made a valuable contribution to the family economy gradually evolved into the "useless" child of the twentieth century who is economically worthless, in fact very costly, to the family, but is considered to be emotionally priceless. The reasons for this transformation were many, including the decline in useful tasks that could be performed by children in a maturing industrial economy, the decline in birth and death rates, and the rise of the compassionate family. Because of this changed concept of the value of children, society began to view them as worthy of protection.[9]

The second general factor that accounts for the emergence of child protection at the end on the nineteenth century is, in fact, one result of the first. Stemming from the changed conception of the value of children, there evolved a change in the common law interpretation of children's and women's rights. Before the nineteenth century the relationship between parents and children in this country generally followed English common law. Under the law at this time children's rights were considered to be relatively unimportant. Likewise, mothers were entitled to "no power but only reverence and respect." The father, in contrast, was given practically absolute control over all matters pertaining to his wife and children. Although fathers were expected to protect and care for their children, the duty was "merely a moral obligation creating no civil liability." In other words, if a father was cruel or neglectful toward his children society would not approve, but was powerless to intervene. In the second half of the nineteenth century the system of family law began to change. Two new legal principles emerged as dominant. One was the recognition of equal rights between mother and father, with the mother's rights, at least in regard to children, often being given preference. The second was the recognition by the legal system of children as being of paramount importance, vital to the future of society, and therefore as appropriate objects of the court's protection.[10]

The Child Rescue Movement

By the second half of the nineteenth century the stage was set for outside intervention into family life for the purpose of protecting children. An incident in New York City in 1873 served to ignite what has come to be called the child rescue movement. Henry Bergh was a prominent philanthropist who had directed his efforts toward the protection of animals and, for this purpose, had in 1866 founded the New York Society for the Prevention of Cruelty to Animals. It was to Bergh and his society that charity worker Etta Wheeler turned with her concern about the treatment of Mary Ellen Wilson, an eight-year-old girl who was being abused and neglected by her stepparents. Bergh directed his attorney, Elbridge T. Gerry, to seek custody of the child and prosecution of the stepparents. Gerry did this and, amidst much publicity, was successful. Media coverage of the Mary Ellen Wilson case caused a flood of public opinion resulting in the passage in New York in 1875 of "an Act of the incorporation of societies for the prevention of the cruelty to children."[11] The idea of organizing to protect children from cruel treatment caught on and in a very few years there was an anticruelty society in every major city in the country. In a manner similar to the SPCA, agents of the new child protection societies were quasi law enforcement officers with power to "prefer a complaint before any court or magistrate having jurisdiction for the violation of any law relating to or affecting children...." In 1877 the American Humane Association was incorporated to provide coordination among the local societies and to disseminate information and provide assistance. By 1900 its membership was composed of one hundred fifty humane societies throughout the country, most dealing with both child and animal protection, but about twenty restricting their activities to protection of children only.[12]

The Societies for the Prevention of Cruelty to Children did not view themselves as social welfare agencies. Rather they viewed themselves as law enforcement agencies specializing in the investigation of charges of child abuse and neglect. When they received a complaint they would conduct an investigation and, if the charge was substantiated, remove the child and prosecute the parents. The child would be turned over to a child placement agency or children's home and the SPCC would close the case and have no further responsibility for the child. Only in cases of lost or kidnapped children did the society ever consider returning the child to its parents. In describing the work of the Massachusetts Society for the Prevention of Cruelty to Children its director, Grafton Cushing, said in 1906 "There is no attempt to discover the cause of the conditions which make action by the [society] necessary, and therefore no endeavor to prevent a recurrence of these conditions. In other words, there is no 'social' work done. It is all legal or police work."[13]

Social Work Takes Over

From its onset there were many problems with the child rescue approach. Among these were that it was not concerned with prevention of child maltreatment; it gave no recognition to the possibility that a child might love his or her family despite its problems and prefer to remain in the family of origin; and it had no concern with the difficulties of establishing a viable life for the child once the child was removed. At the same time the child rescue movement was emerging, social work as a profession and as a scientific approach to social problems was also emerging. It was not long before people both within and outside of the child rescue agencies began to advocate for a social work approach to the problem of child maltreatment.

The foremost advocate for a social work approach to child welfare was C. Carl Carstens, a trained social worker appointed in 1906 as director of the Massachusetts Society for the Prevention of Cruelty to Children. Carstens advanced a new approach to child maltreatment that came to be known as child protection as opposed to child rescue. The child protection approach involved providing personal services to families with the goal of preventing the recurrence of maltreatment, seeking out the causes of abuse, neglect, exploitation, and delinquency, and preventing maltreatment through environmental reforms. When the 1912 annual meeting of the American Humane Association rejected Carstens' proposal that the child rescue approach be replaced by a child protection approach, he withdrew the Massachusetts society from membership in the AHA and founded the Bureau for the Exchange of Information among Child-Helping Agencies which in 1921 became the Child Welfare League of America (CWLA).[14]

Carstens became the first executive director of the CWLA and retained this position until his death in 1939. During his tenure, the CWLA and the AHA remained competitors around the issue of whether a child rescue or a child protection approach was the appropriate response to the problem of child maltreatment. However, gradually the AHA began to change and by the time of Carstens's death had adopted standards that referred to child protection and defined it as "a specialized service in the general field of child welfare" and recognized that the work involved "psychological factors" as well as "standards of physical care." The standards further called for member organizations to employ workers with college degrees and "special training in the social sciences, and knowledge and experience in the social and legal phases of child protection work."[15]

During the same period that social work was taking over the field of child welfare, forces were also at work moving the responsibility from private to public auspices. The American Humane Association, the societies for the prevention of cruelty to children, the Child Welfare League of America, and all of the loosely affiliated agencies, were all privately funded and operated. This arrangement befitted an era where government was quite small and took very little responsibility for anything beyond "protecting our shores and delivering the mail" as the expression went. As the twentieth century progressed, government showed an increasing willingness to be active in the area of social welfare in general and child welfare in particular. The 1909 White House Conference on Children resulted in the establishment in 1912 of the U.S. Children's Bureau, located in the Department of Commerce and Labor. The Bureau was charged with investigation and reporting on "all matters pertaining to the welfare of children and child life among all classes of our people."[16] In 1918 the Infancy and Maternity Health Bill (Sheppard-Towner Act) was passed, which set up infant and maternal health centers administered by state health departments. In

1935, child welfare services became a predominantly public function with the passage of the Social Security Act which, under provisions of Title IV, Grants to States For Aid To Dependent Children, and of Title V, Grants to States for Maternal and Child Welfare, mandated that all states provide services for dependent children and provided funding for these services.

Child Abuse Becomes the Dominant Theme

During the earlier part of this century, when child welfare was becoming a social work function and a responsibility of the public sector, it was a relatively small and broad-based area of social welfare. In 1955, for example, there were only slightly more than 5,000 professional employees of public child welfare agencies nationally.[17] The eleven-page entry on child welfare in the 1949 *Social Work Yearbook* devotes only two paragraphs, less than one-third of a page, to "Protection from Neglect and Cruelty." The remainder of the entry deals with a wide range of child welfare concerns including poverty, health care, disabilities, juvenile delinquency, and the like.[18] A series of related events that began in the 1950's has resulted in the child welfare system experiencing tremendous growth while at the same time narrowing to an almost exclusive focus on child abuse and neglect.

The event that triggered these changes in the child welfare system was the discovery of child abuse by the medical profession. Due to advances in radiological techniques, physicians began to identify traumatic injuries in children that did not fit any known explanation. Physicians were hesitant to blame these unexplained injuries on parents until 1955, when P. V. Woolley and W. A. Evans investigated the home situations of a sample of children displaying such injuries and found that the infants "came invariably from unstable households with a high incidence of neurotic or frankly psychotic behavior on the part of at least one adult."[19] The wide public attention given the findings of Woolley and Evans virtually exploded into an anti–child abuse crusade six years later when pediatrician Henry Kempe published the results of his research on child abuse under the catchy name the "battered child syndrome."

A major result of the "discovery" of child abuse by the medical profession and the corresponding widespread public knowledge and interest in the problem was the development of child abuse reporting laws. In the early 1960s the Children's Bureau developed a model law that was adopted by thirteen states by 1963. By 1966 every state had passed a mandatory child abuse reporting law. The original laws only required physicians to report, but objections by the medical profession led to the laws being quickly broadened to require other professions with frequent contact with children to also report.[20] As a quick inspection of Table 11.1 illustrates, the combination of these reporting laws with the heightened public awareness caused by radio, television, and press

TABLE 11.1   Increase in Reports of Child Abuse

	Abuse Reports	Rate per 1,000 Children
1967	9,563	0.1
1975	294,796	4.5
1980	1,154,000	18
1985	1,919,000	30
1990	2,559,000	40
1994	3,110,000	46

Source: Duncan Lindsey, *The Welfare of Children* (New York: Oxford University Press, 1994) p. 93; Karen McCurdy and Deborah Daro, *Current Trends in Child Abuse Reporting and Fatalities: The Results of the 1994 Annual Fifty State Survey* (Chicago: National Committee to Prevent Child Abuse, 1995) p. 5; and Ching-Tung Lung and Deborah Daro, *Current Trends in Child Abuse Reporting and Fatalities: The Results of the 1995 Annual Fifty State Survey* (Chicago: National Committee to Prevent Child Abuse, 1996) p. 5.

coverage resulted in a huge increase in the number of child abuse reports to public agencies.

The massive increase in child abuse referrals created a major problem for child welfare agencies. The heightened public awareness of the problem led to large increases in staff, but these have not nearly kept pace with the increased demand for services. As Table 11.2 illustrates, the size of the child welfare staff increased by 128 percent between 1967 and 1977; however, during this same time period, the number of child abuse complaints requiring investigation increased by almost 9,000 percent. This trend has continued and has resulted in child welfare agencies assigning an ever increasing proportion of staff to the function of protective services until this one service has virtually taken over

TABLE 11.2   Increase in Child Welfare Staff as Related to
Child Abuse Referrals

	Child Welfare Professional Staff	Child Abuse Referrals
1967	14,000	9,563
1977	32,000	838,000
% Increase	128%	8,763%

Source: Duncan Lindsey, *The Welfare of Children* (New York: Oxford University Press, 1994) p. 20; Karen McCurdy and Deborah Daro, *Current Trends in Child Abuse Reporting and Fatalities: The Results of the 1994 Annual Fifty State Survey* (Chicago: National Committee to Prevent Child Abuse, 1995) p. 5.

public child welfare agencies. In their 1990 analysis of child welfare Sheila Kamerman and Alfred Kahn confirmed this phenomena, concluding:

> *Child Protective Services (CPS) (covering physical abuse, sexual abuse, and neglect reports, investigations, assessments, and resultant actions) have emerged as the dominant public child and family service, in effect "driving" the public agency and often taking over child welfare entirely.... Child protective services today constitute the core public child and family service, the fulcrum and sometimes, in some places, the totality of the system. Depending on the terms used, public social service agency administrators state either that "Child protection is child welfare," or that "The increased demand for child protection has driven out all other child welfare services."[21]*

Foster Care—From Solution to Problem

The beginnings of foster care in the United States were characterized by the same child rescue approach that characterized the societies for the prevention of cruelty to children. The originator of the idea of foster care was the Reverend Charles Loring Brace, who founded the New York Children's Aid Society in 1853. Brace's idea was to take homeless children from the streets of New York, where they were beginning to be perceived as a serious threat to social order, and transport them to rural regions of the country to be placed with farm families. Brace perceived this to be a win-win proposition, as the result would be homes for homeless children and additional hands to help the farm families with their labor-intensive lifestyle.

The technique of the Society was to gather homeless children in shelters in New York City and, when a large enough group was gathered, to send them by train to towns in the Midwest. Agents of the Children's Aid Society would precede the train into each town, organize a local placement committee of prominent citizens, and advertise the location and the date the children would be available for placement. When the day arrived, local families would inspect the children, and families who were deemed suitable by both the Society's agent and the local committee could select one or more children. No money was exchanged between the parents and the Society. As Verlene McOllough reports, "Willing families would sign placing-out agreements guaranteeing the child the same food, lodging, and education children born to them would receive. In return the child would become part of the family, which in the nineteenth century generally meant taking on a sizable share of the work."[22] The work of the Children's Aid Society grew quickly and eventually became quite extensive. By 1873 the Society was placing more than 3,000 children per year. Its peak year was 1875, when a total of 4,026 children were placed.

The policies and techniques of the Children's Aid Society were the target of some well-deserved criticism. A major concern was that, in true child rescue fashion, if a child had living parents the Society made no attempt to work with them so the child could return home. Quite the opposite "as the Children's Aid Society ferreted out neglected children from the poorer districts, they convinced many impoverished parents that a child's best chance lay in permitting the society to find the child a new home far beyond the urban slums and its miseries."[23] Another criticism was raised by Catholics, who felt that the Children's Aid Society, founded and run by Protestants, was snatching Catholic children off the streets and sending them to the west to be reared as Protestants. Many of the states receiving children soon lost their enthusiasm for the Society's work. Many of the children—one study estimated nearly 60 percent—became sources of trouble and public expenditure when their placements failed to work.[24] Finally, the most serious criticism was the lack of study, the generally casual nature of the placement process, and the almost total absence of followup supervision after a placement was made.

Although the Children's Aid Society's program had many flaws, the basic idea of placing dependent children in a family setting caught on and had a tremendous impact on child welfare practice. Toward the end of the nineteenth century, advocates for a social work, child protection approach to child welfare, notably John Finley of the New York State Charities Aid Association, Charles Birtwell of the Boston Children's Aid Society, and Homer Folks of the Children's Aid Society of Pennsylvania, began to develop sound administrative procedures for child placement. These procedures included placement of the child in his or her home community, if possible; thorough study of the child and the prospective foster home; some financial support for the child; and careful supervision of the placement. By the turn of the century, foster care had replaced institutional placement in a number of cities. In 1909, the report of the first White House Conference on Children gave support to the foster care movement with the recommendation that "it is desirable that [children] should be cared for in families whenever practicable. The carefully selected foster home is for the normal child the best substitute for the natural home."[25] The spread of foster care continued until, by mid-century it was the placement of choice for normal children who, for one reason or another, were not able to remain with their natural families.

Foster care became a standard item in the child welfare worker's tool kit and existed with little question or examination until the late 1950s. At this time two things happened which began to profoundly shake social workers' and public policymakers' confidence in the foster care system. The first development was the publication of several studies of foster care which found serious deficiencies in the system. The second was the explosion of child abuse referrals, which lead to a consequent explosion in the number of children placed in foster care and hence a huge increase in cost.

The study that opened the floodgates for criticism of the foster care system, conducted by Henry Maas and Richard Engler, was entitled *Children in Need of Parents,* published in 1959. Maas and Engler chose nine communities that were thought to be representative of America in general. They sent a research team into each community who:

> *studied these nine counties and, simultaneously, the children in care in each of them. Information about the children and their families was gathered from all sixty agencies serving the communities at the time of our study. Key persons were interviewed in each of the communities which produced these dependent children and/or offered placement resources. The legal systems through which many of these children came into care, or which influenced their destinies in care, were studied. And the networks of agencies serving these children and families were also examined.[26]*

As there was no central data reporting mechanism for foster care, the Maas and Engler study provided the first valid look into the overall picture of foster care in America. What they discovered was not comforting. They found that the assumption that foster care was a temporary respite for children and families experiencing difficulty was not true—the average length of a foster placement was three years, many children were destined to grow up in foster care, and in less than 25 percent of the cases was it probable that the child would ever be returned home. Equally disturbing was the finding that the parents of foster children indicated, in most cases, that they either had no relationship or a negative relationship with the child placement agencies, and in only one-third of the cases did a parent ever visit the child in care. In an afterword to the study, Child Welfare League of America Executive Director Joseph Reid referred to foster children as "orphans of the living."[27]

Following the study by Maas and Engler was a series of research studies revealing deficiencies in the foster care system and in the whole concept of foster care as the plan of choice for dependent and neglected children. A 1962 Children's Bureau national survey of child welfare agencies conducted by Helen Jeter corroborated the findings of Maas and Engler, estimating that 31 percent of children in placement were "in danger of growing up in foster care." Jeter found that for 64 percent of the children in public foster care, the only plan the agency had was to continue them in placement. Little evidence was found of work being done to address the problems that lead to children being placed in foster care.[28] In 1966, David Fanshel and Eugene Shinn examined data from 659 children entering the New York foster care system and followed these children for the next five years. They found that the system was not guided by any systematic scientific knowledge or principles. Although they concluded that foster care had little harmful effect on the children, they also found that those children who eventually went home were returned to home situations which were little, if any, better than when they left. As in the Maas and Engler and the Jeter studies, Fanshel and Shinn found that many children were in foster care for long periods of time with little probability of ever returning home, and with virtually no contact with their natural parents.[29]

The studies cited above, along with a number of journalistic and legalistic treatises on foster care, such as Goldstein, Freud, and Solnit's influential *Beyond the Best Interests of the Child,* identified three major concerns regarding foster care. The first is that foster care was in many, if not most, cases not a temporary but rather a long-term situation. The second concern is with what came to be called "foster care drift." This referred to the fact that many children in foster care were not in one stable foster home, but were placed in a series of homes. The final problem was that agencies placing children in foster care rarely had any kind of long-term plan for the children other than for them to remain in care until such time as they could be returned home (often never). As a result of these concerns, a new approach to foster care was developed in the late 1970s and 1980s known as the permanency planning movement.

Permanency planning is based on several interrelated ideas:

1. The child's own home is the best place for him or her, and removal should occur only under extreme circumstances.
2. In instances where a child is removed, a specific plan should be developed immediately, closely monitored, and revised as needed. The focus of the plan should be obtaining a permanent living arrangement for the child in as little time as possible.
3. The primary goal of the plan should be to return the child to his or her own home. If this is not possible, steps should be taken to legally free the child for a permanent placement at the earliest possible time.
4. The preferred plan for a child who cannot return to his or her biological home is adoption. No child is considered unadoptable.
5. If adoption is not an option, then a long-term foster care plan should be developed with the child, the agency, and the foster family all making a commitment to a permanent placement.

Permanency planning became a part of national social welfare policy with the passage of P.L. 96–272, the Adoption Assistance and Child Welfare Act of 1980. This act directs federal fiscal incentives toward permanency planning objectives—namely the development of preventive and reunification services and adoption subsidies. For states to be eligible for increased federal funds, they must implement a service program designed either to reunite children with their families or to provide a permanent substitute home. They are required to take steps, such as the establishment of foster placement review committees and procedures for regular case review, which ensure that children enter foster care only when necessary, that they are placed appropriately, and that they are returned home or else are moved on to permanent families in a timely fashion. The act also creates fiscal incentives for states to seek adoptive homes for hard-to-place children, including children who are disabled, older, or minority group members.[30]

When the permanency planning approach was implemented in the 1970s and 80s, it appeared, for a while, that the problem of foster care was under control. The number of children in foster care declined from 520,000 in 1977 to 275,000 in 1984. However, after 1984 a number of factors in the social environment kicked in and caused this trend to reverse. Among these factors were the crack cocaine epidemic, economic problems leading to increased poverty and unemployment, AIDS, and a sharp rise in births to single mothers, particularly teenagers. By 1991 the number of children in foster care had risen to 429,000 and it is estimated that the number is currently near an all-time high. Compounding the problems caused by the rapid increase in the number of children needing foster placement has been the corresponding decrease in the number of foster families. Between 1984 and 1989 the number of foster homes declined from 137,000 to 100,000.[31] Among the factors generally thought to explain the decline of foster homes are the increased employment of women outside the home, the low payments made to foster parents, inadequate support services for foster parents, and a lack of training opportunities for foster parents.[32]

The Emergence of Family Preservation

Selecting a beginning point for the history of a social policy is always somewhat arbitrary, but the date and event generally cited as the beginning of the family preservation movement is 1974, when the Homebuilders Program was piloted in Washington state. To hear the originators describe the program, it appears to have begun almost by accident. Three psychologists, Jill Kinney, David Haapala, and Charlotte Booth, submitted a grant application proposing to develop "super foster homes" which they conceptualized as foster placements backed up with lots of training and professional consultation.

> *Our funding agent, however, insisted that before placement, we try "sticking a staff member in to live with a family." This idea sounded outlandish, but it also seemed interesting. We knew we would learn about families, and since we wanted the super foster home funding, we decided to try the in-home services, assuming they would fail, our funding agent would be convinced, and we could then continue with our*

super foster home approach.... We were wrong: The approach was sur-
prisingly effective.[33]

Two factors caused the idea of family preservation to be widely and rapidly embraced by the child welfare community. The first is the "reasonable efforts" provision of P.L. 96–272, the Adoption Assistance and Child Welfare Act of 1980. This provision is the requirement that child welfare agencies provide services to prevent the necessity for placement and that courts determine whether the agency has made "reasonable efforts" to accomplish this end. The act does not specify what these reasonable efforts might be, but states have seized upon family preservation services as a way to demonstrate that they are in compliance with the law. The second factor is the explosive increase in the number of children in foster care. Faced with a trend with no end in sight, and the accompanying increase in costs, states began to perceive foster care as a situation that was out of control. Family preservation offered a way to rein in the situation. In 1982 there were 20 family preservation programs nationwide, by 1988 this number had increased to 333, and by 1991, to over 400.[34] Most of these programs were initially funded by federal demonstration grants and by grants from private foundations, notably the Anne E. Casey Foundation and the Edna McConnell Clark Foundation.

In 1993, family preservation became an explicit part of federal policy with the passage of P.L. 103–66, the Family Preservation and Support Program, which was part of the Omnibus Budget Reconciliation Act. The provisions of this act have an estimated federal cost of one billion dollars over five years to provide states with funds for services to avoid foster care placement for children and to preserve and strengthen families. As this act includes a 25 percent matching requirement from the states, the actual amount to be spent on family preservation services over five years is actually 1.25 billion dollars. As reported by the Congressional Research Service, "The legislation was developed in response to a widespread perception of crisis in the child welfare system, as indicated by dramatic growth in the numbers of child abuse and neglect reports and children entering foster care, beginning in the mid-1980s. As the caseload has grown, the child welfare system also has faced high staff turnover and low morale, a shrinking supply of foster parents and foster homes, and a shortage of related support services such as drug and alcohol treatment and mental health care."[35]

The combination of P.L. 96–272, with its requirement that agencies demonstrate "reasonable efforts" to prevent foster home placement of children, and P.L. 103–66, providing massive federal financial incentives to provide family preservation services, has made family preservation the policy of choice in the 1990s for dealing with child maltreatment. Virtually every state in the Union now has some form of family preservation program in place.

Social Analysis

Problem Description

Family preservation is one aspect of society's response to the problem of child dependency. Child dependency as a problem has at least three levels. The primary level is the problem of child poverty. The secondary level, derived from the primary, is the problem of child maltreatment. Derived from the first two levels is the tertiary problem of the explosive growth of the foster care population.

Descriptive Data

A number of statistics regarding child welfare and family preservation were previously cited; a brief recap is provided here. Note that, despite years of concern, there is no good centralized source of data regarding child maltreatment and foster care. From 1974 to 1986 a good source of data was the annual *National Study of Child Neglect and Abuse Reporting,* conducted by the American Humane Association and funded by the federal Children's Bureau. This was funded for a reduced study for 1987 and has not been funded since. The National Study consisted of a nationwide compilation of data derived from official reports of child maltreatment documented by state child protective service agencies. A more limited study collecting the same basic information has been conducted in recent years by the National Committee to Prevent Child Abuse. Data regarding children in foster care is even more limited than that pertaining to reports of maltreatment. Since 1982, limited data has been available through the American Public Welfare Association's Voluntary Cooperative Information System. An effort is currently underway which will, hopefully, provide much better information in the future. This is a system currently under development by the U.S. Department of Health and Human Services called the Adoption and Foster Care Analysis System. This system is designed to collect uniform, reliable information on children in all forms of out-of-home care.

Four levels of data are important for understanding family preservation as a social welfare policy. The first level is data that estimate the actual incidence of child maltreatment—("estimate" because it is not possible to actually know the incidence of abuse and neglect, due to the secret nature of the acts involved). David Gil has estimated the incidence of abuse alone to range from 2,500,000 to 4,070,000. Murray Straus, Richard Gelles, and Susan Steinmetz, who also were concerned only with abuse, suggest that between 1.4 and 1.9 million children are abused each year. Combine these estimates with the fact that the majority of cases of child maltreatment involve neglect rather than abuse, and it is clear that the problem we are dealing with is massive.[36]

The second type of data that are important for understanding family preservation summarize actual reports of child maltreatment. This information is presented in Table 11.1, which indicates that the number of reports has increased from 9,563 in 1967 to 3,140,000 in 1994. Most of this increase is undoubtedly a result of increased public awareness of the problem, and more efficient reporting systems. However, there also is little doubt that a portion of the increase reflects an actual increase in incidence resulting from trends such as increased poverty, homelessness, drug usage, and births to young single mothers.

The third type of data for understanding the family preservation policy is the number of confirmed reports. As the number of reports has increased, the proportion that are substantiated by protective services investigation has decreased. In 1975, about 60 percent of reports were substantiated; by 1987 this had fallen to 40 percent, and currently about one in three reports is substantiated.[37]

The final figure—the one most directly relevant to family preservation policy—is the number of confirmed reports that lead to child placement. This was previously referred to when discussing the development and early success of permanency planning. To review, the number of children in out-of-home placements went from a high of 520,000 in 1977 to a low of 275,000 in 1984, at which time the number began to rapidly increase until it is estimated that it is again near an all-time high.

Relevant Research

There is a huge body of research with relevance to child protective services. However, here we will only address the research that has the most relevance to family preservation as a policy response to child placement. This research regards parent-child bonding, the effect of foster placement on child development, and the relation of poverty to child maltreatment. Research on program effectiveness will be described in the evaluation section.

Although Harry Harlow and his colleagues at the University of Wisconsin Primate Center had no specific interest in child welfare, their findings on infant-parent attachment were extremely interesting to social workers in the field. Duncan Lindsey describes the studies as follows:

> *An experimental psychologist, Harlow wanted to understand the importance of a mother's nurturing on the growth and development of a child. He examined what happened to an infant monkey that was raised in a wire cage that provided necessary physical nourishment but did not permit any emotional interaction or attachment with other monkeys. The monkey's cage allowed it to see and hear other monkeys but did not allow any physical contact. Harlow observed that the infant*

raised in an isolated cage suffered from intense neurotic behavior when compared to an infant monkey raised with a cloth surrogate mother.... Further, the effects of social isolation continued for the experimental monkey into adulthood.... Harlow's experiments provided dramatic evidence of the importance of parental affection and care to the developing child. The research emphasized the importance of providing children with parental nurturing. Children growing up in institutions or in a series of foster homes were deprived of the essential bonding and attachment that comes from a parent.[38]

Research by John Bowlby on children who were separated from their parents at age two or three confirmed Harlow's primate studies. Bowlby found that these children tended to suffer from severe psychological distress, and concluded that separation from parents has severe consequences for a child's development.[39]

Given the importance of the question, it is surprising that there are not more studies of the actual effects of foster placement on the development of children. The one major study of this question is the longitudinal study of children in foster care conducted by Fanshell and Shinn. This study resulted in data contradictory to what would be expected based on the findings of Harlow and of Bowlby. Fanshell and Shinn employed a wide array of behavioral indicators and checklists to assess the adjustment of children returned home, and those still in foster care at the end of the five-year period covered by their study. They conclude, "From our involvement in these data and other investigations, we feel that children who enter foster care as infants and live stable lives in the same setting emerge as teenagers who are relatively free of problems." Children who entered care when they were older, and those who did not have stable, long-term, placements were found to have significant problems.[40] However, this can be at least partially explained by the findings of several studies that children entering foster care at an older age are more likely already to have severe behavioral and adjustment problems.[41]

Unlike the question of the effects of foster placement on children, the effects of poverty are very well researched and consequently well understood. One study concluded that the incidence of abuse and neglect is ten times higher among families with incomes below the poverty line than among those with middle-class incomes. In a 1969 survey of abusive families, Gil found that nearly 60 percent had been on public assistance at some time, and that slightly more than 34 percent were receiving welfare at the time of the report. A journalist looking into abuse and neglect found that more than half the children removed from their homes as a result of abuse or neglect reports came from families receiving welfare. Leroy Pelton surveyed child protective service records in New Jersey and found that 79 percent of the families had incomes below the poverty line. Gelles conducted two nationwide surveys on family violence and found that "violence toward children, especially severe violence, is more likely to occur in households with annual incomes below the poverty line."[42] After two separate, thorough reviews of the research, Lindsey and Pelton conclude that poverty is at the root of nearly all child welfare problems. Making the situation worse are data indicating that the rate of child poverty has been steadily increasing.[43]

Is Family Preservation Policy in Accord with Research Findings?

One of the cornerstones of family preservation policy is the belief that foster care is bad for children. As reviewed above, the research on this question is incomplete and results to date have been contradictory. However, when looked at more carefully, the results do not appear so contradictory. The study by Fanshall and Shinn concluded that children in foster care did not appear to suffer any serious consequences, with the caveat that the children they were talking about were those who entered foster care at a young age and who had stable placements. In *Beyond the Best Interests of the Child,* Goldstein, Freud, and Solnit argue that what is important to a child is a psychological parent, not necessarily a biological parent. A psychological parent is any caring adult who meets the child's day-to-day needs and does so over an extended period of time.[44] It seems clear that the children studied by Fanshall and Shinn were fortunate enough to find psychological parents in their placements. Thus it appears that the attachment and outcome research of foster care would lend support to either permanency planning (strive to provide a psychological parent to a child if the biological parent is unavailable) or to family preservation (support biological parents in their efforts to also be psychological parents).

While family preservation policy may be consistent with the research and theory regarding attachment, it is hard to discount the arguments of scholars such as Lindsey, Pelton, and Gil that the real problem behind child maltreatment is poverty. It is ironic that just as our society is pouring money into family preservation programs in an attempt to hold families together, we are slashing financial assistance programs that provide many of these families their only hope for stability. Lindsey refers to child abuse as "the red herring of child welfare," arguing that it is a highly charged issue that draws attention away from the real and more difficult problem of child poverty.[45]

Major Social Values Related to Family Preservation

Family preservation policy occurs at the intersection of some of the most deeply held, and deeply dividing, values our society holds. These are children's rights, family rights, and the government's right to act in *parens patriae,* the ultimate parental authority. As you saw in the historical analysis section, up until the nineteenth century children were considered to have few rights, and those they did have were clearly subservient to the rights of their parents, particularly their father. As time has passed, children have been given considerably more rights and it now is quite clear that they have a right to a certain—albeit vague—level of care. Lagging only slightly behind the recognition of children as beings with certain rights was the recognition of the right of government to intervene in family life to safeguard the rights of children. Susan Downs, Lela Costin, and Emily McFadden observe that support for government intervention has increased in recent years due to a fear that U.S. society is experiencing breakdown in the family as a social institution, and to "the realization that virtually all governmental actions directly or indirectly affect families."[46] Nevertheless, Americans still have great ambivalence about this, being ever-fearful of government and believing that the government should be allowed in family life only in cases of the utmost urgency.

Family preservation policy represents a very clever attempt to reconcile these seemingly contradictory rights. It recognizes the right of children to be protected, but does it in such a way as to maximize the rights of parents to rear their own children. By its generally time-limited nature, family preservation seeks to make government intervention as short as possible and to get out of family life in the least possible time. This balancing of rights makes family preservation a very marketable policy to legislators and to the general public and, in part, explains its rapid spread.

Family Preservation Goals

Because family preservation policy includes an explicit and well-funded evaluation requirement, the manifest goals of the policy are clearer and more explicitly spelled out than is the case in most social welfare policies. This is because a basic requirement of program/policy evaluations is that goals be specified; if they are not, you have nothing to evaluate. The basic, stated, goals of family preservation are:

1. To prevent placement of children in families in crisis. This is the cornerstone of family preservation. The idea is to intervene in family situations that would normally be assessed as requiring placement of the children with intensive, time-limited, services, which quickly improve family functioning to a degree that the children can remain in the home.
2. Protect children and prevent subsequent child maltreatment. Family preservation policy does not consider it enough to simply prevent placement. This must be done in a way which assures that the children are protected from subsequent harm both in the short and in the long term.
3. Improve family functioning. Family preservation services seek to leave families with better daily living and problem solving skills than were present before intervention.

4. Prevent child abuse and neglect. This goal is sometimes categorized as family support, as opposed to family preservation, but in any case is generally a component of family preservation policy. This goal is to improve the general social environment of families and to enable more families to adequately care for their children without the necessity of intervention of any kind. This may be viewed as an institutional approach to the problem of child maltreatment, as contrasted to the other services which represent a clear residual approach.

Somewhere between a manifest and a latent goal of family preservation is the goal to decrease the cost of child protective services. One of the major motivating factors in the rapid spread of family preservation has been that it is perceived as a cost-efficient way to deal with child maltreatment. This goal lies between *manifest* and *latent* because, while few people would deny it, it is generally not listed among the stated goals. We suspect that if within a few years the costs of child protective services do not decline, or at least the growth show signs of slowing, policymakers will lose considerable enthusiasm for family preservation, regardless of how well it achieves its stated goals.

We are not able to identify any purely latent goals of family preservation policy. A few scholars, for example Ann Hartman and L. Diane Bernard, have argued that a latent goal of all family policy is to preserve the existing patriarchal family structure, and along with it existing power relationships in society. Bernard states:

> *The oppression and exploitation of women in society is reflected and initiated in the family, which reinforces continued gender discrimination. The primary function of the family is to maintain the status quo. Preservation of the family and family stability are the primary goals of patriarchy, ensuring obedience and continuity.... The major purpose appears to be to restore stability and reestablish control by returning to traditional values."[47]*

We see little evidence that this is the case in family preservation policy. Nowhere in the policy is there a definition of the type of family that is to be preserved. In fact, many of the cases described in the literature appear to be female-headed, single-parent households, and changing these to traditional nuclear families is never mentioned.

Hypotheses
There appear to be two major hypotheses derived from family preservation goals. The first can be stated as: "If intensive, time-limited, social work services are provided to families with children at risk of placement, and these services are pro-

vided in a timely fashion, then placement of the children can be permanently avoided." As we will discuss in the evaluation section, we have serious doubts that this hypothesis will be upheld, given the severity of the problems most of the target population are experiencing, the decline of supporting resources and services, and the relatively primitive state of social work intervention technology.

The second hypothesis appears to be: "If child placement is avoided via provision of intensive family preservation services, then reduction in foster home placement will save more money than the family preservation services cost." Once again, given the seriousness of the problems in the target population, we doubt that it will be possible, in most cases, to limit services to a brief period, and therefore services will cost more than anticipated. Also, as will be discussed in the evaluation section, there is some evidence of a "net-widening" phenomena in family preservation. This is a phenomena first identified in probation and diversion services in criminal justice. What appears to happen in some instances is that, with the option of family preservation being available, social workers are referring cases to family preservation that would not have even been opened were these services not available.

Political Analysis

Family preservation is one of those rare social policies that contains significant elements which appeal to stakeholders across the political spectrum. Liberals (a group that includes most social workers) favor family preservation because it operationalizes many of their most sacred values. Among the aspects of family preservation that appeal to this group are:

- It does not blame the victim.
- It proceeds from a strengths perspective.
- It emphasizes cultural sensitivity.
- It emphasizes a belief in people's capacity to change and desire to do so.
- It defines family in a flexible fashion and approaches each family as a unique system.
- It respects the dignity and privacy of family members.

Conservatives also find much to like about family preservation as a response to the problem of child maltreatment. Among the aspects of family preservation this group likes are:

- It shortens the time government is involved in people's lives.
- It emphasizes that people are ultimately responsible for solving their own problems.

- It emphasizes independence and seeks to wean people from the social service system.
- It resonates with the conservative emphasis on "family values."
- It is viewed as a potentially more cost efficient way of protecting children.

Because family preservation policy exists at this intersection of liberal and conservative values, it has—up to this point—experienced little meaningful political opposition. At the Committee on Ways and Means hearing on the legislation which eventually lead to P.L. 103–66, Family Preservation and Support Services, forty-three groups either testified or submitted testimony for the record. Not a single submission expressed any opposition or even reservations to the act.[48]

There are, however, a few groups that oppose family preservation policy. One group consists of those very conservative ideologues who see in family preservation a continuation of trends which they believe are eroding the very foundations of our society. They believe that family preservation is another policy that removes accountability for responsible behavior from the individual and places it upon society. Patrick Murphy, the Cook County (Chicago) Public Guardian, for example, states "The family preservation system is a continuation of sloppy thinking of the 1960s and 1970s that holds, as an unquestionable truth, that society should never blame a victim. But in most cases, giving services and money to parents who have abused their children does nothing but reward irresponsible and even criminal behavior."[49] Murphy introduced a bill into the 1993 Illinois legislature that would require court approval for family preservation in cases of physical or sexual abuse. The bill passed, but in response to strong opposition by the Department of Children and Family Services and the American Civil Liberties Union, among others, Governor Jim Edgar vetoed it. Murphy and his allies persisted, however, and in 1993, in response to the murder of a young girl whose family was receiving family preservation services, Illinois ended its Family First program. However, as Heather MacDonald, another critic of family preservation, reported, "This decision does not mean, however, that Illinois is rejecting family preservation. It is now introducing the original Homebuilders model, which, though it has a vastly better safety record than the Family First program, embodies the identical philosophy."[50]

Opposition to family preservation policy also comes from competing human service providers who see it as cutting into their "market." The National Council for Adoption, a group favoring policies that free more children for adoption, argues that family preservation programs often harm children who could be removed from hopeless parents and placed in good adoptive homes. The group's vice president, Mary Beth Seader, complains: "I know people who have been trying for two years to adopt these crack babies that have been abandoned in hospitals, but...the state is not terminating parental rights even if there is no contact with the biological mother."[51] Residential treatment center personnel are another group who question family preservation. They argue that family preservation is being embraced so enthusiastically by policymakers because it offers an alternative much cheaper than residential treatment for children experiencing severe problems in their family setting. However, the argument goes, in many instances there is no substitute for the more expensive alternative. For example, David Coughlin of Boys Town says: "Family preservation? Who can be opposed to that? But some of these kids are going to be in trouble all their lives. These kids are always going to need help. You can't just blow across the top of a family for three months and expect their woes to go away."[52]

With the exception of Murphy's partial victory in Illinois, groups opposing family preservation policy have had relatively little impact. The reason for this is what Sam Ross, a children's home advocate, refers to as "the liberal-conservative conspiracy." By this he means the intersection of values referred to at the beginning of this section. As the results of the evaluation studies (which will be reviewed later in this chapter) come in, if they are not positive, this situation may well change. Be sure that these opposition groups are waiting in the wings in hopes that this will happen.

Economic Analysis

Although many good arguments have been made for the policy of family preservation, we think it is clear that economic considerations are the driving force behind its rapid growth. In the opening statement to the Committee on Ways and Means, Representative Fred Grandy said, "Principally, federal spending on foster care and adoption through Title IV-E of the Social Security Act has increased from $474 million to $2.5 billion, or roughly a 418 percent increase since 1981. And in the last five years, IV-E has increased by an average of $360 million a year." Policymakers and administrators are desperate to get control of what is perceived as a runaway increase in costs, and family preservation advocates have successfully used this as a way to sell the policy.

If family preservation can produce the results it promises—prevention of foster home or institutional placement through the provision of time-limited, intensive, services—the potential cost savings are significant indeed. The Edna McConnell Clark Foundation has produced media kits stating that family preservation programs cost an estimated average of $3,000 per family per year, as compared to foster care at $10,000 per year per child, or institutional care, which costs $40,000 annually per child. Carolyn Brown and Susan Little, writing about the Full Circle Program, a California family preservation program, assert that "Besides helping children and their families, this work has saved hundreds of thousands of tax dollars: Reunification services for a family cost an average of $2,600...less than one month of residential care in California."[53] Kinney, Haapala, and Booth, founders of the original Homebuilders Program in Washington state, report their costs as $2,700 per family. They report the costs of alternatives as $5,113 for foster care, $19,673 for group care, $25,978 for residential treatment, $42,300 for placement in an acute psychiatric hospital, and $100,200 for long-term psychiatric care. Marianne Berry evaluated a family preservation program in California and kept detailed per-hour cost records. She found that families in the program received an average of 67.35 hours of service at a cost of $41.22 per hour, for a per-case average cost of $2,776.17. Comparing this with foster care costs, she concluded that this "translates into a savings of $4,648 for every foster care placement this program prevented.... When placement is prevented for more than one child in a family, this savings is multiplied, resulting in an even greater economic benefit from this program."[54]

The critical question on which the future of family preservation rests is whether the projected cost savings will actually materialize. To do so, the number of foster placements will have to begin to decrease or, at the very least, the rate of increase will have to slow, and evaluation results will have to establish that family preservation is the reason. If this does not happen, policymakers will doubtlessly lose their initial enthusiasm for family preservation, critics like Patrick Murphy will gain more credibility, and child welfare policy will turn to some other proposed solution. The results of evaluations of family preservation programs are continuing to come in and are being widely disseminated. It is to these results we now turn.

Policy/Program Evaluation

It is probably not stretching the truth to say that family preservation is one of the most carefully studied social welfare innovations in history. There are a number of reasons for this, principle among them that the program involves leaving children in potentially harmful situations, which is believed to call for extremely vigilant monitoring. The increasing skepticism with which policymakers are now receiving claims of social policy advocates also has resulted in calls for close monitoring of innovations. The prototype family preservation program, the Homebuilders Program, was originally funded under a National Institute of Mental Health research grant which, of course, had as a primary goal knowledge development. When the Family Preservation and Support Program was passed in 1993, Congress included $2 million in fiscal 1994 and $6 million per year from 1995 through 1998 to fund research and evaluation as well as training and technical assistance. The act also requires states to develop new foster care and adoption information systems.

When family preservation models were first implemented during the 1970s, they reported wildly positive outcomes. The Homebuilders Program reported placement prevention rates varying from a low of 73 percent to a high of 91 percent of families served. Some of the more recent studies have reported success rates almost as high. An evaluation of a Connecticut program claimed that 82 percent of children at risk of placement were still in their own homes after one year of service. Berry's study of a family preservation program in California concludes: "a full 88 percent of the families receiving services in this program avoided otherwise imminent child removal for a year after being served."[55]

These studies, sometimes referred to as "first generation studies" have come under serious criticism for methodological problems. The major problem identified is that they lack any kind of control or comparison group. Thus, if a study finds that 90 percent of the children in the program were not placed, it cannot, without a control group, conclude that the services prevented placement, because there is no way of knowing if the children really were at risk in the first place. It is possible to argue that, without the services, fewer than 10 percent of the children would have been placed and therefore the program actually *increased* that rate of placement.* In response to these criticisms, a number of more rigorous studies have been implemented. The results of these studies have been mixed. Some have found no significant differences in placement rates between experimental and control groups.[56] An Oregon study found that significantly fewer children in less difficult cases were placed, but there was no significant difference in placement rates for children in families with more difficult problems.[57] In one study, the experimental group—or the one receiving intensive family preservation services—actually experienced a *higher* rate of placement than the control group.[58]

A number of studies have found significantly lower placement rates in the groups receiving intensive family preservation services as compared to groups not receiving these services. The differences have been much smaller, however, than those claimed in the first generation, non-experimental studies. A New Jersey study found 14 percent fewer placements in the experimental group, a California study found 28 percent fewer, and a study in Ramsey County, Minnesota found 22 percent fewer placements.[59]

The most significant study of family preservation to date was conducted in Illinois by the University of Chicago's Chapin Hall Center for Children, under

---

*This has, in fact, been the finding of evaluations of intensive social services to people released from prison on parole. The more services a parolee is given, the more likely he is to be caught for some violation of parole and sent back to prison. It is quite possible that intensive supervision of families with children defined as being at risk of placement could have similar results.

contract with that state's Department of Children and Family Services. The study began in 1989 after Illinois had implemented a version of the Family First program. The study ran for four years and involved three levels of data collection. The first level involved collecting descriptive data from all 6,522 cases involved in Families First in 1989. The second level was a randomized experiment, with a sample of 1,564 cases, to test program effects of subsequent placement and harm to children. The third level, involving a sample of 278 cases, was a series of interviews with parents in both the experimental and control groups to gather data on the effects of the program on child and family well-being over time and to assess clients' experiences and views on the services they received. The results of this study were that the Family First program in Illinois had no effect on either the frequency or the duration of placements.[60]

A number of scholars in child welfare have recently begun to criticize what they believe is the overemphasis on placement prevention as the major criterion for effectiveness of family preservation services. They argue that there are a number of other, equally or more important, possible outcomes from services. Pecora et al., for example, suggest the following additional types of outcomes:[61]

- improvements in child functioning (e.g., behavior, school attendance, school performance, self-esteem)
- positive changes in parental functioning (e.g., depression, employment, substance abuse, anger management, self-esteem) or parenting skills, such as the use of appropriate discipline techniques and child care
- improvements in family functioning (e.g., family conflict, communication, cohesion, adaptability, or social support)
- reunification of families after child placement

Berry has argued that our focus on placement prevention has deflected attention from important questions regarding just which elements of intensive services contribute to family preservation and which do not.[62] This knowledge would lead to an improvement in services rather than a simple judgement of whether or not the services were cost efficient.

We agree that there are a number of dimensions of family preservation services that could profitably be examined for the purpose of increasing social worker effectiveness in designing programs and in responding to family needs. However, keep in mind that the family preservation policy has been touted and implemented based on the belief that it will eventually help manage the child welfare crisis by reducing the population in placement and (consequently) the huge and rapidly increasing cost of services. If family preservation does not live up to the cost efficiency promise, regardless of how effective it is demonstrated to be as a social work practice approach, it will be abandoned by policymakers who will then continue the search for cost containment in child protection.

Current Proposals for Policy Reform

Family preservation has probably reached its zenith as a policy supporting specific program initiatives. In spite of the data coming in indicating a number of areas of effectiveness, it seems clear that it is not leading to a reduction in foster care rates. As this data continues to be collected and disseminated, it is likely that policymakers will begin to look for other answers.

There is a strong reform movement afoot in the area of foster care and family preservation. This is a steady movement toward kinship care. Kinship care is simply the practice of looking to a child's extended family for a placement resource before looking to foster care with an unrelated family. Data reported to the U.S. Department of Health and Human Services by twenty-five states indicates that the percentage of children placed with relatives increased from 18 to 31 percent of the foster care caseload from 1986 through 1990. Most children placed with relatives are members of racial and ethnic groups, mostly African American. In other ways, the population placed in kinship care appears to be identical with the general foster care population.[63]

The movement in foster care policy toward kinship care has been an interesting mix of macro and micro policy initiatives. On the macro level there have been two significant events. The first is the Child Welfare League of America's National Commission on Family Foster Care, which convened in 1991 and developed *A Blueprint for Fostering Infants, Children, and Youth in the 1990s.* One of the major thrusts of this document was to support the significance of kinship care. The other significant macro level event was the 1979 Supreme Court ruling in *Miller v. Youakim,* in which the court ruled that relatives not be excluded from the definition of foster parents eligible for federal foster care benefits.

Mark Courtney makes an interesting observation that the movement toward more kinship care may well be the result of micro-level policy change as much as macro. He observes:

> *Various states, localities, and individual social workers and judges have no doubt contributed to this trend in ways that cannot be easily observed, let alone described, given the decentralized nature of child welfare services.... Current permanency planning philosophy in child welfare places emphasis on keeping children 'with family,' even when they are removed from the home of their birth parents.... Common sense suggests that staying with relatives is likely to be less traumatic for a child removed from parental care than placement with unfamiliar foster parents or group care providers.... Paying kin to care for a child, as opposed to having to find an appropriate foster home, makes the difficult decision to remove a child from home easier for social workers and judges.[64]*

Early data indicates that kinship care is a very effective tool for the goal of permanency, but works to the detriment of family preservation/reunification if the family to be preserved is that of the biological parents. In a rigorous study of reunification of families with children placed in foster care in Chicago, Robert Goerge found that placement in the home of a relative was one of the strongest variables in reducing the probability of reunification.[65] Courtney found that children in kinship care are more likely than children placed in family foster homes or group care to remain in the foster care system for long periods of time.[66]

Kinship care is very appealing to policymakers on two fronts. First, because it leaves children in the care of relatives, although not the parents, it appeals to profamily sentiments. Second, kinship care is cheaper than family foster care. Families are now eligible for licensure and payment as foster parents for related children, but under current policy in 34 states, they can only receive the amount of the child's public assistance payment. This amount is much lower than the prevailing foster care rate in most states, and it is even lower if more than one related child is placed in the same home. It appears that the inequity in this situation is becoming apparent, and pressure is mounting for states to provide the same level of support for children in kinship care as for those in family foster care. Thus this foster care system reform will also prove to eventually be no cost saver.

Conclusion

By way of conclusion, we wish to make several observations regarding family preservation as a policy response to child maltreatment. The first is the recognition of the difference between family preservation as a philosophy behind child welfare policy, and family preservation as a specific programmatic response to the problem of child maltreatment. As a programmatic response implemented in programs such as Homebuilders and Family First, family preservation produces evaluation results that are, at the very least, casting doubt on the claims of the programs' designers that they will save money through placement prevention. Although it may well prove to be true that the programs are effective on a number of other dimensions, such as elevating a family's general level of problem solving ability and child care, this is pretty much beside the point. The programs have been advertised and implemented on the basis of cost effectiveness, and if they do not demonstrate effectiveness according to this criteria, they will lose support.

Family preservation, however, should not be interpreted to only mean one specific type of program or method. Family preservation is first and foremost a philosophy of practice with families in crisis. Robin Warsh, Barbara Pine, and Anthony Maluccio offer the following broader definition of family preservation:

Family preservation is a philosophy that supports policies, programs and practices which recognize the central importance of the biological family to human beings. It underscores the value of individualized assessment and service delivery, with adequate system supports, in order to maximize each family's potential to stay, or again become, safely connected.[67]

This general philosophy of family preservation can be expressed through any number of specific programs and techniques, including kinship care, shared foster care (where the foster family and the biological family are in direct contact and share child rearing responsibilities), open adoption, family reunification programs, and a number of other pro-family approaches, some of which may not have even been thought of yet. Warsh, Pine, and Maluccio argue that defining family preservation in terms of one model, such as Homebuilders, confuses the concept. Thus we conclude that although the specific family preservation models that have recently spread so quickly seem to be falling short of their goals, family preservation as a philosophy of child welfare policy is alive and well.

The second observation we wish to make is that true family preservation will, of necessity, involve a much wider range of interventions and benefits than just a direct response to incidents of child maltreatment. We have reviewed arguments concluding that poverty is actually the central child welfare problem. Lindsey, for example, analyzed national survey data and demonstrated that family income is the best predictor of a child's removal from home.[68] Courtney has analyzed cost data and concluded that it costs the federal government over eleven times as much per child to provide foster care as to provide welfare assistance to the child's family. Putting these findings together, we could argue that if poverty is the leading variable related to placement, and *if* placement is much more expensive than increased welfare payments, *then* we could save money and improve the lives of children and families by increasing welfare benefits to a level that enables people to live and care for their children decently. However, as with specific family preservation services, increased welfare supports are only a small part of the total response needed to adequately deal with the problem of child maltreatment. As Edith Fein and Anthony Maluccio have stated:

No solutions to child welfare issues will be viable without supports to families. These include adequately compensated employment, availability of housing, accessible medical care, and decriminalization of substance abuse to remove the economic incentive for drug dealing. Other supports are also important, such as good day care, parenting education, and readily available mental health services. As we noted over a decade ago, "permanency planning [or family preservation programs] cannot substitute for preventive services and for increased investment in our children."[69]

Thus we conclude that it is unrealistic to expect any one specific approach to have a great impact on placement rates. Perhaps if family preservation programs were evaluated as one of a whole set of interventions to reduce placements, they would fare better.

Our final observation is derived from the first two: while it is understandable to look for a "silver bullet"—a simple one-step remedy to a problem such as child maltreatment—it is highly unrealistic. Child maltreatment results from a huge number of variables, some relating to individual psychology and some to macro social and economic conditions, all interrelated along an almost infinite number of dimensions. As a society, we have a modest understanding of a few of the relevant variables and no knowledge of a number of others; as to how they are interrelated, our understanding is at an even more primitive level. To think that one program approach, such as family preservation, will be *the* solution, is simplistic. The conclusion of Fein and Maluccio regarding permanency planning is also an appropriate conclusion for this policy analysis of family preservation: "The complexity of human interactions precludes simple solutions, and the certainty of having solved a problem is destined to elude our grasp. These considerations, however, are not negative. They help define the dimensions of the problem and provide a challenge to those who choose to work seriously with children, society's most precious resource."[70]

Notes

1. Children's Defense Fund, *S.O.S. America! A Children's Defense Budget* (Washington, DC: Children's Defense Fund, 1990) p. 4.

2. David S. Liederman. "Child Welfare Overview," in Richard L. Edwards and June Gary Hopps, Eds., *Encyclopedia of Social Work,* 19th ed. (Washington, DC: NASW Press, 1995) p. 424.

3. Karen McCurdy and Deborah Daro, *Current Trends in Child Abuse Reporting and Fatalities: The Results of the 1992 Annual Fifty State Survey* (Chicago, IL: National Committee for the Prevention of Child Abuse) p. 22.

4. Joyce E. Everett, "Child Foster Care," in Edwards and Hopps, *Encyclopedia of Social Work,* p. 385.

5. Richard Wexler, *Wounded Innocents: The Real Victims of the War Against Child Abuse,* rev. ed. (Buffalo, NY: Prometheus Books, 1995).

6. David Fanshel and Eugene B. Shinn, *Children in Foster Care: A Longitudinal Investigation* (New York: Columbia University Press, 1978); Ellen Gambrill, *Critical Thinking in Clinical Practice: Improving the Accuracy of Judgements and Decisions*

about Clients (San Francisco, CA: Jossey-Bass, 1990); Duncan Lindsey, *The Welfare of Children* (New York: Oxford University Press, 1994).

7. Elizabeth M. Tracy, "Family Preservation and Home Based Services," in Edwards and Hopps, *Encyclopedia of Social Work,* p. 973.

8. John R. Schuerman, Tina L. Rzepnicki, and Julia H. Littell, *Putting Families First: An Experiment in Family Preservation* (New York: Aldine De Gruyter, 1994) pp. 20–21.

9. Viviana A. Zelizer, *Pricing the Priceless Child: The Changing Social Value of Children* (New York: Basic Books, 1985).

10. Susan Tiffin, *In Whose Best Interest? Child Welfare Reform in the Progressive Era* (Westport, CN: Greenwood Press, 1982) pp. 142–143.

11. Gertrude Williams, "Protection of Children Against Abuse and Neglect: Historical Background," in Gertrude J. Williams and John Money, Eds., *Traumatic Abuse and Neglect of Children at Home* (Baltimore, MD: The Johns Hopkins University Press, 1980) p. 77.

12. Robert H. Bremner, Ed., *Children and Youth in America—A Documentary History,* Vol. II: 1886–1932 (Cambridge: Harvard University Press, 1971) p. 201.

13. *Annual Report of the MSPCC* 26 (December 31, 1906) 4, quoted in Paul Gerard Anderson, "The Origin, Emergence, and Professional Recognition of Child Protection," *Social Service Review* (June 1989) p. 224.

14. Anderson, "The Origin, Emergence, and Professional Recognition of Child Protection," pp. 224–227.

15. Anderson, "The Origin, Emergence, and Professional Recognition of Child Protection," p. 223.

16. Walter I. Trattner, *From Poor Law to Welfare State—A History of Social Welfare in America,* 3rd ed. (New York: The Free Press, 1984) p. 115.

17. Lindsey, *The Welfare of Children,* p. 20.

18. Emma O. Lundberg, "Child Welfare," in Margaret B. Hodges, Ed., *Social Work Yearbook, 1949* (New York: Russell Sage Foundation) pp. 98–109.

19. P. V. Woolley and W. A. Evans, "Significance of Skeletal Lesions in Infants Resembling Those of Traumatic Origin," *Journal of the American Medical Association* 181: pp. 17–24, cited in Lindsey, *The Welfare of Children,* pp. 91.

20. Lindsey, *The Welfare of Children,* pp. 91–92.

21. Sheila B. Kamerman and Alfred J. Kahn, "Social Services for Children, Youth and Families in the United States," special issue of *Children and Youth Services Review* 12, 1, pp. 7–8, quoted in Lindsey, *The Welfare of Children,* p. 96.

22. Verlene McOllough, "The Orphan Train Comes to Clarion," *The Palimpsest* (Fall 1988) p. 146.

23. McOllough, "The Orphan Train Comes to Clarion," p. 146.

24. Trattner, *From Poor Law to Welfare State,* p. 118.

25. Trattner, *From Poor Law to Welfare State* p. 118, 202.

26. Henry S. Maas and Richard E. Engler, Jr., *Children in Need of Parents* (New York: Columbia University Press, 1959) p. 3.

27. Joseph H. Reid, "Action Called For—Recommendations," in Maas and Engler, *Children in Need of Parents,* p. 380.

28. Helen Jeter, *Children, Problems and Services in Child Welfare Programs* (Washington, DC: U.S. Children's Bureau, 1963).

29. Fanshel and Shinn, *Children in Foster Care.*

30. Mary Lee Allen and Jane Knitzer, "Child Welfare: Examining the Policy Framework," in Brenda G. McGowan and William Meezan, Eds., *Child Welfare: Current Dilemmas—Future Directions* (Itasca, IL: Peacock Publishers, Inc., 1983) pp. 120–123.

31. Susan Whitelaw Downs, Lela B. Costin, and Emily Jean McFadden, *Child Welfare and Family Services: Policies and Practice* (White Plains, NY: Longman, 1996) p. 266.

32. Everett, "Child Foster Care," p. 385.

33. Jill Kinney, David Haapala, and Charlotte Booth, *Keeping Families Together: The Homebuilders Model* (New York: Aldine De Gruyter, 1991) pp. 3–4.

34. Peter Pecora, James K. Whittaker, and Anthony Maluccio, with Richard P. Barth and Robert D. Plotnick, *The Child Welfare Challenge: Policy, Practice, and Research* (New York: Aldine De Gruyter, 1992) p. 278; Elizabeth M. Tracy, "Family Preservation and Home-Based Services," in Edwards and Hopps, *Encyclopedia of Social Work,* p. 974.

35. Karen Spar, "The Family Preservation and Support Program: Background and Description," *CRS Report for Congress* (Washington, DC: Congressional Research Service—The Library of Congress, 1994) p. i.

36. David Gil, *Violence Against Children: Physical Abuse in the United States* (Cambridge: Harvard University Press, 1970) p. 59; Murray Straus, Richard Gelles, and Susan Steinmetz, *Behind Closed Doors: Violence in the American Family* (New York: Anchor Press, 1980) p. 64.

37. David Wiese and Deborah Daro, *Current Trends in Child Abuse Reporting and Fatalities: The Results of the 1994 Annual Fifty State Survey* (Chicago: National Committee to Prevent Child Abuse, 1995) p. 5.

38. Lindsey, *The Welfare of Children,* p. 32.

39. J. Bowlby, "The Nature of the Child's Ties to his Mother," *International Journal of Psychoanalysis,* 39, pp. 350–373, cited in Lindsey, *The Welfare of Children,* p. 32.

40. Fanshell and Shinn, *Children in Foster Care,* p. 449.

41. N.J. Hochstady, P. K. Jaudes, D. A. Zimo, and J. Schachter, "The Medical and Psychosocial Needs of Children Entering Foster Care," *Child Abuse and Neglect* 11, pp. 53–62; A. McIntyre and T. Y. Kesler, "Psychological Disorders Among Foster Children," *Journal of Clinical Child Psychiatry* 15, pp. 297–303; M. E. K. Moffatt, M. Peddie, J. L. Stulginskas, I. B. Pless, and N. Steinmetz, "Health Care Delivery to Foster Children: A Study," *Health and Social Work* 10, pp. 129–137.

42. National Center on Abuse and Neglect, *Study Findings: National Study of Incidence and Severity of Child Abuse and Neglect* (Washington, DC: Department of Health, Education, and Welfare, 1982); Gil, *Violence Against Children,* p. 112; Barbara Vobejda, "Are There No Orphanages?" *Washington Post—National Weekly Edition* (October 26–November 1, 1995) p. 32; Leroy Pelton, "Child Abuse and Neglect: The Myth of Classlessness," in Leroy Pelton, Ed., *The Social Context of Child Abuse and Neglect* (New York: Human Sciences Press, 1981) pp. 37–42; Richard J. Gelles, "Poverty and Violence Toward Children," *American Behavioral Scientist* 35 (1992) pp. 258–274.

43. Lindsey, *The Welfare of Children;* Leroy Pelton, *For Reasons of Poverty: A Critical Analysis of the Public Child Welfare System in the United States* (New York: Praeger, 1989).

44. Joseph Goldstein, Anna Freud, and Albert J. Solnit, *Beyond the Best Interests of the Child* (New York: The Free Press, 1973) pp. 16–20.

45. Lindsey, *The Welfare of Children,* p. 157; Pelton, *For Reasons of Poverty.*

46. Downs, Costin, and McFadden, *Child Welfare and Family Services: Policy and Practice,* p. 15.

47. Ann Hartman, "Ideological Themes in Family Policy," *Families in Society: The Journal of Contemporary Human Services* (March 1995) pp. 182–192; L. Diane Bernard, "The Dark Side of Family Preservation," *Affilia; Journal of Women and Social Work,* Vol. 7, No. 2 (Summer 1992) pp. 156–159.

48. Subcommittee On Human Resources of the Committee On Ways And Means, House of Representatives, One Hundred Third Congress, First Session, "Hearings on President Clinton's Budget Proposal For New Funding For Child Welfare Services Targeted For Family Support And Preservation Services," 21 April 1993.

49. Patrick Murphy, "Family Preservation and Its Victims," *New York Times* (19 June 1993) p. 21.

50. Heather MacDonald, "The Ideology of 'Family Preservation'," *The Public Interest* (Spring 1994) p. 52.

51. Quoted in MacDonald, "The Ideology of 'Family Preservation'" p. 51.

52. Quoted in Mary-Lou Weisman, "When Parents Are Not In The Best Interests Of The Child," *The Atlantic Monthly* (July 1994) p. 62.

53. Carolyn L. Brown and Susan Little, "Family Reunification," *Children Today* (November–December 1990) p. 23.

54. Marianne Berry, "An Evaluation of Family Preservation Services: Fitting Agency Services to Family Needs," *Social Work* 37 (July 1992) p. 320.

55. Jill Kinney, David Haapala, and Charlotte Booth, *Keeping Families Together: The Homebuilders Model* (New York: Aldine De Gruyter, 1991) p. 185; Charles E. Wheeler, Grietje Reuter, David Struckman-Johnson, and Ying-Ying T. Yuan, "Evaluation of State of Connecticut Intensive Family Preservation Services: Phase V Annual Report," (Sacramento, CA: Walter R. McDonald & Associates), cited in Schuerman, et al., *Putting Families First,* p. 34; Berry, "An Evaluation of Family Preservation Services," p. 316.

56. D. N. Willems and R. DeRubeis, "The Effectiveness of Intensive Preventive Services for Families with Abused, Neglected, or Disturbed Children: Hudson County Project Final Report," (Trenton, NJ: Bureau of Research, New Jersey Division of Youth and Family Services, 1990); Stephen J. Leeds, "Evaluation of Nebraska's Intensive Services Project," (Iowa City, IA: National Resource Center on Family Based Services, 1984), reviewed in Schuerman, et al., *Putting Families First,* pp. 34–35.

57. Steven A. Szykula and Matthew J. Fleishman, "Reducing Out-of-Home Placements of Abused Children: Two Controlled Field Studies," *Child Abuse and Neglect* 9, pp. 277–283.

58. Hennepin County Community Services Department, "Family Study Project: Demonstration and Research in Intensive Services to Families," 1980, reviewed in Theodore J. Stein, "Projects to Prevent Out-of-Home Placement," *Children and Youth Services Review* 7, pp. 109–121.

59. Sally Wood, Keith Barton, and Carroll Schroeder, "In-Home Treatment of Abusive Families: Cost and Placement at One Year," *Psychotherapy* 25 (3) pp. 409–414; Charles G. Lyle and John Nelson, "Home Based vs. Traditional Child Protection Services: A Study of the Home Based Services Demonstration Project in the Ramsey County Community Human Services Department," Unpublished paper (St. Paul, MN: Ramsey County Community Human Services Department, 1983); G. Halper and M. A.

Jones, "Serving Families at Risk of Dissolution: Public Preventive Services in New York City," (New York: Human Services Administration, Special Services for Children, 1981) reviewed in Schuerman, et al., *Putting Families First*, pp. 35–38.

60. Schuerman, Rzepnicki, and Littell, *Putting Families First,* pp. 53–79, 143–191.

61. Peter J. Pecora, James K. Whittaker, and Anthony Maluccio, with Richard P. Barth and Robert D. Plotnick, *The Child Welfare Challenge: Policy, Practice, and Research* (New York: Aldine De Gruyter, 1992) p. 295.

62. Berry, "An Evaluation of Family Preservation Services: Fitting Agency Services to Family Needs."

63. Everett, "Child Foster Care," p. 383; Child Welfare League of America, *Kinship Care: A Natural Bridge* (Washington, DC: Child Welfare League of America, 1994).

64. Mark E. Courtney, "The Foster Care Crisis and Welfare Reform: How Might Reform Efforts Affect the Foster Care System?" *Public Welfare* (Summer 1995) p. 31.

65. Robert M. Goerge, "The Reunification Process in Substitute Care," *Social Service Review* (September 1990) p. 436.

66. Mark E. Courtney, "Factors Associated with the Reunification of Foster Children with Their Families," *Social Service Review* 68 (March 1994) pp. 81–108.

67. Robin Warsh, Barbara A. Pine, and Anthony Maluccio, "The Meaning of Family Preservation: Shared Mission, Diverse Methods," *Families in Society: The Journal of Contemporary Human Services* 76 (December 1995) p. 625.

68. Duncan Lindsey, "Factors Affecting the Foster Care Placement Decision: An Analysis of National Survey Data," *American Journal of Orthopsychiatry* 6 (Spring 1991) pp. 272–281.

69. Edith Fein and Anthony N. Maluccio, "Permanency Planning: Another Remedy in Jeopardy," *Social Service Review* 37 (September 1992), pp. 344–345.

70. Fein and Maluccio, "Permanency Planning," p. 345.

Chapter *12*

Conclusion—Lessons from Policy Analysis

When in graduate school, one of the authors had a favorite economics professor who was fond of saying that the key to understanding economics is the realization that everything is related to everything else—in at least two ways. This is also a useful observation for social welfare policy. All parts of policy are infinitely complex and interrelated in a seemingly endless variety of ways. This same professor also used to say that if you took all the economists in the world and laid them end-to-end, they would never reach a conclusion. Although a cynic might also say this about social welfare policy analysts, we do not want to end this book on such a note. We think several broad, general conclusions can be drawn from the analyses we have presented, and we will identify these below.

The Bottom Line Is the Bottom Line

The primary issue in practically every area of social welfare policy is *cost*. Put another way, social welfare policy is always subservient to economic policy. Every policy reform we have discussed has as its driving goal the reduction of expenditures, or else a fear that costs will get out of control. The recent welfare reform legislation has as its centerpiece requirements that recipients become employed, with time limits for this to happen. The argument is that we are spending too much, and work requirements will reduce costs. The main argument for family preservation is that by intervening in a family quickly and intensively, we can avoid foster care and thus reduce total long-range cost. Most proposals for reform of Social Security are based on projections that the system will "go broke" at some future date unless costs are reigned in. Managed care is a system designed to deliver medical and mental health services at a cheaper rate. Issues of humanitarianism, quality of life, promoting a good society, and mutual responsibility are all secondary to doing it cheaper.

As social workers we have often been pulled into the cost game and we have sold policies we wished to pursue based on promised cost reductions. Lindblom's notion of partisan policy analysis is why we do this. (If you will remember from Chapter 5, Lindblom is the political scientist who argues that people perform policy analyses directed toward the goals of those they wish to influence.) Realizing that policymakers are greatly concerned with cost, social workers try to sell policies based on cost reduction. Social workers did this in 1962 when we convinced Congress that providing social services to welfare recipients would help them solve the problems leading to their dependency, get them off of welfare, and thus save costs. We did this again in 1993 with arguments advocating for the Family Preservation and Support Program. Legislators quickly soured on the 1962 Social Service Amendments when they did not produce the expected cost savings. Now that family preservation is firmly in place and foster care placement rates—hence costs—are continuing to rise, it is highly likely that Congress will also sour on this, even if it can be demonstrated that by other criteria the concept is a success.

Compassion and Protection: Dual Motivations for Social Welfare Policy

Our review of current social welfare policies has confirmed Ralph Pumphrey's historical review of social welfare in America. He argued that all social welfare is driven by two more or less compatible motives. On the one side is the desire of people to make the lives of others better. "This aspect of philanthropy may be designated as *compassion:* the effort to alleviate present suffering, deprivation, or other undesirable conditions to which a segment of the population, but not the benefactor, is exposed." On the other side are aspects of policies that are designed for the benefit of their promoters and of the community at large. Pumphrey called this motivation *protection* and stated that, "It may result either from fear of change or from fear of what may happen if existing conditions are not changed." Pumphrey concludes by offering the hypothesis that social welfare policies that have proven effective have been characterized by a balance between compassion and protection.[1]

Aspects of compassion and protection have been evident in all the policies we have analyzed. Public welfare policy is concerned with helping poor people (actually the children of poor people) but is also concerned with protecting society against the threat of dependent adults; family preservation policy seeks to help keep families together, but also seeks to protect society from the excessive costs of an escalating foster care population; Social Security is designed to assure that the elderly are afforded a reasonably comfortable retirement, but it also protects families from having to assume responsibility for the care and support of aging relatives.

Ideology Drives Out Data in Social Welfare Policy Making

Social welfare policies are influenced much more by social values than they are by data from empirical research. It causes policy analysts no end of frustration to see situations like the recent welfare reform debate. Even though masses of data have been presented to Congress demonstrating that many poor people can't work, and there are not jobs for a majority of those who can, Congress continues to pass reform packages that feature time limits on assistance.[2] These time limits are based on the work ethic with its assertion that work can be found by anyone who tries hard enough. As empiricists and social scientists we express outrage, sometimes amusement, at what we view as antiscientific, anti-intellectual, behavior.

Is this tendency to promote values over data really so difficult to understand? We don't think that it is. Even social workers and allied social scientists find it hard to accept data that contradicts deeply held values. For example, we are finding the research that casts doubt on the effectiveness of family preservation programs very difficult to deal with because these programs are embodiments of some of our most cherished values. When Richard Herrnstein and Charles Murray published *The Bell Curve: Intelligence and Class Structure in American Life,* social workers immediately rejected the book's main theses, in most cases never having bothered to read the book. We have read the book and found ample grounds upon which to empirically reject Herrnstein and Murray's assertions. However, and this is our point, many of our colleagues rejected it without objectively assessing the arguments because these were so out of line with social work values.

Although we understand the tendency for ideology to drive out data in policy making, we do not excuse it. One of the ongoing challenges to policy makers will always be to make the process more rational and data based. This is the only way we will ever bring about meaningful social change and a more just society.

Policymakers Are Generally More Sophisticated than They Appear

Political scientists Theodore Marmor, Jerry Mashaw, and Philip Harvey argue that the central feature of social welfare policy is misinformation. They say, "A quite remarkable proportion of what is written and spoken about social welfare policy in the United States is, to put it charitably, mistaken. These mistakes are repeated by popular media addicted to the current and the quotable. Misconceptions thus insinuate themselves into the national consciousness; they can easily become the conventional wisdom."[3] However, policy makers themselves generally know better. With the legion of consultants, expert staff members, and social scientists providing testimony before committees, and all of the data and expertise available from government bureaus and private think tanks, all at the beck and call of legislators, they usually have a pretty good grasp on the reality of social welfare problems. Also, some policymakers, for example Daniel Patrick Moynihan, were experts in social welfare–related areas before they were elected to office. Others specialize in one or two areas of policy after election and quickly become quite expert.

With popular misconceptions about social welfare so strongly entrenched, how can legislators make policy in this area and hope to remain in office? Marmor, Mashaw, and Harvey present three options. They can try to correct the conventional wisdom, they can act as if the conventional wisdom is true, "or they can speak in terms that reflect popular understanding but attempt to govern on the basis of their quite different conception of the facts." The first option is a sure road to political death, the second is generally too cynical even for career politicians, so most see "dissembling as the only path available to policy reform combined with political success."[4]

These observations explain why reforms of social welfare policy have such a high failure rate. If reforms are marketed in terms of dominant misconceptions, they are destined to fail. As we saw in the chapter on welfare reform, nearly every politician is currently on the bandwagon advocating a two-year time limit on welfare benefits. However all, except for perhaps the very densest, have seen the data demonstrating that at the end of two years there will be a huge number of welfare recipients for whom there simply is no work. They further realize that taking the steps necessary to guarantee work will result in a more costly, rather than less costly, welfare program. Thus, because social welfare policies are designed and marketed in a way that virtually assures eventual failure, reform will always be a key feature, perhaps even focus, of the system.

Our Expectations for Social Welfare Policy Are Unrealistic

The common denominator of all of the policies we have analyzed, with perhaps the exception of Social Security, is that, for some of the reasons mentioned above, they have had disappointing outcomes. In an interesting analytical twist, the prominent sociologist Amitai Etzioni argues that the problem may well be not that the policies are failures, but rather that people expect too much from them. He argues that human behavior is extremely difficult to change, and the very act of attempting to do so is a tremendous challenge. He says, "We all know how difficult changing human behavior is, but this knowledge has not changed our basic optimistic predisposition. Once we truly accept that human behavior is surprisingly resistant to improvement, however, some rather positive, constructive lessons follow."[5] These lessons are summarized below.

Lower Your Expectations—Expect Change to Cost Much More Than Predicted

Because behavior change is so difficult to accomplish, we should be happy with any positive results at all. Viewed from this perspective, we should celebrate the fact that family preservation programs are successful in reaching and helping a few families, that a welfare-to-work program places 10 or 15 percent of participants in jobs, that boot camps for young offenders have a 50 percent grad-

uation rate. Regarding this last example, Etzioni observes "We must acknowledge that hoping to assimilate people raised for twenty years in one subculture
(say, the inner city, as a gang member) into a different subculture (of work and
social responsibility) in only a few months is laughably ambitious."[6]

Creaming Is Okay

Social programs are often criticized for concentrating on the part of the target
population with the fewest problems. For example, welfare-to-work programs
often admit recipients with a comparatively high level of education, few problems, and recent work experience, because they are easy to place in jobs and
make the program look effective. As we saw in the review of family preservation, that policy is currently under criticism because the clients selected for services are not the most serious cases. Researchers have concluded that most of
family preservation's clients were never in danger of having the children
removed in the first place. Critics say that the practice of creaming is undesirable because it directs services to people who may not even need them and it
avoids dealing with the really tough problems. Etzioni disagrees, arguing that
we never have enough money to help everyone and so it only makes sense to
concentrate our efforts on those most likely to benefit. "The resources saved this
way can then be applied to some of the more difficult cases. Policymakers
should, though, recognize the fact that the going will get tougher and tougher."[7]

Don't Expect to Scrape the Bottom of the Barrel

We must recognize that even with concentrated and persistent effort, no social
welfare policy will ever be able to reach everyone and every social problem. In
a situation analogous to a medical patient with an illness too severe to cure,
there are some people who will never be adequate parents, some welfare recipients who will never be able to get a job, some criminals who see no percentage
in being "rehabilitated," and some social problems, like poverty, that may never
be completely eradicated.

Don't Allow the Best to Defeat the Good

We generally tend to evaluate social welfare policies relative to the original
promises of their sponsors rather than to some reasonable level of achievement.
Because of the nature of the political process, policies are almost always over-
sold initially in order to get enough support to be enacted. Because, as we have
noted over and over, social welfare policies rarely exhibit spectacular success,
they should be measured against other policies rather than against some ideal

standard. For example, a welfare-to-work program that increases the level of paid employment by nine hours a month will be considered a failure if measured against the standard that all participants should find full-time jobs. However, if compared with other programs that only increased work by five hours per month, this program could look very good. "As long as the social goal at hand must be served, we must settle for the comparative best (which is often not so hot), rather than chase elusive perfection."[8]

Be Multi-Faceted But Not Holistic

In social work school we teach students to utilize a systems approach. This approach illustrates how the various aspects of a person's life and problems are related, and that anything impacting on one aspect of a system will reverberate throughout the system. This approach also illustrates that policies must address a number of facets of a person's life to be truly effective. Probably the best example in this book is child welfare policy. It is now quite fashionable to point out that it is impossible to effectively address child abuse and neglect without at the same time addressing poverty. Etzioni accepts this, but argues that a holistic approach would cost so much, and be so complex, it would never be practical for the large number of people who need help. We must search for policies that recognize the systems aspect of problems but are less exacting than a holistic approach. Thus, while we recognize that poverty is the major factor leading to child neglect, we can still provide therapeutic day care programs that address only a few targeted aspects of the neglect, and by doing so make children's lives better. As Etzioni concludes, "It's no use pretending that poverty or welfare will be abolished, AIDS or cancer cured in this century, drug abuse or teen pregnancy sharply reduced. Let's instead dedicate our efforts to effective but clearly delineated projects in each of these areas. This humbler approach is likely to have a very attractive side effect: it may enhance public willingness to pay for such projects and may also restore public trust in our leaders and institutions."[9]

Notes

1. Ralph Pumphrey, "Compassion and Protection: Dual Motivations in Social Welfare," *Social Service Review* 23 (1959) pp. 21–29.

2. For example see "Testimony of Sheldon Danziger, Professor, School of Social Work and School of Public Policy, University of Michigan, Before the Senate Finance Committee, February 29, 1996."

3. Theodore R. Marmor, Jerry L. Mashaw, and Philip L. Harvey, *America's Misunderstood Welfare State* (New York: Basic Books, 1990) p. 213.

4. Marmor, Mashaw, and Harvey, *America's Misunderstood Welfare State,* pp. 213–214.
5. Amitai Etzioni, "Incorrigible," *The Atlantic Monthly* 274 (July 1994) pp. 14–16.
6. Etzioni, "Incorrigible," p. 16.
7. Etzioni, "Incorrigible," p. 16.
8. Etzioni, "Incorrigible," p. 16.
9. Etzioni, "Incorrigible," p. 16.

Appendix A

Library Research for Practitioner Policy Analysis

LYNN TOBOLA, M.L.S.
Social Work Librarian
University of Alabama

Information Self-Reliance

Unquestionably, the process of locating information has changed dramatically in the last few years. In the past, librarians could provide patrons with virtually all of the information available at their fingertips. Now, with the growing numbers of electronic resources available, that is a difficult—perhaps even impossible—task. Therefore, it is essential for social workers to move in the direction of becoming "information self-reliant," which can be defined as the ability to independently identify, locate, and use information effectively. Locating information is a process-oriented task. As you become fluent with the process of identifying and locating print and online resources, you will be empowering yourself with information self-reliance skills.

Get To Know Your Librarians

There is nothing terribly complex about collecting published information for policy analysis. Although the information itself is not unduly complicated, it is vast and is becoming available at a dizzying pace. Many people have the curious idea that the main function of librarians is to check out books and then return them to the shelves. They think that asking a librarian a question is an imposition on the librarian's time and often feel embarrassed to do so. Many times library users approach the reference desk only after failed attempts to locate specific information.

Librarians are professionals trained to help people make efficient and effective use of the library. They assist individual patrons with particular research problems on a daily basis. Modern libraries contain a fascinating yet bewildering new assortment of online, CD, machine-readable, and laser disc information retrieval systems, as well as the older print resources. A few sessions with your librarian, ideally focused on a research problem, will save you an immense amount of time and trouble.

After you have become familiar with the major information retrieval sources available in your library, your dependence on the reference librarians will greatly decrease. However, there will always be valid reasons to consult your librarian. For example, there may be a new resource available of which you are not aware. Stop by the reference desk occasionally and ask if there are any new additions to the collection that might be of value to your current research.

The quickest and easiest way to become information self-reliant is to go to the library and begin exploring the building by simply walking around. Get a visual sense of what is where. Where are the current journals shelved? Where is the Reference Department? What is the location of the Interlibrary Loan Office? Bring a planned research strategy, ask for assistance, follow through on the instructions and suggestions of the librarian, and give it your best shot. You'll probably surprise yourself. You are on the way to becoming an information self-reliant social worker.

Explanation and Organization of Information Self-Reliance Topics

This appendix contains three items. The first two are worksheets designed to assist you in planning research strategies and to practice communication skills with librarians. The third is a set of checklists that you can use to determine whether or not a library has a particular title, to find the locations of those titles, and to make notes on the usefulness of those resources for specific information needs.

The checklists can be used, depending on your strategy, for more than one library to help make the most productive use of your time. Space has been provided next to each title in the lists for you to write call numbers or government document classification numbers and the physical location of materials for any notes you care to include to get back to a particular resource easily.

Space is also included to allow you to review these resources with a critical eye and make notes. Try to include the value of the resource as well as some limitations. For example, a resource could have extensive, up-to-date statistics on mental health services, but be limited to adult populations and you might need statistics on mental health services for children. Making one or two comments on the usefulness of a resource the first time you use it can save time on future projects.

It is important to consider the kinds of information included in each resource (e.g., names and addresses, statistics, or historical information), the subject areas covered (e.g., health, mental health, or child welfare), and the scope (e.g., geographic limitations, specific populations, timeframe, or intended audience). Although this might seem to be a lot of work, it is not. Take a moment to determine whether or not a particular resource is appropriate for your current information needs.

Searching for a known title can often be the simplest strategy for beginning researchers. Most major academic and many large public libraries now have online catalogs. Therefore, the entries on the checklists are arranged by title.

Much of the information appropriate to a given topic should be as current as possible; however, it is important to know the history of a policy when doing policy research. Many of these titles have been published for a number of years and are still updated or published on an annual, biannual, monthly, weekly, and even daily basis. Some titles are updated on an irregular basis. Dates of publication for titles that have been updated either regularly or irregularly will appear as **latest ed.** in the date field. Publication dates of several titles are rather old. They have been included because they have historical value. Speak with a librarian if you have a question regarding the current edition of a title.

To further assist you in building information self-reliant skills, annotations (i.e., brief summaries) of the resources are *not* included. Many of these resources are unique and can provide an abundance of useful information, including names of people to contact, association and research society publications, and information on free publications. The only way you can understand the value of some of these resources is to find a good table and a comfortable chair, and look at them yourself.

The resources listed vary according to level of intensity. Some tend to be more popular than academic, but all are certainly helpful for policy analysis. Both levels are included in order to make the checklist useful for a variety of libraries.

After reviewing the content of each worksheet you can either systematically complete all the checklists or use them selectively to explore resources useful for specific kinds of information.

This appendix is intended to encourage social work students to begin learning information self-reliance skills and to encourage practitioners to redis-cover known resources and explore the changing nature of information retrieval. It is offered in the conviction that careful and skilled research will improve social policy, social programs, social work education, and social work practice. The best way to learn how to do library-oriented research is go out and do it.

Worksheet for a Planned Research Strategy

1. Create a list of possible areas for a policy analysis.
   a. _____
   b. _____
   c. _____

2. What is the purpose of the analysis?
   a. ____course requirement
   b. ____legislative testimony
   c. ____grant proposal
   d. ____job related
   e. ____other

3. Check all of the relevant types of information needed for your policy analysis.
   ____background
   ____charts, graphs, tables
   ____definitions
   ____historical
   ____interview experts
   ____laws/legal information
   ____legislative histories
   ____primary sources
   ____public opinion
   ____statistics

4. Determine the timeframe for completion of the first round of research _____
   Determine the timeframe to begin writing the first draft _____
   Determine the timeframe for the second round of research _____
   Determine the timeframe to begin writing the second draft_____

5. **GO TO THE LIBRARY** to become familiar with the organization (where things are) and with the services (reference assistance, interlibrary loan, photocopying).

continued

6. Stop at the reference desk and determine whether or not there is a social sciences and/or government documents librarian to speak with regarding your information needs. Ask for a brief introduction to the online or card catalog if you are not familiar with the system.

7. Spend some time becoming familiar with the library's catalog.

8. Use the list of indexes, abstracts, journals and other resources in the appendixes as a checklist for the holdings in the library. What does your library have?

9. Begin an initial search for information related to your topic. Locate one or two books, three or four journal articles, and one or two government documents.

10. Begin reading. Concentrate on the information you have located and whether it is what you will need for the analysis. Make some notes on each one of the books or articles. Include bibliographical information in your notes, bearing in mind the information you will need for your reference list should you decide to use a particular source.

11. Determine what resources are available for locating federal, state, and local experts knowledgeable in your policy area. Make a list of names and numbers. Plan ahead. Write down three to five carefully worded questions to ask the experts when you contact them. MAKE THE CALLS.

12. Refine your research question based on the initial review of the literature and your conversations with the experts.

13. Communicate with the librarian to get suggestions regarding additional resources you might need to consult.

14. Communicate with your instructor regarding the results of your initial findings and ask for suggestions.

15. Don't get frustrated. Plan your library time, your reading time, your thinking time, and your writing time. And especially, your *rewriting* time.

16. As you begin to become comfortable using the library resources, you are likely to find additional information that can be added to your analysis. Incorporate new information in your rewrites.

17. *Know when to stop.* There is an enormous amount of information available on topics related to policy analysis. Don't get caught up in the *amount* of information you collect. Concentrate on *relevance* to the analysis.

18. A well-written paper is as important as the resources you choose to use. Ask a friend or colleague to read your analysis for clarity and style.

19. Once you begin following planned research strategies, you should notice a difference in the quality of the finished product.

Worksheet for an Interview with a Librarian

This form was developed to assist students with communicating in an effective and efficient manner when talking to a reference librarian. It can be used in conjunction with the Planned Research Strategy Worksheet. The desired outcome of this worksheet is to instill confidence in students when communicating with a librarian or other information specialist.

Most people feel completely at ease ordering food in a restaurant. We know what we want and how we want it prepared. This is not always true in communicating what we want when it comes to information. Put yourself in control. Make statements as opposed to asking questions. "I would like to find information on...." is a stronger positive introduction than "Can you help me find...?" and they convey the same need for assistance.

Pay attention. Be inquisitive. Librarians are no different from other professionals when it comes to jargon. When something is said that you don't understand, ask for an explanation. "What are 'the stacks'?" "What is a SUDOC number you just mentioned?" "What does 'keyword' mean?" Present yourself in a prepared manner and the results will be a productive exchange between yourself and the librarian. A planned strategy for talking with a librarian is one of the skills needed to become information self-reliant. Complete the following form.

1. Decide on a topic using the Planned Research Strategy Worksheet as a guide.

   _____

2. Form an introductory statement in one sentence. For example, "I would like to find some current articles and a couple of books on [*your topic*]". _____

   _____

3. Write down the next two statements to include more detailed information. The more information librarians have will help them determine their strategy for assisting you. For example, "I am working on a 10-page paper for my social work policy analysis class. I know I'll need some statistics and the historical background of [*your topic*]." _____

   _____

4. *Listen* to the librarian. Are you being asked to clarify your subject? Are you being directed to resources? Do you understand what the librarian is saying? If not, admit it and ask to have the instructions repeated. For example, "Gee! That's great–but I have no idea what you just said. Could you run that by me again?" You are still in control. Practice a couple of positive responses if you are not sure what you have been told.

5. Depending on when you go to the library, there could be a different librarian at the reference desk than the one you spoke with initially. Make use of the variety

continued

of expertise available to you. For example, one librarian might specialize in searching electronic resources, while another might have more experience in locating state or regional resources. Also, you may find that you feel more comfortable with one than another. Practice the communication exercises suggested earlier with more than one librarian.

6. Remember that librarians are there to help you. Help them to help you by coming prepared.

The Internet

It is essential to mention here the vast amount of information available on the Internet that can be used for policy analysis. Many college, university, and public libraries now have computers available for people to connect to the Internet. One of the best ways to learn some of the search strategies is to find someone who has experience and ask for a demonstration. If you don't really know what the Internet is or haven't actually done any searching, find out and devote some time to learning how to locate information on the Net. There are numerous books on navigating the Net, as well as resources that list various sites containing a broad array of information. Check with your librarian or local bookstore to see what is available. As Internet sites change and grow everyday, specific addresses are not included here.

Newspaper Indexes

Newspapers are an excellent source for locating analyses of current or historical events and issues. Policy developments can be followed on a day-to-day basis, whereas magazines and academic journals can be weeks or months behind. Most major libraries subscribe to a variety of national newspapers, such as the *New York Times* and the *Washington Post,* that regularly print in-depth analyses of social welfare policy issues. Check your library holdings for national, regional, state, and local newspaper holdings. Depending on the newspaper subscriptions, find out what commercially or in house indexes are available.

Newspapers

State and local newspapers are an excellent primary source of current and historical information. Determine if your library subscribes to any commercially produced state newspaper indexes. Also, many public libraries maintain newspaper clipping files for local, state and regional newspapers.

Beginning Resources

The titles listed below are general resources that can be helpful when beginning a research project. Names, addresses and telephone numbers in some of the publications can help get you in touch with experts in a given field. Other titles provide guidelines for writing, or recommend additional resources to consider.

Find it Fast: How to Uncover Expert Information on any Subject, by Robert I. Berkman (Harper & Row, 1990).
Call Number _____ Location _____
Notes _____

Guide to Information Sources for Social Work and the Human Services, by Henry Mendelsohn (Oryx Press, 1987).
Call Number _____ Location _____
Notes _____

Guide to Library Research Methods, by Thomas Mann (Oxford University Press, 1987).
Call Number _____ Location _____
Notes _____

How and Where to Find Facts and Get Help (R & E Publishers, 1993).
Call Number _____ Location _____
Notes _____

Professional Writing for the Human Services, edited by Linda Beebe (NASW Press, 1993).
Call Number _____ Location _____
Notes _____

Reference Sources in Social Work, by James H. Conrad (Scarecrow, 1982).
Call Number _____ Location _____
Notes _____

Sources of Information for Historical Research, by Thomas Slavens (Neal-Schuman, 1994).
Call Number _____ Location _____
Notes _____

Sources of Information in the Social Sciences: A Guide to the Literature (American Library Association, 1986).
Call Number _____ Location _____
Notes _____

Encyclopedias/Dictionaries/Directories/Biographies

The titles listed below provide a variety of different kinds of information. For example, the encyclopedias are great resources for a quick review of a given topic. The dictionaries can be useful for providing a specific definition for a word or phrase that plays a key role in your policy analysis. Information on people who played significant roles in developing or changing existing policy can be located in the biographical material. Profiles of interest groups and information on numerous associations, organizations, and societies that can be contacted for information are included in some of the resources.

American Reformers: An H. W. Wilson Biographical Dictionary, edited by Alden Whitman (H. W. Wilson, 1985).
Call Number _____   Location _____
Notes _____

Biographical Dictionary of Social Welfare in America, edited by Walter I. Trattner (Greenwood Press, 1986).
Call Number _____   Location _____
Notes _____

Biographical Directory of the Governors of the United States, 1988–1994, by Marie Marmo Mullaney (Greenwood Press, 1994).
Call Number _____   Location _____
Notes _____

Biographical Directory of the United States Congress, 1774–1989 (U.S. Government Printing Office, 1989).
Call Number _____   Location _____
Notes _____

Biographical Directory of the United States Executive Branch, 1774–1989, edited by Robert Sobel (Greenwood Press, 1990).
Call Number _____   Location _____
Notes _____

Directories in Print (Gale Research, Inc., latest ed.).
Call Number _____   Location _____
Notes _____

continued

Directory of Political Newsletters: A Guide to Sources of Insiders' Information about Government and Politics (Government Research Service, 1995).
Call Number _____ Location _____
Notes _____

Encyclopedia of Associations (Gale Research Co., latest ed.).
Call Number _____ Location _____
Notes _____

Encyclopedia of Social Work, 19th ed. (NASW Press, 1995).
Call Number _____ Location _____
Notes _____

Guide to Multicultural Resources (Highsmith Press, 1995/96) (biennial).
Call Number _____ Location _____
Notes _____

International Encyclopedia of the Social Sciences (Macmillan, ©1968—©1979).
Call Number _____ Location _____
Notes _____

Political Resource Directory (Political Resource, Inc., latest ed.).
Call Number _____ Location _____
Notes _____

Public Policy Dictionary, by Earl R. Kruschke & Bryon M. Jackson (ABC CLIO, 1987).
Call Number _____ Location _____
Notes _____

Public Welfare Directory (American Public Welfare Association, latest ed.).
Call Number _____ Location _____
Notes _____

Social Work Almanac, 2nd ed., by Leon Ginsberg (NASW Press, 1995).
Call Number _____ Location _____
Notes _____

Social Work Dictionary, 3rd ed., by Robert L. Barker (NASW Press, 1995).
Call Number _____ Location _____
Notes _____

Social Work Speaks: NASW Policy Statements, 3rd ed. (NASW Press, 1994).
Call Number _____ Location _____
Notes _____

continued

Think Tank Directory: A Guide to Independent Nonprofit Public Policy Research Organizations (Government Research Service, 1996).
Call Number _____ Location _____
Notes _____

U.S. Aging Policy Interest Groups: Institutional Profiles, by David D. Van Tassel and Jimmy Elaine Wilkinson Meyer (Greenwood Press, 1992).
Call Number _____ Location _____
Notes _____

U.S. Criminal Justice Interest Groups: Institutional Profiles, Michael A. Hallett and Dennis J. Palumbo (Greenwood Press, 1993).
Call Number _____ Location _____
Notes _____

Indexes and Abstracts

The following index and abstract titles refer to the printed version. See the following section for indexes and abstracts that are available electronically. Journals covered by an index or abstract and a user's guide are located at the front of each issue of the index. Subject headings vary from index to index. For example, *Psychological Abstracts* uses "social casework," *P.A.I.S.* uses "social services," and *Social Work Abstracts* uses "social work." Keep this in mind as you look through different indexes and abstracts. Remember to speak with a librarian when you have questions regarding these resources.

ABC POL SCI (ABC-Clio, 1969–   ).
Call Number _____ Location _____
Notes _____

Abstracts in Social Gerontology (Sage, 1990–   ).
Call Number _____ Location _____
Notes _____

America, History and Life (Clio Press, 1964–   ).
Call Number _____ Location _____
Notes _____

Criminal Justice Abstracts (National Council on Crime and Delinquency, Information Center, 1968–   ).
Call Number _____ Location _____
Notes _____

continued

ERIC (U.S. Department of Education, 1968–   ).
Call Number _____ Location _____
Notes _____

Human Resources Abstracts (Sage Publications, 1975–   ).
Call Number _____ Location _____
Notes _____

PAIS (Public Affairs Information Service, 1915–   ).
Call Number _____ Location _____
Notes _____

Psychological Abstracts (American Psychological Association, 1927–   ).
Call Number _____ Location _____
Notes _____

Sage Family Studies Abstracts (Sage Publications, 1979–   ).
Call Number _____ Location _____
Notes _____

Social Sciences Citation Index (Institute for Scientific Information, 1970–   ).
Call Number _____ Location _____
Notes _____

Social Sciences Index (H.W. Wilson, 1974–   ).
Call Number _____ Location _____
Notes _____

Social Work Abstracts [formerly *Social Work Research and Abstracts,* 1977–1993]
(National Association of Social Workers, 1994–   ).
Call Number _____ Location _____
Notes _____

Sociological Abstracts (Sociological Abstracts, Inc., 1952–   ).
Call Number _____ Location _____
Notes _____

Women's Studies Abstracts (Transaction Periodical Consortium, 1972–   ).
Call Number _____ Location _____
Notes _____

Electronic Resources

Many university libraries now have a selection of electronic resources available that can direct you to information related to policy analysis. "Electronic resources" refers to information stored and accessed through a computer. These resources are often accessible through either the online catalog or at individual computer workstations. As many large academic institutions have branch libraries, take the time to determine if there are specialized electronic resources that are only available in those locations.

There continues to be a growing number of people who are just beginning to learn about and use electronic resources. Electronic resources can save time, allow you to search for very specific kinds of information, and sometimes even allow you to print out the full text of an article at the computer. Speak with a librarian to determine which electronic resources are available in your library and how they are accessed. Find out what the library policy is on providing assistance in learning to use the electronic resources or ask for a brief introduction.

Keyword Searching

A reminder regarding differences in subject headings is included in the introduction to printed indexes. It is appropriate to add here a word on searching electronic resources. Information can be located by subject headings in electronic indexes. However, keyword searching is becoming a popular way to search as well. Keyword searching is a request typed into the computer that tells the computer to locate all of the records that contain certain keywords anywhere in the citation (e.g., title, author, name of journal, publisher, subject headings, or abstract). The following is a very basic introduction to keyword searching. The way in which a request is actually typed into the computer will depend on the system you are using.

Keyword searches will often locate an enormous amount of citations, but many of them can be totally irrelevant to your topic. For example, a keyword search for **drugs** might retrieve citations to articles on the drugs used to treat AIDS patients. It might also locate articles on FDA rules for approving new drugs or an article on drugs in the workplace.

There is a strategy for limiting a keyword search to narrow the focus. This is called Boolean logic. Boolean logic allows you to narrow a search by using the word *and,* broaden a search by using the word *or,* and limit the search by using the word *not.* For example, **drugs and policy** would locate citations that have both words in the record. To narrow your request further, **drugs and policy and schools** would retrieve a more focused set of results. The *or* operator can be used when an idea can be expressed by synonyms. For example, **aged or elderly** would retrieve all citations that contain either of those words.

The *not* operator can be used to exclude a concept. For example, **housing not rural** would retrieve only the citations that include the word *housing,* but not *rural.*

continued

Many electronic resources allow you to combine search requests in order to retrieve relevant citations. For example, a search request could be refined to request citations to articles on housing for the elderly, but limited to urban not rural environments.

Although keyword searching can be exact, it is important to keep in mind that keyword searching can also retrieve either too many irrelevant citations or too few relevant ones. Many libraries have tipsheets available to acquaint you with keyword searching and Boolean operators. Ask for assistance as you begin to explore this method of retrieving information electronically.

Listed below are a few of the major and more readily available electronic resources found in major libraries. The subject area has been provided after the name of the database, because titles of some electronic resources are not indicative of the subject area. Dates have *not* been included, as coverage will depend on the kind of subscription your library has to an individual index.

ABI/INFORM [business] (University Microfilms International)
Location _____
Notes _____

AgeLine [aged and aging] (American Association of Retired Persons)
Location _____
Notes _____

EAI [covers a broad range of topics related to social welfare as well as many others] (Information Access Corp.)
Location _____
Notes _____

ERIC [education] (U.S. Department of Education)
Location _____
Notes _____

MEDLINE [health and medicine] (U.S. National Library of Medicine)
Location _____
Notes _____

PAIS [economic, international, and social issues] (Public Affairs Information Service)
Location _____
Notes _____

PsycINFO or *PsycLIT* [psychology/psychiatry] (American Psychological Association)
Location _____
Notes _____

continued

Social Sciences Citation Index [social sciences] (Institute for Scientific Information)
Location _____
Notes _____

Social Sciences Index [social sciences] (H. W. Wilson)
Location _____
Notes _____

Social Work Abstracts [social work] (National Association of Social Workers)
Location _____
Notes _____

U.S. Government Documents

Approximately 1,400 research and public libraries have been designated as selective or regional depository libraries. These libraries, based on their classification, regularly receive either unclassified selected publications from the Government Printing Office (GPO) or all unclassified publications available in the depository program. The U.S. government is one of the most prolific publishers in the world. Government documents are an unparalleled source of information. Locating the closest selective or regional depository library can provide you with extensive information on most topics for doing a policy analysis. Government documents librarians are specially trained to assist you with locating these unique and various kinds of publications. Use their expertise, as they can be tremendously helpful.

What follows is a list of basic relevant resources published by either the GPO or research presses that will aid in policy analysis. Several of the resources belong in more than one of the categories listed below. They have only been listed once in the most appropriate category. Use the spaces provided to check your library's holdings.

Getting Started

Complete Guide to Citing Government Information Resources: A Manual for Writers and Librarians, Rev. ed., by Diane L. Garner and Diane H. Smith (American Library Association, 1993).
Call Number _____   Location _____
Notes _____

Directory of Federal Libraries, edited by William R. Evinger (Oryx Press, 1993).
Call Number _____   Location _____
Notes _____

continued

Directory of Government Document Collections and Librarians, 6th ed., edited by
Judith Horn (Congressional Information Service, 1991).
Call Number _____   Location _____
Notes _____

Encyclopedia of Governmental Advisory Organizations (Gale Research Co., latest
ed.).
Call Number _____   Location _____
Notes _____

Federal Data Base Finder (Information USA, Inc., latest ed.).
Call Number _____   Location _____
Notes _____

Government Online, by Max Lent (Harper Perennial, 1995).
Call Number _____   Location _____
Notes _____

Guide to U.S. Government Publications, edited by Donna Andriot (Documents Index,
latest ed.).
Call Number _____   Location _____
Notes _____

How to use the Major Indexes to U.S. Government Publications, by John M. Ross
(American Library Association, 1989).
Call Number _____   Location _____
Notes _____

Introduction to United States Government Information Sources, by Joe Morehead
and Mary Fetzer (Libraries Unlimited, Inc., 1992).
Call Number _____   Location _____
Notes _____

Subject Guide to Major United States Government Publications, 2nd ed., edited by
Wiley J. Williams (American Library Association, 1987).
Call Number _____   Location _____
Notes _____

*Tapping the Government Grapevine: The User Friendly Guide to U.S. Government
Information Sources, 2nd ed.,* by Judith Schiek Robinson (Oryx Press, 1993).
Call Number _____   Location _____
Notes _____

continued

United States Government Manual (Government Printing Office, latest ed.).
Call Number _____ Location _____
Notes _____

Using Government Information Sources: Print and Electronic, 2nd ed., by Jean L.
Sears and Marilyn K. Moody (Oryx, 1994).
Call Number _____ Location _____
Notes _____

Keeping up with New Government Publications

New Books (U.S. Government Printing Office, latest ed.).
Call Number _____ Location _____
Notes _____

Subject Bibliography Index (U.S. Government Printing Office, latest ed.).
Call Number _____ Location _____
Notes _____

U.S. Government Books (U.S. Government Printing Office, latest ed.).
Call Number _____ Location _____
Notes _____

Names and Numbers

The following resources contain the names, addresses, and phone numbers of people
working with or for the U.S. government. They can be used for contacting individuals or offices for information on the current status of specific legislation or to express
concerns, opinions, or ideas.

American Lobbyists Directory (Gale, latest ed.).
Call Number _____ Location _____
Notes _____

Congress A to Z: A Ready Reference Encyclopedia, 2nd ed. (Congressional Quarterly,
Inc., 1993).
Call Number _____ Location _____
Notes _____

Congress and the Nation (Congressional Quarterly Service, latest ed.).
Call Number _____ Location _____
Notes _____

continued

Congressional Yellow Book (Washington Monitor, latest ed.).
Call Number _____   Location _____
Notes _____

Federal Statistical Sources: Where to Find Agency Experts & Personnel, by William
R. Evinger (Oryx Press, 1991).
Call Number _____   Location _____
Notes _____

Federal Yellow Book (Washington Monitor, Inc., latest ed.).
Call Number _____   Location _____
Notes _____

Washington Information Directory (Congressional Quarterly, latest ed.).
Call Number _____   Location _____
Notes _____

Government Indexes

There are a wide variety of indexes for locating government documents. The appropriate resource to use depends on what kind of information you are looking for. Depository libraries now have many of their indexes available on CD-ROMs. Find out what your library has in electronic format that relates to government publications.

The indexes listed below will direct you to hearings, reports, debates, articles published in government publications, as well as other relevant information related to your policy area. Other indexes and finding aids are listed in more specific sections of this appendix. Please also refer to the section on Legal Resources.

CIS/Index to Publications of the United States Congress (Congressional Information Service, latest ed.).
Call Number _____   Location _____
Notes _____

Index to U.S. Government Periodicals (Infordata International, 1970–1987).
Call Number _____   Location _____
Notes _____

Monthly Catalog of U.S. Government Documents (U.S. Government Printing Office, latest ed.).
Call Number _____   Location _____
Notes _____

U.S. Government Periodicals Index (Congressional Information Service, latest ed.).
Call Number _____   Location _____
Notes _____

continued

Government Bibliographies

Bibliography of United States Government Bibliographies, 1968–1973, by Roberta A. Scull (Pierian Press, 1975).
Call Number _____ Location _____
Notes _____

Bibliography of United States Government Bibliographies, 1974–1976, by Roberta A. Scull (Pierian Press, 1976).
Call Number _____ Location _____
Notes _____

Cumulative Subject Guide to U.S. Government Bibliographies, 1924–1973 (Carrollton Press, ©1976).
Call Number _____ Location _____
Notes _____

***see also *Subject Bibliography Index* listed in the New Government Publications section for more current bibliographies.

Statistical Sources

American Statistics Index (Congressional Information Service, latest ed.).
Call Number _____ Location _____
Notes _____

Guide to U.S. Government Statistics (Documents Index, latest ed.).
Call Number _____ Location _____
Notes _____

Historical Statistics of the States of the United States: Two Centuries of the Census, 1790–1990, by Don Dodd (Greenwood Press, 1993).
Call Number _____ Location _____
Notes _____

Historical Statistics of the United States, Colonial Times to 1970 (U.S. Government Printing Office, 1975) [and supplements].
Call Number _____ Location _____
Notes _____

Statistical Abstract of the United States (U.S. Government Printing Office, latest ed.).
Call Number _____ Location _____
Notes _____

United States Census of Population and Housing (U.S. Bureau of the Census, latest ed.).
Call Number _____ Location _____
Notes _____

Legislative Histories

A thorough policy analysis requires a detailed review of the information provided to the policymakers that leads to the passing of a law. The resources listed below all have a unique role in tracking past and present policy histories at the federal level. Remember, making good notes the first time you use a resource is important. Working with a number of resources that provide similar kinds of information in a variety of ways can be confusing. Two or three comments about a resource can save time when you go back to use them again. Several of the resources listed in the 'Getting Started' section of this appendix provide descriptions of the content of the following titles and why and when to use them. Please also refer to the section on Legal Resources.

Code of Federal Regulations and Index (U.S. Government Printing Office, latest ed.).
Call Number _____   Location _____
Notes _____

Congressional Record Daily Digest (U.S. Government Printing Office, latest ed.).
Call Number _____   Location _____
Notes _____

Federal Legislative Histories: An Annotated Bibliography and Index to Officially Published Sources (Greenwood Press, 1994).
Call Number _____   Location _____
Notes _____

Federal Register (U.S. Governmemt Printing Office, latest ed.).
Call Number _____   Location _____
Notes _____

Legislative Histories (Congressional Information Service, latest ed.) [volume 3 of the CIS/Index listed above].
Call Number _____   Location _____
Notes _____

United States Code (U.S. Government Printing Office, latest ed.).
Call Number _____   Location _____
Notes _____

United States Code Congressional and Administrative News (West, latest ed.).
Call Number _____   Location _____
Notes _____

United States Statutes at Large (U.S. Government Printing Office, latest ed.).
Call Number _____   Location _____
Notes _____

Selected U.S. Government Department and Agency Periodical Publications

The following periodicals are published by departments or agencies within the federal government. This is only a short selected list. There are many more. These sources often provide useful and easy to follow summary material on policy issues. Articles in these publications can be located using the U.S. Government Periodicals Index and the Monthly Catalog.

Aging [quarterly]
AIDS Bibliography [monthly]
Child Support Report [irregular]
Children Today [bimonthly]
Health [annual]
Health Care Financing Review [quarterly]
Juvenile Justice [quarterly]
Mental Health, United States [annual]
Psychopharmacology Bulletin [quarterly]
Public Health Reports [bimonthly]
Social Security Bulletin [quarterly]
Social Security Handbook [annual]
Sourcebook of Criminal Justice Statistics [annual]
Schizophrenia Bulletin [quarterly]

State and Local Information Resources

There are a variety of places to locate information at the state and local level. State departments of public health often publish vital statistics on an annual basis. Departments of human resources can provide statistics on social services, program and project status reports, and information related to the elderly, children, youth, families, health, mental health, and crime in the state. Many state universities publish economic almanacs and statistical atlases. Contact your state department of human resources and state university to obtain information on regularly published newsletters, reports, and factsheets. Many of these can be subscribed to on a minimal or no-cost basis. Chambers of commerce and county courthouses can also provide valuable information at the local level.

Almanac of the 50 States: Basic Data Profiles with Comparative Tables, by Edith R. Horner (Information Publications, 1995 or latest ed.).
Call Number _____ Location _____
Notes _____

continued

Bibliography of State Bibliographies, 1970–1982, by David W. Parish (Libraries Unlimited, 1985).
Call Number _____   Location _____
Notes _____

Book of the States (Council of State Governments, latest ed.).
Call Number _____   Location _____
Notes _____

County and City Data Book (U.S. Government Printing Office, latest ed.).
Call Number _____   Location _____
Notes _____

Directory of State Court Clerks and County Courthouses (WANT Publishing, latest ed.).
Call Number _____   Location _____
Notes _____

Encyclopedia of Associations. Regional, State, and Local Organizations (Gale Research, latest ed.).
Call Number _____   Location _____
Notes _____

Governors' Staff Directory (National Governors' Association, latest ed.).
Call Number _____   Location _____
Notes _____

Municipal Government Reference Sources: Publications and Collections, by Peter Hernon et al. (Bowker, 1978).
Call Number _____   Location _____
Notes _____

State and Local Statistics Sources (Gale Research, latest ed.).
Call Number _____   Location _____
Notes _____

State and Metropolitan Area Data Book: A Statistical Abstract Supplement (U.S. Government Printing Office, latest ed.).
Call Number _____   Location _____
Notes _____

State Documents Checklists: A Historical Bibliography, by Susan L. Dow (W. S. Hein, 1990).
Call Number _____   Location _____
Notes _____

continued

State Government Research Directory (Gale Research, 1987 or latest ed.).
Call Number _____ Location _____
Notes _____

State Publications and Depository Libraries: A Reference Handbook, by Margaret T.
Lane (Greenwood Press, 1981).
Call Number _____ Location _____
Notes _____

*State Reference Publications: A Guide to State Blue Books, Legislative Manuals and
Other General Reference Sources* (Government Research Service, latest ed.).
Call Number _____ Location _____
Notes _____

Statistical Reference Index (Congressional Information Service, 1980–   ).
Call Number _____ Location _____
Notes _____

United States Census of Population and Housing (U.S. Bureau of the Census, latest ed.).
Call Number _____ Location _____
Notes _____

Bibliography

The article cited below lists resources for doing legal research at the state level.

Deel, N. A., & James, B. G. (1994). "An annotated bibliography of state legal research guides." *Legal Reference Service Quarterly, 14,* pp. 23–77.

Legal Resources

A large number of public documents related to social welfare policy are in the form
of laws or regulations. Many of these can be located in the federal and state documents collection of most large libraries. However, a thorough analysis will generally
require the resources available in a law library and the services of a trained law
librarian. Listed below are some of the most widely available resources in academic,
public, and law libraries that are useful for policy analysis. Also included below is a
brief summary of the different types of law and resources specific to those laws to
assist in clarifying what kinds of resources to use related to your particular policy.

Brief Description of Laws and Basic Resources

Statutory Law

Statutory law consists of session laws—a collection of federal laws in chronological order
of their enactment—and statutory codes which arrange statutes according to subject matter. The publisher of the three following titles is the U. S. Government Printing Office.

continued

Statutes at Large—Used to locate federal session laws in their chronological order of enactment.

United States Code—Used to locate federal statutory laws by subject.

United States Code Annotated and the *United States Code Service*—Provide more than just the text of the laws. Each includes: 1. Notes of court decisions interpreting, construing, and applying code sections; 2. Editorial notes and analytical discussions on particular statutes or provisions; and 3. References to attorney general opinions, administrative regulation, various secondary sources, and legislative history. Morris L. Cohen and Kent C. Olson, *Legal Reseach in a Nutshell* (St. Paul, MN: West Publishing Co., 1992) p. 113.

Administrative Law

Much authority has been delegated to administrative agencies by Congress and the president. The administrative rules of these agencies can be located using both government and commercial indexes.

The Federal Register—Chronologically arranges all new rules adopted by federal agencies, gives a brief synopsis of the content of the regulation, a preamble to clarify the contents, and then the complete text of the regulation.

The Code of Federal Regulations and the *Index to the Code of Federal Regulations*—Provide subject access to regulations listed in the *Federal Register.* Each volume contains an alphabetical list of federal agencies indicating the title and chapter of each agency's regulation.

Shepard's Federal Citations—Citations to cases at the federal courts of appeals as well as district court levels.

Shepard's United States Citations—Citations to U.S. Supreme Court decisions and Congressional statutes, trademarks, copyright, and patents.

Common Law

Common law is created by judges' rulings in trial, intermediate appellate, and final appeals courts on the federal, state, and local level. Decisions of these courts are collected chronologically in volumes called 'case reporters,' and summarized by subject matter in references works called 'case digests.'

Federal Reporter—Contains United States Court of Appeals decisions.

Supreme Court Reports—Official government report of Supreme Court decisions.

United States Supreme Court Reports: Lawyers Edition—Similar to the *Supreme Court Reports,* but also includes editorial comments on decisions.

Getting Started

Almanac of the Federal Judiciary, by Stephen Nelson et al. (Prentice Hall, latest ed.).
Call Number _____   Location _____
Notes _____

Black's Law Dictionary, by Henry Campbell Black (West, latest ed.).
Call Number _____   Location _____
Notes _____

continued

Encyclopedia of Legal Information Sources, by P. Wasserman, G. McCann, and P. Tobin (Gale Research Co., 1988).
Call Number _____ Location _____
Notes _____

Guide to American Law: Everyone's Legal Encyclopedia (West Publishing Co., 1983) [and annual supplements].
Call Number _____ Location _____
Notes _____

Law and Legal Information Directory, edited by P. Wasserman (Gale Research, latest ed.).
Call Number _____ Location _____
Notes _____

Legal Newsletters in Print (Infosources Publishing, latest ed.).
Call Number _____ Location _____
Notes _____

Legal Research in a Nutshell, by Morris L. Cohen & Kent C. Olson (West, 1996).
Call Number _____ Location _____
Notes _____

Legal Indexes

Current Law Index (Information Access Corp., 1980–   ).
Call Number _____ Location _____
Notes _____

Index to Legal Periodicals (H. W. Wilson Co., 1908–   ).
Call Number _____ Location _____
Notes _____

Electronic Legal Indexes

As mentioned in the earlier section on electronic resources, dates are not included. The coverage will depend on the kind of subscription your library has.

Legal Resources Index (Information Access Corp.).
Location _____
Notes _____

LEXIS/NEXIS (Mead Data Central).
Location _____
Notes _____

WESTLAW (West Publishing Co.).
Location _____
Notes _____

Journals

The following list of journals is provided for two purposes. First, it can be used as a checklist to determine what titles are in a library. Secondly, it is an attempt to demonstrate the variety of publications that contain information related to policy analysis.

There are a couple of things to keep in mind when searching for articles in journals. The most current issues of a journal, usually located in a current periodicals section of the library, are not yet indexed in printed resources. However, more and more journals are being included in online indexes available through your library's computer. These indexes are generally updated often enough to include current articles. For each research project in progress, make a list of a few journals most relevant to those topics. Train yourself to regularly browse through the current issues for articles not yet indexed.

A second reason to browse the current as well as the previous issues of a journal is that not all of the articles in any given journal are indexed. Some indexing is done selectively, depending on the policies of the publishers. This means that a relevant article might not be located if you rely strictly on print or online indexes. This is not as time consuming, tedious, or boring as it might sound. After a couple of browsing sessions, you'll be surprised at how quickly you can go through an enormous amount of published information and determine whether or not it is relevant to your research needs.

Descriptions of content for several of the titles listed below are given in the two following publications.

An Author's Guide to Social Work Journals (3rd ed.) by Henry Mendelsohn (NASW Press, 1992).
Call Number _____ Location _____

Understanding Social Problems, Policies, and Programs (2nd ed.) by Leon Ginsberg (University of South Carolina Press, 1996). (See appendix.)
Call Number _____ Location _____

Place a checkmark next to the titles held by your library.

AAA
____ABS, American Behavioral Scientist
____Administration in Social Work
____Administration and Policy in Mental Health
____Affilia: The Journal of Women and Social Work
____American Journal of Public Health

BBB
____Behavioral Sciences and the Law
____British Journal of Social Work

continued

CCC

____Child Abuse and Neglect

____Child and Youth Services

____Child Welfare

____Children and Youth Services Review

____Children's Health Care

____Community Alternatives

____Community Mental Health Journal

____Congressional Quarterly Researcher

____Congressional Quarterly Weekly Report

____Crime and Delinquency

EEE

____Evaluation and Program Planning

____Evaluation and the Health Professions

FFF

____Families in Society

____Family Perspective

____Family Process

____Family Relations

GGG

____Gallup Poll Monthly

____Gerontologist

HHH

____Health Affairs

____Health and Social Work

____Home Health Care Services Quarterly

____Human Service in the Rural Environment

JJJ

____Journal of Aging and Social Policy

____Journal of American History

____Journal of Applied Gerontology

____Journal of Criminal Justice

____Journal of Drug Issues

____Journal of Family Issues

____Journal of Gerontological Social Work

____Journal of Gerontology

____Journal of Health and Social Behavior

____Journal of Health and Social Policy

____Journal of Progressive Human Services

____Journal of Research in Crime and Delinquency

____Journal of Social History

continued

____Journal of Social Issues
____Journal of Social Policy
____Journal of Social Service Research
____Journal of Sociology and Social Welfare

LLL
____Legislative Studies Quarterly

NNN
____NASW News

PPP
____Policy Evaluation
____Policy Review
____Policy Studies
____Policy Studies Journal
____Policy Studies Review
____Political Science Quarterly
____Public Administration
____Public Administration Quarterly
____Public Administration Review
____Public Health Reports
____Public Interest
____Public Policy
____Public Welfare

RRR
____Research in Social Problems and Public Policy

SSS
____Social Action and the Law
____Social Forces
____Social Philosophy and Policy
____Social Policy
____Social Policy and Administration
____Social Problems
____Social Science Research
____Social Security Bulletin
____Social Service Review
____Social Work
____Social Work in Health Care
____Social Work Research

YYY
____Youth and Society
____Youth Policy

Associations/Organizations/Societies Publications

In addition to journal articles, books, government documents, and newspapers, the publications of national, regional, state and local associations and organizations are excellent resources for information. Included in newsletters, factsheets, bulletins, and reports are calendars of upcoming events, such as political rallies related to pending legislation, status reports on programs funded by state and federal laws, as well as the names and addresses of experts who can be contacted for specific information. Both the national and state and local editions of the *Encyclopedia of Associations* provide names, phone numbers, addresses, member information, conference announcements, and titles of publications of thousands of large and small associations including the ones listed here. Many of the publications are free. Check with your librarian if you have questions related to locating association and organization information.

The following list is intended as a small example of the variety of associations, organizations, and societies that can be contacted for information related to policy that impacts whole populations at the federal, state and local level as well as for specific populations, such as Alzheimer's patients and their families or the homeless.

Alzheimer's Association
Alzheimer's Association Newsletter
Brochures / Factsheets / Video kits

American Association of Retired Persons
AARP Fact Sheets
AARP Public Policy Institute Papers
Profile Of Older Americans [annual]

American Public Welfare Association
Public Welfare
W-Memo

American Society on Aging
Aging Today: The Bimonthly Newspaper of the American Society on Aging
Generations: The Journal of the American Society on Aging

Bazelon Center for Mental Health Law
Factsheets / Handbooks / Manuals

Center on Hunger, Poverty and Nutrition Policy
Research in Progress
Working Papers

Children's Defense Fund
CDF Reports

continued

Child Welfare League of America
Children Today
Child Welfare
Washington Social Legislation Bulletin

Council on Social Work Education
Social Work Education Reporter

Institute for Research on Poverty/University of Wisconsin-Madison
Focus

National Alliance for the Mentally Ill
NAMI Advocate

National Association of Social Workers
NASW News
Social Work Speaks: NASW Policy Statements

National Coalition for the Homeless
Safety Network

Social Welfare History Group
Newsletter

INFORMATION SELF-RELIANCE STATEMENT
School of Social Work
The University of Alabama

The following is a statement approved by the faculty at The University of Alabama School of Social Work regarding information self-reliance competencies for students in the social work program. It is included as an example and as encouragement for other schools to adopt similar statements to demonstrate a common goal of working toward information self-reliant social work students.

> *The School of Social Work is dedicated to preparing social work students with the ability to retrieve, identify, and assess information relevant to professional social work practice during their course of study at the school. Our goal is that students be competent to identify, locate, and effectively use information in print, machine-readable, and electronically-transmitted formats. These skills are essential to the competent practice of professional social work.*
>
> *The faculty believes that these competencies not only contribute to the quality of professional practice and scholarship, but can also enhance an individual's lifelong information needs and quality of life.*

Appendix *B*

Historical Policy Analysis Research

Research for a historical policy analysis may draw upon some of the library sources described in Appendix A, but will generally rely on more specialized historical resources. Several of these are described in Appendix A, such as *Historical Statistics of the United States, Colonial Times to 1970* and Thomas Slavens' *Sources of Information for Historical Research*. This appendix will give you more extensive information on the types of sources necessary for understanding the history of a social welfare policy.

As we described in the chapter on historical policy analysis, historians distinguish between primary and secondary sources of data. Primary material consists of records made at the time an event occurred by participants or direct observers of the event. Secondary sources are reconstructions of an event by persons without first-hand knowledge of the event. Secondary sources often do an important job of orienting you to the area you want to study. They can provide an overview and a context for your policy history. However, they generally present conclusions drawn by the author, based on his or her interpretation of the evidence existing at the time the material was written. These conclusions may not always be accurate. If you want to draw your own conclusions based on the evidence, and particularly to use new data that has come to light or new theories about the development and nature of social welfare policies, you will need to examine the original sources yourself.

This is not to say that primary sources are bias-free. They too represent the values, judgements, and preconceptions of the observer or participant recording an event. However, historians attempt to control for bias by using a variety of primary sources, and indeed of secondary sources. If you were investigating the history of an agency decision regarding which sorts of client problems to deal with and which to refer, for example, you would want to interview staff at various levels and not just the agency director.

In using secondary sources for social policy history, the library is a basic place to start; bibliographic and catalogue subject headings such as "Child Welfare" often include "History" as a subheading. Abstracts of historical articles can be found on laser disk, as well as hard copy, in sources such as *American History and Life, Historical Abstracts, and Historical Abstracts on Disk.* Other tools for finding books and articles on social welfare history include a new heading ("Social Welfare and Public Health") in the Recent Scholarship Section of the *Journal of American History,* a category on "Social Work Profession—History" in *Social Work Abstracts,* Trattner and Achenbaum's *Social Welfare in America: An Annotated Bibliography,* and the annual annotated bibliography, including books, articles, and dissertations, produced by the Social Welfare History Group.[1]

Among social work journals, *The Social Service Review* and *The Journal of Sociology and Social Welfare* are particularly likely to publish historical articles. Review articles in *Reviews in American History* offer excellent orientations to current trends and debates in social welfare history.

The Encyclopedia of Social Work covers historical topics and biographies of social welfare leaders; Walter Trattner's *Biographical Dictionary of Social Welfare in America* is also a good source of information about important figures in social welfare.[2] *The Dictionary of American Biography, Dictionary of American Negro Biography,* and *Notable Women: The Modern Period* are other helpful sources of biographical data.

Once you have an overview of a policy history area, you will want to turn to the original sources. Using original sources may seem daunting at first. The range of evidence is vast: memoirs, correspondence, minutes of committees, agency manuals containing rules and policies, client case histories, court testimony, government reports, and census reports. You may be further intimidated to learn that the historical evidence is not always written, and can include interviews with key policymakers and staff of social work agencies, oral histories, photographs, films, and even songs. Our policy history of the Benton Park Crisis Center, for example, drew in part from a large scrapbook which included news clippings, photographs, and other material documenting major events in the life of the agency. Yet as you pursue a historical analysis, you may find yourself caught up in the fun of this "sleuthing" game, where you use your imagination to determine what has gone on in the past. Occasionally one stumbles across an exciting "find" like a mouldering box of case records in an agency basement, dating back to the early 1900s. More usually a painstaking search is involved, in state and local libraries, archival collections, organization headquarters, individual agencies, and collections of oral histories, in order to locate pertinent sources. Fortunately, there are guides to a number of these holdings and collections.

Archives are places where unpublished records are collected, catalogued, and made available to researchers. They may be housed in libraries, organizations, universities, and museums. Tracking where the records of particular individuals or organizations are stored can be a tricky task. One help is the *National Union Catalogue of Manuscripts,* available in libraries. There are several important archival collections in social work and social welfare; these include the Social Welfare Archives at the University of Minnesota, the Social Work Archives at the Smith College School for Social Work, and the records collection at the Center on Philanthropy, Indiana University, Indianapolis. Individual archives have their own directories, for example, the directory of the University of Minnesota's Social Welfare History Archives Center (1970) and supplements to it.

The articles "Archives of Social Welfare" by Clarke Chambers in the 18th edition of the *Encyclopedia of Social Work* and "Social Welfare History Archives" by David Klaassen in the 19th edition are excellent starting points for locating primary sources. The 19th edition also contains Leslie Leighninger's entry "Historiography," which gives an overview of the use of historical sources.[3] In addition, authors of books on social work and social welfare history generally describe the archival sources they have used in their notes and bibliographies.[4]

Libraries can also be sources of primary material on social welfare history topics. The social work collection will often include issues of social work journals dating back to the early 1900s, as well as the complete *Proceedings* of the National Conference of Social Work (formerly National Conference of Charities and Correction), dating from the 1980s back to 1874. You will also find the annual published reports of various social welfare organizations, such as your state's public welfare or mental health departments and selected private agencies and institutions. A search in the Louisiana State University library, for example, produced a fascinating set of reports regarding the patient census, types of treatment, and size and condition of the physical plant in large state hospitals in the 1930s and 1940s.

Newspapers and newsmagazines provide first hand reports of social welfare developments and interviews with both policymakers and the recipients of social services. Many of these, such as the *New York Times* and the *Washington Post,* have their own indexes. As we noted earlier, the *Times* index goes back to 1851. Finally, the Government Documents departments of libraries offer a wealth of information regarding the history of public social welfare policies.

A special kind of individual record is the oral history, which is a tape-recorded interview with a person about his or her past and often about that person's participation in particular historical events. These interviews are transcribed and then made available through special oral history collections, often housed in university libraries. Historians may use oral histories conducted by others, or carry out their own.[5] The Smith College Social Work Archives and the Social Security Project at the Oral History Collection of Columbia University are important repositories of oral histories related to social work and social welfare.

Related to oral history is a research technique known as interviews with key informants. This technique, more familiar to journalists than to social scientists, consists of interviewing people who by virtue of job and/or training are recognized as experts. People commonly used as key informants are academic researchers, agency executives, legislators and their aides, and social activists. Often forgotten, but possessing an important perspective, are clients of programs created by social welfare policies. Gaining the first-hand perspective of people actually involved in the policy you are analysing can be extremely useful, whether their perspective is from the top down or the bottom up.

Social welfare organizations, agencies, and Schools of Social Work also create their own unpublished records. These include annual reports, minutes of committee meetings, agency manuals and regulation books, memos, client surveys, and case records (such as those used by Eve Smith in her study of orphanages). Sometimes these are still locked in some dusty file cabinet in a school or agency office. Sometimes they have been donated to local or state libraries, archives such as the Social Welfare History Archives, or state history collections. In figuring out if these records still exist and where they are located, one place to start is the organization itself. The records of many national social welfare organizations can be found at the Social Welfare History Archives, as can the committee minutes, yearly conference proceedings, and other memorabilia of professional associations like the National Association of Social Workers.

The case records of social agencies are particularly helpful to social welfare historians as they try to understand the lives of ordinary citizens.[6] If you are planning to use an agency's client records, you must be sure to receive permission from the agency administration and to follow your university's Human Subjects Review Board policies for protecting subject rights.

The addition of a client perspective helps to make policy histories more complete. So does attention to the issues of women and minorities, who constitute a large proportion of the clientele of social welfare programs and who have also played significant roles in the development of the social work profession. In addition, women and minorities have been a driving force behind informal self-help organizations. There is a growing body of historical literature on the roles and position of women and minorities in the social welfare system. These include studies of women and public welfare by Abramovitz and Gordon, biographies of African American social welfare leaders by LaNey, Peebles-Wilkins, and Rouse, and histories of the women's clubs and self-help movement by

Lerner and Scott.[7] The works of these authors include a number of references to archival and other sources related to race and gender in social welfare. There are, for example, specialized oral history collections, such as the Black Women Oral History Project at the Schlesinger Library, Radcliffe College; archival collections at Howard University and other institutions; and programs such as the Center for Research on Women, Memphis State University, which provides computerized searches of data bases in their particular topic area.

The list of sources in this appendix is extensive, but necessarily so, since the best history relies on a variety of kinds of data. Taking the time to learn the history behind a policy, whether it's the federal Equal Opportunity Act or your field agency's rules on eligibility for services, will greatly enrich your understanding of the policy's goals, scope, weaknesses, and strengths.

Notes

1. Walter I. Trattner and W. Andrew Achenbaum, Eds., *Social Welfare in America: An Annotated Bibliography* (Westport, CT: Greenwood Press, 1983). The annual Social Welfare History Bibliography is available through membership in the Social Welfare History Group, School of Social Work, East Carolina University, Greenville, NC 27858–4353.

2. Walter I. Trattner, *Biographical Dictionary of Social Welfare in America* (Westport, CT: Greenwood Press, 1986).

3. The directory of the University of Minnesota's Social Welfare History Archives can be found in many university libraries. Other useful archives include the U.S. National Archives, the Archives of Labor and Urban Affairs at Wayne State University, Temple University's Urban Archives Center, and the Rockefeller Archive Center in North Tarrytown, NY. The social work and other libraries at Columbia University in New York have an extensive collection of materials on social welfare history, including a large collection of annual reports, publications, and conference proceedings from leading social agencies and organizations. Many states maintain archives that include material on public social welfare programs and policies, and some agencies also store their administrative and client records.

4. In fact, portions of this appendix were adapted from Leslie Leighninger, "Historiography," in Richard L. Edwards and June Gary Hopps, Eds., *Encyclopedia of Social Work,* 19th ed., Vol II (Washington, DC: NASW Press, 1995) pp. 1253–1254.

5. B. Allen and W. L. Montrell, *From Memory to History: Using Oral Sources in Local Historical Research* (Nashville: American Association for State and Local History, 1981).

6. See, for example, Linda Gordon, *Heroes of Their Own Lives: The Politics and History of Family Violence* (NY: Penguin Books, 1988); Beverly Stadum, *Poor Women and Their Families: Hardworking Charity Cases* (Albany, NY: State University of New York Press, 1992).

7. Mimi Abramovitz, *Regulating the Lives of Women: Social Welfare Policy from Colonial Times to the Present* (Boston: South End Press, 1988); Linda Gordon, *Pitied But*

Not Entitled: Single Mothers and the History of Welfare (NY: Free Press, 1994); Iris Carlton-LaNey, "The Career of Birdye Henrietta Haynes, A Pioneer Settlement House Worker," *Social Service Review* 68 (June 1994) pp. 254–271; Wilma Peebles-Wilkins, "Black Women and American Social Welfare: The Life of Fredericka Douglass Sprague Perry," *Affilia* 4 (Spring 1989) pp. 33–44; Jacquelyn Anne Rouse, *Lugenia Burns Hope: Black Southern Reformer* (Athens, GA: University of Georgia Press, 1989); Gerda Lerner, "Community Work of Black Club Women," *Journal of Negro History* 59 (1974) pp. 158–167; Ann Firor Scott, *Natural Allies: Women's Associations in American History* (Urbana: University of Illinois Press, 1992). See also Steven J. Diner, "Chicago Social Workers and Blacks in the Progressive Era," *Social Service Review* 44 (December 1970) pp. 393–410; Linda Gordon, "Black and White Visions of Welfare: Women's Welfare Activism, 1890–1945," *The Journal of American History* 78 (September 1991) pp. 559–590; Robyn Muncy, *Creating a Female Dominion in American Reform, 1890–1930* (NY: Oxford University Press, 1991); Susan Kerr Chandler, "Almost a Partnership: African Americans, Segregation, and the Young Mens' Christian Association," *Journal of Sociology and Social Welfare* 21 (March 1994) pp. 97–111; and N. Yolanda Burwell, "North Carolina Public Welfare Institutes for Negroes, 1926–1940," *Journal of Sociology and Social Welfare* 21 (March 1994) pp. 67–82.

Index